COMPUTER ARCHITECTURE:
A MODERN SYNTHESIS

VOLUME 1: FOUNDATIONS

COMPUTER ARCHITECTURE:
A MODERN SYNTHESIS

V. 1

VOLUME 1: FOUNDATIONS

Subrata Dasgupta
Edmiston Professor of Computer Science
University of Southwestern Louisiana
Lafayette, Louisiana

WILEY

John Wiley & Sons, Inc.
New York   Chichester   Brisbane   Toronto   Singapore

Copyright © 1989, by John Wiley & Sons, Inc.

All rights reserved. Published simultaneously in Canada.

Reproduction or translation of any part of
this work beyond that permitted by Sections
107 and 108 of the 1976 United States Copyright
Act without the permission of the copyright
owner is unlawful. Requests for permission
or further information should be addressed to
the Permissions Department, John Wiley & Sons.

Library of Congress Cataloging-in-Publication Data:

Dasgupta, Subrata.
  Computer architecture : a modern synthesis / Subrata Dasgupta.
    p.   cm.
  References: v. 1, p. 331–366
  Includes index.
  Contents: v. 1. Foundations.
  ISBN 0-471-82310-4 (v. 1)
  1. Computer architecture. I. Title.
QA76.9.A73D35   1989   87-37188
004.2′2 — dc19   CIP

Printed in the United States of America

10 9 8 7 6 5 4 3 2 1

To
Sarmistha

PREFACE

The casual reader turning the pages of a comprehensive text or survey article on computers will be struck by the *diversity* of computers that have emerged over the past four decades.

This diversity manifests itself across several dimensions. One of these is the *technological* dimension—that is, the physical basis for their construction and implementation. Most strikingly, however, other sources of computer diversity lie in their *functional* characteristics—their externally observable behavior, properties, and capabilities—and in their *internal structure and organization*. Collectively, these essentially abstract properties define what has come to be known as *computer architecture* and constitute the architectural dimensions of computer diversity.

Thus, one view of computer architecture sees it as the study of such abstract characteristics of computers and their interrelationships that have led to the "evolution" and proliferation of computer species. The analogy between computer architecture and the anatomical and evolutionary studies in biology is, in some sense, evident.

Unlike organisms, however, computers are designed and built entities; they are *artifacts*. Thus, from another viewpoint computer architecture is seen as a *design discipline* concerned with the design, development, description, and verification of computer *architectures*. Here the appropriate analogy is perhaps with *building architecture*. Indeed, in the latter context we use the term "architecture" both in the declarative sense as defining some set of abstract properties, plan, or theme that a building exhibits as well as in the procedural sense of a design discipline concerned with the process of producing these abstract properties.

The analogy between computer architecture and building architecture is really striking in this respect: they are both concerned with abstract properties that ultimately depend on appropriate technologies for their effective implementation; yet each has its own autonomous vocabulary, heuristic rules, and scientific principles—constituting a universe of discourse—that are distinct from the vocabulary, rules and principles of its underlying technology; the efficacy of both architectural disciplines and principles are ultimately tested in social (i.e., human) environments; and finally, they are both, again as disciplines, preoccupied with the problem of organization.

However, this text and its companion volume are not about these analogies, fascinating though they are. In these two volumes I have attempted to deal simultaneously with the two faces of computer architecture—its compendium of architectural *principles* and the issues related to architectural *design*. The first is concerned with parts or subsystems viewed in convenient isolation. The second with the design of the whole. The "synthesis" in the title refers, first, to the unification of these two facets and, second, to my attempt to organize the diversity of architectural principles within a single integrated framework.

The two texts are intended to form a coherent whole. However, they have been written and organized so that each volume can be read, studied, and used independently of the other. The present volume, *Foundations,* is intended for senior undergraduate students of computer science and engineering and consists of a set of topics that can be covered in a one-semester senior undergraduate course in computer architecture. In contrast, the companion volume, *Advanced Topics,* is suitable as a graduate-level text. There are, however, two aspects common to the two books: shared References and an identical first chapter, which establishes a common framework and terminology for both *Foundations* and *Advanced Topics.*

Volume 1 is organized into two parts. Part I deals with issues common to all computer architecture. In particular, Chapter 1 introduces the important idea of *architectural levels*—a notion that pervades the entire book—and establishes the connections between architecture on the one hand and design methodology, compilers, microprogramming, software technology, and implementation technology on the other. Chapters 2 and 3 discuss, respectively and in more detail, the issues of implementation technology and design methodology as they relate to architecture.

Part II discusses various facets of the architecture of uniprocessors. At its heart is the register machine, which is discussed at different abstraction levels in Chapters 4 and 5. Since the register machine is historically tied to the emergence and development of microprogramming, a substantial part of Chapter 5 is devoted to this topic.

Chapters 6 and 7 present two contrasting approaches to the development of "language directed architectures"—alternatives to the register machine style. The first is the (now almost "classical") stack machine approach; the second is the very recently developed idea of reduced instruction set computers, much in vogue at this time.

Finally, Chapter 8, discusses various fundamental and important issues related to the memory aspects of architecture.

In concluding, I would like to note an important feature of the problem sets at the end of each chapter: and that is (in keeping with the view of computer architecture as a design discipline), the emphasis on *design problems.* Some of these are suitable for solution as normal "assignments" whereas others are more in the nature of "projects" that can be pursued in the course of an entire semester.

Lafayette, Louisiana
July 31, 1987   Subrata Dasgupta

ACKNOWLEDGMENTS

A project of this kind can only be conducted in an atmosphere in which one's research, teaching, and writing can be carried out in symbiotic harmony and where one is relatively free of administrative duties. I have been fortunate in enjoying, for several years, precisely such a climate at the Center for Advanced Computer Studies of the University of Southwestern Louisiana. Its Director, Terry Walker, has had much to do with this pleasant state of affairs. I thank him for the environment and his support.

I also must thank the National Science Foundation for supporting my recent studies of computer architecture as a design discipline. The fruits of these studies have advertently and inadvertently influenced several parts of this book. These same researches formed the basis of continuing discussions of many aspects of architecture with my students (and collaborators), notably Philip Wilsey, Ulises Aguero, Alan Hooton, Cy Ardoin, and Sukhesh Patel. My ideas were also formed under the influence of an ongoing transatlantic dialogue (stretching over 6 years) with Werner Damm formerly of Aachen Technical University and now with the University of Oldenburg, West Germany. I thank them all for the pleasure of their intellectual company.

A part of this work was done while I was a visiting fellow at Wolfson College, Oxford, and the Oxford University Computing Laboratory in the summer of 1986. I am very grateful to Professor C. A. R. Hoare and to Sir Raymond Hoffenberg, President of Wolfson College, for providing me the facilities and an enchanting physical environment in which to work.

Several persons were kind enough to read and review selected chapters from the two volumes. I thank, in particular, Laxmi Bhuyan, Dipak Ghosal, John Gurd, Steven Landry, and Robert Mueller for their many helpful comments. I also thank William M. Lively and James L. Beug who provided very useful reviews of the manuscripts. For any residual errors that may be found in the text, may I say, in the time-honored tradition: *mea culpa*!

In the course of this work I received enormous logistical help from several persons. In particular:

Cathy Pomier, who typed the manuscripts and undertook their many revisions with invariable and sustained good humor. For her, the adjective "unflappable" is truly apt.

Nancy Pellegran, who typed the problem sets and the index and helped put the finishing touches to the manuscript.

Philip Wilsey and Ulises Aguero who exercised their computational ingenuity in producing the computer generated diagrams that appear in the text, and who assisted me in innumerable ways.

ix

Richard Bonacci, my original editor at Wiley, who warmly supported this project.

Gene Davenport, Senior Editor at Wiley, who provided firm, wise, and invaluable advice during the later, crucial stages of my writing.

Joe Dougherty, Editor, Gilda Stahl, Senior Copy Editor, and Dawn Reitz, Senior Production Supervisor at Wiley, for their assistance during the physical production of this book.

I am grateful to each one of these individuals for their help.

My thanks to Robert Mueller, Werner Damm, Gert Dohmen, Philip Wilsey, the Institute of Electrical and Electronic Engineers, Intermetrics, Inc., the Association for Computing Machinery, Digital Equipment Corporation, John Wiley & Sons, Academic Press, McGraw-Hill, and MIT Press for granting me permission to reproduce diagrams and excerpts from their publications. I also thank George Spix and Linda Turpin of Cray Research for providing information on some recent Cray systems.

Finally, a note of gratitude to my wife, Sarmistha, and sons, Jaideep and Monish, for living patiently with this, seemingly interminable, project and for their love and support.

CONTENTS

PART ONE

INTRODUCTION AND BACKGROUND

CHAPTER 1

THE SCOPE OF COMPUTER ARCHITECTURE

In this book the term *computer architecture* will be used in two complementary ways. It will refer to certain *logical* and *abstract properties* of computers, the nature of which will be described herein. The term will also be used to denote the art, craft, and science — or more generally, the discipline — involved in *designing* these same logical and abstract properties. Thus, computer architecture (or more simply, when there is no room for ambiguity, architecture) refers both to certain characteristics of computers and to the design methods used in realizing these characteristics.

1.1 EXO-ARCHITECTURE

What are these logical and abstract properties that are of interest to the computer architect? There are first the *functional* characteristics of computers: their externally observable behavior, properties, and capabilities that are of fundamental interest to a certain group of users. These users include, in particular, system programmers responsible for the construction of operating systems and compilers for a given computer and the applications programmers involved in writing programs in the computer's assembly language.

The collection of externally observable behavior, properties, and capabilities goes by several names in the architectural literature, including, simply, computer *architecture* (Myers, 1982), the *instruction set processor* (ISP) level (Siewiorek, Bell, and Newell, 1982), the *conventional machine level* (Tanenbaum, 1984), and *exo-architecture* (Dasgupta, 1984). I will employ this last term in this book to remind you that these properties reflect the *external* functional and logical features of computers.

The primary components of a computer's exo-architecture are

1. The organization of programmable storage.
2. Data types and data structures, their encoding and representation.
3. Instruction formats.
4. The instruction (or operation code) set.
5. The modes of addressing and accessing data items and instructions.
6. Exception conditions.

3

A computer's exo-architecture represents a particular abstraction level at which we may choose to view it. An *abstraction* is a simplified or selective description of a system that highlights some of the system properties while suppressing others. In the case of complex systems, we may need to perform *different kinds* of abstraction depending on the purpose at hand. Furthermore, these different kinds of abstractions may be so selected as to form a hierarchic relationship with one another. In that case, we talk of the existence of different *abstraction levels.*

The abstraction level of a computer that we call exo-architecture defines the interface between the physical machine and any software that may be superimposed on it (Fig. 1.1). Indeed, the establishment of such a user interface is the *purpose* of this abstraction level. The "users" of this interface are the operating system and compiler writers and, generally, those who wish to program in assembly language.

It is important to note that abstractions and abstraction levels are *artifacts*. We invent them so that we have a means for organizing and understanding complex phenomena, but there is nothing sacrosanct about them. Thus, two different designers of an exo-architecture may choose and define two very distinct sets of functional capabilities, depending on what they consider to be useful for the "user."

Example 1.1

For most conventional single-processor systems the exo-architecture will consist of the features cited earlier; namely, the instruction set, operand addressing modes, the word length, the number of words (or bytes) of available main memory, the number and types of high-speed programmable registers, and so on. The user may never need to know such "internal" details as the precise mechanisms by which instructions are interpreted by the hardware or whether, for example, instructions are "pipelined."

In contrast, the user of a *vector processor* may well have to know some details of its internal processor organization in order to effectively exploit the potential parallelism that such processors offer. The exo-architecture of these machines may then be defined to reveal such details rather than to hide them as in conventional processors. ∎

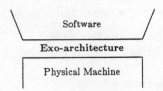

FIGURE 1.1   Exo-architecture: The interface between software and physical machine.

1.2 ENDO-ARCHITECTURE

An exo-architecture is realized by mechanisms implemented in hardware and microcode (or firmware). We can, in fact, describe these mechanisms and their interactions at various levels—for example, the circuit, logic (gate), or register transfer levels. However, important as these levels are, for many purposes they are too detailed—they contain too much information. To understand how the hardware/firmware complex realizes an exo-architecture may require us to abstract from the details of logic or even register transfer levels. This abstraction of the hardware/firmware details has been given several names in the literature, including *processor architecture* (Myers, 1982), *computer organization* (Hayes, 1978), and *endo-architecture* (Dasgupta, 1984). I will use this last term in this book to emphasize that these characteristics constitute a description of a computer's *internal* organization.

Basically, a computer's endo-architecture consists of the following descriptions.

1. The capabilities and performance characteristics of its principal functional components.
2. The ways in which these components are interconnected.
3. The nature of information flow between components.
4. The logic and means by which such information flow is controlled.

It is important to realize that the purpose of this abstraction level is really to aid *understandability.* This abstraction is necessary not only for the "reader" of the design but also for the designer so that he or she need not have to manage and master too many "low-level" details.

The relationship between exo-architecture, endo-architecture, and the next lower (e.g., register-transfer) level representation of the circuits that interpret and realize these architectural levels is illustrated in Figure 1.2.

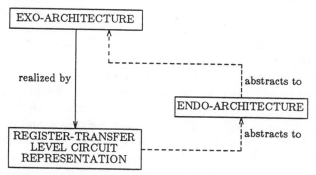

FIGURE 1.2 **The relationships between exo-architecture, endo-architecture, and the register-transfer level.**

1.3 MICRO-ARCHITECTURE

As described in the foregoing sections, a processor's endo-architecture is an abstracted view of its internal hardware organization. However, architects in practice may exercise considerable freedom in deciding how detailed the endo-architectural design and description should be. A very special situation arises in the cases of *microprogrammed* and *user microprogrammable* computers because, for these machine classes, the architect specifies the endo-architecture at a level of detail necessary for the microprogrammer to write and implement the microcode for such machines.

I will reserve the term *micro-architecture* to denote the internal architecture — the logical structure and functional capabilities — of a computer as seen by the microprogrammer.

Remarks

Several points about micro-architecture are worth noting.

1. The *purpose* of micro-architecture as a distinct abstraction level is to establish and define *the interface between the hardware* and the *superimposed* firmware (microcode). Thus, micro-architecture is to the microprogrammer what exo-architecture is to the (assembly language) programmer.
2. Extending this parallel, and given the recent trend toward the use of high-level microprogramming languages (HLMLs) and their compilers, the micro-architecture of a processor defines those aspects of the hardware system required either by the microprogrammer or by the HLML compiler writer.
3. Although a micro-architecture may be viewed as a special version of a machine's endo-architecture, it is important to keep in mind that the latter may be defined independent of (a) whether microprogramming or hardwired logic is used to implement the processor or (b) the precise style, logic, and organization of the control unit. In other words, a given computer may be designed and described meaningfully in terms of its exo-architecture, its micro-architecture on which the microprogram is run so as to realize the exo-architecture, and an endo-architecture that is an abstraction of the micro-architecture/microprogram complex. The relationship between these levels is shown in Figure 1.3.
4. The micro-architecture of a processor, depending on how detailed it is, may or may not coincide with the *register-transfer level* description. At the latter level, computer structures are described in terms of such primitives as terminals, registers, delays, counters, clocks, memories, and combinational circuits. The primitives from which such a description is composed bear obvious one-to-one correspondences with common medium-scale integration (MSI) logic circuits. Generally speaking, the register-transfer level description will contain more information than the microprogrammer needs to know, hence the micro-architecture abstracts somewhat from this level (Fig. 1.3).

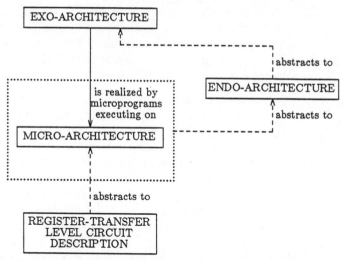

FIGURE 1.3 The relationships between architectural and register-transfer levels.

5. Finally, note that the foregoing "definition" of micro-architecture and its relationship to endo-architecture as depicted in Figure 1.3 is universally valid only for *single processors*. In the case of a *multiprocessor* system, you may refer to the endo-architecture of the system as a whole—that is, to the collective, internal structure of the whole, integrated complex. However, it does not *usually* make sense to talk of the micro-architecture of the multiprocessor. The individual processors comprising the system—if microprogrammed—will, of course, have their own, *local* micro-architectures.

1.4 EXAMPLES OF ARCHITECTURAL LEVELS: THE VAX FAMILY

I will illustrate the typical characteristics of, and the distinctions between, architectural levels using as an example, Digital Equipment Corporation's VAX family of 32-bit processors (Digital, 1981a, 1981b). There are several members of this family, including the VLSI VAX microcomputer (Brown and Sites, 1984), the VAX-11/750 and VAX-11/780 systems (Digital, 1981b), and, most recently, the VAX 8600 (Digital, 1985).

1.4.1 Exo-architecture

The VAX family of processors was designed to share a common exo-architecture, which is described in the *VAX Architecture Handbook* (Digital, 1981a).[1]

---

[1]As we have noted earlier, various names are used to designate what has been called exo-architecture here. In the VAX literature, this is simply referred to as the "architecture" of the VAX family. See the Bibliographic and Historical Notes at the end of this chapter for further remarks on this matter.

The commonality of exo-architecture assures *compatibility* among the individual family members—that is, it ensures that software originally intended for execution on one member-processor may be transported for execution on some other member-processor with a minimum of reprogramming.

The VAX exo-architecture contains the following features.

1. A 4 gigabyte (2^{32} bytes) virtual address space.
2. A set of numeric data types for the representation, storage, and manipulation of 8, 16, 32, 64, and 128 bit integers; 32, 64, and 128 bit floating-point numbers; data types representing packed decimal strings up to 16 bytes long with two digits packed per byte; unpacked numeric strings up to 31 bytes with one digit per byte; character strings; and queue data types allowing the representation and manipulation of circular, doubly linked lists.
3. A high-speed register space consisting of 16 32-bit registers of which some have special roles such as the program counter, stack pointer, and stack frame pointer.
4. A repertoire of operand addressing modes—that is, means for specifying (either directly or indirectly) operands located in either main memory, the registers, or within the instruction stream itself.
5. The VAX exo-architecture also provides several mechanisms for supporting multiprogramming. However, such features are not part of the "user-visible" exo-architecture. Rather, they are part of the more general interface visible to the systems programmer. Thus, for instance, context switching between processes may be performed by the operating system, using such special instructions as *save process context* and *load process context.*
6. A variable-length instruction format consisting of a 1 or 2 byte opcode field followed by 0 to 6 operand specifiers whose number and type depend on the opcode.
7. A general instruction set for the manipulation of the various numeric and nonnumeric data types, a repertoire of control instructions, special instructions for manipulating special data types such as addresses and queues, and a privileged instruction set available only to the systems programmer.
8. Specification of various exceptions and interrupts. In the VAX terminology, *exceptions* are unusual events that may occur in the context of the "currently" executing process. These include, for example, various arithmetic overflow and underflow conditions. *Interrupts* are events that may have been generated on a systematic basis or outside the context of the currently executing process. These include, for example, interrupts induced by device errors or a device completion condition.

1.4.2 Endo-architecture

Figure 1.4 shows the principal endo-architectural components of the VAX-11/780 processor and their interconnections. The *data cache* is an 8K byte, two-way set associative memory (see Chapter 8, Volume 1) that is used for all information coming from main memory, including data, addresses, and instructions.

The *address translation buffer* (TB) is a cache containing 128 virtual-to-physi-

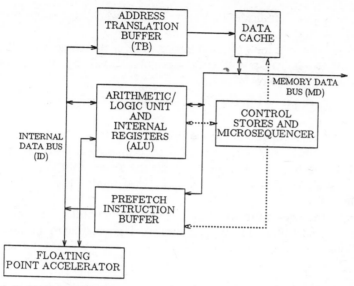

FIGURE 1.4 VAX-11/780: The endo-architecture (Reprinted with permission from *The VAX Hardware Handbook* © Digital Press/Digital Equipment Corporation, Bedford, Mass, 1981).

cal page address translations that is used to reduce the time required for dynamic address translation.

The *prefetch instruction buffer* (IB) is 8 bytes long and is used to improve the performance of the central processing unit (CPU) by prefetching instructions. The control logic continuously fetches data from memory to keep the buffer full.

In addition, the (optional) floating-point accelerator executes arithmetic operations on single- and double-precision floating-point data, while the control unit includes a 96-bit wide, 4K word read-only memory holding the principle microprogram implementing the VAX-11 instruction set, a 1K 96-bit word writable diagnostic control store holding diagnostic microroutines, and an optional 1K 96-bit word user writable control store.

The distinction between exo- and endo-architecture, and the idea that the former is an abstraction of the latter, can be more clearly appreciated when we examine the dynamics of instructions execution. Consider as a specific example the interpretation of the VAX-11

CLRL RO

instruction, assuming it is stored at virtual address V. At the exo-architectural level, the meaning of this instruction is simply given by the equations

$$
\begin{aligned}
\text{reg.RO}' &= 0 \\
N' &= 0 \\
Z' &= 1 \qquad \text{Condition codes} \\
V' &= 0 \\
C' &= C
\end{aligned}
\tag{1.1}
$$

where the symbol X′ indicates the *new* value of X whereas the unprimed symbol denotes its old value.

However, when we look at the interpretation of this same instruction at the endo-architectural level, several events take place involving the functional components shown in Figure 1.4.

1. The virtual address V is converted to a physical address P by the translation buffer TB.
2. The data cache is queried to see if it contains P.
3. Assuming this is not so, a block of bytes beginning at P in main memory is fetched and the addresses and contents are loaded into the cache.
4. The first few of these same bytes are also loaded into the prefetch instruction buffer.
5. Finally, the relevant instruction is read from the buffer, decoded, and executed by the arithmetic and logic unit (ALU), resulting in the effects shown in Equation (1.1).

Remarks

1. Note, in this example, that for a complete understanding of the endo-architecture and how it supports the execution of the (CLRL) instruction, it is necessary to understand the *functional behavior* of such components as the data cache, the translation buffer, and the prefetch instruction buffer as well as how information is transferred between these components.
2. On completion of the instruction execution the state of the machine at the exo-architectural level is identical to that prior to its execution except for the changes shown by Equation (1.1). On the other hand, the state change of the same machine at the endo-architectural level will include, in addition to those shown by Equation (1.1), changes to the states of the two caches and the instruction buffer in addition to those of register RO and the condition code flags. The exo-architectural state of the machine is, thus, an abstraction of the endo-architectural machine state — that is, there is, in general, a many-to-one mapping from the latter state space to the former state space (Fig. 1.5).
3. Finally, note that the foregoing description of instruction execution remains valid regardless of whether or not the processor is microprogrammed.

1.4.3 Micro-architecture

Finally, when we move down to the micro-architecture of the VAX-11/780 processor,[2] the state space is further enlarged since many additional components are visible at this level. Most importantly, the microprogrammer must have precise knowledge of the internal organization of the control unit, including the microinstruction word format, the semantics of each of the micro-operations that may be encoded within a microinstruction, and the mechanism used by the microsequencer to generate the successive addresses of microinstructions. An-

[2] Also called the KA780 central processing unit in the VAX literature (Digital, 1979).

Exo-architectural state space

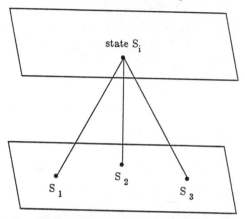

state S_i

S_1 S_2 S_3

Endo-architectural state space

FIGURE 1.5 Mapping between exo-architectural and endo-architectural state spaces.

other important component of the micro-architecture is the clocking (or timing) system that guides the synchronized execution of micro-operations, microinstructions, and the sequencing logic. This information was factored out at the endo-architectural level.

A highly selective view of the VAX-11/780 micro-architecture contains the following components.

1. A 96-bit wide ("horizontal") control store with a single microinstruction format containing some 30 fields. These fields enable the microprogrammer to encode concurrently executable micro-operations, including a variety of 8-, 16- and 32-bit arithmetic, logical, and shift operations (Fig. 1.6).

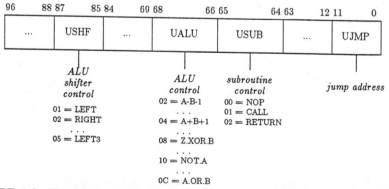

FIGURE 1.6 The VAX-11/780 microinstruction format (Reprinted with permission from *KA780 Central Processor Technical Description*. © Digital Equipment Corporation, Maynard, Mass, 1979).

2. A 200 ns, four-phase system clock, each phase being 50 ns long.
3. A "microstack" capable of saving up to 16 control store addresses and used for calling and returning from subroutines within a microprogram. The call/return signal originates in the microinstruction (Fig. 1.6).
4. A sequencing mechanism that may generate the next executable microinstruction address from a number of different sources. The normal source is a 13-bit "jump" field in the current microinstruction logically added to special 3-, 4- or 5-bit "branch input" entities. A second address source is the top element of the microstack, used when control returns from a (micro)subroutine (Fig. 1.7).

1.5 STRUCTURE AND BEHAVIOR

Every architectural level contains both structural and behavioral components. By *structure* we mean the set of important static (time invariant) components of

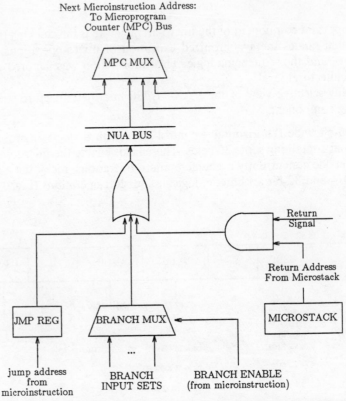

FIGURE 1.7 Next microinstruction address generation logic in the VAX-11/780 microarchitecture (Reprinted with permission from *KA780 Central Processor Technical Description*. © Digital Equipment Corporation, Maynard, Mass, 1979).

the architecture and their static (time invariant) relationship. Because of their nature, structural aspects of an architecture can be easily described and even be represented diagrammatically.

Thus, the data types, data structures, and instruction formats in an exo-architecture, or the microinstruction format in a micro-architecture — that is, its internal organization and the names and encodings of their constituent operations (Fig. 1.6) — are often pictorially represented. The "block diagram" form, as shown in Figure 1.4, is a common representation of the structural aspect of endo-architectures, whereas Figure 1.7 is a hybrid diagram consisting of functional blocks (the NUA bus, microstack), register-transfer-level elements (the JMP register, and the two multiplexers) and gate level elements (the OR and AND gates). The components in both diagrams are connected by lines denoting data and control paths.

The structural aspect of an architecture establishes the basis for formulating how it should behave. By *behavior* we mean the dynamics of the abstract machine that the architecture represents: what the functions of its components are and how information and control actually flow between the components.

In an exo-architecture, it is therefore necessary to know not only how an instruction is represented and encoded but what the *meaning* of an instruction is: the mapping it performs between its input and output storage elements. Similarly, the name of an operand addressing mode (e.g., "autoincrement" in the VAX-11) and its encoding in an instruction is a structural feature; the corresponding computation performed by the machine hardware/firmware to generate the effective real address is a behavioral component.

Behavior becomes particularly crucial in endo- and micro-architectures since the source of complexity at these levels lies in their behavior. The problem of designing or analyzing the endo-architecture of the VAX-11/780, for instance, lies in one's ability to comprehend the dynamic relationships between the components depicted in Figure 1.4. Questions are, typically, of the form:

- What is the mapping performed by the address translation buffer?
- How is this unit activated and which of the other components have the power to activate it?
- Can two or more of the components shown become active concurrently? What if one needs the result of the other — how are they synchronized to exchange information at the right time?

Concurrency and synchronization are, thus, notable factors contributing to the behavioral complexity of architectures.

1.6 COMPUTER ARCHITECTURE AS A DESIGN DISCIPLINE

In the preceding sections I described those properties of computers that fall within the scope of computer architecture. A major part of research, development, and innovations in this field is concerned with the identification, development, refinement, and implementation of such architectural properties at one or more of the architectural levels. The totality of our knowledge of these properties at any particular time constitute what might be termed architectural *principles*.

However, computers and their properties are artifacts; architects must, therefore, also deal with how an appropriate subset of these principles are selected, composed, and integrated during the *design* of a particular architecture. The subject of computer architecture, then, deals not only with the description, analysis, and understanding of architectural principles; it is also a *design discipline* concerned with how the *total architecture* of a computer may be derived.

A *discipline* means, among other things, "a system of rules of conduct."[3] This meaning is particularly relevant to our context: A discipline of computer architecture design may be defined as *a system of rules and procedures governing the design of computer architectures*.

Interest, among theorists and practitioners, in formulating such a discipline— a rational, formal, "scientific" basis for architectural design—is of relatively recent origin (Dasgupta, 1984). At the time of this writing, it is not yet a major movement, although there are signs that the movement as such is steadily gaining momentum.[4] It is, therefore, important to examine the causes of this newly emergent interest in a discipline of computer architecture.

The first and probably the most vital of these causes is technology. The development of very large scale integration (VLSI) semiconductor technology has resulted in a potential for processor chips of enormous circuit density. On the one hand, this has led to entire processors being embedded on a single chip or a few chips. On the other, the atoms from which larger, more powerful computer systems may be built are no longer simple circuits but entire (micro)processors. Thus, whether they are designing and building single-chip processors or multichip multiprocessor systems, computer architects are having to grapple with design issues and the problems of "complexity management" that are quite different from those of a decade or so ago.

Taking their cue from other fields—in particular, software technology (Wegner, 1979)—many architectural theorists and practitioners have turned their attention to a more careful examination of the design process in the conviction that only the development of highly ordered, disciplined, and logical methods of design can control and solve these newly emergent problems of complexity (Mead and Conway 1980; Dasgupta 1984).

Second, substantial parts of the computer design process have been fully or partially automated. Much of *design automation* has traditionally been concerned with the low-level or physical aspects of computer design, such as the

---

[3]J. B. Sykes (ed.): *Concise Oxford Dictionary, 6th ed.* Oxford: Clarendon Press, 1976.

[4]One such sign is of an institutional nature: the ninth (1982) and tenth (1983) International Symposia on Computer Architecture—the premier international conference on the subject—had entire sessions on design methods. The "call for papers" for the eleventh and twelfth symposia (1984 and 1985, respectively) identified "methods for the design and description of architectures" as one of the selected topics of interest.

design, simulation, and testing of logic level and electrical circuits and the solution of chip layout problems (Breuer, 1975; Rabbat, 1983). More recently, efforts have been directed to the more difficult, high-level stages of the design process, including the synthesis of register-transfer-level systems (Parker, 1984), and microcode and micro-architecture synthesis (Dasgupta and Shriver, 1985; Mueller and Varghese, 1985; Nagle, Cloutier, and Parker, 1982).

Finally, as observed by Dasgupta (1984), the ad-hoc, informal and intuitive nature of conventional architecture design has proved to be highly unsatisfactory for a number of reasons. In particular, because architects have, by and large, ignored the use of formal methods of modeling, describing, and documenting their designs, it has proved difficult to demonstrate design correctness and accurately predict the performance of an architecture without actually implementing it in the form of a physical system.

Thus, much interest has recently been shown, and some progress made, in the construction of unified, theoretical frameworks within which one may systematically and formally design, describe, model, verify, and evaluate computer architectures prior to undertaking the costly endeavor of physically realizing such systems. Note that this program of research and development rests on its own merit quite independent of any desire to automate the design process.

1.7 THE INTERACTION OF COMPUTER ARCHITECTURES AND COMPILERS

The task of a compiler is to transform a program written in some high-level, machine-independent language into an efficient, functionally equivalent representation in the target machine's instruction set.[5] Thus, there is an obvious interaction between the design of a computer's exo-architecture and the design of compilers intended to generate code for that computer. In particular, the complexity of the compiler itself, the difficulty of writing it, the ease and efficiency with which the compiler generates code, and the efficiency (in both time and space) of the executable code are all profoundly influenced by the nature of the target exo-architecture as well as by the harmonious relationship between the exo-architecture and the source (high-level) programming language.

1.7.1 The RISC Philosophy

A widely discussed architectural topic in recent years is the philosophy of the reduced instruction set computer (RISC) (Patterson and Ditzel, 1980; Patterson, 1985), which not only illustrates how technology influences architecture design

---

[5]In the compiler literature, the machine that will execute the compiled code is referred to as the *target* machine. In contrast, in microprogramming terminology, the machine that executes the microcode is called the *host* machine whereas that which the microprogram emulates is referred to as the target.

(see Section 1.9) but also demonstrates how compiler-related issues may influence architecture. It puts forth a view of exo- and endo-architecture designs intended to both ease the compilation process and enhance the efficiency of the compiled code.

RISC architectures are discussed in some detail in Chapter 7, (Volume 1), but we can summarize the issue in relation to compilers as follows.

Basically, it has been observed that for various reasons exo-architectures have evolved over the years toward greater complexity—as manifested in larger instruction sets and more complex ("powerful") instructions. Because of the widespread replacement of assembly languages by high-level programming languages the burden of using such instruction sets falls on the compiler, which very often is unable to exploit the more complex instructions.

The result is that only a small subset of the instruction repertoire is actually used by the compiler. Empirical observations of this phenomenon have been reported by several investigators. For example, in their study of the XPL compiler for the IBM System/360, Alexander and Wortman (1975) found that only 10 instructions accounted for 80% of the instructions executed and 99% of executed instructions were accounted for by 30 instructions.

Thus, the proponents of the RISC philosophy suggest that rather than design architectures with large instruction sets, most of which are ignored by the compiler, one should strive to select a small (or "reduced") set of instructions that are sufficiently simple to be exploited fully by the compiler.

1.7.2   Architectural Ideals from a Compiler Writer's Perspective

The design of a small number of relatively simple instructions is, in fact, one of a number of exo-architectural features that influences compilers and the compilation process. A more comprehensive set of issues from the compiler writer's perspective was discussed by Wulf (1981). He identified a collection of "ideal" characteristics or principles that should guide the definition of exo-architectures.

1. **Regularity**   If a particular feature is realized in a certain way in one part of the architecture, then it should be realized in the same way in all parts.

Example 1.2

There should only be one way of encoding or representing a particular operand address in an instruction, regardless of the instruction type or format.

As another example, if a set of programmable general purpose registers are defined for a machine, these registers should indeed be usable in a general, uniform way by all instructions. It should not be the case, for instance, that certain instructions can only reference certain registers and not others, or that one or more of these "general purpose" registers have special roles.   ■

2. **Orthogonality**   This is also referred to as the "separation of concerns" principle. The overall architecture should be partitionable into a number of independent features, each of which can be defined separately.

Example 1.3

The definitions of opcode (instruction) set and the set of operand addressing modes should be mutually independent — that is, orthogonal — issues. ∎

3. **Composability** By virtue of the two foregoing principles, it should be possible to compose the separate, orthogonal features in arbitrary ways.

Example 1.4

Given that the instruction (opcode) set and operand addressing modes are regular and orthogonal, the compiler would be able to combine any opcode with any addressing mode. ∎

4. **The one or all principle** From the compiler's point of view, there should be either only one way to do some something or all ways should be possible.

Example 1.5

For generating conditional branching code if the only available branch instructions are ones for testing "equality" and "less than," then the compiler has only one way to generate each of the six possible relations; or if all six test relations are defined in the exo-architecture, there is, again, only one method of generating code for these relations. The problem arises when some *arbitrary* subset of the relations are defined in the architecture, in which case the compiler has a nontrivial analysis on hand to determine how to implement one of the undefined or "nonprimitive" relations. ∎

5. **Provide primitives not solutions** This ideal has a bearing on the interaction of architectures with both compilers and programming languages. The point is, that from the compiler's point of view it is better for the architecture to provide good "primitive" features that can be used efficiently by the compiler to solve code generation problems than for the architecture itself to provide these solutions.

   This principle is, in fact, the cornerstone of the RISC philosophy (see Section 1.7.1). Its validity rests on the observation that certain "powerful" instructions — solutions — are often available in a machine to support a particular high-level language construct. Precisely because of this, however, such instructions represent solutions to *particular* code generation problems and may not be usable to solve even slightly deviating problems.

Example 1.6

1. Subroutine call instructions that support only some parameter passing mechanism.
2. Looping instructions that support only a certain type of high-level language iteration construct. ∎

It is preferable for the compiler to have access to more primitive general features that can be used to support all programming language constructs rather than a subset.

The point of this set of ideals is that the code generation and optimization phases of a compiler essentially involve an enormous *case analysis,* the objective of which is to extract and use information from both program and architecture to generate the most efficient possible code in the best possible way. It is because of this case analysis that the foregoing principles are so important: Any deviation constitutes a special case to be analyzed separately in a possibly ad-hoc manner. The greater the number of such deviations, the larger the number of special case analyses that must be done by the compiler.

1.7.3 Microcode Compilers and Micro-architectures

Since the relationship between compilers and exo-architectures directly affects the performance of both system and application software, the nature of this interaction has been widely discussed. A far less appreciated fact is that one of the very real obstacles that has hitherto prevented the widespread development and acceptance of compilers for *high level microprogramming languages* (HLMLs) is the inherently complex, and frequently convoluted, nature of micro-architectures for which such compilers are supposed to generate microcode.

The crucial problem is that a microcode compiler *must* generate microcode that compares favorably with conventional hand-produced and assembled microprograms. Furthermore, most micro-architectures support horizontal micro-instruction formats that can encode and store several primitive micro-operations intended for execution in parallel. Thus, a microcode compiler must have the capacity to generate sequential code, optimize it, detect which operations can be done in parallel, and, based on this analysis, *compact* the sequential code into a sequence of horizontal micro-instructions. Figures 1.8 and 1.9 contrast the compilation processes for conventional single-processor exo-architectures and horizontal micro-architectures.[6]

Research into high-level microprogramming languages began only in the early 1970s (Dasgupta and Shriver, 1985), and the full-scale development of microcode compilers is of even more recent vintage. At the time of this writing, only a few compilers capable of producing good quality microcode have actually been completed (Baba and Hagiwara, 1981; Ma and Lewis, 1981; Sheraga and Gieser, 1983). There is no doubt that *one* of the major reasons for the paucity of such systems is the sheer difficulty of coping with the idiosyncrasies of micro-archi-

---

[6]Note that Figures 1.8 and 1.9 depict in a very general way the structure of these two types of compilers. One can also point to exceptions. Thus, there is a class of exo-architectures (vector processors) for which compilers must incorporate compaction techniques in order to produce acceptable executable code. Likewise, there are some micro-architectures that may not necessitate compaction at all.

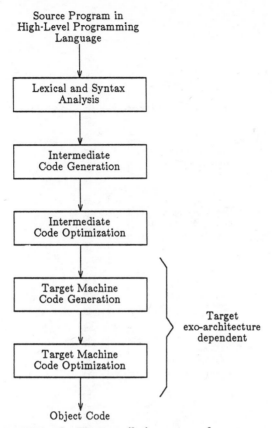

FIGURE 1.8 **The compilation process for programs.**

tectures. Because of the relative youthfulness of microcode compiler technology, very little exists in the way of a careful analysis and documentation of how micro-architectures could be changed to help the compilation process. Instead, firmware engineers[7] have been content to construct progressively more powerful *models* of micro-architectures, hoping that these would allow them to represent larger classes of host machines. These models then form the basis for the code-generation and compaction phases of the compiler.

---

[7]*Firmware engineering* is the discipline concerned with the identification of scientific principles underlying microprogramming and the application of these principles to the firmware development process (Dasgupta and Shriver, 1985). The firmware engineer is, then, typically interested in constructing tools and techniques to support the various phases of the firmware life cycle, that is, functional specification, design, verification, implementation, and maintenance of microcode. Refer to Volume 2, Chapter 5, for further details.

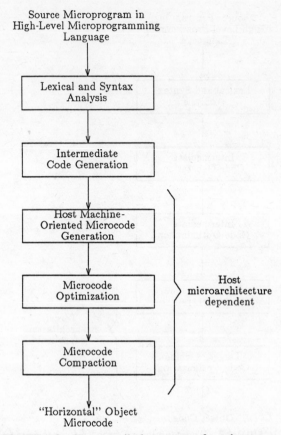

FIGURE 1.9 The compilation process for microprograms.

1.8 THE INFLUENCE OF SOFTWARE TECHNOLOGY ON ARCHITECTURES

As I have noted in Section 1.1, an exo-architecture provides the interface between the computer's *inner environment* — its internal structure — and its *outer environment* (the terms are from Simon, 1981). One of the main reasons why the design of exo-architectures poses difficulties for the architect is because the outer environment is often wide ranging and not predictable to any degree of precision.

The architect has traditionally dealt with this problem by assuming an arbitrary environment and designing exo-architectures that are adapted to this "virtual" environment. The result of this is the now well known *semantic gap* (Myers, 1982) between real and virtual outer environments (Fig. 1.10). The task of bridging this gap is then delegated to compilers and operating systems.

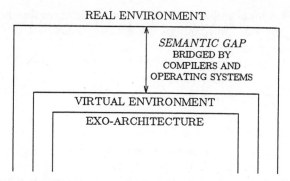

FIGURE 1.10 **The semantic gap (Dasgupta 1984; © 1984, John Wiley & Sons; reprinted with permission).**

Fortunately, this situation has been changing (albeit slowly) over time. From 1961 onward, the Burroughs Corporation has developed and marketed the B5000/B5500/B6500/B6700/B7700 series of general-purpose computers, largely dedicated to the direct architectural support of Algol-like programming languages (Lonergan and King, 1961; Barton, 1961; Organick, 1973; Doran, 1979). In the United Kingdom, beginning in 1968, International Computers Limited initiated the design and production of the ICL 2900 series intended to support efficiently a range of common programming languages (Buckle, 1978). Many of the ideas embodied in this series of machines were first developed by Iliffe (1968) in his Basic Language Machine and by the designers of the Manchester University MU5 (Kilburn *et al.*, 1969; Morris and Ibbett, 1979). Other, more contemporary systems embody similar principles.

To emphasize this relatively new direction in which the real outer environment provides the springboard for designing exo-architectures, such phrases as *software-directed, high-level language,* and *language-directed* are used to describe these architectures. In this book, I will use the last-named term and contrast such language-directed architectures with the more *conventional* exo-architectural styles.

The sources of the mismatch between real and assumed outer environments in conventional machines are many, but they all ultimately appear to originate in the fact that conventional architectures—even contemporary ones—are, largely, evolutionary offsprings and close descendents of the original, so-called *von Neumann computer model* of the 1940s.[8] As Myers (1982) has pointed out, most of these architectural features were more or less identified in the early 1950s—that is, in an era when the programming craft was scarcely understood, operating systems were primitive, and high-level programming languages had yet to be invented. The semantic gap in its present form came into being because exo-architecture design has evolved *much* more slowly than software technology.

[8]For an explanation of this term and a brief account of the controversy surrounding it, see Section 1.10, "Bibliographic and Historical Notes," at the end of this chapter.

Thus, the conventional exo-architectures contain features that have little or no direct bearing on how computations are actually conceived, designed, and described by programmers.

The issue of language-directed architectures are dealt with further, in Chapters 6 and 7 of Volume 1. However, it may be useful to state briefly here the principal causes of the semantic gap. These have been identified by Myers (1982) as

1. *Language-related causes.* Programming languages embody many concepts that are not directly reflected in the underlying architecture. Examples include (a) the explicit separation of data and executional statements (instructions) in high-level language programs; (b) the definition of data types as a set of values together with a set of operations that may be applied to these values; (c) a concept of storage that is intrinsically nonlinear and nonmonolithic; and (d) the notion and use of multidimensional and nonregular data structures.
2. *Operating system-related causes.* Modern operating systems provide several functions. These include (a) utility services such as storage and other resource allocation functions, process synchronization, and interprocess communication; (b) the creation of abstract virtual machines and memories; and (c) the enforcement of both information sharing and protection.

Again, some very critical aspects of these operating systems functions are poorly supported by conventional machines. For example, Denning (1978) has pointed out that while the working-set concept (see Volume 1, Chapter 8) is crucial in paged virtual memory mechanisms, there are no contemporary architectures in which this concept is implemented in hardware—although studies (Morris, 1972) have demonstrated its economic feasibility. Myers (1982) has also noted that the long-established and central notion of the *process* as the basic unit of parallel execution and owner of resources has no support in conventional architectures.

1.9 IMPLEMENTATION TECHNOLOGY AND COMPUTER ARCHITECTURE

Regardless of the extent to which compilers, programming languages, and computational issues exert their influence, the dominant force on architecture and computer design has, and will continue to be, the implementation technology prevalent at a given time. It is the technology that determines the potential performance and the cost of a computer and the latter's form and function are inevitably dictated by, and the result of, these technology-determinant parameters. We may illustrate the nature of the interaction between technology and architecture through several examples.

Example 1.7

In a sense, the most celebrated instance of this interaction—and how implementation technology may influence the success or failure of an architectural proposal — is Charles Babbage's work on the Difference and Analytical Engines, the former occupying him between 1822 and 1833 and the latter for the rest of his life till he died in 1871.

The Difference Engine — in modern terms, a special-purpose processor — was intended to generate successive values of algebraic functions by means of the method of finite difference. However, it was Babbage's conception of the Analytical Engine that was more remarkable since in the course of its design, Babbage discovered most of the key principles of a programmable general-purpose computing device consisting of a store, an arithmetic unit, punched card input/output, and a card-controlled sequencing mechanism that allowed for both iteration and conditional branching (Randell, 1975, Chapters 1 and 2; Wilkes, 1977). In fact, it has been pointed out by Wilkes (1977) that Babbage was essentially dealing with what we now call problems of logical design and architecture.

The reason why Babbage failed to complete the construction of these two machines is complex and diffuse. Certainly, it must have had something to do with whether the ethos of the time was receptive to his ideas on computing engines. But it is equally clear that a *major* factor was that the successful construction and operation of these machines *lay beyond the available technology of the day.* In the case of the Difference Engine, in fact, a master machine-tool builder, Joseph Clement, was hired to work on the project; Randell (1975, Chapter 1) has pointed out that the engineering demands exerted by the Difference Engine actually resulted in significant improvements in machine-tool technology.

As for the Analytical Engine, a committee appointed in 1878 by the British Association for the Advancement of Science to advise it on the construction of the Analytical Engine, although recommending highly its conceptual design, voiced its scepticism concerning the physical realizability of the machine.

Herein lies the essential tension between the vision and concepts of an architect and the hard reality of the technology available at the given time. ■

Example 1.8

Jumping forward some 150 years to the present, the way in which technology may influence architecture is most dramatically illustrated by developments in very large scale integration (VLSI).

The essential point about VLSI is that while it offers the enormous benefits of low-cost fabrication and high chip density, it also imposes significant constraints, one of which is that if VLSI is to be used effectively, then systems must be of an *orderly, regular,* and *repeatable* form. Thus, the technology places the very real constraint of regularity on VLSI-based endo-architectures (Mead and Conway, 1980; Snyder, 1984) whether that architecture is realized on a single chip or through multiple chips.

As a good example of such architectures, Kung and coworkers (Kung and Lieserson, 1980; Foster and Kung, 1980; Fisher and Kung, 1983) have developed a whole class of structures called *systolic* systems that are particularly suited for VLSI implementation. The basic idea is to use a highly regular

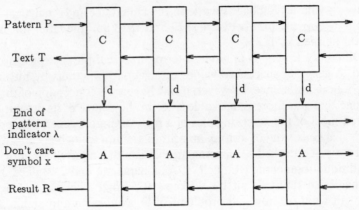

FIGURE 1.11 **Structure of a systolic pattern matching system (Foster and Kung 1980; © 1980, IEEE; reprinted with permission).**

configuration of identical cells that realizes a particular function in the form of a special purpose processor.

Figure 1.11 depicts the general architecture for a systolic pattern matching system. It consists of a one-dimensional array of two types of cells. The *comparator* cell (C) receives a single character from a pattern P and from a text string T flowing in opposite directions. It compares them and passes the text character to the left adjacent cell and the pattern character to the right adjacent cell. The result of the comparison is a match signal d that passes down to the *accumulator* cell (A).

Inputs to an accumulator cell are an end-of-pattern indicator λ and a "don't care" symbol x, entering from the left; the match signal d entering from the top; and the intermediate result signal R flowing from right to left. The accumulator cell maintains a temporary result T, and at the end of the pattern it uses T to replace the result R according to the computation

$$\lambda_{out} := \lambda_{in}$$
$$x_{out} := x_{in}$$
If λ_{in} **then** $R_{out} := T$; $T := TRUE$
else $R_{out} := R_{in}$; $T := T \wedge (x_{in} \vee d)$

It is interesting to note that the idea of using highly ordered structures of identical cells was formulated almost 20 years ago under the name of *cellular logic* (Minnick, 1967; Kautz, 1971; Mukhopadhay and Stone, 1971), in anticipation of large-scale integration (LSI) technology. Systolic arrays represent a modern reincarnation largely driven by the arrival of the necessary technology. ■

Example 1.9

Finally, we return once more to the Berkeley RISC machines, which exemplify in a different way how VLSI technology may influence architectural design. We have already noted (see Section 1.7) that one of the objectives of the reduced instruction set philosophy was to ease the task of efficient compilation. A second major objective was to effectively use "scarce" silicon area to implement a single-chip processor comparable in performance to more complex processors such as the VAX-11/780 (Patterson and Sequin, 1981; Patterson, 1985).

These two objectives matched one another well. By analyzing the frequency of various types of instructions generated by compilers the RISC architects identified a set of 31 instructions. Implementing such a small set resulted in a substantial saving in control logic—from about 50% of the chip area on typical microprocessors to about 6% in RISC-I (Patterson, 1985). The saved area was then used to hold a large set of internal registers [138 in the case of RISC-I (Patterson and Sequin, 1981)], which, in turn, was used to implement a scheme called *overlapping register windows* for improving procedure calls and returns.

The net result was a distinctive architectural style (spanning both exo- and endo-levels) that achieved a performance comparable (in some ways) to that of the so-called "complex" instruction set computers.   ■

1.10 BIBLIOGRAPHIC AND HISTORICAL NOTES

The word "architecture" appears to have been used for the first time in the early 1960s by the designers of the IBM System/360 series (Amdahl, Blaauw, and Brooks, 1964). They used this word to denote the attributes of the machine as seen by the programmer, that is, the conceptual structure and functional behavior of the machine as distinct from the organization of the data flow or the logical and physical design. This definition has since been adopted by other authorities, for example by Fuller and associates (1977a) in their work on the computer family architecture (CFA) project, Myers (1982), and the VAX designers (Digital, 1981a).

Unfortunately, there has never been any consistency in the use of this word, either in the published literature or in the institutional setting in which computer architects practice their craft. An inspection of the actual topics that are the subject of their research, writing, and discussion reveals that architects are as much interested in internal structure and behavior of processors as in their external characteristics. For instance, a very active area of investigation is the design of interconnection networks—a quintessential characteristic of the internal structure of a system. Moreover, some architects, for example, those designing single-chip processors, are interested in the relatively low-level structure of machines as seen at the microprogramming level.

These inconsistencies with respect to the original definition have, in fact, been recognized by several authors, for example, Baer (1980), and Dennis and co-workers (1979). The terms "exo-architecture" and "endo-architecture" were coined by Dasgupta (1981) largely to reflect this social reality and was used widely in Dasgupta (1984).

"Micro-architecture" has been in reasonably common use, especially in the microprogramming literature (Salisbury, 1976). For another viewpoint on the concept of architecture, refer to Zemanek (1980).

The name of the Hungarian born mathematician John von Neumann (1903–1957) has become permanently associated with the style that has dominated computer design since the mid-1940s. At the heart of the so-called *von Neumann machine model* is the stored program idea. The question of who originated this fundamental concept has generated controversy that remains unabated almost to this day.

The key figures in the earliest development of the electronic computer were J. Presper Eckert (b. 1919) and John W. Mauchly (1907–1980) on the one hand, and von Neumann on the other. Eckert and Mauchly were the principle designers of the ENIAC, the very first electronic computer, built at the Moore School, University of Pennsylvania, between 1942 and 1946 (Randell, 1975, Chapter 2; Stern, 1981). This was not a stored program computer—the program was manually loaded through external pluggable cables and switches.

Very soon after the ENIAC design had been frozen (in 1944), von Neumann became associated with the Moore School group as a consultant, and the planning of a new computer named EDVAC soon followed. The basic design of this machine was outlined in a memorandum authored by von Neumann (1945). This widely distributed report contained, apparently for the first time, the description of the role of a memory "organ," including its need to hold instructions. Furthermore—and this is significant—the report noted that although the "different parts" of the memory were to perform different functions (e.g., holding input data, intermediate results, instructions, tables), it should be conceived as a single organ with the different parts being "interchangeable." Thus was born the stored-program computer concept with a homogenous multifunctional memory.

As Stern (1980) has pointed out, because this report was authored only by von Neumann, and contained neither references to, nor acknowledgements of, any other contributor, the stored program principle was widely believed to have been invented by von Neumann. A later, more detailed, report on the stored program computer by Burks, Goldstine, and von Neumann (1946) that, over the years, has been widely reprinted in various anthologies (Randell, 1975; Bell and Newell 1971; Swartzlander, 1976) further helped to strengthen this general belief.

However, according to several other participants of the ENIAC and other projects that followed, the stored-program concept had emerged within the ENIAC group consisting of Eckert, Mauchly, von Neumann, and others in the course of their many discussions at the time (Stern 1980). Both Wilkes (1968) and Metropolis and Worlton (1980) state very clearly that Eckert and Mauchly had *conceived* the stored-program idea during the ENIAC development period —that is, before von Neumann became associated with the Moore School.

For further discussion of the stored-program controversy, refer to Randell (1975, Chapter 8); Stern (1980); Metropolis and Worlton (1980); and Goldstine (1972, Part 2).

Quite apart from the debate it generated over the stored-program concept, one very important aspect of the initial EDVAC report (von Neumann, 1945) must be noted. And that is, its remarkable focus on the *logical* principles and organization of computers in contrast to the electrical/electronic means of realizing these principles; in other words, in the modern history of the computer, the EDVAC report appears to have been the first to make a clear distinction between what we now call the architecture and the technology of computers.

PROBLEMS

1.1   The adoption of the term *computer architecture* seems to imply an analogy of some sort between computers and buildings. However, scientists also talk about the *architecture of matter,* the *architecture of the brain,* and so on. Thus, the word "architecture" seems to be used to designate some set of *shared properties* present in very dissimilar objects.

 Using these and other relevant objects as examples, identify exactly what these common properties are that justify the use of the word "architecture" in the context of such diverse objects as computers, buildings, matter, and brains.

1.2   One of the hallmarks of a complex system — whether natural or made by humans — is that it can be described at several different *abstraction levels* such that each abstraction level serves a specific purpose that is not served by any of the other levels. Furthermore, the different abstraction levels are related to one another in some fashion.

 Consider an arbitrary computer program P.

(a)   Identify at least three distinct levels at which P may be meaningfully designed (or described). Also describe the purpose of each of these abstraction levels.

(b)   Explain how these different levels are related to one another.

 [*Hint*: It might be helpful to answer this question by considering a specific program that you have written or are familiar with.]

1.3   The exo-architecture of a pocket calculator may be defined as the structure and behavior of the calculator that need to be known by the "user." Write a concise but complete description of your pocket calculator's exo-architecture. Keep in mind that from your description it should be possible for others to learn to use your calculator correctly.

1.4   Consider the "exo-architecture" of an automobile. As with all architectural descriptions, this will consist of a structural component and a behavioral component.

(a)   Characterize the structure of an automobile at the exo-architectural level.

(b)   Characterize the behavior of an automobile at the exo-architectural level.

1.5 Is it possible to define the structure of a system without any reference to the system's behavior? Justify your answer.

1.6 Is it possible to describe the behavior of a system without any reference to the system's structure? Justify your answer. [*Hint*: It might be helpful to answer both 1.5 and 1.6 by referring to a specific system.]

1.7 We talk about a particular person being the *architect* of a plan or a policy. We also say that a person has *engineered* some particular event. Using these figures of speech as clues, explain what you think is the real distinction to be made (if any) between the disciplines of computer architecture and computer engineering.

1.8 Consider a vending machine that will dispense three types of soft drinks, one priced 40 cents, the second 45 cents, and the third 50 cents. For each of these services the machine will accept only exact amounts as combinations of quarters, dimes, and nickels. After inserting the coins, the consumer presses one of three buttons corresponding to the three types of drinks, and, if the correct coinage has been inserted, the machine responds by dispensing the drink. Otherwise an error light comes on.

Prior to actually building the vending machine, it is required to implement a program that will *simulate* the device.

(a) Design the *exo-architecture* of the simulated machine.

(b) Design an *endo-architecture* for the simulated machine such that your exo-architecture design is a correct abstraction of the endo-architecture.

(c) *Implement* the endo-architecture in the form of a fully executable computer program.

1.9 Given the experience gained from solving 1.8, what conclusions do you reach regarding the role of architecture in the design and implementation of a system and the distinctions (if any) between "architecture" and "implementation"?

1.10 The basic premise behind the design of RISC architectures (see Section 1.7.1) is that for "typical" computers only a very small subset of the instruction set is actually used by the compiler during code generation. Based on your experience in programming in high-level languages such as FORTRAN, Pascal or C, identify what in your opinion are likely to be the 10 most important instructions that a computer must contain as part of its exo-architecture. Justify each of your choices.

CHAPTER 2

THE TECHNOLOGICAL FRAMEWORK

2.1 INTRODUCTION

The word *technology* when used in connection with computer design refers to the electronic, physicochemical, or mechanical means for the *physical implementation* of processors and other components. The word is used to denote the entire range of implementation techniques as well as to specific methods; in the latter case, one may legitimately speak of different *technologies.*

The relationship of computer architecture to technology is somewhat analogous to that of, say, structural engineering to structural and building materials. It is absolutely imperative for the structural engineer to be fully cognizant of the strengths and limitations of materials so that the structures he or she designs are realizable. Conversely, knowledge of some particular properties of materials may be exploited by the engineer and brought to bear in a particular structural design. This knowledge used by the engineer is highly selective: metals, alloys, concrete, wood, and other materials have many different kinds of characteristics, only a few of which are of interest to the structural engineer, notably their mechanical properties and the factors that affect these properties. The (building) architect, in contrast, may be interested in very different kinds of properties — their textures, for example, or how they symbolize some aesthetic or functional aspect of the building as a whole.

We make these preliminary observations to emphasize that in discussing the technological framework of computer architecture one is (once again) posed a problem of abstraction: Among the many features and characteristics of the various available technologies, which are the ones relevant to the computer architect and why? And in what fashion can such technological knowledge influence architectural designs or styles?

The aim of this chapter, then, is to discuss those aspects of the technologies of processors (*logic technology*) and memory systems (*memory* or *storage technology*) that are relevant to computer architecture.

2.2 LEVELS OF INTEGRATION

Certainly the dominating evolutionary theme in both logic and memory technology has been the remarkable increase in the number of logic gates or components per integrated circuit (IC) chip since about 1959 when the first discrete transistors were used in digital computers. This growth in circuit density has been succinctly described in terms of what has come to be known as *Moore's law.*

This "law" in its original form states simply that the number of components per circuit doubles every year. This trend was first predicted in 1964 by Gordon E. Moore and, as Figure 2.1 indicates, the growth for the period 1959–1975 followed this prediction.

This rate of growth, however, has tended to decelerate from the mid 1970s onward. Moore (1979) himself noted this and suggested that the component count would double every 2 years rather than every year. This is shown in Figure 2.1 by the slight flattening of the curve from about 1975 onward. It is further obvious that even this growth rate cannot continue indefinitely, since there are physical limitations to the size of circuits.

The technological basis for this growth in the density of IC chips is essentially twofold: reduction in feature size and increase in chip area.

The *feature size* is the width of the smallest dimension to be fabricated in silicon and determines the size of the transistors and width of the wires. Feature size has dropped from about 37 microns in 1960 to 2 microns in 1984,[1] although

---

[1] 1 micron $= 10^{-6}$ meters.

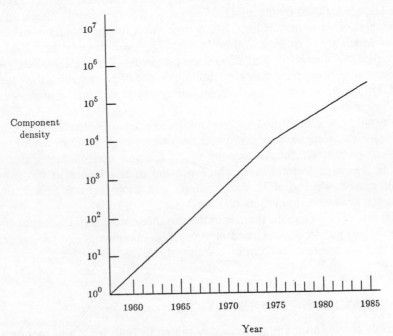

FIGURE 2.1 The Moore Plot.

Burger and colleagues (1984) have pointed out that laboratory devices with 0.3-micron feature size have been developed.

Similarly, over the past two decades, chip size (chip area) has increased by an order of magnitude — from about 4 mm² in 1965 to 40 mm² in 1982 (Burger *et al.*, 1984).

For many years now, it has become customary to partition ICs among the following classes according to the extent of integration:

Small-scale integration (SSI).

Medium-scale integration (MSI).

Large-scale integration (LSI).

Very-large-scale integration (VLSI).

To these, a fifth class, ultra-large-scale integration (ULSI), has sometimes been added. Unfortunately, there is considerable discrepancy among different author-ities as to the range of circuit densities for each of these classes, as Table 2.1 shows. The matter is further confused in that the scale of integration is some-times quantified according to the number of *gates* (the first and second column, Table 2.1), the number of *devices* (transistors, resistors, etc.), or the number of *components* (without further explanation — see the third column of Table 2.1) per chip. In general, the device count per chip can be obtained from the gate count by multiplying the latter by from 3 to 5 (Muroga, 1982).

Rather than relying too much on the numbers, you can better appreciate these scales of integration by considering the functional power (or "functionality") of the circuits when viewed as building blocks in digital systems and computer design. Table 2.2 lists examples from each of the classes of ICs. Again, because the boundaries are somewhat fuzzy, you may disagree about the placement of some of the circuits in one class rather than another.

TABLE 2.1 Circuit Density/Chip for Various Scales of Integration

Scale of Integration	Circuit Density/Chip		
	Siewiorek, Bell, and Newell (1982)	Muroga (1982)	Burger *et al.* (1982)
SSI	1–10 gates	<10 gates	2–64 components
MSI	10–100 gates	10–100 gates	64–2,000 components
LSI	100–10,000 gates	100–100,000 gates	2,000–64,000 components
VLSI	10,000–100,000 gates	>100,000 gates	64,000–2,000,000 components
ULSI	>100,000 gates		2,000,000–64,000,000 components

TABLE 2.2   Functionality of Building Blocks per Scale of Integration

Scales of Integration	Building Block and Circuit Examples
SSI	4 two-input NAND gate packages 3 three-input NAND gate packages 6 INVERTER packages 4 two-input XOR gate packages 2 master-slave JK flip-flop packages 2 edge-triggered D flip-flop packages
MSI	4-bit ALU with up to 32 functions 8-input multiplexor/selector Decimal decoder 4-bit synchronous binary counter 8-bit serial-in, parallel-out shift register
LSI	16K-bit (2048 × 8) read-only memory 12-input, 12-output programmable logic array 300-gate array 4-bit ALU/register bit-slice device 4-bit microprogram sequencer 8-bit microprocessors
VLSI	16-bit and 32-bit microprocessors Programmable systolic chip

2.3 TECHNOLOGIES AND THEIR CHARACTERISTICS

The properties of IC chips are intimately connected to the technology used to fabricate the chips. ICs are basically built from conducting material deposited on a substrate (usually) of silicon. The different technologies arise because of the different kinds of materials that may be used to form the layers and the different methods used to deposit them. The actual details of materials and fabrication underlying these technologies are beyond the scope of this book; however, the Bibliographic section at the end of this chapter discusses several references for further reading.

Our perspective and understanding of technologies will, instead, be based on a few key features that are of immediate interest to the computer architect. We will, therefore, attempt to provide a characteristic "profile" of each of the more well-known technologies, with minimal reference to the internal physical causes underlying these profiles.

The most widely used ICs fall into two main categories according to the transistor type. The first uses the *pnp* or *npn junction transistor*, which are commonly known as *bipolar transistors* since charge carriers of both polarities (electrons and holes that are, respectively, the negative and positive charge carriers) are involved. The second category is based on the unipolar or *field effect transistor* (FET) involving a single charge carrier. These are more commonly referred to as *metal-oxide semiconductor* (MOS) devices because of the materials used in their fabrication.

Bipolar devices can be from one of several technology or logic families. Of these, the most widely used are the *transistor-transistor logic* (TTL) and *emitter-coupled logic* (ECL) technologies. A third, more recently developed bipolar family, is *integrated-injection logic* (I²L). Several other bipolar technologies that we will not be considering here have also been developed.

MOS devices fall principally into three classes, called *p-channel* MOS (PMOS), *n-channel* MOS (NMOS), and *complementary* MOS (CMOS), depending, respectively, on whether the charge carriers are positive (holes) or negative (electrons) or whether the devices include both types of transistors. PMOS technology, although used in the past, has been largely replaced by the faster NMOS technology and will not be further discussed here. We will consider, rather, a high-performance version of NMOS, called HMOS.

The properties that are most likely to be of interest to the architect are summarized in Table 2.3 for the three principal bipolar technologies (TTL, ECL, and I²L) and the three most significant MOS technologies (NMOS, HMOS, and CMOS). It is important to note that the values of the different parameters are "typical" and there are higher and lower performance versions of each of the technology families that yield different values for these parameters. Furthermore, whenever there is a sharp discrepancy in values given by different authorities for a given parameter, these variants are listed. The sources for all the data are cited at the bottom of Table 2.3.

Based on the data of Table 2.3 and other considerations, the following, very general, statements can be made.

1. The most attractive characteristics of NMOS and HMOS devices are their high packing density and low power consumption (relative to bipolar devices). Compared to NMOS, HMOS yields even better density and power consumption characteristics. Because of these basic properties, MOS technology has been traditionally used for semiconductor memories and most microprocessors. NMOS was used in the 8-bit microprocessors whereas HMOS has been employed in both 16-bit and 32-bit microprocessors. The low speed (high gate propagation delay) characteristics of NMOS have also been circumvented in HMOS technology.

2. CMOS technology gives still lower power consumption. It has other advantages not shown in Table 2.3, namely, a wider operating range with respect to power supply voltage and operating temperatures. As Table 2.3 shows, the speed of CMOS devices and the achievable density of chips are low compared to NMOS and HMOS logic. However, these problems are being resolved by continuous improvements in CMOS technology (Muroga, 1982).

3. ECL is the fastest of the currently prevalent commercial technologies, although this speed is accompanied by high power consumption and low chip density. ECL technology is mostly used to achieve small-scale-integration building blocks and also gate arrays and, because of its speed characteristics,

TABLE 2.3 Comparison of Technologies

Technology/ Year of Introduction	Propagation Delay/Gate (ns)	Power Consumption/ Gate (mW)	Relative Density (1 = densest)	Delay (speed)— Power Product (pj)	Integration	Uses
TTL (1963; Sylvania)[3]	2 – 10[1,2]	1 – 19[1,2]	5[1]	20[1,2]	MSI, LSI	Midrange processors (e.g., VAX-11/780, PDP-11/34);[2] bit-slices (e.g., AM2901 alu/register slice).[1]
ECL (1961; J. A. Narud)[3]	0.2 – 2[1]	20 – 60[1]	5[1]	20[1]	SSI, small, medium LSI	Gate arrays; high-performance processors [e.g., CRAY-1 (SSI)[2] IBM 370/168, Amdahl 470/v6 (gate arrays);[2] MC 10800 processor slice].[1]

Technology						Applications
I²L (1972; IBM Germany and Philips)	5–35[1]	<0.5[1]	2[1]	0.5[1] 3.75[4]	Small, medium LSI	Bit-slices (e.g., TI SBP0401A 4-bit ALU/register slice).
NMOS (1968)	20–90[1] 4[2,5]	0.1–3[1] 1[2]	2[1]	4[1,5]	LSI/VLSI	8-bit microprocessors (e.g., Intel 8080, Motorola 6800)
HMOS (1977; Intel)[5]	1[1] 0.2 (1982)[5]	1[1]	1[1]	1[1] 0.25 (1982)[5]	LSI/VLSI	16-bit and 32-bit microprocessors (e.g., Z8000[6]; Berkeley RISC-11[7])
CMOS (1967; RCA)[3]	>10[1] 25-35[8]	<0.1[1]	4[1]	3[1]	LSI/VLSI	Some bit slice devices (e.g., Fairchild Macrologic 4705 ALU/register slice)[1] calculators

Sources
1. Myers (1980), p. 16
2. Bell, Mudge, and McNamara (1978), pp. 36–40.
3. Muroga (1982), p. 239.
4. Muroga (1982), p. 123.
5. Muroga (1982), p. 143.
6. Shima (1979). Reprinted in Rice (1980), pp. 274–282.
7. Katevenis (1985).
8. Muroga (1982), p. 204.

is employed in high performance processors. Some bit slices are also based on ECL technology.

4. Because of its overall set of characteristics, TTL is the most widely used technology for a large variety of medium-range processors and bit-slice components. It provides the basic technology for medium-scale integration. I^2L is a much more recent bipolar technology, the most attractive features of which are low power consumption and relatively high density. Thus, it is used for the low- to medium-end of large-scale integration.

5. The *delay-power product* of a gate defined as (delay time) $\times$ (power dissipation) and measured in picojoules (pj) is a metric that is used to denote the amount of energy required to change the state of a device. It is used to compare different logic technologies as well as variants within a given technology. Generally speaking, the smaller the delay-power product, the better is the technology. However the delay-power product is usually measured under the best conditions (using a ring counter consisting of a ring of logic gates where each gate has only one fan-out connection).[2] It turns out that when networks are constructed with gates having relatively large fan-outs a low-power-based technology such as MOS shows a much greater delay-power product. Thus, the latter as normally measured does not properly reflect the influence of the number of fan-out connections. Because of this, the delay-power product is considered a reasonable but not very precise metric for comparing technologies (Muroga, 1982).

We have reviewed here briefly the relevant characteristics of the most important silicon-based technologies currently in use. Before concluding this section, we must mention two other technologies that are presently of interest, at least at the laboratory level.

The mobility of electrons is 6 to 10 times faster in gallium arsenide than in silicon. Thus, *gallium arsenide metal semiconductor field-effect transistors* (GaAs MESFETs) are being studied as possible high-speed logic devices. Such devices with a gate delay of about 100 picoseconds (psec)[3] at a power consumption of 1 milliwatt (mW) have been demonstrated (Muroga, 1982) while propagation delays as low as 30 psec at room temperature and 17.5 psec at 77°K (liquid nitrogen temperature) have been reported (Lee *et al.*, 1983). Such delays are comparable with the best speeds obtained in Josephson technologies (see the next paragraph). The delay-power product is also very low, measurements of 0.057 pj being obtained (Lee *et al.*, 1983). However, GaAs has certain problems, in particular, its high cost and the fact that high levels of integration have yet to be achieved. As reported by Lee and coworkers (1983), a 1008 gate 8×8 multiplier and several circuits with 100 gates or more have been demonstrated, giving some indication of the level of integration currently attainable.

Research into IC technology will continue to improve speed and power consumption characteristics by scaling-down devices; however, heat dissipation will

---

[2]*Fan-out* denotes the number of inputs (to gates) that can be driven by one output (of a gate).

[3]1 picosecond $= 10^{-3}$ nanoseconds.

increasingly become a problem in high-speed logic. Thus, the feasibility of high-speed devices that work at superconducting temperatures and generate little heat are also being investigated. The most prominent example of such devices is the *Josephson junction*, which currently has the highest speeds. For example, gate delays of 13 psec for 2-input OR gates (at 2.6 μW) have been demonstrated. The delay-power product of a Josephson junction is even lower than that of GaAs circuits — of the order of 0.001 to 0.0001 pj (Muroga, 1982). A disadvantage of the Josephson junction is its greater sensitivity to temperature relative to MOS or GaAs technologies.

2.4 THE PIN-LIMITATION PROBLEM

I have already noted the problem of excessive heat generation and the consequent necessity for its dissipation when IC performance is improved by scaling down the size of circuit elements and increasing the level of integration. Another problem associated with IC chip manufacture and packaging is that of pin limitation.

During the fabrication process IC chips are bounded or mounted on a ceramic substrate. The terminals on the chip (i.e., the inputs to and outputs of the circuits, the ground, and the power supply) are called *pads*, and these are connected to *pins* — the terminals of the ceramic container (Fig. 2.2).

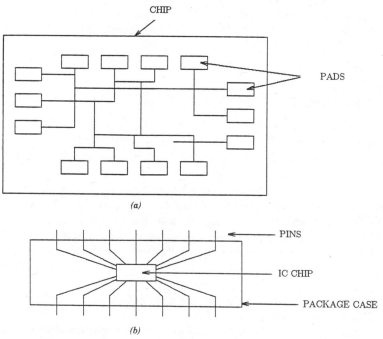

FIGURE 2.2 *(a)* Integrated circuit chip. *(b)* Packaged chip.

The number of pads (or pins) that can be provided on a chip is a vitally important factor affecting the speed of digital systems: It is desirable to minimize the number of pins, since otherwise many interchip connections would be required with an attendant slow down of the overall speed of the digital network.

Rent's rule (devised by E. Rent of IBM in 1960) yields the average number of pads (P) required for a chip of G gates according to the formula

$$P = a*(G**b)$$

where *a* is approximately 4 and *b* is approximately 0.6 (Muroga, 1982). This rule appears to hold well when the overall digital network is partitioned into a number of chips; however, when the level of integration increases, entire networks are often contained in a relatively small number of chips and, consequently, the required number of pads tends to be smaller than the value of P computed according to Rent's rule.

The number of pads (or pins) that can actually be provided on a chip is limited by the two-dimensional geometry of the chip and is usually much smaller than the number that would be required by all the gates on the chip; this is especially so if the pads are restricted to the chip periphery. Up to 150 pads have been obtained this way (Muroga, 1982). However, the pad count can be greatly increased by placing pads throughout the chip, as was done by IBM, which used a chip with a matrix of 17×17 (289) pads in their 4300 series of computers (Muroga, 1982). When the number of pins is too small for the number of signals to be transmitted across the chip boundary, the usual solution is to time-multiplex the available pins. However, this obviously reduces the signal transfer speed greatly. On the other hand, when a network requires a large number of pads, the use of the chip area may be inefficient, thereby reducing the effective level of integration.

2.5 IMPLEMENTATION COMPONENTS

As already noted in Sections 1.9 and 2.1 the architect must be fully aware of the characteristics of the various technologies and components out of which an implementation of a given architectural design will be forged. Some examples of how architecture design and implementation issues can interact were given in Section 1.9. To understand this relationship in more detail, consider the stages in the design and implementation of architectures (Fig. 2.3). It must be emphasized that this is a very general schematic: A particular design and implementation project may omit one or more of the stages shown in the diagram. The extent to which this schematic will be adhered to will depend on the size and complexity of the system being developed, the kinds of design tools and techniques at one's disposal, the organization of the design team, and the extent to which the designers are willing to accept the various stages of the design process shown in Figure 2.3 as separate entities.

Figure 2.3 should be read in conjunction with the various abstraction levels discussed in Chapter 1 (see, in particular, Figures 1.2 and 1.3). A basic assump-

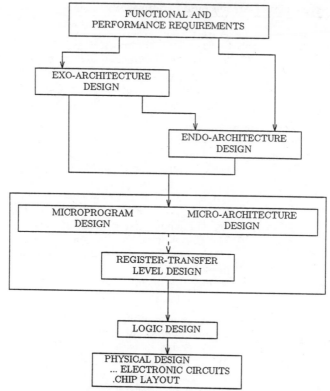

FIGURE 2.3 Steps in the design and implementation of architectures.

tion here is that design proceeds in a top-down fashion (see Chapter 3 for further discussion of design methods); that is, the single line edges denote direct precedences between the stages.

As noted in Section 1.3, and keeping in mind our definitions of these concepts, the micro-architectural and the register-transfers levels may or may not be viewed as distinct. Because of this, these two stages of design are encapsulated in a single box and the dotted line shown between the two inner boxes indicate that these steps are not necessarily viewed as distinct stages. When the micro-architectural level of design *is* viewed as a distinct step, we include it in the range of architectural design activities.

The set of requirements that the computer as a whole must (attempt to) satisfy includes both qualitative and quantitative elements. Among the latter, the two that are most influenced by technology are *performance* and *cost.*

There are, in fact, a variety of performance measures depending in part on the architectural level of interest and in part on the context in which one wishes to evaluate a system. The design goals for all computers will not necessarily involve the same measures, and, sometimes, performance may not be the primary or most important design objective.

Table 2.4 lists some of the more important measures used to assess the

TABLE 2.4 Examples of Architectural Performance Measures

Level	Performance Measures
Micro-architecture	1. Cycle time for control store. 2. Average microinstruction execution rate. 3. Average execution time for benchmark instruction emulation. 4. Total storage space (in control store) for benchmark instruction set emulator.
Implemented (technology-dependent) endo-architecture	1. Average instruction execution rate. [Number of (millions of) instructions/second (MIPS).] 2. Operand processing rate. [Number of (millions of) operands processed/second.] 3. Average execution rate of key operations [e.g., number of floating-point operations/second (FLOPS); number of logical inferences/second (LIPS)]. 4. The CFA R measure: the number of bytes transferred among internal registers of the processor during execution of benchmark. 5. Memory bandwidth: number of bits transferred between memory and CPU/second.
Exo-architecture	1. The CFA measures: S: the number of bytes used to store benchmark programs. M: the number of bytes transferred between main memory and processor during the execution of benchmark programs. 2. The Flynn ratios: M-ratio, P-ratio, and NF-ratio.

performance of architectures. Note that many of these—especially those to do with the design of endo- and micro-architectures—are heavily dependent on technology. Indeed, once such performance goals as MIPS or FLOPS or cycle times are included in the initial set of requirements, the architect can hardly ignore thinking about technological factors.

Suppose otherwise; in particular, assuming that the overall system design proceeds top down as shown in Figure 2.3, suppose that the exo-architecture is first designed *without* taking into account technological factors. Decisions made at the exo-architectural level will establish new constraints and requirements that the endo- and micro-architectures must meet. To satisfy these emergent requirements, the design of the lower architectural levels may necessitate, in turn, certain technological choices that are simply unacceptable from the viewpoints of either performance or cost. The original exo-architecture design becomes infeasible.

Under such circumstances, the architect will be forced to iterate the overall design process using the previous sequence of stages as the basis for feedback information.

In general, even the most careful designer may not be able to foresee every implication of the decisions of an earlier stage of the design; consequently, iterations of the type indicated will hardly be avoidable; that is, design is necessarily of an *evolutionary* nature (see Chapter 3). However, the architect in solving some "architectural problem" must at all times have the capacity and knowledge for testing the *feasibility* of implementation of the design and for estimating whether the design satisfies a priori cost/performance objectives. The iterative design process will then converge to an acceptable solution much more rapidly. To achieve this, the architect must be aware of, and be able to identify beforehand, the kinds of technology that may reasonably support his or her architectural objectives.

Example 2.1

Consider the development of the MU5 computer system (Morris and Ibbett, 1979; Ibbett, 1982). A major initial design objective was that the throughput would be some 20 times that of its predecessor, the Atlas machine. Furthermore, this speedup would be achieved by means of the following features (Morris and Ibbett, 1979, pp. 2–3).

1. State of the art off-the-shelf integrated circuits and interconnection techniques that would give a basic computing speed of seven times that of the Atlas.
2. A 250 nsec main store that would be eight times faster than the Atlas main store.
3. Inclusion of fast operand registers, register-to-register arithmetic, and multiple ALUs.
4. An instruction set designed for ease and efficiency of compilation.
5. Special hardware to support the operating system.

Note the use of both technological and architectural means for achieving the given end. Indeed, the concern for achieving this performance objective influenced almost every aspect of the architecture design, and the project demonstrated very clearly the constant interplay of technological and architectural (especially endo-architectural) decision making.

As a specific case in point, the chosen processor technology was small-scale integration ECL with a circuit delay of 2 nsec. Design of the index arithmetic (Fig. 2.4)—after taking into account packaging considerations—revealed that the time to input operands into the BIN register, perform an add or subtract operation, and output into the B register would be 45 nsec. This is very much

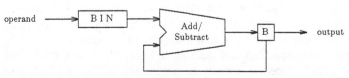

FIGURE 2.4   MU5 index arithmetic unit (based on Ibbett, 1982).

smaller than the cycle time (260 nsec) of the plated wire main memory. To eliminate this mismatch between operand accessing rate (from main memory) and the index arithmetic execution rate (for index arithmetic instructions), an associative store or cache (see Chapter 8) called the *name store* was introduced into the processor. This would hold up to 32 most-recently-accessed operands and deliver the values at a rate almost comparable to the index arithmetic unit speed (Ibbett, 1982, pp. 3–5). ∎

The architect, then, must not only be cognizant of the technologies that go into the fabrication of digital systems, he or she must also possess knowledge of the different kinds of components or building blocks that the technologies make available, since it is from these components that architectural designs are assembled.

For the present discussion, I will not discuss SSI and MSI components any further; it is assumed that you are familiar with the structure and function of such components as they are presented in most modern texts on logic design (see Hayes, 1984, for example). Rather, in the rest of Section 2.5, I will discuss some of the characteristics of LSI/VLSI components that are particularly relevant to computer architecture.

2.5.1 Semiconductor Memories as LSI/VLSI Components

One of the most significant consequences of the scaling up of integrated circuits has been the development and use of semiconductor memories. Because of their regular structure, such memories are very compact, easy to layout, and continue to become cheaper, faster, and more compact every year. These same characteristics have led to the consequence that memories and logic networks can now be combined and distributed throughout a digital system, leading to new choices for design and performance. In particular, memories that have hitherto been used for the traditional purpose of storing programs and temporary data are now used for a variety of functions that were traditionally realized through logic circuits. In fact, as Muroga (1982) and other authorities have noted, modern logic design depends considerably on how well memories are used as components in logic networks.

Basically, of course, all computer systems incorporate some variation of the *memory hierarchy* shown in Figure 2.5, which consists of

1. A small but fast *local store* located within the processing unit. In most processors the local store—also called a *register file*—consists of an array of 8 to 32 registers, although in some recent computers more than a hundred registers have been provided (Patterson and Sequin, 1981; see also, Chapter 7). The main role of a local store is to serve as temporary memory for parameters and variables local to a block or procedure (see Chapters 6 and 7) or the operands for arithmetic and logic operations (see Chapters 4 and 7).

2. A larger, perhaps (but not necessarily) slightly slower *cache memory* (or simply, *cache*) used essentially to hold small segments of program or data

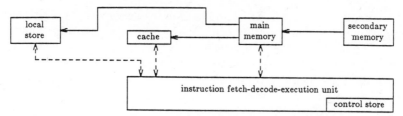

FIGURE 2.5 The "standard" memory hierarchy.

that may be rapidly referenced without the need to access main memory (Chapter 8). Cache sizes usually range up to 8K bytes or words.

3. A far larger and relatively slower *main memory*, the capacity of which is up to the order of *megabytes* [1 megabyte (Mbyte) = 2^{20} bytes]. It is used to hold programs and data segments in preparation for processing.

4. A very large and (relatively) very slow *secondary memory*, typically consisting of magnetic disks and tapes, having a capacity measured in *gigabytes* (1 gigabyte (Gbyte) = 2^{30} bytes) and used to hold, in archival fashion, large quantities of programs and data.

From the perspective of LSI semiconductor technology, the main and cache memories are of most interest to us. In addition, semiconductor memories are used for a variety of purposes within the instruction fetch-decode-execution unit, for example, to hold microprograms in the *control store* (see Section 2.5.3 and also Chapter 5).

The principal types of LSI memories may be described according to the hierarchic scheme of Figure 2.6. At the highest level we distinguish between

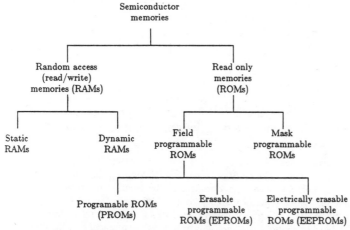

FIGURE 2.6 Types of semiconductor memories.

random access memories (RAMs) and *read-only memories* (ROMs).[4] The main distinguishing characteristic is that in a RAM information can be both written (altered) and read "on line" (i.e., while the system is in operation) whereas in a ROM information can be read on line but not written.

RAMs are further divided into static and dynamic types. In a *static* RAM, information stored in a memory cell can be retained for an indefinite period. In contrast, the information placed in a *dynamic* RAM decays over time and must therefore be periodically refreshed. From the architect's perspective, there are three important points to note about the static/dynamic dichotomy among RAMs. First, the basic storage cell in a static RAM is a flip-flop, whereas the storage cell in a dynamic RAM consists of a capacitor and a transistor. Thus the dynamic storage cell is a simpler circuit so that *the same chip area may contain a much larger capacity dynamic RAM than does its static counterpart.* The difference in memory size may vary from 4 to 10 times, depending on the technology (Muroga, 1982).

Second, reading a static RAM cell is *nondestructive*, whereas reading the contents of a dynamic RAM cell is *destructive.* Thus, an extra write step is required in the latter case; because of this, *the access time for dynamic RAMs are higher than that for static RAMs.*

Finally, because static RAMs do not need to be refreshed as do dynamic RAMs, the *former are simpler to use* in a digital system.

The principal subclasses of ROMs are also shown in Figure 2.6. In a *mask programmable* ROM (sometimes simply referred to as a ROM) data are stored during the chip fabrication process by the manufacturer; it cannot thereafter be changed in any fashion. A *field programmable* ROM can be programmed by the user. As Figure 2.6 shows there are a variety of such ROMs. In what is simply referred to as a *programmable* ROM (PROM) each basic storage cell contains a fusible link that may be opened electrically (or otherwise left intact) after the memory has been fabricated by the manufacturer. Thus, information may be stored in the ROM by the user once, and it will remain unalterable thereafter.

The other varieties of ROMs do allow erasure of stored information. In an *erasable programmable* ROM (EPROM), the contents of all the storage cells are simultaneously destroyed by exposure to ultraviolet light and new information is written electrically. In an *electrically erasable programmable* ROM (EEPROM), data are both erased and written electrically.

The basic structure of a semiconductor memory chip (whether RAM or ROM) is depicted in Figure 2.7. It consists of *an array of store cells*, an *address decoder*, some *control logic*, and *address* and *data buses.* Most of the chip area is

---

[4]The term *random access memory* is truly a misnomer as far as its relevance to distinguishing between these two memory classes. Both RAMs and ROMs are "randomly" accessible — that is, the time to access a memory word is independent of the location or address of the word. A more accurate name for "random access memory" is *read/write memory*, a term that is sometimes used, especially in the context of control stores (see Chapter 5). The uses of the term *random access memory* and the abbreviation *RAM* are, however, so well entrenched in the literature it would be futile to ignore them.

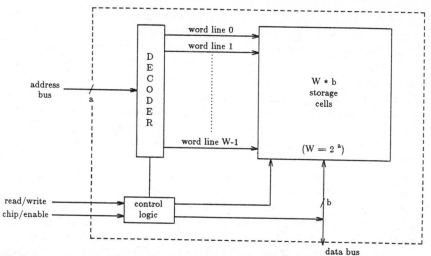

**FIGURE 2.7 General structure of semiconductor memory (based on Hayes 1984 ©
1984, McGraw-Hill Book Company; Used with permission).**

occupied by the storage array. The a-bit address supplied to the memory is
decoded, causing one of the word select lines, w, to be activated. This enables the
b storage cells (where b is the "word length' of the memory) in the w-th word to
be accessed. In the case of a ROM, the contents of the b cells thus selected are
transferred to the data bus. In the case of a RAM, an additional *read/write*
control line will signal what kind of operation is to be performed. Both ROMs
and RAMs have an additional *chip enable* line that must be activated for the
memory to respond to access requests. The role of the chip enable line will be
discussed in Section 2.5.2.

From an architectural vantage point, developments in semiconductor memory technology are of interest insofar as they affect a number of key parameters
and issues that are relevant to architecture design. These are:

1. The speeds and costs of random access and read only memories.
2. The available sizes of memory chips.
3. The uses of memory as implementation components.

I will summarize the present status and trends related to speed, cost, and size
in this section. The question of memory as an implementation component is
discussed in Sections 2.5.2 and 2.5.3.

Speed and Cost

Two basic performance measures for memories are their access and cycle times.

The *access time* t_A is defined as the maximum time required to read a word
from memory. It is measured from the time an address is placed on the memory

address bus to the time at which the contents of the referenced word appears on the memory data bus.

The *memory cycle time* t_C is defined as the minimum time that must be allowed between the initiation of two successive memory operations (read or write). The cycle time may actually differ for read and write operations, although they are often identical, in which case the memory is characterized by a single cycle time. Generally speaking, $t_C = t_A$ for ROMs and static RAMs whereas $t_A < t_C$ for dynamic RAMs because of the destructive nature of the read operation in the latter case and the subsequent need to regenerate the stored information.

There is a trade-off between the speed of memory and the cost per bit: The cost of memory generally declines as the cycle time increases and, indeed, this forms the technoeconomic basis underlying the development of memory hierarchies. Typical cycle times for RAMs and ROMs of various technologic persuasions are shown in Table 2.5. The general evolution of main memory speeds is exemplified by the graph of Figure 2.8. The cost per bit of memory has diminished at an average rate of about 0.76 of the cost of the previous year (Pohm, 1984).

Memory Size

We have already noted Moore's law concerning the increase in circuit density over time in Section 2.2. The growth in the sizes of memory chips has followed this general curve, increasing at the rate of about 1.66 per year (Pohm, 1984). As a specific example for the 1970–1980 period, the density of static RAM chips rose from 256 bits to about 16K bits whereas that of dynamic RAM increased from 1K bits to 64K bits (Rice, 1980). Currently, 256K bit dynamic RAM chips are available (Pohm, 1984).

TABLE 2.5 Typical Speeds (in Nanoseconds) of Semiconductor-Memories

	ROMs				RAMs		
	Mask Programmable		PROMs	EPROMs	MOS		Bipolar
	MOS types	Bipolar types	Bipolar types	MOS with ultra-violet erase	Dynamic	Static	Static
Read time	200–500	10–60	30–60	220–500	100–400	30–400	5–100
Write time	—	—	—	—	100–400	30–400	5–100

Source: Muroga 1982; © 1982 John Wiley & Sons, Inc.; reprinted with permission.

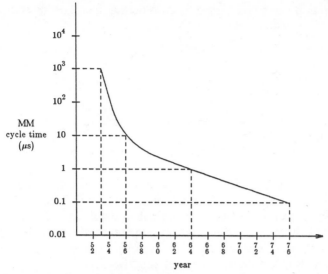

FIGURE 2.8 Growth of main memory speed over time (Matick 1977; © 1977, John Wiley & Sons, Inc.; Reprinted with permission).

2.5.2 Random Access Memories

The main role of random access memories in computer architecture is to serve as components in the implementation of memory hierarchy schemes of the type shown in Figure 2.5. Indeed, one should note that the concept of a hierarchic memory system was only made feasible by developments in semiconductor technology, that is, by the availability of memories with differing cost/speed characteristics. This provides an outstanding example of a situation where an architectural design principle was predicated on the availability of a particular technological phenomenon. Hierarchic memory systems will be discussed further in Chapter 8.

RAMs are also used to implement *writable control stores* in user-microprogrammable computers (see Chapter 5).

RAMs are now available in a variety of technologies and sizes. These include, at the low end, 64- and 256-bit chips organized, respectively, in the form of 16 word × 4 bits/word and 256 word × 1 bit/word arrays (Texas Instruments, 1981); 1K bit static NMOS circuits organized as 1024 word × 1 bit/word or 256 word × 4 bits/word arrays, and 4K bit static NMOS devices organized as a 1K word × 4 bits/word array; and large, dynamic memories available in the form of 64K word × 1 bit/word and 256K word × 1 bit/word arrays.

From the architect's viewpoint, the basic question of interest is: Given the availability of a memory chip of some specific size, how does one organize such chips so as to realize a target memory of some desired dimensions?

This question can be addressed by considering the following two possibilities (Matick, 1977, 1980).

1. The number of words required in the target memory equals the number of bits/chip.
2. The number of words required in the target memory exceeds the number of bits/chip.

Considering situation 1., suppose that the target is a 1K word × 64 bits/word memory (Fig. 2.9). Such a memory size would be desired, for example, in the case of a writable control store for holding microcode. Suppose further that we have at our disposal 512 × 2 static RAM chip arrays with an on-chip address decoder, sense amplifiers, appropriate 2-bit data input and output lines, and a 9-bit address bus (Fig. 2.10). With additional read/write and chip enable lines and lines for power and ground, the chip is available as a 20-pin package.

Figure 2.11 shows one possible way in which the chips may be organized, the resulting form often being called a *2D organization.* For the sake of clarity, the data input lines to the chips have been suppressed.

The target memory of capacity $2^{10} \times 2^6$ bits is decomposed into 64 (2^6) $2^9 \times 2^1$ bit chip arrays each of the type shown in Figure 2.10. The 10-bit *memory address register* (MAR) is composed of a 9-bit low-order part and a 1-bit high-order part. The 9-bit component is fed into the address lines (A) of each RAM, thereby activating the same corresponding word lines. The high-order MAR bit passes to the *chip select* logic and activates either each of the upper set of 32 chips or each of the lower set chips through their respective *chip enable* (E) lines. Thus only one of the two sets is selected. For each enabled word line the two data bit lines are sensed and, thus, the 64 data output lines send their signals to the *memory buffer register* (MBR).

Quite obviously, the overall organization and complexity of a target memory implementation will depend on the target memory dimensions and the compo-

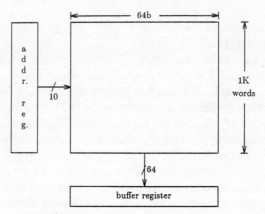

FIGURE 2.9 Target memory structure.

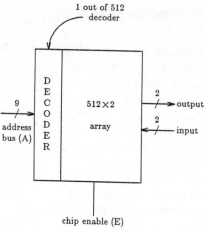

FIGURE 2.10 Available RAM chip.

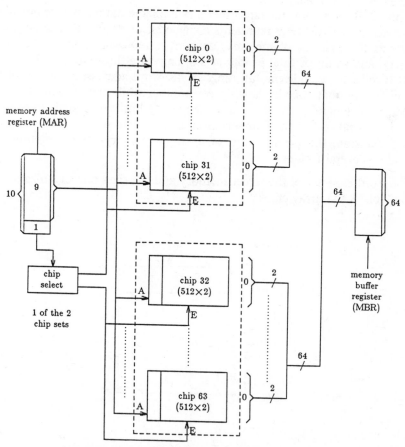

FIGURE 2.11   2D Organization of target memory.

sition of available chips. Supposing our building block is the 1K-bit RAM shown in Figure 2.12. In this case, in contrast to the *word organized* RAM of Figure 2.10, a single memory cell is selected on the *coincident selection* principle; that is, the cell at coordinates (x,y) is selected for reading or writing when the address lines A_1 and A_2 encode, respectively, for selection of the x-th row and y-th column of the array. The input and output lines are now only 1 bit each. Taking into account lines for read/write control, chip enable, power and ground, the chip may be encased in a 16-pin package.

Figure 2.13 shows what is often called a 2½ D organization of the target memory. Here, each chip represents a single bit of the target memory word, hence a total of 64 chips are required. For any given value in MAR, *all* the chips will need to be selected.

Consider now, situation 2, that is, the number of target memory words exceeds the bit capacity of the RAM chip. As an example, suppose we wish to implement a 4K word × 64 bits/word writable control store with the 32 × 32 bit array RAM of Figure 2.12.

Figure 2.14 shows how the target memory implementation may be organized. As before, each RAM chip represents a single bit of a word so that chip set 0 represents the first 1K of memory, chip set 1 represents the second 1K of memory, and so on. A total of four sets of chips are thus required. The 12-bit MAR (needed to encode the full range of 4K word addresses) consists of two high-order bits that encode the chip set number while the remaining 10 bits encode as in Figure 2.13. The chip set encoding bits send signals to the chip select logic, and one of the four sets of chip are thus enabled.

In conclusion, the precise form of a target memory implementation will depend on several factors:

• The word capacity of the target memory and the sizes and organizations of available RAM array chips.

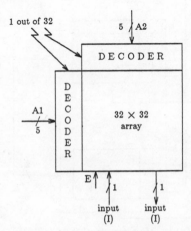

FIGURE 2.12   32 x 32 Coincident selection memory chip.

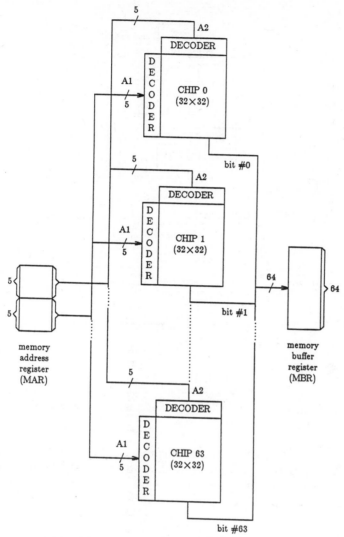

FIGURE 2.13 $2\frac{1}{2}$ D—organized target memory.

- The relative complexities and speeds of the chips and the desired cycle time for the target memory (note that, given the same technology, the longer a single path through a chip the slower the memory; similarly, the longer the number of logic levels the lesser will be the speed of the circuit); and, finally,
- The amount of additional (extra-RAM chip) logic and memory (e.g., registers) required.

Comparing Figures 2.11 and 2.13, for example, whereas the same number of RAM arrays are needed in the two cases, the overall complexity is somewhat less

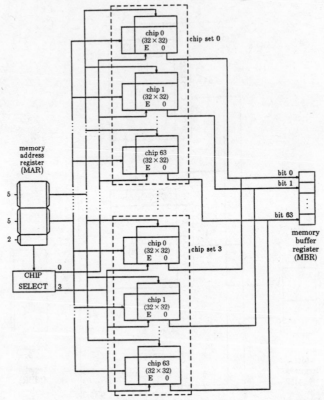

FIGURE 2.14 Memory organization when target memory size exceeds chip capacity.

in the second implementation since the chip select logic is not required nor the OR-ing of corresponding outputs from the two chip sets. The on-chip decoder on the component chip of Figure 2.11 will also be more complex than those on the component of Figure 2.13.

2.5.3 Read-Only Memories

A ROM has the functional structure depicted in Figure 2.15 (see also Fig. 2.7). It consists of a $b \times W$ *memory array* (with $W = 2^q$ for some integer q), *address inputs* $A_0, A_1, \ldots, A_{q-1}$, *data outputs* $B_0, B_1, \ldots, B_{b-1}$, and a *chip enable* line CE. When a signal arrives on CE and an address is supplied on the input lines $A_0, \ldots, A_{q-1}$, then the contents of the addressed b-bit word is read out onto the output lines $B_0, \ldots, B_{b-1}$.

ROMs have been, and continue to be, used in computers for storing small, frequently used or important constant items of information. However, their most celebrated and "traditional" uses is as a control store in which microprograms reside (Dasgupta, 1979; also, Chapter 5). Figure 2.16 shows, in simplified

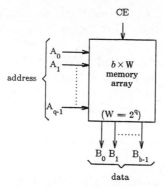

FIGURE 2.15 Functional structure of a ROM.

form, the archetypal organization of a microprogrammed control unit. Note its similarity to the typical structure of a main memory module (as shown, for example, in Fig. 2.9).

In this particular context, the contents of each ROM word is termed a *microinstruction*. On presentation of an address from the *control store address register* (CSAR) a microinstruction is read out into the *microinstruction register* (MIR). Each microinstruction encodes a set of more primitive *micro-operations* and, on decoding of the contents of the MIR, control signals corresponding to the particular micro-operations encoded in the microinstruction are issued to relevant units in the data path. At the same time, or perhaps in serial fashion, the *sequencing logic* updates the state of CSAR with an address value that is a function of either its current state (e.g., the current value of CSAR incremented by 1) or the contents of the currently executing microinstruction (which may

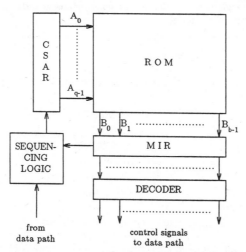

FIGURE 2.16 Simplified organization of a microprogrammed control unit.

store the branch address if an unconditional or conditional branch is specified in the current microinstruction; see Chapter 5 for a detailed discussion of these issues).

Microprogramming was invented by Wilkes (1951) as a technique for implementing control logic. The use of ROMs in such structures illustrates the remarkable concept of *substituting conventional logic circuits by functionally equivalent memory circuits*. This concept has in recent times been exploited for the realization of several other logic functions as I next discuss.

The basic *advantages* of replacing (where possible) "random" logic[5] by memory are as follows:

1. ROMs are dense, regular, and repetitive structures, consequently, they require much less time to design, lay out, and debug than do functionally equivalent logic networks.

Example 2.2

The data in Table 2.6 compares some design parameters for two well-known 16-bit microprocessors, the Motorola MC68000 and the Zilog Z8000. The MC68000 was designed using microprogrammed control—the microcode, in fact, resides in a *two* level ROM-based control store (Stritter and Tredennick, 1978; see also Chapter 5)—whereas the Z8000 control unit was implemented in random logic. What is notable about the data is that although the circuit count of the MC68000 was roughly four times that of the Z8000, the design time was only 0.67 greater, the layout time was the same whereas the debugging time for the 68000 was actually half that for the 8000. ∎

[5]As in the use of the term *random access memory*, the term *random logic* is another notable and, to the uninstructed, confusing misnomer. There is nothing "random" about random logic. The term is simply used to denote logic networks that are irregular or unstructured in contrast to the highly ordered and regular form of memories.

TABLE 2.6 A Comparison of Some Design Parameters for the MC68000 and Z8000 Microprocessors

	Motorola MC68000	Zilog Z8000
Number of transistors	68,000	17,500
Design time	100 man-months	60 man-months
Layout time	70 man-months	70 man-months
Elapsed time to first silicon	30 months	30 months
Elapsed debugging time[a]	6 months	12 months

[a]This is the time from the first silicon to a working production version (with no known bugs) of the chip.

Source: Frank and Sproull (1981). © 1981. Association for Computing Machinery, Inc. Reprinted with permission.

2. Because the *contents* of a ROM and its *layout* are quite independent of each other, changes in design leading to changes in the information stored in the ROM can be easily accommodated. This is not the case with random logic.
3. Finally, the regularity of ROM structures enhances the *testability* of the resulting network (Frank and Sproull, 1981).

The main *disadvantage* of ROMs compared to random logic is that they are slower, primarily because of the long signal paths in ROM arrays.

The general basis for using a ROM to implement a combinational logic circuit is as follows. Consider, again Figure 2.15. A signal appearing on output line B_i is a Boolean function of the values on the input address lines $A_0, A_1, \ldots, A_{q-1}$; thus

$$B_i = f_i(A_0, \ldots, A_{q-1}) \quad \text{for } i = 0, \ldots, b-1 \quad (2.1).$$

In other words, one may view $A = <A_0, \ldots, A_{q-1}>$ as a set of q Boolean variables in which case the ROM circuit is seen to realize a Boolean function

$$F(A) = [f_1(A), f_2(A), \ldots, f_{b-1}(A)] \quad (2.2)$$

where the output signals are produced after a time t, the access time of the memory. Equation (2.2) represents, then, a truth table involving q input and b output variables (Fig. 2.17).

In general, ROMs may be regarded as *universal logic modules*, since a $b \times W$ ROM array (where $W = 2^q$) can be used to realize *any* combinational logic circuit involving q input and b output variables.

ROMs are commonly used to implement a number of different types of combinational circuits, including

1. Code converters (e.g., Gray-to-binary, BCD-to-decimal).
2. 1-out-of-n detectors.
3. Arithmetic circuits (e.g., adders, multipliers, square root extractors, trigonometric functions).
4. Character generators (i.e., circuits that transform coded alphanumeric characters into two-dimensional display forms).

A_0	A_1	$\cdots A_{q-2}$	A_{q-1}	B_0	B_1	$\cdots B_{b-1}$
0	0	$\cdots$ 0	0	0	1	$\cdots$ 0
0	0	$\cdots$ 0	1	1	1	$\cdots$ 0
0	0	$\cdots$ 1	0	0	1	$\cdots$ 1
$\cdots$				$\cdots$		
$\cdots$				$\cdots$		
1	1	$\cdots$ 1	0	0	0	$\cdots$ 1
1	1	$\cdots$ 1	1	0	0	$\cdots$ 1

FIGURE 2.17 Truth table for a *q*-input, *b*-output logic function.

Several examples of ROM-based logic circuits are found in Muroga (1982) and Hayes (1984).

It is important to realize that the size of the ROM array increases exponentially (2^q) as the number of input variables q. Thus, for large values of q the ROM size may rapidly explode and, furthermore, lead to slower speeds. In such cases, *networks of ROMs* may be effective in reducing both memory space and access time.

Example 2.3 (Muroga, 1982)

The AND-ing of four input variables A_0, A_1, A_2, A_3 can be realized by a single 16-bit ROM array (Fig. 2.18). However, this same function can be implemented using a 2-level cascaded network of 4-bit ROMs (Fig. 2.19). In this particular case, the memory space saved is 4 bits. The effect of increasing input sizes on the respective space requirements for single and two-level cascaded ROMs is shown in Table 2.7. ∎

2.5.4 Programmable Logic Arrays

In the programmable logic array (PLA), a variant of the read-only memory concept, MOS transistors are arranged in the form of a two-dimensional array and the connections between the transistors and the horizontal and vertical lines are established during fabrication by the manufacturer (Fig. 2.21). Since only one mask needs to be made, PLAs are economical when the production volume is sufficiently high. As in the case of ROMs, we distinguish between such *mask-programmable* PLAs and *field-programmable* PLAs (FPLAs) in which the user establishes the necessary connections between transistors and lines by opening or leaving intact fusible links. Since additional area is needed for the fuses as well as the circuitry to blow the fuses, the area requirements of FPLAs are higher than those of their equivalent mask-programmable cousins — by about 40% (Muroga, 1982). FPLAs are most helpful when only a small number of PLAs are required, since the user can "program" them cheaply and rapidly.

A ROM, you will recall, stores information in the form of a truth table such that the input variables correspond to the address lines of the decoder, the number of words in the ROM array correspond to all possible combination of

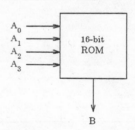

FIGURE 2.18   Single ROM array for a 4-input AND function realization.

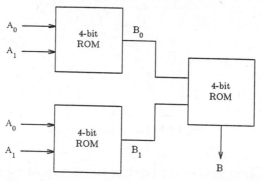

FIGURE 2.19   **Cascaded ROM network for a 4-input AND function realization.**

input variable values, and the number of bits/word correspond to the output variables of the truth table (Fig. 2.15).

A PLA, in contrast, is composed of two substructures termed, respectively, an AND-array and an OR-array, which together store information in the form of Boolean expressions—specifically, the sum-of-products form of Boolean expressions. Generally speaking—with the exception of the so-called *decoded* PLAs (see following)—PLAs do not require decoders.

Consider, as an example, the truth table of Figure 2.20. The corresponding Boolean sum-of-products expressions are

$$F_1 = \bar{X}\bar{Y}Z + \bar{X}Y\bar{Z} + X\bar{Y}\bar{Z} + XYZ \tag{2.3}$$

$$F_2 = \bar{X}YZ + X\bar{Y}Z + XY\bar{Z} + XYZ \tag{2.4}$$

Figure 2.21 is a PLA realization of these two expressions. Here, the upper matrix is the AND-array and the lower part, the OR-array. Each dot at the intersection of horizontal and vertical lines denotes the presence of a transistor connecting the two lines. A vertical line in the AND-array passing through two or more transistors realizes the logical product of the corresponding horizontal lines. For example, the left most vertical, or *product-line*, represents the term $\bar{X}\bar{Y}Z$. Each horizontal line in the OR-array passing through two or more transis-

TABLE 2.7   **Space Requirements for AND Function Realization Using Single and Two-level Cascaded ROMs**

Number of Input Variables	Memory Space Requirements (bits)	
	Single ROM	Cascaded Two-level ROM Network
4	16	12
5	32	16
6	64	20
7	128	24

Source: Muroga. (1982); © 1982 John Wiley & Sons; reprinted with permission.

x	y	z	F_1	F_2
0	0	0	0	0
0	0	1	1	0
0	1	0	1	0
0	1	1	0	1
1	0	0	1	0
1	0	1	0	1
1	1	0	0	1
1	1	1	1	1

FIGURE 2.20   A truth table.

tors realizes a logical sum of the product terms corresponding to the product lines.

Logically, then, the PLA of Figure 2.21 is equivalent to a two-level AND-or circuit realizing the functions F_1 and F_2 (Equations 2.3 and 2.4). Any two-level combinational network can, thus, be realized by a PLA.

An attractive characteristic of PLAs is that the minimization techniques developed in classic switching theory for multiple-output Boolean functions (see, for example, Kohavi, 1982) can be used to minimize the size of a PLA). For a given number of input lines I and output lines O, the size of a PLA is $(2I + O)P$, where P is the number of product lines. By minimizing the number of AND gates in a two-level AND-or network, you can minimize P and, therefore, the PLA size.

In commercially available PLAs, the input and output lines both range between 10 and 30 and the number of product lines varies between 50 and 150 (Muroga, 1982). The array size of a PLA is essentially limited by speed considerations.

If we compare ROMs and PLAs, we see that in the former case the AND part (represented by the address decoder) is fixed and the OR part (represented by the contents of the ROM array) is programmable, whereas in the latter case both AND and OR arrays are programmable. The so-called *programmable array logic* (PAL) is a variation of this theme in that the AND-array of an FPLA is

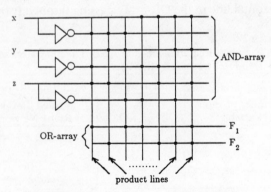

FIGURE 2.21   A 3-input, 2-output PLA.

programmable whereas the OR-array is fixed (Monolithic Memories, 1982; Muroga, 1982). The advantage of PALs lies in the significant reduction in area given to the OR-array due to the elimination of programmable fuses and the associated circuitry. PALs are particularly effective for implementing single output sum-of-products functions.

Additional variants of the basic PLA structure discussed thus far include the *decoded* PLA and the *folded* PLA. A discussion of these are beyond the scope of this book but the interested reader may refer to Muroga (1982) for further details.

2.5.5 Gate Arrays

The use of PLAs to realize logic functions is an instance of *semi-custom* logic design; that is, the circuitry corresponding to some target logic network has been determined in advance to some extent. What remains is to tailor or *customize this predetermined structure to solve the problem at hand.*

Another approach to semi-custom logic design that has assumed some importance in the last decade is the use of the *gate array*—also called *masterslice* or *uncommitted logic array.* This is an LSI chip that contains an array of unconnected identical cells or "gates," each of which, in turn, is an identical arrangement of circuit elements (transistors, diodes, and resistors). A given network may be implemented (and the array thereby customized) by mapping elements of the target design onto gates of the array (the so-called *placement* problem) and suitably connecting the selected gates (called the *routing* problem).

A specific example of such a device is the gate-array chip used in the VAX-11/750 processor (Armstrong, 1981). The array consists of 400 basic cells surrounded by 44 I/O gates. The basic cell is a 4-input NAND gate, although an 8-input NAND gate can be produced by combining two adjacent cells.

The major advantage of gate arrays lies in the fact that the realization of a particular logic function involves only the tasks of placement and routing. Furthermore, because of the predetermined nature of the positions of cells, placement and routing can be effectively achieved using *computer-aided design* (CAD) programs. Gate arrays are thus used primarily because of their low design time and (consequently) design cost. At the same time, it must be pointed out, gate-array chips require more area (relative to fully customized chips; see Section 2.5.6) and do not lend themselves easily to very high levels of integration (Muroga, 1982).

Gate arrays come in a variety of technologies (ECL, TTL, I^2L, NMOS, CMOS) and, consequently, vary considerably in gate density. For example, arrays used in AT&T Bell Laboratories from 1977 on range from 200 gates/chip to as high as 2250 gates/chip (Katz, 1983). In 1980, IBM reported the use of a 7640-TTL gate array for an implementation of a System/370 processing unit. Some 65% of the gates were used (Davis *et al.*, 1980).

It is interesting to observe some of the data reported on the basis of this experience (Feuer, Khokhani, and Mehta, 1980):

1. The total time for automatic placement and routing of all but 68 of the 11,000 connections took about a month. However, the manual routing of the remaining 68 connections took a month.
2. The actual running time for the CAD placement program was 208 minutes on an IBM System/370 model 168 and routing time was 87 minutes.

A notable aspect of gate arrays is its use in the implementation of mini- and mainframe computers. One of the reasons for this is that such machines are manufactured in relatively low volumes (of the order of hundreds or thousands). For such volumes, full-custom design is economically unviable. Gate arrays, thus, constitute a step toward the adoption of large- and very-large-scale integration for mainframe computers.

This trend appears to have begun with the extensive use, in 1975, of ECL gate arrays by Amdahl Corporation for the 470 series of mainframes. The 470/v6 processor, for example, contained about 2000 gate-array chips, each chip consisting of 100 gates (Muroga, 1982).

In 1978, IBM began using ECL and TTL gate arrays in their machines: The implementation of the IBM 370'/138' mentioned earlier had been preceded by the use of 700-cell gate arrays in the System/38 and the 4300 series (Feuer, Khokhani, and Mehta, 1980).

As another example, some 90% of the processor logic in Digital Equipment Corporation's VAX-11/750 was realized using 27 different types of low-power Schottky TTL gate-array chips (Armstrong, 1981). The use of this technology, together with the extensive use of CAD programs apparently lowered the design time and cost to about 15% of what it would have been had full-custom design been used.

2.5.6 Fully Customized LSI/VLSI Implementations

Full-custom implementation of an architecture represents the most extreme exploitation of large- and very-large-scale integration. It also signifies a reverse swing of the pendulum in the sense that, rather than assume the availability of implementation modules that, with appropriate tailoring, can be assembled to form the target system, the full-custom approach takes cognizance of the availability of MOS technology, a philosophy of design, and a body of tools and techniques to create a "supercomponent": a chip that embeds some significant and functionally powerful organ of a computer—a central processing unit, an "intelligent" I/O processor, a memory management unit, or such.

The *microprocessor*—a (more or less) complete general purpose processing unit with ALU, a file of registers, some amount of program memory, and control logic all within a single chip—denotes the most widely publicized instance of a fully customized module. A *microcomputer* is a (more or less) complete computer system (excluding peripherals, however) synthesized from a very small number of IC chips.

The microprocessor excites three somewhat different kinds of attention. First, it provides a very cost effective and—because of its programmability—highly flexible component that can be used in an unlimited variety of products that have very little resemblance to what we traditionally view as computational systems. These include video games, toys, home appliances, watches, control and diagnostic systems in automobiles, and health-care products (Muroga, 1982). This aspect of the microprocessor is of only marginal interest to the computer architect.

From another perspective, the microprocessor is an expression of how one may exploit IC technology to realize, partially or wholly, a computer architecture design on a single chip. Full-custom LSI/VLSI circuits thus constitute an *architecture implementation technique*, and it is this that is of primary interest in this section.

Finally, from a third perspective, the microprocessor may be viewed as a cheap computational module or building block for creating computers of enormous information-processing capabilities—that is, as a building block for multiprocessors and supercomputers (Siewiorek, Thomas, and Schanfeller, 1978; Snyder, 1982, 1984). Within this same perspective, we include an alternative LSI/VLSI component, the *bit-slice device*, which is used as a module to implement mainframe computers (Borgerson, Tjaden, and Hanson, 1978).

Note that the use of such LSI/VLSI modules places microprocessors and bit-slices back into the tradition emphasized in the preceding sections. Bit-slice devices and microprocessors viewed as implementation components are discussed in Sections 2.5.7 and 2.5.8, respectively.

Our immediate interest in this section lies in the factors that dictate the choice of the full-custom LSI/VLSI approach as an architecture implementation technique and the influence this technique has on architectural design.

The salient characteristics of full customization may be summarized as follows.

1. For a given set of performance and functional characteristics, the full-custom approach yields the smallest or most compact implementation with the lowest speed-power product. The reliability will also be very high.
2. However, full customization demands very large investments in design time: the design, verification, and, in particular, layout of VLSI chips is extremely time consuming, especially when random logic networks are being implemented.

   In response to the challenge of complexity posed by VLSI, the twin philosophies of *well-structuredness* and *hierarchic design*—already well entrenched in the consciousness of the software designer—came to be advocated, most influentially by Mead and Conway (1980). At the heart of this philosophy are

   a. The use of a systematic, hierarchic design approach involving backward chaining (or top-down reasoning) and/or forward chaining (or bottom-up reasoning) strategies (see Chapter 3).
   b. The use of highly regular structures (e.g., PLAs, ROMs) for subsystems

and the composition of these into larger systems in a highly regular way.[6] Indeed, regularity of structure both inside a single chip and of an ensemble of chips is a profoundly significant characteristic in the case of VLSI implementations (Mead and Conway, 1980; Lattin *et al.*, 1981; Snyder, 1984).

In addition to the adoption of such structured design techniques, it is widely conceded that the complexity of customized LSI/VLSI circuits of ever-increasing density demands, for their successful realization, sophisticated computer-aided design (CAD) techniques for describing, designing, testing, verifying, and laying out VLSI structures (Frank and Sproull, 1981; van Cleemput and Ofek, 1984; Rice, 1982; Muroga, 1982; Shahdad *et al.*, 1985). This influence of both design methods and CAD tools on the implementation of specific customized VLSI processors has been widely documented (Fitzpatrick *et al.*, 1981; Lattin *et al.* 1981; Gries and Woodward, 1984; Samudrala *et al.*, 1984).

3. Because of this large initial investment, the full-custom approach is the most cost-effective if the volume of production is very high—certainly of the order of several hundred thousands, preferably in the range of several millions. This economic fact forms the basis for the production by semiconductor manufacturers of the various 8-, 16- and, now 32-bit microprocessors.

It is worth noting that these characteristics may often suffice as a basis to take a first-order decision as to whether for a given architectural project the implementation should be customized.

Example 2.4

An interesting instance of why full-custom implementation was *not* selected, has been described by Armstrong (1981). The machine in question was the VAX-11/750, chronologically, the second member of the VAX-11 family (Digital, 1981a, 1981b).

The primary architectural design goals for this machine were that

1. It would support the same exo-architecture (the "VAX architecture") as its predecessor, the VAX-11/780, and, therefore, be software-compatible with the latter; and
2. It would achieve this functional power with about 60% of the VAX-11/780's performance at 40% of the latter's price.[7]

Additional (non-architectural) goals and constraints included:

---

[6]The impact of regularity on design and layout times has already been commented on in Section 2.5.3.

[7]The VAX-11/780 had been implemented using mostly off-the-shelf Schottky TTL logic with some additional ECL technology and custom LSI components (Armstrong, 1981).

3. A propagation gate delay of between 5 and 10 nsec and a significant (≥ 10) fan-out capability.
4. An implementation technology and associated design system that could be applied most effectively by a design team experienced mostly in logic design using off-the-shelf TTL parts.

The technology options considered were: off-the-shelf TTL/ECL components; custom LSI chips; a combination of off-the-shelf and customized components; and gate arrays.

The use of off-the-shelf components was rejected on the grounds of high cost. The second option was to use customized chips designed and fabricated by a semiconductor manufacturer. However, initial analysis indicated that some 30 distinct chip designs would be required. Each of the semiconductor companies approached indicated its lack of sufficient engineering resources for the design of so many different chips. Even otherwise, it was felt that the design time incurred for the development of such a large number of unique chips would have been unduly high.

The third option was rejected essentially because it appeared to combine the disadvantages of both the first two options, although, admittedly, the design costs for customization would have been less in this case.

The fourth option was the use of gate-array technology. The use of off-the-shelf gate arrays was rejected on the grounds of propagation delays in the 50 to 75 nsec range. The eventual choice of designing and manufacturing in-house gate arrays was based on at least three facts:

1. Sufficient manpower resources were available within Digital Equipment Corporation for developing both the gate arrays and the necessary CAD system.
2. The in-house approach would be most cost-effective.
3. It would maximize the use of automation in all the steps, starting from the integrated circuit design through mask production.

The total time for this entire sequence of steps was 10 to 12 weeks compared to (an estimated) 5 to 6 months for fully customized design; the additional time to the delivery of components was 2 to 3 weeks for the gate arrays compared to about 13 weeks for full-custom chips. ■

Many authors have pointed out that the advent of VLSI technology marks a stage in computer science and engineering at which a new paradigm of design, theory, and analysis has had to be established. In the context of the present discussion, it is worth considering, at least briefly, this new paradigm.

Area as a Measure of "Goodness"

Probably the most significant aspect of the new paradigm is the emergence of *area* as a measure of the "goodness" of VLSI design. The measure is used by computational complexity theorists, algorithm designers, and computer designers alike.

The reason for this is one of the realities of the technology of chip fabrication: the larger the area the greater the probability that a chip will be defective and, therefore, the smaller the yield of chips of that area. In fact, the cost of fabricating a chip is an exponential function of the chip area. A specific form of this cost function for NMOS chips, cited by Flynn (1981) and based on an earlier formulation by Cragon (1980) is

$$\text{cost} = K(10^{.0368A})$$

where A = area of the chip in square millimeters and K is a constant for a given process.

The exponential dependence of manufacturing cost on chip area exerts an obviously fundamental pressure on the designer of VLSI chips to implement processors or circuits in the smallest area possible. At higher levels of abstraction the VLSI algorithm designer is correspondingly concerned with *area-efficient* VLSI algorithms (Ullman, 1984).

Time as a Design Parameter

The second basic design parameter is *time* (or speed). Area and time, thus, capture two distinct aspects of a system's cost—whereas area is a measure of the cost of manufacture, time measures the executional cost of the circuit.

Time, of course, has always been a fundamental complexity measure for computing systems. The significant change that VLSI has introduced is that, because of the dominance of *wires* (signal transmission paths) over processing logic—for reasons stated below (see: The Planarity Problem II)—signal propagation time along wires assumes greater significance in VLSI circuits. The time to propagate a signal along a wire of length l is proportional to l^2 (Bilardi, Pracchi, and Preparata, 1981; Ullman, 1984) and, as Wilkes (1983) has pointed out, propagation delays due to intrachip interconnections are a major issue with which chip and computer designers must constantly contend.

The Planarity Problem I: The Perimeter Constraint

At the heart of VLSI design is the fact that the technology is a *two-dimensional* one:[8] the circuits are all laid out on the plane. Snyder (1984) refers to this as the *planarity problem* and has pointed out two important effects that result from the planar nature of integrated circuits.

The first of these is the "perimeter constraint," which I have already introduced in Section 2.4 as the pin limitation problem. Stated briefly, the issue here is that the number of wires leading out from a chip is proportional to the length

---

[8]Current research in VLSI theory and design includes, however, the study of three-dimensional VLSI chips (Rosenberg, 1981).

of the chip perimeter. Since chips are approximately square, the number of external connections or pins is proportional to $A^{1/2}$, where A is the chip area. This exerts a fundamental constraint on the amount or rate of information that may be exchanged across a chip boundary.

As Synder (1984) also notes, this limit on the amount of external connections is not because the pads on the chip are placed on the perimeter — they can, in fact, be located anywhere on the chip as they were in the case of the IBM 4300 series (see Section 2.4). The problem is that the wires are attached to the packaged chip *in the same plane as the chip* so that, regardless of where the pads are, wires must cross the chip boundary.

The implication of the perimeter constraint is obvious: VLSL technology will be more favorable to architectural designs and implementations that can exploit increases in chip density without the need for additional pins.

The Planarity Problem II: The Wire Dominance Effect

I have previously remarked that wires become a dominant factor in VLSI circuits. This is also a consequence of the planar nature of the technology and the fact that chip designers need to avoid an excessive number of wires crossing over one another (otherwise, undesirable electrical effects arise) (Muroga, 1982).

To further understand the wire dominance effect, consider the topology of a circuit. In VLSI models of computation, a circuit is usually viewed as a *graph* whose vertices denote devices and whose edges represent wires.

Viewed as graphs, circuits are not usually planar; that is, they cannot be drawn in the plane such that no two edges cross one another. Consequently, when a given circuit graph is laid out on the plane its edges must be spread out to minimize wire crossovers.

The overall result is that wires can well become the dominant component in a chip layout, reducing the proportion of chip area given to processing logic. Routing of wires in an area-efficient manner is, thus, an important aspect of VLSI implementation.

Architectural Aspects of the New Paradigm

In the foregoing discussions I have already mentioned some of the implications of VLSI for the architect of single-chip, customized processors. In concluding this section (2.5.6), it is useful to summarize, in one place, the more important of these architectural issues (Cragon, 1980; Patterson and Sequin, 1980; Muroga, 1982).

1. **Constraints on chip boundary bandwidth** Because of differences in electrical characteristics, the delay-power product (see Section 2.3) of a connection residing inside a chip is significantly lower than that of an interchip path. Thus, transmitting a signal from one chip to another involves a major performance drop either because of increased power consumption or be-

cause of signal propagation delay. Thus, it behooves the designer to place all high-bandwidth data paths inside the chip. This implies that as much memory as possible should be placed in the same chip as the processing unit.

2. **Program memory size**   Because of the importance of chip area and the need to minimize the area requirements for a given subsystem, the static size of programs becomes a significant parameter in order to save chip area dedicated to program memory.

3. **On-chip memory hierarchy**   Even within a given technology, different types of memories exhibit different density and speed characteristics (see Section 2.5.1). Generally speaking, ROMs are denser than RAMs and, within the latter class, dynamic RAMs are at least four times as dense as static RAMs. Although the access times of MOS static RAMs and ROMs are comparable, static RAMs are three to four times faster than dynamic RAMs (see Table 2.5). These comparative characteristics have the following implications: first, whenever possible, ROMs should replace RAMs as program storage in order to conserve area. Second, it becomes reasonable to think in terms of an on-chip memory hierarchy in which a faster static RAM is used to implement a small cache while slower, denser dynamic RAMs may implement a larger "main" memory (Fig. 2.22). The overall memory systems could, with the proper design, achieve an effective density close to that of the dynamic RAM and an effective access speed near to that of the static memory.

4. **Reduced instruction set philosophy**   Area constraints also imply more careful consideration (than has been done traditionally) of what architectural functions should be directly cast in silicon and what to omit. The larger the set of implemented functions, the greater the proportion of the chip given to processing circuits and control logic. The choice of instructions will then be dictated by their dynamic execution characteristics—that is, given limited "silicon real estate" only the most frequently used instructions should be supported by the hardware, leaving other functions to be synthesized by the compiler or the programmer. This, or course, is the basis for the RISC style of architecture (see Chapter 7).

2.5.7 Bit-Slice Devices

The omnipresent technoeconomic pressure to raise the integration level of components has culminated in the past decade and a half in the development of

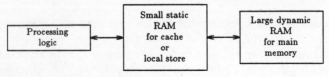

FIGURE 2.22   **An on-chip memory Hierarchy (based on Patterson and Sequin 1981).**

powerful computational modules whose integration levels range from the mid-LSI to the mid-VLSI scales—that is, from the equivalent of about 500 to 500,000 gates (Table 2.1). The two principal classes of such modules are the *bit-slice* device, which we discuss in this section, and the *microprocessor*, described in Section 2.5.8. The first microprocessor, the 4-bit Intel 4004 was marketed in 1971 (Noyce and Hoff, 1981); the very first bit-slice component, produced by National Semiconductor Corporation, appeared in 1973 (Hayes, 1984).

A *bit-slice* is essentially an integrated circuit module that combines and raises the functionality of typical MSI components. The archetypal bit-slice device is a *low-width* processor slice containing one or more functional units, a register file, and an associated data-path structure connecting these components. The typical width of the slice is 4-bits.

The internal (micro-) architecture of a very widely used 4-bit processor slice, the Am 2901, is shown in Figure 2.23. Its main components are a 16 word × 4 bit dual port RAM that serves as a register array, a 4-bit wide ALU capable of performing three arithmetic and five logical operations, two 4-bit shifters, and some multiplexing and decoding logic.

The input and output ports by which the 2901 interfaces with its environment are shown in Figure 2.24. The device accepts input data through the 4-bit D bus

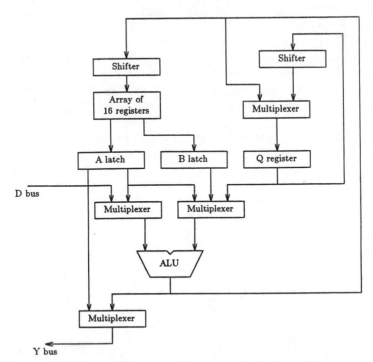

FIGURE 2.23   Architecture of the AM2901 ALU register slice (Myers 1982; © 1982, John Wiley and Sons, Inc.; Reprinted with permission).

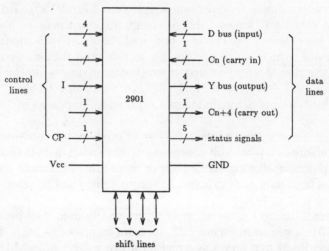

FIGURE 2.24 External ports in the AM2901 (based on Myers 1982).

and the carry-in line Cn and outputs data onto the 4-bit bus, a carry-out line Cn+4, and a set of five other status lines indicating the outcome of the ALU operation. The four lines shown at the bottom can each be used for input or output or be left in a high-impedance state. The remaining input lines are for control signals, power, and ground, making a total of 40 pins for the 2901 chip.

The important functional property of a bit-slice device is that several copies can be cascaded together to form a device of much larger width that can perform the same functions as the original slice. Figure 2.25 shows schematically how four 2901 slices may be composed to form a 16-bit ALU/register/data path component.

The bit-slice device, it may be inferred, is much simpler and less dense than a complete microprocessor. The width of its components are low, typically, as we have noted, 4 bits, although some 8-bit slices have also appeared. The character-

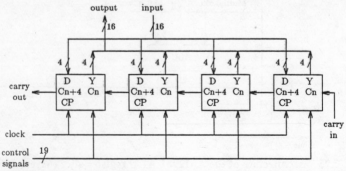

FIGURE 2.25 16-bit ALU/register component composed from four AM2901's.

istic density, for example, of the Am 2901 bit-slice [there are, in fact, several versions of the 2901 with varying performance and chip-area characteristics (Advanced Micro Devices, 1983)] is 540 gates. The architectural implications are the following.

1. The faster technologies such as TTL and ECL can be used for their manufacture.
2. The pin limitation problem is essentially eliminated.
3. Several bit-slice devices may be required to build a processor of some given capability.

To use bit-slices as implementation components, several types of such components are required to build a computer. Thus, bit-slice devices are commercially available as *families* of components usually manufactured and marketed by one manufacturer. The most well known of these is the Am 2900 family produced originally by Advanced Micro Devices (AMD) but now "second-sourced" by other semiconductor manufacturers. The first of these devices were marketed in 1976, and they mostly use low-power Schottky TTL technology, although the higher performance devices are made in an AMD-proprietary bipolar technology called IMOX.[9] Other important bit-slice families are the Intel 3000, the Motorola 10800, Texas Instruments' SN 74S480, and the Fairchild 100220. The last-named two use ECL technology, and the 100220 is one of the earliest to include an 8-bit processor slice (Hayes, 1984).

The rest of our discussion in this section will use members of the 2900 family as examples. For a very comprehensive discussion of bit-slice technology, refer to Myers (1980).

A fundamental characteristic of the bit-slice approach is the assumption that processors built from such devices would be microprogrammed (see Chapter 1,

[9]IMOX is a registered trademark of Advanced Micro Devices, Inc.

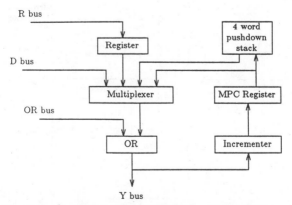

FIGURE 2.26 Internal organization of the AM2909 microprogram sequencer (Myers 1982; © 1982, John Wiley & Sons, Inc.; Reprinted with permission).

Sections 1.3, and 1.4 and Chapter 5; it must be noted, though, that the use of bit-slice does not *necessitate* the use of microprogrammed rather than any other form of control logic). Thus, in addition to the ALU/register slice, a major member of a bit-slice family is the microprogram sequencer. Figure 2.26 describes the internal organization of the Am 2909, a 4-bit, low-power Schottky TTL microprogram sequencer slice, *n* of which can be cascaded to form a 4*n*-bit address sequencer.

The function of this device is to transfer a 4-bit address from one of several sources (either internally stored in REGISTER, MPC, or the stack or supplied through the D or R buses to the device) to the output address bus (Y), which would be connected to the address port of a control memory. At the same time, additional functions such as incrementing the contents of the MPC register or storing or popping an address from the stack would be done.

The overall relationship between processor and microprogram sequencer slices in the organization of a microprogrammed computer is depicted schematically in Figure 2.27. This gives the outline of a 16-bit processor controlled by microcode residing in a 4K word control memory. The 12-bit control store address is generated by cascading three sequencer slices of the 2909 type.

To the architect, the use of bit-slices as components becomes attractive for some obvious reasons, namely: (1) the flexibility they provide for implementing target architectures of any particular word size; (2) the use of microprogramming (with *its* attendant advantages—see Chapter 5) to implement exo-architectures; and (3) the fact that bit-slice devices are built out of the faster TTL and ECL technologies.

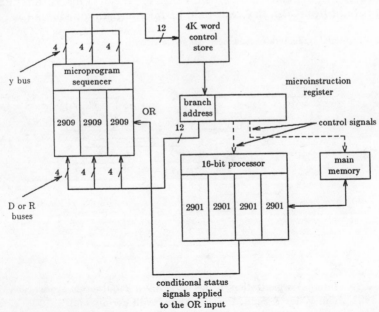

FIGURE 2.27 Organization of a bit-sliced microprogrammed computer.

2.5.8   Microprocessors

As we have already noted, the microprocessor is of most interest to the computer architect as an inexpensive module for designing and constructing systems of enormous computational capabilities. This, of course, is not the only matter of architectural significance. Other important applications include the use of microprocessors as components in personal computer systems (Siewiorek, Bell, and Newell, 1982), minicomputer-compatible microcomputer systems—for example, the DEC LSI-11 (Severn, 1976)—and as elements in special purpose computers—for example, for on-board spacecraft control (Rennels, 1978). Nonetheless, it is in the context of general purpose multiprocessing and "supercomputing" that the microprocessor has most excited the architect's imagination.

In Section 2.5.6 we have discussed some of the technological issues surrounding the design of single-chip processors. As regards the architecture of specific microprocessors, such descriptions will appear in various sections in Part 2 to illustrate specific architectural issues.

2.6   BIBLIOGRAPHIC REMARKS

The theory and technology of integrated circuits is discussed in several books, including Millman and Halkias (1972), Colclaser (1980), and Muroga (1982). For a briefer, but truly scintillating account, see Clark (1980). Much of the discussion in this chapter is based on Muroga (1982). A recent, but brief, review of IC technology is Burger, *et al.*, 1984. The seminal work on VLSI design is, of course, Mead and Conway (1980); Ayres (1983) is concerned more specifically with the problem of automatic VLSI chip design. A pioneering monograph on the design and analysis of algorithms for VLSI implementation is Leiserson (1983), based on his 1981 doctoral dissertation. Ullman (1984) is a thorough summary of a broad range of algorithmic, computational, and theoretic aspects of VLSI. For an excellent, up to date discussion of integrated circuit chips and the way they are structured in digital systems, see Hayes (1984). A standard designer's reference on TTL circuits is Texas Instruments (1981). One of the most authoritative texts on memory technology and architecture is Matick (1977); a more recent, though brief, discussion is Pohm (1984).

For an account of the development of microprocessors at Intel Corporation, refer to Noyce and Hoff (1981). Myers (1980) is a good discussion of several well known families of bit-slice devices. There are, of course, many books and articles on microprocessors. Hayes (1984) has several excellent chapters on the architecture, interfacing, and programming of 8- and 16-bit microprocessors. Two papers by Gupta and Toong (Toong and Gupta, 1981; Gupta and Toong, 1983) give valuable comparative studies of the architecture of the more well known 16- and 32-bit reprocessors. Blakeslee (1979) describes the uses of MSI and LSI components in designing digital systems.

For a viewpoint on the design issues surrounding single-chip processors, see Patterson and Sequin (1980).

PROBLEMS

2.1 The widespread use of semiconductor chips in all types of consumer and engineering products is a relatively recent phenomenon. What are the principal technological reasons for this "microchip revolution"?

2.2 Recall (from Chapter 1) that an *abstraction* is a selective view of a system. Thus, the assembly language programmer "sees" a particular abstraction of his or her computer. Clearly, if the programmer has *some* knowledge of the computer's technological characteristics, then the programmer would be able to write more efficient programs. At the same time, it seems reasonable to suppose that the assembly language programmer's technological view of the computer need not be the same as that of the architect who designed the machine's architecture.

Describe those aspects of a computer's technological features that are likely to be useful to the programmer, and in what way the programmer can effectively use this knowledge in order to write efficient programs.

2.3 (a) Define a microprocessor in terms of its *functional* characteristics (that is, in terms of what its capabilities are).

(b) From a functional viewpoint, what, if any, are the distinctions between a microprocessor and a computer?

2.4 (a) Define a bit-slice family in terms of its functional characteristics.

(b) What, if any, are the distinctions between bit-slice devices and a microprocessor?

2.5 Microprocessors and bit-slice devices are both examples of integrated circuits that have a high level of "functionality." However, in general, bit-slice devices can be realized in faster technologies than can microprocessors. Explain the reasons for this.

2.6 Analyze the trade-offs that should be considered by the computer designer when a choice has to be made between semi-custom and fully customized components.

2.7 Analyze the trade-offs that must be considered by the computer designer when a choice has to be made between off-the-shelf MSI components and semi-custom components such as gate arrays or PLAs.

2.8 (a) Give a general, technological profile of microprocessors.

(b) Describe what, in your opinion, is an appropriate technological profile of the computer that *you* use for your programming tasks.

(c) Based on (a) and (b), explain why the microprocessor is (or is not) an appropriate building block for your particular computer.

2.9 One of the consequences of the scaling up of integrated circuits is that "memories and logic networks can now be combined and distributed throughout a digital system leading to new choices for design and performance . . . memories are now used for a variety of functions that were traditionally realized through logic circuits" (Section 2.5.1).

What are the advantages of using memory instead of conventional logic circuits to realize logic functions? What are the disadvantages?

2.10 Referring to Problem 2.9, describe with at least two examples how memory devices are used in digital systems to implement common logic functions.

2.11 The computer architect has determined that the control (or microcode) memory in the system being designed will have a word length of at least 84 bits and must consist of at least 9000 words. The available memory chips are the 512×2 array shown in Figure 2.10 and the 32×32 array shown in Figure 2.12

(a) Give block diagrams showing how the target control memory can be organized using each of these two memory chips.

(b) Based on (a), choose which of these organizations will be adopted for the actual implementation. Provide arguments in support of your choice.

CHAPTER 3

THE DESIGN PROCESS

3.1 INTRODUCTION

In its broadest sense, design is one of the most ubiquitous of human activities. As Simon (1981) has pointed out, anyone who devises courses of action intended to change an existing state of affairs to a preferred one is involved in the act of design. As such, it is of central concern across a huge range of human activities, dealing not only with the production of material artifacts (structures, machines, tools, factories), but also with the generation of symbolic devices (plans, policies, programs). Design, in fact, is the defining characteristic of the artificial sciences, the one characteristic that distinguishes an artificial from a natural science.

In this chapter, I discuss the act of design—the design process—in the context of computer architecture. The questions that will be addressed are of the following kinds: What are the issues and factors that play significant roles in the creation of designs? What kinds of intellectual concepts need be used by the designer in managing the complexity of the design process? How can the designer acquire confidence in the output of his or her design activity?

Although these questions are framed here in the specific context of computer architecture, they have been posed extensively in the past in a variety of other contexts: software, building architecture, urban planning, and large-scale integrated circuits. We will, therefore, bring to bear on the topics of design ideas from a variety of sources. The problems of design are, indeed, so similar across most of the artificial sciences that *design theory*—the study of design methods in general—has emerged in the past quarter century as a discipline in its own right.[1]

3.2 THE RELEVANCE OF DESIGN METHODS FOR COMPUTER ARCHITECTURE

In Chapter 1 (Section 1.6) I pointed out that the systematic study of computer architecture as a *design discipline* is of very recent origin (Dasgupta, 1984). Perhaps one reason for this is that the "architecture of a computer" by itself is often viewed as a nebulous entity, the reality of which, independent of a hard-

---

[1]See the Bibliographic Remarks at the end of this chapter for a discussion of the literature on design theory.

ware implementation, is held in doubt. Thus, in this view, the design of an architecture is but one part of the physical computer design and hardly merits any separate consideration.

We will deal with this issue of the autonomy or "realness" of architectures later in Section 3.4. There is, however, another possible reason why design methods have not, till recently, excited much attention among architects: and that is, unlike many of the other artificial sciences — in which design theories, techniques, and tools emerged in response to a crisis within the discipline — architecture was not perceived as being threatened by any such crisis.

There is, however, every indication that because of remarkable developments in technology (see Chapter 2) architects are already having to come to terms with the problem of complexity management so familiar to software designers (Wegner, 1979). Possibly the most significant issue of complexity lies in the problem of constructing high-performance, highly concurrent computers composed of several hundreds, thousands, or even millions of processors (Snyder, 1984). Clearly, in such situations architects will have to cope with design and complexity problems that are significantly different from those of the past (Snyder, 1984; see also Chapter 2, Section 2.5.9).

If the development of highly concurrent multiprocessors pose problems of what might be called large-scale complexity, the design and implementation of single-chip (or a few chips) processors of ever increasing computational power involve complexity issues of a different kind. Because of chip area and pin limitations (see Chapter 2, Section 2.5.9) the architect is forced to consider very carefully — more than ever before — not only trade-offs regarding which functions to implement in silicon and which to leave out, but also the allocation of areas of the chip to specific functions. One might term the problem here as one of small-scale complexity. The techniques, ideas, and tools that are being used to evolve the design from architecture to chip layout (Lattin, *et al.*, 1981; Hammerstrom, 1983; Katevenis, 1985) are novel as far as the design and implementation of architectures are concerned. We must, however, point out that as of this writing much of design methodology has been concerned with the lower levels of abstraction — logic level, microcode, and chip layout.

Even if we choose to ignore these issues, there still remains a compelling reason why the study of design methods is relevant for architecture; that is, quite simply, that the architect's business is design and the evaluation and verification of the designs. It is, thus, *imperative* for us to understand the architectural design process in order that we may make interesting, objective (and thus testable) statements about the architectures we design. Because computer architecture is an artificial science, design is at its core; unless we understand the *process* of design, we can hardly claim to understand the *products* of that design process.

3.3 CHARACTERIZING "DESIGN"

Just what design is — that is, characterizing what one does when one designs — has been discussed at length in the context of building architecture (Alexander,

1964; March, 1976), software (Freeman, 1980a, 1980b), computer architecture (Dasgupta, 1984), and firmware (Dasgupta and Shriver, 1985) and in the literature of "general" design theory (J. C. Jones, 1980, 1984; Simon, 1981; Lawson, 1980). Recent attempts at *automating* the design process have also produced new "models" of design couched in the vocabulary of computer science and artificial intelligence (Mostow, 1985).

On the basis of these various perspectives, it becomes possible to characterize the design process in terms of some fundamental attributes. In this section I identify these attributes and examine their ramifications.

3.3.1 Design as Change

In an ultimate sense the purpose of design is to alter the world. We design in response to a perception that some aspect of our universe is imperfect. We design to *improve* the state of affairs. Although this may seem in the nature of a "motherhood" statement, it does have an important implication: If we accept the view that design is concerned with how things *ought* to be, then the question of *values* crops up and it does so in at least two ways.

First, the selection of the problem for which we seek to design a solution is often determined by the designer's "value system." What *ought not* to be the case for one person—which is thus a valid design problem in the context of that person—may be a matter of indifference to another; and for a third person, it may denote a state of affairs that should remain unchanged.

Example 3.1

One of the most visible examples of the role of values in the identification of design problems is the discussion by Weizenbaum (1976) a few years ago on whether one *should at all* attempt to devise computer programs that emulate psychotherapists or, indeed, any other human activity that involves interpersonal relationship. The problem of values that one encounters here is one of morality. ∎

Example 3.2

Since the early 1970s, many researchers have been involved in the design and implementation of high-level microprogramming languages (Dasgupta and Shriver, 1985; Dasgupta, 1980). The "problem" at hand was to move the microprogramming effort to a more abstract and intellectually manageable plane. The technical benefits that would accrue seemed obvious to the researchers involved. Yet till very recently industrial microprogrammers seemed to regard this as a "nonproblem" or at best of marginal interest. The disparity of views on this particular design research problem[2] hinged essentially on the fact that what seemed important as a goal to one was not so to another. ∎

---

[2]Note that just as values determine valid design problems, they also determine valid *research* problems in the artificial sciences since much of such research is given to design methods and design issues. This, of course, has obvious implications for the role of values in the *funding* of research in the artificial sciences.

Second, even given agreement on what constitutes a valid design problem, the solution to the problem—that is, *what* ought to be the case—may again be determined by (among other things) the designer's system of values.

Example 3.3

In designing and implementing a programming environment for a multiprocessor system a decision must be made as to whether the user should specify concurrent segments explicitly in the program or whether the concurrency should be determined by the "system." Note that one can make reasonable arguments for either case. For example, on one hand: "the user will be in the best position to uncover and exploit the parallelism in the problem, and thus, should be given the freedom to specify concurrency in the program;" and on the other: "the user has only limited capacity to optimally detect the parallelism in the program. This task can only be effectively achieved automatically." The eventual choice may well be based on the designer's personal beliefs and opinions about the "right" partitioning of concerns between the system and the user. The decision, then, is fundamentally a value judgment. ■

3.3.2 To Design Is to Represent

The immediate result of the design activity is a description or a *representation* of the object in some symbolic medium. The fact that an activity called "design" is at all necessary is, thus, indicative of the expected complexity of the artifact. For according to J. C. Jones (1980), the traditional craftsman does not distinguish the conceptualization of an object from its making. The separation of the two came about when the target object became too large or complex for the artisan's cognitive capacity; it then became necessary to conceptualize and capture the concept in a representational language—that is, to design the object and then to make it based on the representation.

Just how one chooses to represent the artifact is, of course, determined by the nature of the artifact concerned. There is, however, a very real constraint on the mode of representation: The aim in all cases of design is to produce a *form*—that is, a description of the static structure or composition of the artifact—*from which the artifact's behavior and function may be recovered or inferred.* This property of a representation is essential if the design activity is to be truly useful—for reasons that will become apparent in Section 3.3.4.

At the heart of design, then, is the problem of representation. Indeed, when we talk about "a design" we are really referring to a description or representation. A design discipline can only emerge when appropriate *design* (*representation*) *languages* are available.

Although it is not too difficult to grasp the notion of using abstract or symbolic forms for representing *physical* artifacts, certain kinds of information processors present a more novel problem. An operating system, a real-time control program, and any other piece of software are *abstract* artifacts; they are made out of symbols. Thus, the design of such systems entails, in addition to a *programming language* out of which the artifact is composed, a *design language* in which the program design is expressed. For many years these two languages were identical; that is, the design and implementation of a software system were considered as one activity. Programming was craftsmanship in the traditional sense. With the development of software engineering, *program design languages* (PDLs) began to emerge (Teichrow and Hershey, 1977; Ross, 1977; Linger, Mills, and Witt, 1979; Zelkowitz, Shaw, and Gannon, 1979; Sommerville, 1985; Freeman and Wasserman, 1980; Liskov, 1980). Thus, even in the case of abstract artifacts like software systems, a separation of design from implementation took place.

When we consider the design of computer architectures we face a still more perplexing problem. The phrase "design of a computer architecture" implies that the artifact in question is "an architecture" and that we wish to develop an abstract representation of this artifact. Architectures, like software, are abstract entities, since they are abstractions of physical computers. To this extent software and architectures are similar. However, a software system when it has been implemented is *still* an autonomous software system except that now it is *operational*: one can compile it, load it into a computer's memory, execute it, and, so to speak, watch the artifact in action.

In contrast, it is not at all clear what the implementation of the *artifact* called "architecture" means. Certainly an implemented architecture does not retain its autonomy in the sense that software does. Indeed, by "implementation of architecture" we usually mean that there exists physical computers that behave in ways that conform to the architecture. Architecture as artifact loses — or appears to lose — its autonomy when it has been implemented.

This, of course, is the problem of the autonomy or "realness" of architectures briefly mentioned earlier. I will propose a solution for this problem in Section 3.4. It is mentioned here simply to point out that the view of design as representation, which is surely a valid view, leads to some real problems in the specific domain of computer architecture.

3.3.3 Design Begins with Requirements

If the purpose of design is to improve the world, the designer must know in which direction the improvement is to take place. Thus, the starting point for any design activity is a *specification of requirements*. Some of these may designate the desired *functional capabilities* of the target artifact — what the artifact is required to do; others may stipulate lower bounds on the artifact's *performance characteristics*. Still others may state upper bounds on other kinds of characteristics, for example, cost or chip area constraints.

Stating requirements in such a fashion so that the design can be demonstrated to meet or violate them is an extremely difficult problem. Many requirements can indeed be stated in such a testable form; for example, the typical functional capabilities demanded of an architecture or a software system. Others are far less easy to capture in a form in which the design may be unequivocally shown to meet or contradict them.

Example 3.4

A commonly stated objective in designing computer languages (for programming, microprogramming, or hardware design) is that the language be "easy to learn" or "simple to handle." Similarly, the computer architect is often faced with the requirement that the exo-architecture must be "easy to program."

It may indeed be the case that after the design has been completed, the artifact implemented, and some experience has been gained in the use of the artifact that a consensus may emerge within the user community as to whether or not such requirements are met. This does not, however, make it any easier for the designer to show that the design reflects these requirements using either logical arguments or experimental data.   ■

3.3.4   A Design Finishes as an Assembly

A design, then, is a representation of the target artifact. Just as the latter in its finished state can be analyzed in terms of components or subassemblies, a design when completed, can be understood in terms of components and the way that they have been assembled. These components are themselves representations, and, to distinguish them from the components of the target artifact, I call them *design components* or *design subassemblies.* A design in its finished form is, thus, an assembly, possibly hierarchically structured (Fig. 3.1).

Unfortunately this fact may tell us nothing about *how* this assembly came about. Depending on the initial state of the design, the same final form may, in fact, be produced by different methods.

Example 3.5

It may be the case that the components available to the designer are so primitive that there is a substantial gap between the requirements and the properties of the design components. In that case, the designer may assemble the components into more powerful subassemblies in a hierarchic fashion till the design is

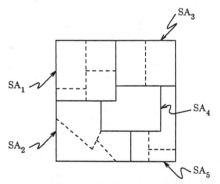

FIGURE 3.1   A design is an assembly of design components.

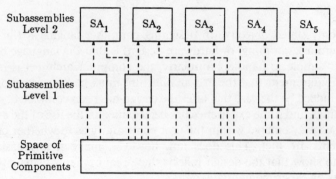

Subassemblies Level 2

Subassemblies Level 1

Space of Primitive Components

FIGURE 3.2   Bottom-up design.

completed (Fig. 3.2). Alternatively, starting with the requirements, the designer may hypothesize a set of subassemblies with specified behavior and interaction such that the composition of these subassemblies meet the given requirements. The subassemblies may, in turn, be refined into sets of smaller subassemblies and so on (Fig. 3.3).

The former approach is usually called *bottom-up design* and the latter *top-down design* or the *method of stepwise refinement*. They are, of course, the most commonly discussed methods of design. In either case, the assembled form may not necessarily reflect the particular method used. ∎

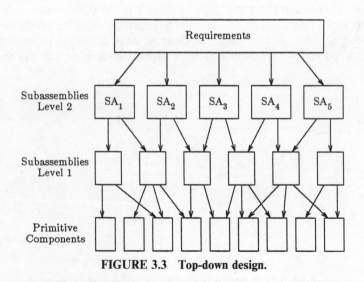

Requirements

Subassemblies Level 2

Subassemblies Level 1

Primitive Components

FIGURE 3.3   Top-down design.

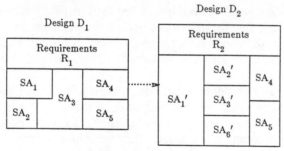

FIGURE 3.4 Redesign.

Example 3.6

Often, however, the designer's task is not to synthesize a representation from scratch but to *modify* an existing design. Jones (1984) refers to this as *redesign*; this is one of the predominant activities in designing software. The problem here, is that given a design D_1 meeting some set of requirements R_1, to modify the design so as to meet a modified set of requirements R_2 (Fig. 3.4). Again, the final design D_2 will appear as an assemblage of design components that will give very few clues as to the fact that the method followed was a case of redesign.

■

3.3.5 Design Is Mostly a Satisficing Process

Regardless of what kind of design method is followed, the process of design necessarily involves making decisions that are typically of the form

1. Given a number of (possibly interacting) goals to achieve, how should these goals be prioritized?
2. Given a number of alternative design subassemblies that are (approximately) equivalent in their functional or performance capabilities, which of these subassemblies should be selected?
3. Given a "space" of design components and subassemblies, which part of this space will most likely yield the most promising solution for the problem at hand?

A fundamental problem in this context is that there are some severe limits to the *rationality* of the decisions that can be made. The rationality is bounded (a) in part by the designer's limited mental capabilities; (b) in part because a decision may have to be made in the face of potential conflicts between two or more desirable goals; and (c) in part by the designer's imperfect knowledge of all the relevant information pertaining to the consequences of a particular chain of decisions.

This notion of *bounded rationality* was first formulated by Simon in 1947 and led to his suggestion that for design problems of any reasonable complexity one must be content with "good" rather than the "best" solutions. In Simon's terms, most design procedures yield *satisficing* rather than *optimal* solutions (Simon, 1981, 1982).

The use of computer-aided design alleviates to some extent the problems of bounded rationality, since the machine may be made to "look ahead" at the potential consequences of some current decision. However, even if the design process is partly or totally mechanized, there are inherent limits to the practical attainment of optimal solutions. It may indeed be theoretically possible to obtain optimal solution to some particular design problem, but as the theory of computational complexity amply illustrates (Aho, Hopcroft, and Ullman, 1974; Horowitz and Sahni, 1978) most of the interesting optimization problems encountered in design produce solutions that are known to require *exponential time or space*. That is, the time (or space) required is of the order of k^n, where k is a constant and n is a parameter specific to, and characterizing the size of, the design problem.[3]

The very high computational cost would suffice to discourage the attainment of such an optimum.

Example 3.7

In the design of microprogrammed control units by adopting the so-called minimally encoded control store word format (see Chapter 5), the derivation of the word length of the control store can be formulated as an optimization problem. The problem is, however, of exponential complexity (Robertson, 1979). Thus, the actual word length of the control store is usually derived using heuristic (satisficing) procedures. ■

3.3.6 The Evolutionary Nature of Design

The main consequence of bounded rationality is that the later effects of design decisions or a chain of such decisions cannot always be logically deduced. Each such decision may also have unintended side effects. Furthermore, one may not be able rigorously to demonstrate that a particular set of design decisions intended to fulfill some requirement do, in fact, satisfy the latter.

Under such conditions a design can only be viewed as a *tentative hypothesis* whose appropriateness vis-à-vis the requirements has to be *tested empirically*. Such tests must necessarily be of a highly *critical* nature since their aims are to reveal *errors* in the design. The design is, then, *modified* to eliminate errors, thus producing a new design hypothesis (Fig. 3.5).

This view of design recalls Popper's well-known theory of the scientific

---

[3]More precisely stated, such problems are said to be *NP-hard* or *NP-complete* problems (Horowitz and Sahni, 1978, Chapter 11).

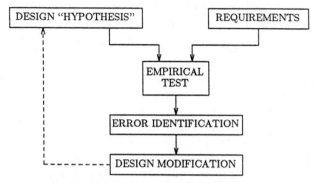

FIGURE 3.5   Evolution of a design—I.

method (Popper, 1968, 1972), which is schematically summarized as (Popper, 1972, p. 145):

$$P_1 \longrightarrow TT \longrightarrow EE \longrightarrow P_2$$

where P_1 is the initial problem situation; TT is a tentative theory advanced as an explanation for the problem situation; EE is the process of error elimination applied to the theory; and P_2 the resulting situation with new problems. Popper likens the development of a science to an evolutionary process in the Darwinian sense that the science develops by continually eliminating errors in whatever is the "current" tentative theory.

Similarly, viewing designs as testable hypotheses that pass through the cycle shown in Figure 3.5, it is reasonable to suggest that *design is an evolutionary process.*

In the specific domain of computing systems, the evolution of a design may occur in two distinct time scales. One form of evolution, which is *highly localized in time*, is the process that takes place between when a problem is given to the designer and when it is passed on to the implementer. This is what is conventionally referred to as the *design phase*; it is during this activity that such strategies as top down, bottom up, or redesign is applied. The cycle shown in Figure 3.5 takes place here primarily because of bounded rationality. What really happens is that the design evolves or unfolds from an initial state over a relatively short period of time to the desired state. Using the biologic analogy, we refer to this form of design evolution as *ontogenic* evolution.[4]

Example 3.8

The first complete design of a software system, a microprogram, an architecture, or an entire computer evolves ontogenically. For instance, a first version of a program (or a microprogram)—the hypothesis—is systematically tested module by module and in its integrated form. The object of program (or micropro-

---

[4]*Ontogeny:* "the life history of an individual, both embryonic and postnatal" (Gould, 1977, p. 483).

gram) testing procedures is to systematically identify errors, which when eliminated produces an "improved" or "more correct" design.   ■

In the context of ontogenic evolution there is a further important parallel
between the empiric test/error identification parts of Figure 3.5 and the error
elimination (*EE*) phase of Popper's scheme. A cornerstone of Popper's theory of
the scientific method is that the experiments used during *EE* are so constructed
that they attempt to *refute* the tentative theory (*TT*).

Briefly stated, the argument is that any number of confirming experiments
will not *logically imply* the truth of *TT* (this is the so-called "problem of
induction") whereas only one refuting experiment will logically imply the *nega-
tion* of *TT*. Hence, from a logical point of view, *EE* can only attempt to refute
TT by revealing errors.

The more stringent the experiment, the better it is; For if *TT* still holds up
after each such experiment, the scientist's *confidence* in *TT* will be greatly
enhanced although the theory still remains tentative.

The problem of induction in a more restricted form is also encountered when
we consider the testing of design hypotheses. Given a design representing a
program or a microprogram, for instance, it is computationally infeasible to test
the design under all possible conditions (states) for which the program (or
microprogram) has been designed. Thus, in analogy to the scientific experiment,
any number of confirming tests will not logically imply the correctness of the
design whereas a test that reveals an error suffices to establish its incorrectness.
This asymmetry between confirmation and refutation in the context of programs was captured in Dijkstra's (1972) celebrated aphorism: "Program testing
can be used to show the presence of bugs but never to show their absence."

It follows then, that empiric tests (of a design hypothesis) should attempt to
refute the hypothesis—that is, be as stringent or as critical as possible. They
should, in fact, test the *limits* of the design.

The second form of design evolution, which occurs over much longer spans
than in the case of ontogenic evolution, represents the *course of change of
implemented designs.* This form of evolution usually reflects changes over time
in the environment of the artifact in question; such environmental changes are,
in turn, reflected in changing contexts for the design and, hence, the design
evolves. Again, drawing on the obvious biologic analogy, we refer to this as
phylogenic evolution of a design.[5,6]

Example 3.9

A well known instance of phylogenic evolution is given by the successive versions or "releases" of the large-scale software systems studied by Lehman and

[5]*Phylogeny:* "the evolutionary history of a lineage conventionally . . . depicted as a sequence of
successive adult stages" (Gould, 1977, p. 484).

[6]By using the adjectives "ontogenic" and "phylogenic" we are, of course, *not* suggesting any
resemblances in the *mechanisms* of evolution between biologic and artificial systems.

Belady (Lehman, 1974, 1984; Belady and Lehman, 1976, 1979). An example is the IBM OS 360/370 operating system, which, in the course of roughly 10 years went through over 20 "releases" and grew some fivefold in size (Belady and Lehman, 1979). ∎

Example 3.10

Consider the Burroughs B5000/B5500/B5700/B6500/B6700/B7700 series of machines (Doran, 1979). The evolution of this series — over roughly a decade, from the early 1960s to the early 1970s — reflects changes and improvements in technology, incorporation of features to meet new needs, and the necessity to correct deficiencies in predecessor designs. The first two are instances of environmental (or design context) changes; the last exemplifies the effect of bounded rationality. ∎

Note that the scheme of Figure 3.5 also holds in the case of phylogenic evolution, except that the empiric test/error identification activities are conducted over larger periods of time "in the field;" furthermore, each design modification phase will *internally* involve ontogenic evolution.

3.3.7   Designs Are Sometimes Theorems

Consider the design of information processing systems (rather than artifacts in general): programs, microprograms, architectures, logic circuits, and so on. On the basis of the foregoing discussion we may agree that a given design is a description or representation of the system in question that allegedly satisfies some given set of requirements. The requirements may pertain to (Mostow, 1985):

1. Functional characteristics.
2. Performance goals.
3. Technological constraints.
4. Constraints on the use of resources — such as time, space, power, cost, work force — during design, implementation, and operation of the system.
5. Other criteria, such as reliability, simplicity, maintainability.

We may also agree that, for reasons having to do with bounded rationality, the design is very much in the nature of a hypothesis. Indeed, some of the alleged properties of the design can only be tested for during or after the system has been implemented. It is highly desirable, though, that the design itself be tested as critically as possible and evolved into the strongest possible hypothesis prior to being passed on to the implementer (Fig. 3.5). In section 3.3.6 I likened the design process to the method of the experimental sciences (Fig. 3.6).

Suppose, however, that we are able to present both the requirements and the design within the common framework of a formal mathematical system. A very different model of the design activity appears to emerge: The design can now be viewed as a mathematical proposition or *theorem* that allegedly solves the

Natural Sciences	Design
Problem	Requirements
Theory/Hypothesis	Design
Experiment	Critical test/ Error identification

FIGURE 3.6 Parallels between the design process and the method of science.

problem as captured by the specification of the requirements. It then becomes the responsibility of the designer to *prove* (or *verify*) that the design/theorem is indeed a solution to the requirements/problem. In this view the design process is likened to the methods of mathematics (Fig. 3.7).

Treating designs as mathematical entities has been the cornerstone in the development of formal programming techniques. As is well known, the foundations for this approach were laid in seminal papers by Floyd (1967) and Hoare (1969).[7] Extensive developments have since taken place in the theory of program correctness (Dijkstra, 1976; de Bakker, 1980; C. B. Jones, 1980; Gries, 1981; Hoare and Sheperdson, 1985) and mechanical verification technology (Boyer and Moore, 1981b; Hoare and Sheperdson, 1985). In recent years the view of designs as verifiable entities has also found its way into the design of hardware (Moszkowski, 1985, 1986; Shostak, 1983), computer architectures (Dasgupta, 1984) and firmware (Damm *et al.*, 1986; Dasgupta and Wagner, 1984; Marcus, Crocker, and Landauer, 1984; Mueller and Duda, 1986; see also, Volume 2, Chapter 5).

In light of the foregoing sections, the obvious question that comes to mind is: How does one reconcile a view of designs as theorems for which formal proofs of

[7]See, however, the Bibliographic Remarks at the end of this chapter for a discussion of some lesser known "prehistory" of this topic.

Mathematics	Design
Problem	Requirements (Specifications)
Theorem	Design
Proof	Verification

FIGURE 3.7 Parallels between the design process and the mathematical method [based on de Millo, Lipton, and Perlis (1979) and Scherlis and Scott (1983)].

correctness can be constructed with the evolutionary nature of the design process depicted herein? This question is also related to an important and highly influential critique by de Millo, Lipton, and Perlis (1979) of the parallel between programming and mathematics.

Let us consider the latter issue first. Briefly stated, de Millo and colleagues pointed out that the mere *existence* of a proof of some mathematical theorem by itself means little; the proof must be *accepted* by the relevant mathematical community in order to become meaningful. And, acceptance of the proof is largely founded on the *social processes* within that community: the proof is discussed, criticized, and worried over by members of the community, and it is largely this sort of social process that either results in the proof being believed or in it being rejected. Indeed, a proof may be accepted for a considerable period of time before a flaw is detected, at which point it would be rejected or modified.

The program verification process, according to de Millo and colleagues, is of a very different nature. Verifications—that is, proofs of programs, especially those generated by the computer—are long, tedious sequences of logical deductions that look and are very different from the proofs that mathematicians pour over. Mathematicians do not, in fact, produce completely formal logical derivations of their theorems; if they did so, it would be most unlikely that their proofs would ever get read and thus be accepted. Thus, because of their very nature, program verifications, except for very short ones, have not been, nor are likely to be, subject to the social process so characteristic of mathematics.

The publication of the de Millo, Lipton, and Perlis (1979) paper generated considerable discussion.[8] More recently, Scherlis and Scott (1983) provide a most cogent response to the basic issue raised by de Millo and colleagues. Scherlis and Scott do not question the thesis that the acceptability of mathematical proofs lies in social processes. However, they object strongly to the assertion that verifications—especially, machine-generated verifications—are not or cannot be subject to similar processes. Using as a case study the celebrated four-color theorem[9] and the computer-aided proof discovered by Haken, Appel, and Koch (1977) for this theorem, Scherlis and Scott show that such machine-generated proofs may undergo precisely the kind of public discussion and analysis that traditional mathematical proofs go through. As they have documented, mathematicians have examined the proof of the four-color theorem, debated on the nature of such evidences and whether they constitute what are traditionally viewed as proofs in mathematics, compared the Haken-Appel-Koch proof with other subsequent machine-generated proofs, and have even pointed out a flaw in the original proof and how it could be removed.

It is, thus, fair to conclude that while de Millo and colleagues made an

---

[8]See, for example, the "ACM Forum" section of *Communications of the ACM*, November 1979, pp. 621–630. See also, the review of this article by C. A. R. Hoare in the *ACM Computing Reviews*, Vol. 20, No. 8, August 1979.

[9]The four-color problem is: Can a finite planar map be colored with four colors so that no two adjacent regions have the same color?

important contribution to our understanding of the methodology of mathematics by making explicit the importance of the social phenomena at work, their implication that program verifications deviate, or must necessarily deviate, radically from this model has been very successfully and convincingly challenged and refuted by Scherlis and Scott.

This brings us back to the question posed earlier: How does one reconcile the idea of verifying designs-viewed-as-theorems with the notion of designs-viewed-as-evolving-objects?

As long as one adheres to a picture of the mathematical process as consisting of constructing an inexorable chain of deductions from axioms to theorems, then there is indeed a conflict. But as has been shown, this picture is a myth. The mathematician and the natural scientist go about solving their problems in very similar fashion: posing theories/theorems and the relevant evidences/proofs within a shared framework of knowledge; publicly debating and criticizing the evidences/proofs; and accepting or rejecting theories/theorems according to whether or not the evidences/proofs stand up to close scrutiny. The difference lies in the manner and language in which the arguments are conducted. Thus, drawing a parallel between design and the method of natural science on one hand and drawing a parallel between design and the method of mathematics on the other are not conflicting actions. In the latter case, instead of Figure 3.5, the model of the design process is given by Figure 3.8. The main points to note here are the following.

First, as in Figure 3.5, a design evolves into a final shape. However, whether the design "proposition" meets the requirements or not is determined by formal reasoning rather than experimental procedures. Second, the design transformation itself may be guided by formal reasoning rather than empiric arguments. The outcome of one iteration of this cycle is a new design "proposition."

Example 3.11

One approach to program design, advocated mainly by Dijkstra (1976) and Gries (1981), is based on the idea of developing a proof of correctness and the

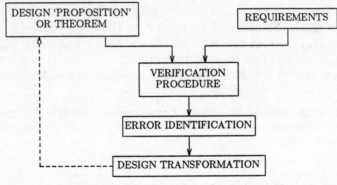

FIGURE 3.8 Evolution of a design—II.

program together, preferably allowing the proof to guide program development. For future reference this will be called the *design-while-verify* approach. I illustrate this approach here, and how it adheres to the evolutionary picture of Figure 3.8, with a trivial example.

We are required to develop a program (i) in the programming language L, which, (ii) given nonnegative integers x, y, sets a variable Z to the maximum of x and y. Call this program-to-be, MAX. Requirement (i) is essentially an implementation constraint whereas (ii) is a functional constraint.

1. The initial design is formulated as follows: The functional requirement is captured in the form of a pair of *assertions* expressed in the predicate calculus. One of the assertions, called a *precondition* (and denoted by PRE), is a predicate that all possible initial states of the relevant variables will satisfy. PRE is, thus, a predicate that will always be true when MAX begins execution. The other assertion, called a *postcondition* (and denoted by POST), is a predicate that all possible final states of the variables will satisfy. That is, POST will always be true when MAX terminates. In general, given a precondition PRE, the objective is to design a system S such that if S begins execution when PRE is true, then when (and if) S terminates, POST will be true. Notationally, this is stated as

    {PRE} **S** {POST}

    If we can prove that this formula holds, we also say that S is *partially correct* with respect to PRE and POST.[10]

    For the problem at hand the appropriate instance of this formula is

    D1:   {PRE: $x \geq 0 \wedge y \geq 0$}
                  MAX
            {POST: $Z \geq x \wedge Z \geq y \wedge (Z = x \vee Z = y)$}}

Here, POST expresses the goal that Z is to be the maximum of x and y. *The initial design proposition is the entire formula D1.* It is a proposition in that it is tentative: We must still *determine* whether or not it is a correct design — that is, whether or not D1 is a true formula — and whether it satisfies all other requirements.

2. In comparing D1 with the requirements, the verification procedure finds that D1 does not satisfy the implementation constraint. The "error" is that "MAX" is not a statement in the language L. Thus, until the error is eliminated, we cannot undertake any program proving.
3. A transformation is then performed on D1. In the verify-while-design approach the transformation procedure attempts to replace some portion of the executable part of the design — in the case of D1 this happens to be the symbol "MAX" — with some other executable component such that (a) it

---

[10]The significance of the word "partial" lies in that the proof of {PRE}S{POST} does not include a proof that S *terminates*. It only assumes termination. If, in addition to the proof of the formula, S is also shown to terminate, then S is said to be *totally* correct.

comes closer to the goal of expressing the program in the specified language (L); and (b) the designer believes that the component is correct with respect to the pre- and postcondition. The outcome is a new design proposition (see Fig. 3.8).

For our example, suppose we replace "MAX" by the assignment statement

$$\text{MAX}': Z: = \max(x, y)$$

where "max" is a function that returns the maximum of x and y. The resulting new design proposition is

D2: {PRE: $x \geq 0 \wedge y \geq 0$}
     MAX': $Z: = \max(x, y)$
     {POST: $Z \geq x \wedge Z \geq y \wedge$
             $(Z = x \vee Z = y)$}

4. The verification procedure reveals that MAX' still does not meet the language requirement. Thus we are still unable to confirm that D2 is correct.
5. Our next transformation is to replace MAX' such that we obtain the design:

D3:   {PRE: $x \geq 0 \wedge y \geq 0$}
          MAX" : $Z: = $ if $x \geq y$ then x else y
          {POST: $Z \geq x \wedge z \geq y \wedge$
                 $(Z = x \vee Z = y)$}

6. The verification procedure now finds that the implementation constraint is indeed satisfied: MAX" is a legitimate statement in L; we can now attempt to confirm that the logical formula expressed by D3 is indeed true by proving that MAX" is correct with respect to PRE and POST. ∎

3.4 THE PLAUSIBILITY OF ARCHITECTURAL DESIGNS

It was briefly noted, in Section 3.2, that the idea of computer architecture as a design discipline is of relatively recent vintage (Dasgupta, 1984). It seems that a rather fundamental reason for this concerns the *plausibility* of architectural design proposals. It is widely believed (if not always explicitly stated) that a description of some new architecture carries little credibility until and unless the design is supported by some sort of physical implementation. Indeed, the term "paper design" is used often disparagingly to designate such proposals.

One of the reasons why new architectural design proposals are viewed with a skeptical eye is the traditionally informal nature of such proposals. Architectures are most usually described and discussed using a mixture of natural language, diagrams, and (only occasionally) some formal notation. The very nature of these descriptions, with their resulting lack of precision, makes it difficult to assess a design objectively for its feasibility, correctness, or performance. Indeed, one can often *neither confirm nor refute* the design against any given set of criteria simply because of the informality, ambiguity, and omissions of relevant details in architectural design proposals. The philosopher of science, K. R. Popper (1968) termed statements possessing this lack of testability or refutability, "metaphysical statements" and in this sense, architectural designs may be regarded as "metaphysical proposals."

Clearly, the only way by which we can assess such a proposal is by waiting till it is implemented and then transferring our critical attention to the physical system. Alternatively, we can attempt to make our designs less "metaphysical"; this can be achieved by using an architecture description language (see Volume 2, Chapters 3 and 4). The description *is* the design — no more and no less.

There is, however, a second vital reason behind the general skepticism with which architectural design proposals are received; this has to do with the uncertain status of computer architecture itself in relation to the physical, tangible computer. Thus, even when design, description, and evaluation tools are available, there still remains a residue of unease within the computer design community: a belief that an "architecture" *in itself* is a nebulous entity, the reality or *plausibility* of which, independent of a physical implementation, is in doubt.

This issue of the plausibility of architectural designs is of considerable importance. From a *practical standpoint,* it has significant implications for what kinds of claims one can or should make about a design proposal and how much confidence can be acquired in such claims prior to physical implementation. From a more *theoretical viewpoint*, an understanding of the plausibility problem may be useful in the ongoing goal of transforming computer architecture from the somewhat arcane craft that it still is to a scientific discipline.

As Popper (1968) and Kuhn (1970) have in their different ways pointed out, the hallmark of any *scientific* discipline is the development of an *objective* (or *public*) and *testable* matrix of knowledge. Objectivity allows propositions to be stated in terms of a universe of discourse shared, understood, and accepted by the relevant community of practitioners.[11] Testability allows for open, critical discussion and the development of sharable procedures for confirming or refuting such propositions.

The problem of the plausibility of architectural designs is very much along these lines: that is, what kind of objectivity can the computer architect bring to bear on a design such that (1) he or she may be able to make believable claims about the design; and (2) given the availability of a shared or sharable collection of formal and experimental tools, *anyone else* may critically scrutinize the design in order to either refute or validate these claims?

3.4.1 Architectural Designs as Specifications of Hardware Systems

Given an *implemented* computer, it is very obvious what purposes architectural descriptions serve: Exo-architectures (micro-architectures) provide the details

---

[11]It is this shared universe of discourse to which Kuhn (1970) gave the name *paradigm.* Unfortunately, this word has assumed a "cult" status in recent times and is both overused and misused.

needed to develop executable programs (microprograms) for the computer. An endo-architectural description helps us to *understand* the internal design better, since, by its very nature, it provides an abstraction level that mediates between the exo-architecture and the myriads of circuit elements that cooperate to realize the exo-architecture.

However, when we *propose* an architecture we are, in effect, suggesting an abstraction (or a set of abstractions) of something *that does not yet exist.* This, it appears, is the source of the skepticism surrounding architectural designs.

Now, the one way in which one may legitimately design abstractions of nonexisting entities is when these abstractions are intended to serve as *specifications* for how an entity when built *should* appear (or behave, or perform). Thus, given the objective of building a computer to meet certain requirements, *an architectural design should be viewed as a specification of functional, structural, and performance constraints* that are to be met by a system that will be implemented by a combination of hardware and firmware. Henceforth, I will refer to the latter as the *physical implementation* and will also use the terms *architecture* and *specification* interchangeably.

There are several implications of this architecture-as-specifications model:

1. It may now be seen in what sense an architecture may be deemed "real." Since, in the life cycle of a system a specification generally precedes an implementation, it is possible for a specification to exist at a time that the implementation does not. Thus, an architecture *qua* specification may be considered "real" in that it may exist autonomously. Furthermore, providing that the specification is expressed in formal language and the right kinds of tools are available, such specifications can, within limits, be analyzed, manipulated, and reasoned about. An architecture *qua* specification may thus be considered "real" in this latter sense also.

2. Like all theoretical descriptions of (intended) physical systems, the constraints appearing in an architectural design may not all be satisfiable; the assumptions about the physical world (e.g., propagation delays through circuits or electrical properties of devices) underlying these constraints may be simply wrong or mutually inconsistent. Thus, the *ultimate* test of the believability of an architecture must lie in the physical implementation.

   This may seem so obvious as to be hardly worth stating. It is stated, nevertheless, because the central matter of interest is the extent to which we can *defer* putting an architectural design (specification) to the physical test and the extent to which believable claims can be made about an architecture *prior* to physical implementation.

3. The fundamental distinction between specification at the exo- and the endo-architectural levels lies in the fact that the latter, being closer to physical implementation, will incorporate many more structural and performance constraints than the former. In exo-architectures, the emphasis is more on overall functional constraints.

4. Given an initial architectural specification, the transition to physical implementation may be too complex to be conducted in a single, undifferentiated

step. *Intermediate specifications* that are *abstract* implementations of a prior specification may be found necessary. A general picture of the architecture design process thus emerges, as shown in Figure 3.9.

Two aspects of this schematic must be emphasized. First, as discussed in Section 3.3, the act of design is inevitably an evolutionary process. Thus, any subsequence of the process shown in Figure 3.9 may have to be iterated in order to converge to a satisficing solution. The feedback arrows have been omitted simply to keep the diagram "clean." What is explicitly suggested by the diagram is that the locus of the design process *progresses* from a more abstract form to a less abstract form.

Second, the abstraction level of a specification may have nothing to do with the *abstractness of the decisions* underlying the specification. For example, the architect may right at the onset decide that a particular technology is to be used for the physical implementation. This (very "low-level") decision could well influence the development of the highest level of specification, as indeed it did in the design of the Berkeley RISC architectures (Katevenis, 1985).

Returning to the problem of plausibility, if an architectural design is indeed viewed as a specification of constraints that some eventual physical implementation has to satisfy, then the plausibility of the overall design will be determined by the plausibility of the constraints themselves. Very recently, a *theory of plausible designs* has been developed by Agüero and Dasgupta for this purpose (Agüero, 1987; Agüero and Dasgupta, 1987). Although it is too early to discuss this theory in any detail—extensive testing on actual design problems need to be conducted to assess its viability—it appears to provide valuable and unexpected insights on the nature of the design process in general and, in particular, on the evolutionary characteristics of design.

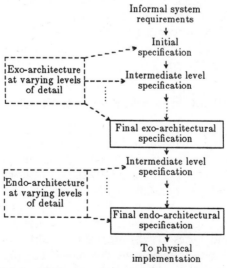

FIGURE 3.9 Schematic of the architecture design process.

3.5 BIBLIOGRAPHIC REMARKS

Design Theory

A substantial part of the literature on design theory has sprung from the disciplines of (building) architecture and urban planning. One of the most influential examples of this *genre* is Alexander's (1964) monograph in which he discusses the process of design in the context of built forms and introduces a formal design method using ideas from elementary set and graph theories.

A well-known general text on design methods is by J. C. Jones (1980). Of particular interest here is the author's insight on the transition from the "craft" stage to the "design-by-drawing" stage in the evolution of a technology. A more recent publication by the same author (Jones, 1984) contains several interesting articles, including one on the notion of "continuous design" or "redesign" — a topic of great relevance for the software engineer.

Several other publications from outside the computer field are of interest: Steadman (1979 is a detailed examination of the oft-drawn analogy, over the centuries, between artifacts and organisms from the perspective of design. Broadbent (1973) provides an extensive survey of design methods and tools in building architecture, including the roles played by the modern sciences of operations research, cybernetics, and computer science. Finally, Schön (1983) is an original study, by a social scientist, of what that author calls "professional knowledge" — the kind of knowledge used by the professional practitioner (designers, doctors, engineers, managers, and such). The relevance of this work to the topic of design should be obvious, as well as its connection to the kinds of knowledge embedded in contemporary "expert systems."

Certainly the most significant set of ideas on the design process from the viewpoint of computer science is contained in Simon (1981). The important notions of bounded rationality and the satisficing nature of decision-making processes summarized in this book, have been discussed by Simon in many places. The reader is recommended, particularly, to the set of papers on "Substantive and Procedural Rationality" appearing in Simon (1982) and to the first five chapters of Simon (1976).

Programming Methodology and Program Verification

From the perspective of computer systems design, much of the early thinking on the design process originated within the programming community. Dijkstra's "notes" on structured programming (Dijkstra, 1972) and the celebrated papers by Hoare (1969), Wirth (1971), Parnas (1972), and Mills (1972) established the theoretical and conceptual foundations of modern programming methodology and software engineering. More recent views of the interaction of design methodology and software engineering are given by Freeman (1980a, 1980b). Yourdon (1979, 1982) and Gries (1978) are valuable anthologies of some of the important papers in software design methodology. The theory of program correctness, though still susceptible to a great deal of skepticism in its applicability to large-scale software design, has evolved to a very mature level, at least in the domain of sequential programs. Important books on this topic are Dijkstra (1976), de Bakker (1980), Alagic and Arbib (1978), Gries (1981), and Hoare (1985).

A Note on the Prehistory of Program Verification

Although the theory of program correctness as we now know it originated with the well-known papers by Floyd (1967) and Hoare (1969), there is, in fact, an interesting prehistory to these developments. In 1949, Alan Turing wrote a short paper in which he discussed the germinal ideas underlying what we now call program verification (Turing, 1949). This paper appeared in the Proceedings of what was probably the first British conference on computing. The main ideas that he presented are as follows.

First, "checking" whether a program is correct or not can be greatly facilitated if the programmer states assertions that are expected to be true at certain points in the program. These assertions are to be such that once they are checked individually the correctness of the whole program easily follows.

Second, Turing makes the distinction between what we now call partial and total correctness—the former concerned with the correctness of a program assuming that it terminates; the latter is additionally concerned with the problem of termination. Furthermore, addressing the problem of program termination, Turing points out that the programmer should also provide a further assertion defining a quantity that decreases continually and "vanishes" when the machine halts.

Turing's third important idea, although not explicitly stated, is that the correctness of a procedure (or "routine" as it was then called) should be done independent of the actual machine code. A final point of interest is that in Turing's scheme, "checking" (i.e., proving correctness) should be done by a "checker" who may be someone other than the programmer.

Most of Turing's paper consists of an example illustrating these ideas. The problem he uses is the computation of $n!$ without using a multiply operator, multiplication being carried out by repeated addition. In the absence of what Turing calls "a coding system sufficiently generally known" (i.e., presumably, a machine-independent programming notation), the algorithm is represented by means of a flowchart. An interesting aspect of his original notation is the use of primed variables (r', n', etc.) on the left side of assignments to denote "new" values of variables while the unprimed symbols denote "old" values. Two decades later, a variant of this primed notation was used by Parnas (1972) to serve the same function for program specifications.

The discipline of the History of Science and Technology is concerned with the genesis, propagation, and evolution of scientific and technical ideas, and Turing's paper raises some interesting questions in this regard. There seems little doubt that Turing had identified the essential ideas underlying program correctness. Strangely enough, the word "proof" does not appear in the text, and it remains unclear as to the checker's *modus operandi* for verifying the various assertions. The historian of computing will, however, be more intrigued by the question of whether Turing's ideas were further pursued by himself or by anyone else in those early days of the electronic digital computer. After all, the Proceedings of this particular conference being one of the first of its kind must have been widely circulated in Britain, Europe, and the United States.

From Floyd's (1967) discussion it is clear that he was unaware of Turing's paper. Thus, unless further evidence comes to light, it would appear that the ideas expressed in 1949 by Alan Turing died a quiet death and some 15 years had to pass before their rediscovery in a form more in tune with the then prevalent notions of programming.

The connection of Turing's paper to the modern theory of program correctness was discovered by Morris and Jones (1984) and, independently, by Dasgupta (1983).

The Design Process in VLSI, Architecture, and Microprogramming

In very recent years, developments in VLSI technology on one hand and expert systems on the other have brought about an examination of design models with a view to design mechanization using heuristic programming (i.e., artificial intelligence) techniques. Mostow (1985) provides some important insights from this perspective.

Myers (1982) discusses, in a brief chapter, some of the factors that impinge on the architecture design process. A more extensive treatment of computer architecture as a design discipline appears in Dasgupta (1984). This work draws on many of the ideas from general design theory, software engineering, programming methodology, hardware description languages, and microprogramming.

The nature of the design process relevant to the design and implementation of firmware is discussed by Dasgupta and Shriver (1985). Finally, Giloi and Shriver (1985) bring together a number of papers on design methodology as it applies across several levels of the computer system. Of special interest in this collection are descriptions of the SARA design system (Seewaldt and Estrin, 1985; Estrin, 1985b; Vernon and Estrin, 1985) and the MIMOLA system (Marwedel, 1985).

PROBLEMS

Consider the problems of designing a vending machine (see also, Problem 1.8, Chapter 1). The requirements are given as follows.

(a) The machine is to dispense 10 types of candies. Of these, types A, B, and C are priced at 50 cents. Types D and E are priced at 65 cents. Types F, G, and H each cost 75 cents. And types I and J are priced at $1.

(b) The machine will only accept coins.

(c) The machine will only accept exact amounts for each candy type as combinations of quarters, nickels, and dimes. That is, no change or coin return will be produced by the machine.

(d) After inserting the exact amount, the consumer presses one of the 10 buttons corresponding to the 10 types of candies and, if the correct coinage has been inserted, the machine responds by issuing the requested candy.

Prior to building a prototype, it is required to develop and implement a program that simulates the vending machine. You are given the problem of designing the *exo-architecture* and the *endo-architecture* of the simulated vending machine. The objective is to ensure a vending machine design that exhibits the "correct" behavioral and functional characteristics. Thus, the architecture must be such that the functional and behavioral characteristics of the future physical machine can be closely monitored and understood from the simulated version.

The following problems are mostly related to this design problem and your solution to it.

3.1 In Section 3.3.3 it was stated that "design begins with requirements." However, it is not always possible to specify or identify all the requirements in advance. Thus, we may augment this statement with the assertion that "design also *generates* requirements." In other words, it may be claimed that the development and identification of requirements is an integral part of the design activity.

In developing a design of the simulated vending machine, show how new requirements are generated as an integral part of your design process.

3.2 "A design finishes as an assembly" (Section 3.3.4).

(a) What are the primitive or most elementary components that appear in your design? How did you select or identify these components?

(b) The principles of structured programming has given us reasonably firm ideas as to what it means for a program to be "well-structured." Based on these principles, define a set of characteristics corresponding to the idea of a *well-structured design*. Referring to these characteristics, comment on the extent to which your simulated vending machine design is well-structured.

3.3 In the development of any system or product, "design" stops at some stage and "implementation" takes over. In the case of your vending machine problem:

(a) At what level of detail did you terminate the design?

(b) What were the factors or reasons that prompted you to terminate the design when you did?

(c) In hindsight, do you think you would have benefited from carrying the design down to a further level of detail? Justify your answer.

(d) Again, in hindsight, would you have benefited from terminating the design at an earlier (less detailed) stage than you did? Give reasons for your answer.

3.4 In Section 3.3.5 it was noted that design is mostly a satisficing process. Describe the two most important features or components of your design that involved satisficing decision making. Your discussion should address such issues as:
(a) Why you were forced to satisfice rather than optimize.
(b) What would have been the consequences had you attempted to optimize.
(c) The criteria you used to judge the "goodness" of the satisficing decisions.

3.5 "Design is an evolutionary process" (Section 3.3.6). By this it is meant that the development of a design evolves by a process of proposing a design hypothesis, testing the hypothesis, identifying errors, modifying the design so as to eliminate errors thus creating a new design hypothesis, and so on.

This is a descriptive model or a "theory" of design processes in general, although designers may not actually view their activity in such terms. However, it may be advantageous to explicitly design according to this evolutionary model — that is, to view the evolutionary model of a design as a *design method.* Being required to construct design components as testable hypotheses, and actually testing these hypotheses, is likely to make each step of the design far more deliberate and thoughtful than may otherwise be the case.

Design the architecture (at either the exo- or endo- levels) of the simulated vending machine by explicitly following the evolutionary model. In particular
(a) Describe in detail at least three important testable design hypotheses that were formulated in the course of the design.
(b) Explain how you tested these hypotheses and how you interpreted the results of your tests.
(c) Discuss the advantages and disadvantages of evolutionary design as a systematic design method.

3.6 This question concerns the evolutionary model of design (see also Problem 3.5). A palindrome is a sequence of characters that reads identically, whether read from left to right or from right to left. Examples of decimal numbers that are palindromes are 44, 121, and 343.

You are required to develop a program that will list all integers between 1 and 10,000 whose *squares* are palindromes (e.g., since 121 is both a palindrome and a square, 11 would be one of the numbers that would be listed). However, the program must be developed strictly according to the evolutionary model.
(a) Describe in detail at least two of the most important testable design hypotheses that were formulated in the course of program development.
(b) Explain how these hypotheses were tested.
(c) How similar or dissimilar are the evolutionary model (as a design

method) and the more familiar method of top-down design (also called stepwise refinement).

3.7 Designing is clearly a type of problem solving. Yet, the design of an artifact such as a building, a piece of hardware, or a computer program seems to require a special kind of problem-solving approach. In particular, consider the following two types of problems.

(a) Given variables x, y, and constants A, B, C, D, E, F, such that

$$Ax + By = E$$
$$Cx - Dy = F$$

solve this pair of simultaneous equations for x and y.

(b) Given an array A of n integers, sort the elements of A in nondescending order—that is, such that after sorting is complete, for $i < j$:

$$A[i] \leq A[j] \qquad \text{where } 1 \leq i < n, \ 1 < j \leq n$$

Compare these problems with the problem of designing the simulated vending machine. More specifically, compare the structure or characteristics of the two problems (a) and (b) (or approaches to their solution) with the characteristics of the simulated vending machine design problem and identify the fundamental differences between them.

[*Hint*: In answering this question it might be especially helpful to establish a framework and a vocabulary based on the concepts of *algorithms, heuristics,* and *search.*]

PART TWO

UNIPROCESSORS

CHAPTER 4

REGISTER MACHINES
I. THE OUTER ARCHITECTURE

4.1 INTRODUCTION

Certainly, the most well established and stable style of exo-architecture is what is often called the *register machine* style. In its present form, it is the main evolutionary offspring of the architecture (or, as it was then called, "logical design") proposed by Burks, Goldstine, and von Neumann (1946) and is typically represented among contemporary systems by the IBM System/370, 3030, and 4300 family of machines (Siewiorek, Bell, and Newell, 1982), the DEC VAX series, namely, VAX 11/750, 11/780, and 8600 (Digital 1981a, 1981b, 1985), and the Intel 8086 (Morse *et al.*, 1978).

This chapter and the chapter that follows will examine the register machine style. However, simply *describing* the architecture of register machines will only provide a partial picture of this style. Because of the close historical-evolutionary connection between the original proposal by von Neumann and colleagues of what has come to be known as the *von Neumann model*[1] and the register machine style, there is a continuity between the principles underlying the von Neumann design, at both exo- and endo-architectural levels, and those present in register machines. That is, the register machine style captures, both at the exo- and endo-architectural levels, a great deal of the spirit and the specifics of the von Neumann-Burks-Goldstine design. Accordingly, this chapter starts with a brief description of the original design proposed by the von Neumann group since this is "where it all began."

One further historical connection is relevant to this discussion. The use of *microprogramming* for the design of a computer's control unit was conceived by Wilkes (1951) at a time when the few computers then extant followed the von Neumann model very closely. EDSAC 2, designed and implemented by Wilkes and colleagues (Wilkes and Stringer, 1953) was both a von Neumann machine and the first microprogrammed computer. Full-scale commercial exploitation of microprogramming, however, had to wait till the 1960s, when IBM developed its System/360 range of processors; these were register machines in most of which

---

[1]See the Bibliographic Remarks section of Chapter 1 for a discussion of the controversy surrounding this term.

microprogramming was used to implement a common exo-architecture on micro-architectures of varying cost/performance characteristics (Blaauw and Brooks, 1964).

Thus, in an obvious historical sense, the development of micro-architectures and microprogramming is intimately related to both the original von Neumann model-based designs as well as its register-machine descendents. To emphasize this relationship, microprogramming is introduced as part of the discussion of the endo-architecture of register machines in Chapter 5.

4.2 THE VON NEUMANN MODEL

At the *exo-architectural* level, the von Neumann machine may be characterized as follows.

1. A main memory of 4096 words with a word length of 40 bits.
2. A repertoire of primarily *1-address* instructions of the form

< operand, opcode>

where "operand" is the address in memory of one of the operands and "opcode" is the operation.[2] The second operand is, implicitly, one of two programmable registers in the processor: an *accumulator*, which is a general purpose register, and an *arithmetic register*, which is used basically for multiplication and division. Just which register is being referenced in a particular instruction is determined by the operation.

3. Instructions are 20 bits long and consist of a 12-bit address field and an 8-bit operation field. Since memory words are 40 bits long, two instructions are packed to a word; these will be distinguished here as the "left instruction" and the "right instruction," respectively (Fig. 4.1).

4. The full repertoire of instructions are listed in Table 4.1. The meanings of these instructions are stated in a semiformal language. Most of the symbols should be easily understood except, perhaps, "pc," which denotes program counter, "@" used to denote concatenation, and "| . . . |" which signifies the absolute value of a quantity. It should be noted that the instructions and

---

[2]In the terminology of the early computer literature the term "order" is commonly used to denote an instruction or an operation. The phrase "order code" is synonymous with "instruction set."

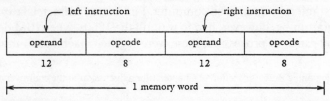

FIGURE 4.1   Instruction format in the von Neumann model.

TABLE 4.1   Instruction Set for the von Neumann Model

Instruction	Example	Meaning
Load acc	LD m	acc <= mem[m]
Load acc neg	LDN m	acc <= −mem[m]
Load acc abs	LDAB m	acc <= |mem[m]|
Load acc neg abs	LDNAB m	acc <= |−mem[m]|
Load reg	LDR m	reg <= mem[m]
Load acc from reg	LDAR	acc <= reg
Store acc	ST m	mem[m] <= acc
Add	ADD m	acc <= acc+mem[m]
Subtract	SUB m	acc <= acc−mem[m]
Add abs	ADDAB m	acc <= acc+|mem[m]|
Subtract abs	SUBAB m	acc <= acc−|mem[m]|
Multiply	MPY m	acc @ reg <= reg*mem[m]
Divide	DIV m	reg <= quotient(acc/mem[m])
		& acc <= remainder(acc/mem[m])
Shift left	SHL	acc <= shift left(acc)
Shift right	SHR	acc <= shift right(acc)
Branch left	BRL m	**goto** left inst(mem[m])
Branch right	BRR m	**goto** right inst(mem[m])
Branch left pos	BRLP m	**if** acc ≥ 0 **then** "Branch left"
Branch right pos	BRRP m	**if** acc ≥ 0 **then** "Branch right"
Store partial left	STPRTL m	left hand 12 bits of
		left inst (mem[m])
		<= left hand 12 bits of acc
Store partial right	STPRTR m	left hand 12 bits of
		right inst (mem[m])
		<= left hand 12 bits of acc

the examples are given in contemporary symbols and terminology rather than those used by von Neumann et al.

The instruction set includes, perhaps most interestingly, two special instructions (STPRTL, STPRTR) that allow the high-order (left-most) 12 bits of an instruction—the memory operand address part—to be altered. This, in a sense, is at the heart of the *stored program* concept: The fact that instructions are held in the same memory as the data means that instructions can be treated as data and can, therefore, be altered. The same instructions can then be used to access operands located in different addresses in memory by simply altering the operand field with the STPRTL or STPRTR instructions.

Also present in the instruction set are two forms of an unconditional branch and a conditional branch: the only condition that can be tested is "accumulator greater than or equal to zero." Note that when a branch takes place the meaning as shown denotes that control is transferred to the left or right instruction (as the case may be) of the addressed memory word.

5. The basic data type is a 40-bit signed binary number with the left-most (high-order) bit designating the sign.

6. The input/output (I/O) subsystem is far less precisely specified than the other aspects of the architecture. Basically, all I/O was conceived as being under program control. Information would be transmitted from an input device to the accumulator and thence to memory. Conversely, data would be sent to the output device from the accumulator.

A number of alternative I/O devices were discussed, although no specific decision was made in the 1946 report. One possible type of device suggested was a "magnetic wire" memory, which appears to be a sequential access device such as the contemporary magnetic tape. Without actually giving the specifications for the instructions for transmitting between wires and the accumulator, the following kinds of operation, strongly suggestive of tape operations, are mentioned

(a) Move wire forward.

(b) Move wire in reverse.

(c) Stop the wire.

(d) Transfer from wire to accumulator.

(e) Transfer from accumulator to wire.

It is interesting to note that von Neumann and his colleagues recognized the possibility of overlapping I/O and processor operations, although the idea is not further pursued in their model.

Consider now the *endo-architecture* of the von Neumann machine. Although the details of the information flow is not stated very precisely in the 1946 report, a block diagram of the principal endo-architectural components may be reconstructed as shown in Figure 4.2. In this diagram, the labels of the various components correspond to the names originally used by von Neumann et al. The legend expands on these labels and also shows the modern names.

Of particular interest is the manner in which the instructions of a program are actually executed, since this, along with the stored program concept, is at the heart of the so-called von Neumann architecture. The instruction interpretation cycle is as follows.

```
Repeat
        address portion of FR <=CC;
        SR <=Memory [address portion of FR];
        FR <=0;
        FR <=Left instruction of SR;
        CR <=Right instruction of SR;
        CC <=CC+1;
        Execute instruction in FR;
        FR <=CR;
        Execute instruction in FR;
Until   Halt
```

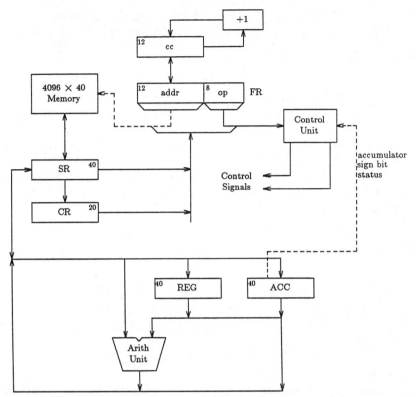

FIGURE 4.2   Block diagram of the von Neumann model. SR = selection register (memory buffer register); CR = control register (auxiliary instruction register); FR = function table register (instruction register and memory address register); CC = control counter (program counter).

Note that since a memory word stores two instructions, instructions are fetched in pairs. The second instruction is saved in CR, an auxiliary buffer register, while the first instruction is executed. Note also that FR doubles as an instruction register holding the "current" instruction and as a memory address register that holds the address of a memory word to be read or written to.

The entire sequence of operations was planned to be fully synchronized by a single clock.

One of the most widely discussed issues at the time that this machine was being planned was the technology for the main memory (Goldstine, 1972, pp. 262–264; Wilkes, 1985, pp. 127–128, 134–135). In the case of the von Neumann machine, it was decided to use a set of 40 cathode ray tubes, each capable of storing an array of 4096 bits. These devices were conceived along the lines of the *Selectron* tube then being developed at RCA's Princeton laboratories. All 40 bits of a word of memory could be accessed in parallel by simultaneously selecting the corresponding bit positions in the 40 tubes.

The Selectron was also considered as a possible graphic output device. Being a CRT, the Selectron could display its patterns of 1's and 0's. Thus, by writing the desired bit patterns onto a "viewing" Selectron, the pattern could be displayed and observed.

This, then, is the root design from which the basic style of register machines has evolved. However, even if the model had proved to be an evolutionary dead end, the Burks, Goldstine, and von Neumann (1946) paper would still be significant because of the depth and care of the analysis that went into each major design issue and the measured descriptions of the rationale underlying the important decisions. These included discussions of the word length, the nature of the instruction set, the encoding of instructions in memory words, and in particular, the design and implementation of the arithmetic subsystem. As Bell and Newell (1971) have remarked, if all computer designers were to analyze and specify their machines in this way before implementing their designs, there would be better (though fewer) computers.

Recall from Chapter 1 that the principal characteristics of a machine's exo-architecture are

1. **Storage organization** The types and organization of storage objects at the exo-architectural level.
2. **Data types** Definition and characterization of the data types and their representation in storage.
3. **Addressing modes** The methods of specifying the addresses of stored objects.
4. **Instruction set** Specification of the form and meaning of the instructions; that is, definition of the operational capabilities of the machine as a whole.
5. **Instruction formats** Representation of instructions in storage.

Accordingly, we will examine the register machine style within this framework.

4.3 THE COMPLEXITY OF EXO-ARCHITECTURES

It is important to note at this stage a rather fundamental attribute of exo-architectures and that is the extent to which exo-architectural components *interact*.

Example 4.1

We will see in the balance of this chapter the following kinds of interaction:

1. The influence of data types on storage organization.
2. The influence of storage organizations on instruction sets and instruction formats.
3. The relationship between data types and the instruction set.
4. The influence of the instruction set, data types, and addressing modes on the instruction format. ∎

A key issue that must be dealt with in the design of a system is deciding the most appropriate way to partition the overall system into subsystems so as to minimize the interaction between subsystems. The designer can then concentrate on the design of the individual subsystems in a largely independent fashion.

Indeed, a basic tenet underlying modern ideas on design methods is that one can, in fact, structure the system under development into a collection of *nearly decomposable* subsystems.

The concept of near decomposability (Simon, 1981; Courtois, 1977) is the idea that in many large and complex systems variables can, in some manner, be aggregated into a small number of groups such that (1) the interactions among the variables within a group may be studied as if interactions among groups did not exist, and (2) interactions among groups may be studied without reference to intragroup interactions.

Unfortunately, in the case of exo-architecture this assumption does not appear to hold, in general. An exo-architecture is almost a *nondecomposable* system in that its components exhibit strong interactions. And if one were to accept Simon's (1981) idea that nontrivial interaction between components is a hallmark of a complex system then exo-architectures are, indeed, rather complex entities.[3]

This observation may come as something of a surprise to some. *Finished* exo-architectures seem deceptively simple and easy to understand, and they are indeed so if one ignores such crucial issues as:

- The rationale underlying the completed design.
- The rationality of the decision-making processes contributing to the design.
- The extent to which the finished design actually meets the initially established goals.

The complexity surfaces whenever we try to address these kinds of issues.

Obviously, then, unless reliable data are available on the precise nature of the interactions between components — and such data are extremely scarce — the architect must necessarily *prioritize* the requirements and (consequently) the order in which the principal components will be designed. The design of the exo-architecture can then proceed on the basis of this ordering. The rationality of the design decisions will, then, be largely determined by this ordering.

4.4 STORAGE ORGANIZATION

At the heart of the register machine style is a storage organization (Fig. 4.3) consisting of a slow, large *main store* in which programs and most of their

---

[3]There are also other ways in which exo-architectures may be deemed complex; in particular, an exo-architecture is, after all, a specification of the capabilities of the computer as a whole, intended to meet the requirements imposed by the *environment* in which the machine is to operate. Part of the complexity of exo-architecture design stems from the high *variability* of this environment.

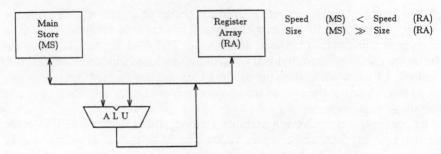

FIGURE 4.3 The storage hierarchy in register machines.

immediate data reside and a fast, much smaller *array of registers* that are primarily intended:

1. To hold intermediate (and temporary) results of a computation.
2. As the source of one or more operands for an arithmetic, logical or shift operation.
3. As the destination of the results of such operations.

The rationale for this storage hierarchy is founded on the following set of facts.

1. Main stores have traditionally been much slower than processors; typically, the ratio of memory to processor speeds are of the order of $1:3$ or $1:4$ (see Chapter 2, Sections 2.5.1 and 2.5.2).
2. The von Neumann model requires a centralized computational (processing) unit to which the arguments of an operation (arithmetic/logical/shift) must be brought, where these operations are performed, and that will hold the immediate results of the operations.
3. Because of facts 1 and 2, there is a substantial time overhead in transmitting information between main store and the processor.[4]
4. Assuming that the principal task of a computer is to evaluate arithmetic or logical expressions [e.g., $(A + B)*(C - D)$] and that only the *final value* of such expressions are needed by other parts of the program, *intermediate values of subexpressions* (e.g., "$A + B$" or "$C - D$") need not be transmitted back to main store; instead, they can be held in temporary fashion in fast processor registers until they are consumed.

The register machine is, thus, an obvious generalization of the original von Neumann model in that the single accumulator and the arithmetic register of the latter has evolved to a collection (usually between 8 and 32) of registers, all of which are intended to be used in the same general way (in theory if not in fact; see Examples 4.2 and 4.3).

---

[4]This is the so-called *von Neumann bottleneck*, as named by Backus (1978). The elimination of this bottleneck has been the goal of much recent researches in computer architecture (see Volume 2, Part 3).

From an evolutionary perspective, the register machine is not a *direct* descendent of the accumulator-based von Neumann model. One important intermediate stage was the emergence, around 1951, of *index registers* for fast address modification. This concept was developed jointly by the University of Manchester and Ferranti Ltd. during the implementation of the Ferranti Mark I Computer (Lavington, 1978).

Recall from Section 4.2 that an important feature of the original von Neumann model is the ability to modify the address part of an instruction, thereby allowing the "same" instruction to access different parts of memory at different times. The main problem with this capability is that the original form of the instruction gets destroyed, a disadvantage that will be evident to anyone who has debugged such "self-modified" programs.

The index register allows for address modification without the need to alter the address specified in the instruction itself. Given such an address A and an index register X, the effective address can be computed as

$$A + X$$

Simply by altering the value of the index register, different effective addresses are obtained.

The advent of a register array thus allowed such registers to be used not only as arithmetic and temporary registers but also as index registers.

Additional uses of the general register were also discovered. In particular, developments in programming techniques and computer systems principles between the mid-1950s and early 1960s led to, among other things, the concepts of *relocatable programs* and *relative addressing.* By loading the starting address (in main store) of a program or data segment into a special, fast *base register*, and by specifying all referenced operands or instructions as *offsets* or *displacements* relative to the contents of such a base register, program instructions and data objects were not bound to any specific location of main memory until execution time. Nor did such segments have to be stored contiguously. Thus, given an operand address in the form of an ordered pair

$$<B, D>$$

where B identifies a base register and D a numeric offset relative to the value of the base register, the effective address can be computed as

$$B + D$$

The outcome of all this was that by the early 1960s the array of registers in a typical register machine had become multipurpose.

Example 4.2

Consider the IBM System/370 exo-architecture (IBM, 1981). In addition to a main store address space of 2^{24} 8-bit bytes, the 370 contains 16 32-bit *general purpose registers* (GPRs), numbered 0–15, and 4 64-bit *floating-point registers* (FPRs) (Fig. 4.4). The FPRs are, of course, dedicated to the performance of

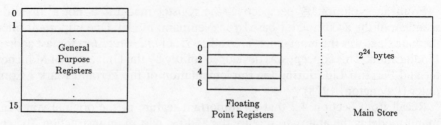

FIGURE 4.4   System/370 programmable stores.

floating-point computations and are, therefore, special purpose programmable registers. The GPRs can be used for holding base addresses, as index registers, as accumulators or as "scratchpad" (i.e., temporary) stores.

GPRs are also used for controlling subroutine calls. The return address is loaded into one of the GPRs prior to control being transferred from the calling to the called routine. In fact, this particular function illustrates the fact that certain general registers are not that "general" after all. For instance, one of the GPRs (say GPR1) by convention will always be used to hold the address of an area in main store that points to the parameters being passed between the calling and the called routines (Fig. 4.5). Another of the registers (GPR 14) will, by convention, be used to hold the return address within the calling routine. Yet a third register (GPR 13, say) will be reserved to point to an area of main store in which the contents of other registers can be saved during a subroutine call. The called routine can thus use the freed registers. The saved values must, of course, be restored when control returns from the subroutine.

Notice, then, that once such conventions are established, these registers be-

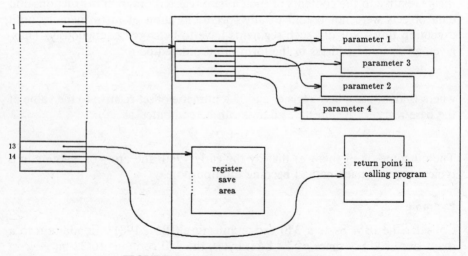

FIGURE 4.5   "Special purpose" GPRs.

come, in some sense, "dedicated;" in effect they reduce the set of available registers that can be used as accumulators or as scratchpad store.   ■

Example 4.3

In the case of the VAX-11 exo-architecture (Digital, 1981a), in addition to a 2^{32} byte (virtual) main store address space,[5] there is a bank of 16 32-bit general purpose registers, numbered $0-15$. However, certain of the registers have specific uses.

1. Register 15 serves as the *program counter.*
2. Register 14 serves as the *stack pointer* (see Chapter 6).
3. Register 13 serves as the *frame pointer*—that is, it is used to point to the starting address within the stack of a new "frame" or "activation record" (see Chapter 6).
4. Register 12 serves as an *argument pointer*—that is, it provides the base address of the argument (parameter) list during a procedure call.   ■

4.5 SOME CONSEQUENCES OF THE USE OF REGISTERS

There are, of course, many issues in the architecture of register machines that are related to the storage organization thus far described. These different aspects will be gradually uncovered as we proceed through this chapter. In this section we consider a few of the important consequences of having programmable registers.

We begin with two observations:

1. Registers have faster access times than does main store. Hence, it "pays" to do as much computation as possible using registers as the source of operands and as the destination of results. The object code, whether generated automatically by a compiler or produced by assembling an assembly language program, should be "optimized" for register use.
2. Because the *register address space* is far smaller than the main store address space (there are typically between 8 and 32 registers), the number of address bits required to specify a register within an instruction is correspondingly much less than that required to specify the address of a main store word. For instance, to reference any word of a 2^{24} byte main store requires 24 address bits/operand. To access one of 32 registers requires only 5 bits. This means that instructions involving registers only will be significantly shorter than instructions involving main store operands (Fig. 4.6). Programs can, then, be expected to be correspondingly shorter.

---

[5]The concept of *virtual memory* is discussed in Chapter 8, Section 8.4.

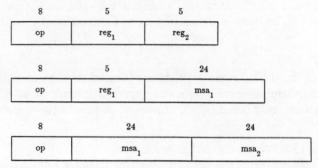

FIGURE 4.6 Effects of register and main store operands on instruction size. op = operation code; reg_1, reg_2 = register addresses; msa_1, msa_2 = main store addresses.

These are the *significant* advantages that have been claimed for registers and have provided the main motivation for the development of the register machine style. Let us now consider the implications of these characteristics.

4.5.1 Code Generation

To understand the code generation issue, I will use, for illustrative purposes, a simple model of a register machine that is somewhat similar to one presented in Aho and Ullman (1977). This machine has the following characteristics.

1. A 2^{16} byte, 16-bit/word main store.
2. An array of 8 16-bit registers identified as RO,R1, . . . ,R7.
3. Instructions (other than branch instructions) of the format

   OPCODE, SOURCE, SOURCE/DESTINATION.

4. Three addressing modes—that is, methods of specifying the address of a source or destination operand (see Section 4.7 for more details):
   - *Register mode,* denoted by mnemonic symbols of the form "Ri." The register Ri itself contains the source operand or is the destination of a result (Fig. 4.7a).
   - *Absolute mode,* denoted by a symbolic identifier, for example, "S." This signifies that the word following the instruction contains the absolute main store address of the operand S or of the destination of a result (Fig. 4.7b).
   - *Immediate mode,* denoted by symbols of the form "#C." This signifies that the word following the instruction contains a 16-bit literal operand, C (Fig. 4.7c).
5. Denoting by "r" and "s," register and main store operands respectively, the instruction set will include the following instructions.

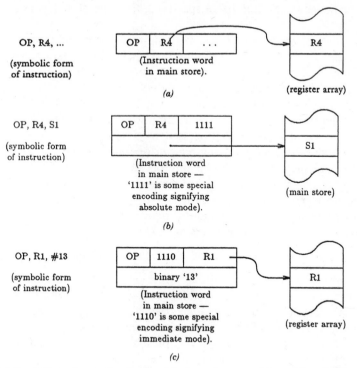

FIGURE 4.7 Addressing modes in the simple register machine: *(a)* register mode; *(b)* absolute mode; *(c)* immediate mode.

*	**MOVES**	s source	to	s	destination
*	**MOVER**	r source	to	r	destination
*	**LOAD**	s source	to	r	destination
*	**STORE**	r source	to	s	destination
*	**ADD**	s source	to	r	destination
*	**SUB**	s source	from	r	destination
*	**ADDR**	r source	to	r	destination
*	**SUBR**	r source	from	r	destination
*	**ADDS**	s source	to	s	destination
*	**SUBS**	s source	from	s	destination
*	**ADDI**	s source	to	r	destination
*	**ADDSI**	s source	to	s	destination

Note that although this is a register machine, the exo-architecture allows for operations involving not only just register operands such as ADDR, MOVER, SUBR ("register-register" instructions) but also main store operands only as exemplified by ADDS, SUBS, and MOVES ("storage-storage" instructions). This kind of capability is present in many register machines, although the actual method of specifying the type of instruction may vary widely.

6. Clearly, each type of instruction will require a specific amount of main store *space* and a specific amount of *processing time*. These parameters are listed in Table 4.2 The processing times are given as integer multiples of some predefined "time units" (tu's) and include the times to access instructions and operands in main store and the time to execute arithmetic operations. The times are computed on the assumption that a word operand of main store can be accessed and processed by an instruction in 3 tu's and an instruction execution involving register operands only requires 1 tu.

Table 4.3 shows, for each of a number of commonly occurring forms of the assignment statement, different versions of code that could be generated by a compiler. In all cases, version 1 involves instructions with one register operand and one storage operand ("register-storage" instructions) whereas at least one of the other two versions use storage-storage instructions only.

Several observations may be made about these examples.

1. The compiler must use appropriate strategies for which variables to assign to registers and, for each such variable, which register to use. Collectively, this is referred to as the *register allocation problem*. For a discussion of the theory and practice of register allocation, refer to (Aho and Ullman, 1977, Chapter 5). It suffices to say for our present purposes that this is a difficult problem demanding sophisticated tactics to be employed by the compiler. The compiler's task may, in general, be further aggravated by the fact that the registers in a register machine are not all available for allocation to program variables (see Chapter 1, Section 1.7).

2. It will be seen for most of the examples in Table 4.3 that in terms of the space and time measures used, code sequences involving storage-storage

TABLE 4.2   Space/Time Requirements for Instructions

Instructions	Time Units for Processing	Number of Main Store Words
MOVES	15	3
MOVER	4	1
LOAD	9	2
STORE	9	2
ADD	9	2
SUB	9	2
ADDR	4	1
SUBR	4	1
ADDS	18	3
SUBS	18	3
ADDI	7	2
ADDSI	12	3

TABLE 4.3 Object Code for Various Assignment Statements

Source Statement	Object Code		
	Version 1	Version 2	Version 3
A := B	LOAD B,R1 STORE R1,A	MOVES B,A	—
space time	4 18	3 15	
A := A+B	LOAD A,RO ADD B,RO STORE RO,A	ADDS B,A	LOAD A,RO LOAD B,R1 ADDR RO,R1 STORE R1,A
space time	6 27	3 18	7 31
A := B+C	LOAD B,RO ADD C,RO STORE RO,A	MOVES B,A ADDS C,A	—
space time	6 27	6 33	
A := A+1	LOAD A,RO ADDI #1,RO STORE RO,A	ADDSI #1,A	—
space time	6 25	3 12	

W :=
  (A−B)+(C−D)
	LOAD A,RO
	SUB B,RO
	LOAD C,R1
	SUB D,R1
	ADDR RO,R1
	STORE R1,W
		MOVES A,W
		ADDS C,W
		SUBS B,W
		SUBS D,W
			LOAD A,RO
			ADD C,RO
			SUB B,RO
			SUB D,RO
			STORE RO,W

space time	11 49	12 69	10 45

instructions appear to perform almost uniformly better than register-storage instruction sequences.

Using similar examples and performance measures, the relative performances of register-based and storage-based code have been discussed by Myers (1977, 1978a, 1978b) and Keedy (1978a, 1978b, 1979) in a lively debate. They have both pointed out the general inferiority of register-based code as compared to storage-storage and other forms of code. Quite a different perspective on this issue will be presented in Chapter 7.

3. The space/time measures for register-based instruction sequences may, however, be improved by more *global analysis and optimization* of the object code—that is, analysis of code spanning several high-level language source statements. Consider, for example, the following sequence of assignments:

```
A : = B;
B : = B + 1
D : = B
```

It can be confirmed that using the data of Tables 4.2 and 4.3, and generating code for each of these assignments independently, the following performances would obtain:

(a) Storage-storage code: space = 9 words, time = 42 tu's.
(b) Register-storage code: space = 14 words, time = 61 tu's.

However, by taking into account the *data dependencies* between statements —that is, the manner in which data flow from one statement to another— an "optimizing" compiler could generate the following code:

```
LOAD    B,RO
STORE   RO,A
ADDI    #1,RO
STORE   RO,B
STORE   RO,D
```

You can easily confirm that the optimizations done here take advantage of the fact that RO contains, first, the value of B to be incremented and, later, the incremented value itself. Hence an instruction for loading the value of B into a register prior to incrementing and storing back in B, and an instruction for loading B into a register and storing back in D are saved. The resulting space and time requirements are 10 words and 43 time units, respectively. This is a considerable improvement over the unoptimized register-storage code sequence and is comparable to the storage-storage version.

4. Table 4.3 also reveals the preponderance of LOAD and STORE instructions. This is caused partly by the inherent style of von Neumann machines and in part by the nature of typical assignment statements; for, it has been observed empirically by many investigators (Alexander and Wortman, 1975; Tanenbaum, 1978; Elshoff, 1976; Patterson and Sequin, 1981; Olafsson, 1981) that

(a) The assignment statement is consistently one of the two most frequently occurring statements in high-level language programs, both with respect to their number of occurrences in the program text (*static frequency*) and the number of times that they are executed (*dynamic frequency*. Table 4.4 summarizes some of the data supporting this proposition. The actual experiments from which these data were obtained are described in Dasgupta (1984).

TABLE 4.4   Frequencies of Assignment Statements

Source	Language	Static Frequency	Dynamic Frequency
Tanenbaum (1978)	SAL	46.5	41.9
Alexander and Wortman (1975)	XPL	42	—
Olafsson (1981)	C	40.1	—
Patterson and Sequin (1981)	Pascal	—	36±5
Patterson and Sequin (1981)	C	—	38±5
Elshoff (1976)	PL/1	41.2	—

Source: Dasgupta, 1984; © 1984, John Wiley & Sons, Inc.; reprinted with permission.

(b)   The most common forms of the assignment statement are A : = B, A : = const., A : = A op B, and A : = A op const., where A, B denote variables or array elements and const. denotes a constant. Table 4.5 summarizes some of the data supporting this proposition.

It follows, then, that the corresponding code generated by the compiler will also be dominated by "overhead" LOAD and STORE instructions.

4.5.2   Some Performance Studies on Register Machines

A quantitative investigation of the nature of such overheads in well-known architectures was conducted by Flynn (1974). He began by partitioning instructions into three broad classes:

1.   **F-type**   "Functional" instructions that actually perform the data-transforming operations (e.g., arithmetic, logical) observed in higher-level languages.
2.   **M-type**   "Memory" instructions that merely rearrange or set up data in preparation for other operations to be performed (e.g., LOAD or STORE).

TABLE 4.5   Breakdown by Assignment Type

Source	Assignment Statement Type	Static Frequency	Dynamic Frequency
Tanenbaum (1978)	**(a)** Assignments with 1 right-hand side term	75.1	64.3
	(b) Assignments with 2 right-hand side terms	15.2	20.4
Olafsson (1981)	**(a)** A := B, A := A op B	23.8	—
	(b) A := const., A := A op const.	35.5	—
	(c) A := B op const.,		
	A := A op (B op const.)	31.2	—
Elshoff (1976)	**(a)** A := B, A := const.	77.6	—
	(b) A := A op B, A := B op C,		
	A := A op const.,		
	A := B op const.	20.5	—

3. **P-type** "Procedural" instructions, involved in the transfer of control within programs (e.g., BRANCH, COMPARE).

Clearly, M-type instructions represent the overhead induced in register machines because of their inherent von Neumann nature. Accordingly, as measures of code efficiency, Flynn proposed the following ratios.

$$\text{M-ratio} = \frac{\text{Number of M-type instructions}}{\text{Number of F-type instructions}}$$

$$\text{P-ratio} = \frac{\text{Number of P-type instructions}}{\text{Number of F-type instructions}}$$

$$\text{NF-ratio} = \frac{\text{Number of (M-type } + \text{ P-type) instructions}}{\text{Number of F-type instructions}}$$
$$= \text{P-ratio} + \text{M-ratio}.$$

The last is the ratio of *nonfunctional to functional* instructions.

It is obvious that these measures must be interpreted with some caution. Flynn, for instance, points out that whether a LOAD, a MOVE, or a COMPARE instruction is nonfunctional or not depends on the nature of the computation: In a sorting program, COMPARE is very much a functional operation, whereas in a machine with index registers an ADD when used to increment index registers may well be viewed as an overhead operation. For certain kinds of computations (or "job mixes"), however, these ratios do provide a quantitative idea of the nonfunctional overheads imposed on register machines. In fact, Flynn (1974) pointed out that these measures were essentially devised for scientific code only.

These ratios have been computed from instruction use frequencies for several computers, notably, the IBM System 7090, IBM System/360, DEC-10, and the PDP-11 (Flynn, 1974, 1980)—all instances of register machines. The corresponding NF ratios obtained were 2.8, 5.5, 2.6, and 6.3, respectively.[6]

Flynn (1974) suggested several reasons for the high nonfunctional overheads in the 360 and the 7090 machines, particularly the former. Keeping in mind that the NF ratio is simply the sum of the P and M ratios, a high M ratio would directly influence the NF ratio and would clearly indicate high memory-register traffic and, therefore, poor register use.

For the IBM 7090, the M-ratio was computed as 1.96. This overhead was attributed to the fact that the 7090 was a single-accumulator machine and that, although there were several index registers, there were no arithmetic facilities associated with the latter. Hence, considerable data traffic was routed through the accumulator.

---

[6]The 360 and 7090 figures were presented in Flynn (1974) and were stated to be based on a mix of programs (primarily scientific) devised originally in 1959 by J. Gibson of IBM for the purpose of studying the instruction use frequencies in the IBM 704 and 650 computers. This mix has subsequently come to be known as the *Gibson mix* (see also Siewiorek, Bell, and Newell, 1982, pp. 53–54). The measures for the PDP-11 and the DEC-10 were given in Flynn (1980). It is not clear, however, what distribution of code yielded these ratios. Thus, the rest of this discussion is restricted to the 7090 and 360 analyses.

The M-ratio for the 360 was 2.9. Compared to the 7090, the 360 had considerably more general purpose registers, thus one would expect much lower memory-register traffic. Yet there is a significant deterioration in the M-ratio. Among the reasons for this, Flynn includes the facts that

1. The base register in the 360 is really an address extension register and necessitates additional loads and stores.
2. In the 360 some of the general purpose registers were reserved for specific purposes — either operating system use or subroutine linkage. This effectively reduced the number of truly general purpose registers.

The P-ratios for the 7090 and the 360 series are 0.81 and 2.5, respectively. Again, one notices the considerably higher procedural overhead in the case of the 360. Flynn points out that the 7090 COMPARE instruction performs both a test and a three-way branch, whereas the 360 COMPARE merely sets a condition code. Another reason for the high 360 P-ratio is that the conditional branches are bicondional whereas the actual path to be tested is often multidirectional. This results in chains of BRANCH ON CONDITION instructions.

One could well conclude from this study that the 360, though conceived as a successor to the 7090 and other earlier IBM machines, appears to be less well-adapted to its operating environment than was the 7090 to its environment.

Another important performance investigation pertaining to register machines was by Lunde (1977), who studied the exo-achitectural properties of the DEC-10 system. This is also a register machine with 16 general purpose registers and a very large instruction set (of more than 400 instructions). This investigation used a task environment consisting of a collection of numeric and nonnumeric algorithms programmed in four different high-level languages (ALGOL, BLISS, FORTRAN, and BASIC), and some compilers written in both high-level and assembly languages. The result was a total of 41 programs generating 5.3 million instructions of which 38 were written in high-level languages.

Of particular relevance to our present discussion was Lunde's analysis of *register use*, the most interesting conclusions being that

1. Ten registers would be sufficient 90% of the time for all 41 programs.
2. Ten registers would be sufficient 98% of the time for 36 of the 41 programs.
3. The size, complexity, and efficiency of the programs did not seem to imply the use of many registers.

Thus, Lunde concludes that as far as the DEC-10 was concerned, programs would run almost as efficiently on a similarly structured machine with fewer registers, perhaps of the order of 8.

4.6 DATA TYPES

A *data type* is a set of values together with a repertoire of operations defined on those values. For instance, an integer data type may be defined as a set of integers (perhaps within a particular range) together with the arithmetic operations { $+$, $-$, $*$, $/$} that take integer values as input and return integers as output. A Boolean data type is given by the set of Boolean values {TRUE, FALSE} along with a set of Boolean operations { $\wedge$, $\vee$, $\neg$, $\oplus$, . . . }. Note that once a data type is defined in this way the only operations allowed on values of a given type are those specified as part of the type.

Henceforth, whenever there is no chance of any ambiguity, I will simply use the word "type" for data type.

In discussing architectures, two classes of types can be distinguished. There are, first, types that are explicitly visible because of the very nature of the physical storage resources themselves. These are the data types out of which main stores and registers are composed. I will refer to these as *intrinsic* data types.

On the other hand, there are also types that are implicitly supported by the hardware by virtue of (1) an encoding or representation of the values of this type in terms of intrinsic data types; and (2) specific type-related operations or instructions implemented in the hardware. These will be termed *supported* data types.

Example 4.3

The basic intrinsic data type is the *bit*, since in most technologies this is the unit of stable information storage in digital systems. Viewed as a data type, the bit is the set of binary digits {0,1} along with a collection of logical { $\wedge$, $\vee$, $\neg$, $\oplus$, . . . } and arithmetic { $+$, $-$, $*$, $/$} operators.

A second basic intrinsic type is the *bit sequence* (or *bit string*). More specifically a bit sequence of a given *length L* is a data type consisting of the set of binary numbers {00 . . . 00,00 . . . 01, . . . , 11 . . . 11} of length L together with a set of logical { $\wedge$, $\vee$, $\neg$, $\oplus$, . . . }, arithmetic { $+$, $-$, $*$, $/$}, and, possibly, shift {shift left (shl), shift right (shr), . . . } operations. A particularly common and important bit sequence is that of length 8, called a *byte*. ∎

From one point of view, the bit sequence may be regarded as a *primitive* type in the sense that transformational operations are defined on values of this type. From another viewpoint, the bit sequence appears to be a composite or *structured* type since it is composed out of bits. Other important structured data types of an intrinsic sort are the *array*, whose elements are all of identical types, and the *record*, which is an ordered set of other (not necessarily identical) intrinsic types.

In architectures, bit sequences are the types for such storage devices as registers or memory words. A file of registers or the main store are instances of the array type. Finally, an instruction register consisting of a 5-bit operation code field, a 3-bit register address field, and a 12-bit main store address field (the latter two denoting source and destination operands, say) can be viewed as an instance of a record data type.

Figure 4.8 shows examples of intrinsic data types both pictorially and as they would be defined textually in an architecture description language such as S*M (see Volume 2, Part 2).

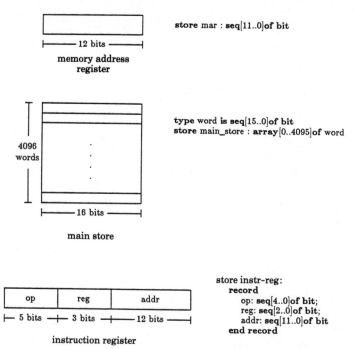

store mar : **seq**[11..0]**of bit**

12 bits

memory address
register

type word **is seq**[15..0]**of bit**
store main_store : **array**[0..4095]**of word**

4096
words

16 bits

main store

store instr-reg:
  record
    op: **seq**[4..0]**of bit**;
    reg: **seq**[2..0]**of bit**;
    addr: **seq**[11..0]**of bit**
  end record

op	reg	addr

5 bits 3 bits 12 bits

instruction register

FIGURE 4.8 **Examples of intrinsic data types: As pictures and in an architecture description language.**

Example 4.4

In exo-architectures the *character* or the *decimal number* are common examples of supported data types. A complete definition of a character data type would involve (1) an encoding or representation of the values of type "character" in terms of bits or a "bit sequence"; and (2) one or more operations (e.g., MOVE CHARACTER) defined as part of the instruction set, which can be used on values of the type in question to produce results of the same type. Other common supported data types are the *integer* (also called *fixed-point numbers*), the *real* (also called *floating-point numbers*), and the *Boolean*. ∎

Two points are worth noting here: First, intrinsic data types are used to implement (or represent, or encode) supported types; thus the two classes of types really belong to two distinct levels. We will next see the representations of the better known supported types.

The second point of interest is that completely specified *instructions* are also supported data types in that (1) they are implemented as structured intrinsic data types, and (2) well-defined operations that *fetch* instructions and *execute* instructions are available. However, as Section 4.2 shows, these operations are not visible at the exo-architectural level. They are characteristics of the endo-architecture.

I next describe some of the supported data types available in contemporary exo-architectures.

4.6.1 Fixed-Point Numbers (Integers)

The integer or fixed-point number has several different representations.

1. **Sign and magnitude** Given an n-bit representation, the left-most (high-order) bit denotes the sign, with 0 denoting positive and 1 negative, while the value or magnitude is encoded in the remaining $n-1$ bits. Thus the *range* of integers is

$$< -(2^{n-1} - 1), \ldots, (2^{n-1} - 1)>$$

Table 4.6 column (a) shows the sign and magnitude form of 4-bit quantities. Note that in this form there are two zeros. This may create a problem when one wishes to distinguish between a true negative from zero.

2. **One's complement** In this form, nonnegative numbers are represented in ordinary binary notation with the left-most (sign) bit being 0. Negative numbers are represented by *complementing* all n bits of the corresponding positive value.

Table 4.6 column (b) shows the one's complement representation of 4-bit

TABLE 4.6 Representation of Fixed-Point Numbers

(a) Sign and Magnitude $b_3b_2b_1b_0$					(b) One's Complement $b_3b_2b_1b_0$					(c) Two's Complement $b_3b_2b_1b_0$				
sign					sign					sign				
+7	0	1	1	1	+7	0	1	1	1	+7	0	1	1	1
+6	0	1	1	0	+6	0	1	1	0	+6	0	1	1	0
+5	0	1	0	1	+5	0	1	0	1	+5	0	1	0	1
+4	0	1	0	0	+4	0	1	0	0	+4	0	1	0	0
+3	0	0	1	1	+3	0	0	1	1	+3	0	0	1	1
+2	0	0	1	0	+2	0	0	1	0	+2	0	0	1	0
+1	0	0	0	1	+1	0	0	0	1	+1	0	0	0	1
+0	0	0	0	0	+0	0	0	0	0	+0	0	0	0	0
−0	1	0	0	0	−0	1	1	1	1	−1	1	1	1	1
−1	1	0	0	1	−1	1	1	1	0	−2	1	1	1	0
−2	1	0	1	0	−2	1	1	0	1	−3	1	1	0	1
−3	1	0	1	1	−3	1	1	0	0	−4	1	1	0	0
−4	1	1	0	0	−4	1	0	1	1	−5	1	0	1	1
−5	1	1	0	1	−5	1	0	1	0	−6	1	0	1	0
−6	1	1	1	0	−6	1	0	0	1	−7	1	0	0	1
−7	1	1	1	1	−7	1	0	0	0	−8	1	0	0	0

quantities. Notice that once again there are two zeros. The range of integers representable in n bits are

$$< - (2^{n-1} - 1), \ldots , (2^{n-1} - 1>$$

3. **Two's complement** In this representation the left-most bit denotes, as usual, the sign with 0 encoding for positive and 1 for negative. Positive values are encoded in the remaining $(n - 1)$ bits in the usual binary form. However, a negative number of absolute value v is represented as a positive integer of value

$$2n - v$$

That is, the negative values are formed as the *two's complement* of the corresponding positive value. This is simply done by complementing the n-bit positive representation and adding (in the binary arithmetic system) a 1 to the lowest-order bit.

Table 4.6 column (c) shows the two's complement representation for $n = 4$. Notice that there is only one form of zero and, consequently, an asymmetry in the range of positive and negative integers.

$$< - 2^{n-1}, \ldots , (2^{n-1} - 1)>$$

Because of the uniqueness of the zero and the relative ease of implementing arithmetic units using two's complement arithmetic, this has been the most common form of integer representation in most computers of the last three decades.

Example 4.5

In the VAX-11 (Digital, 1981a) integer data types of 8-, 16-, 32-, 64-, and 128-bit sizes are supported. These are referred to, respectively, as byte, word, longword, quadword, and octaword integers. These bit sequences can be interpreted as unsigned binary integers or as two's complement representations. The range of values will depend on which of these representations are used. ∎

Example 4.6

In the IBM 360/370 families (IBM, 1981) the basic integer data type is the 32-bit, two's complement form. In addition, 16-bit integers may be specified, and, for denoting the result of a multiplication, 64-bit integers are also supported.

In most register machines based on the von Neumann model, the operations of the integer data type (and of other data types also) are defined explicitly by distinctive *instructions* within the instruction set. That is, given an intrinsic type variable (e.g., a byte or a 16-bit sequence) holding an operand, its interpretation as an integer during the execution of a program is entirely determined by the nature of the instruction referencing that variable.[7] The main outcome of this is that if a particular architecture supports several forms of integer data types (say), then distinctive instructions are required for each such form. ∎

Example 4.7

The VAX-11 contains distinct arithmetic instructions for its different types of integers. For instance, the mnemonics ADDB, SUBB, MULB, DIVB denote instructions for byte length integers; ADDW, SUBW, MULW, DIVW are word length (16-bit) integer instructions; and ADDL, SUBL, MULL, DIVL represent instructions for long-word (32-bit) integers.

It should be noted that the proliferation of instructions for distinct representations of data types is not an inherent characteristic of the register machine style. One observes this phenomenon in machines of very different styles. ∎

Example 4.8

The Intel iAPX 432 (Myers, 1982) has no register set at the exo-architectural level. It supports short (16-bit) and "normal" (32-bit) integers and has corresponding sets of arithmetic instructions. Examples of such instructions are: INCREMENT-INTEGER, INCREMENT-SHORT-INTEGER, ADD-INTEGER, ADD-SHORT-INTEGER, NEGATE-INTEGER, NEGATE-SHORT-INTEGER. ∎

4.6.2 Floating-Point Numbers

Strictly speaking, the fixed-point integer format can be used to represent real numbers such as 63.821 or -42.0124 except, of course, that in the binary representation the binary point would be implicit and one would have to keep track of its position during a computation.

More seriously, scientific computations often involve very large or very small numbers. In ordinary scientific discourse such numbers are themselves expressed in a standard, concise fashion. For instance, a number such as 426000000000 would be expressed as 42.6×10^{10} or as 4.26×10^{11}. Thus, the fixed-point representation is not the usual format for denoting very large or very small numbers. Furthermore, the numbers encountered in scientific computa-

---

[7]That is, the instruction determines the interpretation of a data item—whether it is to be interpreted as an integer or some other data type. This, of course, is another attribute inherited from the von Neumann model. In an architectural variation called *tagged* architectures it is the type of the data item that determines the interpretation of an instruction. A data object stored in memory contains, in addition to the value, a *tag* indicating the type. Thus, for example, data objects for integers and reals are distinguished by the tags; a "generic" arithmetic instruction such as ADD is interpreted by the machine during execution to mean an integer or a real operation by virtue of the specific tag present in the operands. Tagged architectures are not discussed any further in this book. The interested reader may refer to Myers (1982) for more on this topic.

tions are frequently well beyond the range of values that can be captured in fixed-point form.

Real numbers are, thus, expressed in the *floating-point* format, which is the binary equivalent of the standard scientific notation; that is, in the form:

$$M \times R^E$$

where M is called the *mantissa*, R is the *radix* (or *base*), and E is the *exponent* (or *characteristic*). Thus, for instance we could express the numbers 63.821 and -42.0124 as, respectively:

$$.63821 \times 10^2$$
$$-4201.24 \times 10^{-2}$$

Since floating-point numbers have to be implemented on bit sequences, the choice of the format for representing real numbers and the lengths of the bit sequences encoding M and E will depend on the desired *range of values* and the desired *precision*. The exponent E will determine the former and the mantissa, the latter. Given a fixed number of bits in which floating-point numbers are to be held, there is an obvious trade-off between the two: increasing the range (and, consequently, the number of bits to encode E) will lower the number of bits available to encode M (and, hence, the precision of numbers).

Generally speaking, floating-point formats consist of three fields to represent the sign of the mantissa, the exponent (an integer), and the mantissa. Sometimes the sign of the exponent may be explicitly represented by a fourth field. When an exponent sign bit is not explicitly represented by a distinct field, positive and negative exponents are encoded in an *excess notation*. That is, if the exponent field is N-bits long, an exponent E is actually denoted in the exponent field by the value

$$E + 2^{N-1}$$

The exponent is said to be *biased* by 2^{N-1}.

Example 4.9

Consider a 4-bit exponent field ($N = 4$) without an explicit sign bit. In excess notation, a value of $E = 7$ would be represented as $7 + 2^3 = 15$, that is, 1111 in binary. A value of $E = -4$ would be encoded as $-4 + 8 = 4$, that is, 0100 in binary. With $N = 4$, then, the range of binary integers 0000, . . . , 1111 would represent the exponent range -8 to $+7$. ∎

One other characteristic of the floating-point representation must be kept in mind. In general, a given real number can be stated in several ways. For example, alternative forms for the number 42.6×10^{10} are 4.26×10^{11}, 426×10^9, $.426 \times 10^{12}$, $.0000426 \times 10^{16}$. Obviously, it is desirable to have a standard or *normalized* form for such numbers. The usual normalized form is that (1) the mantissa is expressed as a fraction (i.e., < 1) and (2) there are no leading zeros in the fraction. For the foregoing example, the normalized form in the decimal system would be $.426 \times 10^{12}$.

Some examples of floating-point representations follow.

Example 4.10

Figure 4.9 shows the 32-bit (or *single-precision*) representation for the IBM System 360/370 families of machines (IBM, 1981). Such single precision numbers can be held in one word.

The mantissa is in sign and magnitude representation with the highest-order bit denoting the mantissa sign and the low-order 24 bits representing the mantissa. The latter is always represented as a normalized fraction and is interpreted to consist of six hexadecimal digits. This yields approximately seven decimal digits of precision. The radix R is 16, so that a change of 1 in the exponent is equivalent to a 4-bit shift of the mantissa. The exponent is represented in excess-64 code—that is, it is a 64-bias code.

As an instance of this encoding, the number 0.125×16^9 will be represented as:

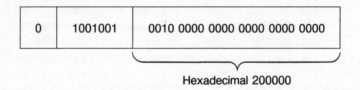

Hexadecimal 200000

Note that because the mantissa is viewed as containing hexadecimal digits the fact that the two highest-order bits are 0 is not significant. The high-order *hexadecimal* digit is 2. Hence the mantissa is in normalized form. ∎

Example 4.11

Figure 4.10 shows the single-precision (called "F-floating") and one of the *multiple-precision* (namely, the "D-floating") representations used in the VAX-11 machines. The mantissas are in sign and magnitude form and yield, respectively, approximately 7 and 16 decimal digits of precision. In addition to

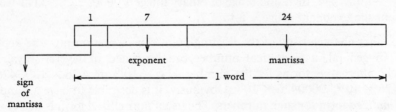

FIGURE 4.9   System/370 single-precision floating-point format.

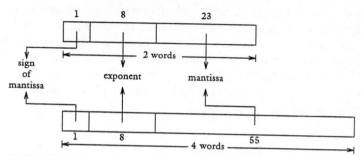

FIGURE 4.10   VAX-11 F-floating and D-floating representation.

the D-floating, the VAX-11 supports two other types of multiple-precision representations of 4 words (64 bits) and 8 words (128 bits). The radix of the exponent is 2, exponents are encoded in excess 128 form, whereas the mantissa is always a normalized fraction.

As in the case of integer data types, the precise set of operations for floating-point numbers are explicitly defined by the repertoire of floating-point instructions.   ∎

Example 4.12

The VAX-11 contains a large number of instructions for operating on floating-point numbers. Indeed, it has distinct subsets of instructions for each type (or precision) of floating-point representation. Thus, for F-floating, it contains, among others, the standard arithmetic instructions, denoted mnemonically as ADDF, SUBF, MULF, DIV, a convert (CVTRF) instruction to round floating to integer, and a special instruction (POLYF) to help in the fast evaluation of polynomial functions.   ∎

4.6.3 Characters and Character Strings

The *character* data type supported in a particular architecture is defined in terms of a set of characters, their representations, and the collection of instructions that may be used to manipulate variables involving characters.

The two standard representations of characters are

1. The 7-bit code devised by the American Standards Committee on Information Exchange (ASCII).
2. The 8-bit Extended Binary Coded Decimal Interchange Code (EBCDIC).

Appendixes A and B at the end of the book lists the main alphanumeric characters and their representations in both these codes. The notion of a *byte* of information was essentially developed as the basic intrinsic data type to support characters. Thus, depending on whether the ASCII code or EBCDIC is used, a byte is defined as 7-bits or 8-bits, respectively.

The most common instructions for this data type are those for the movement of *character strings* from one part of main store to another and for the comparison (for equality) of two character strings. The operand identifying a character string typically specifies the *starting address* of the string in main store and the *length* of the string. In addition, depending on the extent to which the computer is intended to provide support for character manipulation, additional instructions may be defined.

Example 4.13

Consider the IBM System/370 (IBM, 1981). Characters are encoded in EBCDIC form. Instructions include

1. **Move type instructions** For example, MVC (move character) transfers character (byte) strings of length from 1 to 256 bytes from one specified area of main store to another. In contrast MVI (move immediate) transfers a byte of "immediate" data located in the instruction itself into a specified byte area of main store.
2. **Load/store type instructions** For example, IC (insert character) moves a character from a specified byte address in main store to the low-order byte of a specified register. STC (store character) performs the converse transfer.
3. **Compare instructions** CLC (compare logical character) permits comparison of two character strings of lengths from 1 to 256 bytes, both strings being located in main store. The CLI (compare logical immediate) compares a character at a specified byte address in main store with a byte of "immediate" data contained in the instruction itself. ∎

Example 4.14

In the VAX-11 (Digital, 1981a), characters are also encoded in EBCDIC form. As in the case of the 370, instructions are provided to move character strings from one main store area to another and to compare character strings. Additional instructions include:

1. MATCHC (match characters): This searches a specified character string for the presence of a specified substring.
2. LOCC (locate character): This determines whether a specified character is contained in a specified string. ∎

4.6.4 Decimal Strings

A special case of characters are the *decimal digits*. From Appendixes A and B it will be noted that the low-order four bits encoding the decimal characters are identical to the binary representation of decimal digits (that is, the binary-coded decimal, BCD form). Thus, decimal numeric strings may be more economically represented as a string of BCD digits such that, given an 8-bit byte, two such digits can be held in a byte instead of just one EBCDIC character. Thus, decimal strings may be viewed as constituting a distinct data type with its own representation and set of operations.

Example 4.15

In the VAX-11 (Digital, 1981a), one way of representing decimal integers is by placing two digits per byte. When encoded in this way, the integers are termed *packed decimal strings.* Each half byte (or *nibble*) encodes in BCD form a digit 0 through 9, except the low-order-most nibble of the last byte, which encodes the sign of the decimal string (Fig. 4.11). The positive sign may be represented by hexadecimal A, C, E, or F and the negative sign by hexadecimal B or D, although the "preferred" sign representations are hexadecimal C and D, respectively; that is, the signs of decimal numbers that are computed by the machine will use these as the sign representations. When specifying a decimal string as an operand, the starting address and the length *in digits* (not counting the sign) have to be stated.

Instructions for packed decimal strings include

1. MOVP (move packed), which moves a packed decimal string from one specified main store area to another.
2. CMPP (compare packed), which compares two packed decimal strings.
3. ADDP (add packed): This adds two decimal packed strings. Other arithmetic instructions are SUBP, MULP, and DIVP.
4. CVTLP (convert long to packed): This converts a long word (32-bit) integer to packed decimal form; the instruction CVTPL (convert packed to long) performs the converse operation. ∎

The data types just described are, in a sense, "classic" in that they have become firmly established in mainframe computer architectures from the early 1960s onward. They are, also, the kinds of data types around which the most general repertoire of instructions are designed.

In contemporary machines one may observe many other data types that have been implemented to provide specific capabilities. These include, for instance, the *stack*, which, to a greater or lesser extent, is supported in many machines both within the register machine style and without (see Chapter 6); the *queue* data type available on the VAX-11 (Digital, 1981a); and the *capability*, a structured data type used to enforce memory protection in such machines as the Cambridge CAP computer (Wilkes and Needham, 1979; see also, Chapter 8, Section 8.6).

digit	digit	digit	digit	digit	digit	digit	digit	digit	sign

FIGURE 4.11   Representation of packed decimal strings in the VAX-11.

4.7 ADDRESSING MODES

Just as an exo-architecture includes a collection of data types or a repertoire of instructions to manipulate instances of such data types, it also contains a set of *addressing modes* that can be used to specify explicitly the whereabouts of an operand.

In the case of the von Neumann model (Section 4.2) we saw that an operand could be either in main store or in one of the two programmable registers (the accumulator and the arithmetic register). References to the registers are always implicit. The addressing mode for main store operands in this model is about the simplest one can imagine in that the actual address of the main store word is specified in the instruction. This is an instance of what is called *direct addressing.*

To establish a context for discussing addressing modes, Figure 4.12 shows the characteristic storage hierarchy of the register machine (Fig. 4.3) augmented with an *instruction register* that always holds the instruction that is "currently" being executed (recall that in the von Neumann model, Figure 4.2, FR serves as the instruction register). We assume, further, that this instruction is located in main store at address IL.

In a register machine, in general, each instruction specifies the location of one or more operands needed for the instruction to execute. The operand may be in main store, in one of the registers, or may be contained in the instruction itself. The addressing mode determines where precisely the required data item is — that is, its *effective address* — and, for each operand, is encoded in the *operand field* of the instruction (Fig. 4.12). In some situations, the addressing mode may be encoded using a combination of an operand field and the operation code.

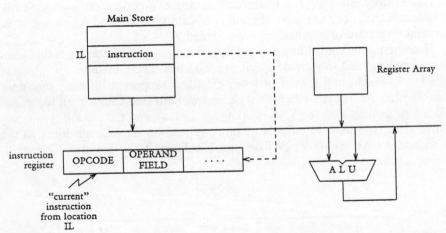

FIGURE 4.12 Canonical register machine storage organization with instruction register.

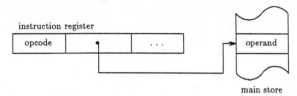

FIGURE 4.13   Direct addressing.

4.7.1   Direct Addressing

The operand is contained in main store and the address of the operand is specified in the operand field of the instruction itself (Fig. 4.13). The size of the operand field must, then, be large enough to encode the entire addressable space; for a main store of 2^{24} bytes, say, an operand field of 24 bits is required.

4.7.2   Register Addressing

The required data item is located in one of the programmable registers, and its address is specified in the instruction's operand field (Fig. 4.14). Such a field must be sufficient in size to encode the total register space. For instance, given an array of 32 registers, a field of 5 bits is necessary.

4.7.3   Immediate Addressing

In the case in which a constant (or a *literal*) is to be used as an operand, this may be specified as part of the instruction itself. The operand field may hold the literal if it is large enough to represent the latter (Fig. 4.15a). For instance, if the operand field is 10 bits long, it may hold signed constants in the range <−512, . . . , +512> using sign and magnitude notation. When larger constants than can be held in the operand field are desired, the word or bytes following the instruction in main store may be used to hold the immediate operand (Fig. 4.15b).

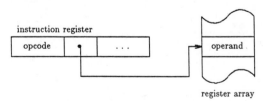

FIGURE 4.14   Register addressing.

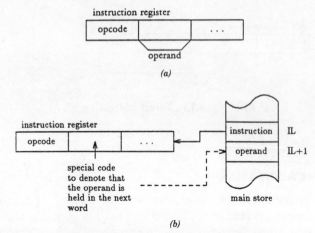

FIGURE 4.15 Immediate addressing.

4.7.4 Indirect Addressing

Instead of the operand field specifying the address of the operand as in direct or register addressing, this field may specify the address of an "intermediate" storage element that contains the address of the desired operand. This is termed *indirect* addressing. The intermediate storage element may be a register (Fig. 4.16a) or a word of main store (Fig. 4.16b). Note that an indirect addressing scheme in which the location of the operand is held in a register will require a smaller number of bits to encode the register identifier in the operand field than if the intermediate storage is a main store word.

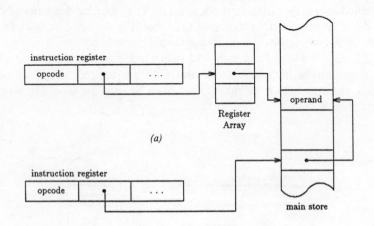

FIGURE 4.16 Indirect addressing.

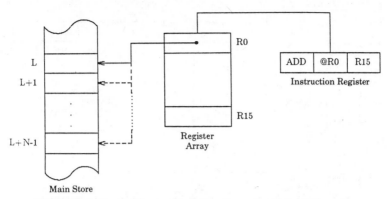

FIGURE 4.17   Indirect addressing through a list of N words.

In fact, this is one of the advantages of using indirect addressing: you can specify the main store address of the desired operand indirectly by establishing a *pointer* to another main store word that actually contains this address.

As an example of the use of indirect addressing, suppose a set of N numbers located in adjacent words of main memory are to be added and the result left in register R15 (Fig. 4.17). The starting address L of these numbers is loaded into a register RO, and R15 is initialized to zero. Let us signify by the symbol "@R" the use of a register R as a source of an address rather than an operand, and by the symbol "#I" that I is an immediate operand. Thus, a sequence of instructions

```
ADD @RO, R15
INCR RO, #1
```

when iterated N times will add the N numbers in main store locations L, $L + 1, \ldots, L + N - 1$ and leave the result in R15.

4.7.5   Indexed Addressing

The problem of accessing these N successive words of main store can be solved in another way. The starting address, L, of the array is specified as a literal and the displacement of the i-th element ($i = 0, 1, \ldots, N - 1$) is held in a register called the *index register*. Suppose we designate this register as X. Then the effective address of the i-th array element can be computed as

$$L + X$$

Suppose, for example, that the register R1 is used as an index register. Keeping in mind that L is a literal denoting an actual address, the successive array elements may be added and the result left in register R15 by first initializing R1 and R15 to 0 and then executing N times, the sequence of instructions

```
ADD #L, R1, R15
INCR R1, #1.
```

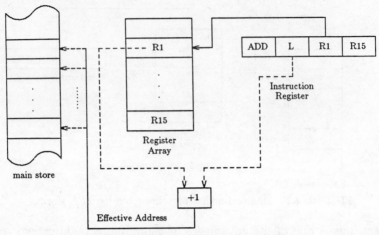

FIGURE 4.18   Indexed addressing.

Here, the effective address of the first operand is computed as R1 + L (Fig. 4.18), the resulting main store operand at this address is added to the contents of register R15 and the result left in R15. The INCR instruction simply increases the value of the index register by 1.

As this example illustrates, an operand specified in the indexed addressing mode consists of two parts: a literal constant and an index register. A particular computer may have one or more registers that are used *only* as index registers. Alternatively, as is the case with most contemporary register machines, one or more of the general purpose registers may be used for this purpose. Furthermore, because of the inevitable need to increment or decrement the contents of an index register, some machines provide special instructions for this purpose whereas others implement mechanisms that cause the index register to be *automatically modified* as a side effect of accessing an indexed operand. This latter feature is called *autoindexing* and first appeared in the DEC PDP-11 (Digital, 1978).

4.7.6   Base-displacement Addressing

In the base-displacement addressing mode (Fig. 4.19), an operand is specified as consisting of a register termed the *base register* (B) and a literal numerical constant termed the *displacement* (D). The latter is often called the *offset*. The specified base register holds some main store address, and the effective address of the desired operand is then computed as

$$B + D$$

The base-displacement addressing mode originated because of two reasons.

First, it provides direct support for the *relocatability of program and data segments*—that is, the capability of a computer system to allocate a program or

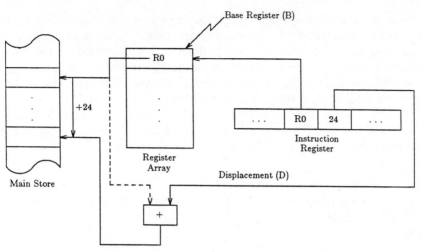

FIGURE 4.19 Base-displacement addressing.

data segment to different areas of main store at different times. This capability became particularly necessary with the emergence of multiprogramming and virtual memory during the latter half of the 1960s (see Chapter 8, Section 8.4).

Base-displacement addressing supports relocatability in the following manner. When a program or data segment S is assembled or compiled into machine code, the translator will not be aware of where this code will reside in main store at execution time; indeed, the segment will be loaded into different main store areas on different instances of execution, depending on the availability of free areas. Thus, the object code must be so generated that all references to instructions and data within S are stated as *displacements* relative to the contents of some specified *base register*, B. When S is actually loaded into main store its starting address will be automatically placed in the base register. During operand access, the effective address of the operand is computed by adding the contents of B to the displacement.

Example 4.16

Consider the following IBM System/370 Assembler code:

```
        BALR    15,0
        USING   *, 15
        L       10, INTERVAL
        . . . .

        . . . .
INTERVAL  DC F'1'
        . . . .
```

In general, the BALR instruction loads the register specified as the first operand with the address of the next instruction and branches to the address specified as the second operand. When the latter is 0, the branch does not take place and control transfers to the next instruction. USING is an instance of a *pseudo operation*—that is, it serves as a directive to the assembler rather than as an executable instruction; it instructs the assembler that the register specified as the second operand will hold the (relocatable) address of the next instruction—that is, the register is to serve as a base address.

Thus, when this segment is *assembled*, USING tells the assembler that register 15 will hold the base (or relocatable) address; hence during assembly of the L instruction the address of INTERVAL will be generated as the ordered pair

<15, D>

where D is the displacement of INTERVAL relative to the contents of register 15. When this code is *executed*, BALR will ensure that register 15 holds the right value.   ∎

A second reason for the emergence of base-displacement addressing is to reduce the number of bits required to specify an operand address. Suppose the main store consists of 2^{24} bytes. Thus, when a main store operand is specified directly in the instruction, or when a displacement relative to some base address is to be given in the instruction, the field must be large enough to reference the entire store; in our example, a 24-bit address field must be available.

However, it is a well-established empirical fact that the references made by a program segment are not scattered all over memory. They are, rather, contained within particular localized regions of the memory space. For example, one segment may reference memory words between locations 1000 and 1150 whereas very rarely will it access words in the 4000 address range; in contrast, a different program segment would have references localized to the latter area rather than the former. Thus, given a 2^{24} byte memory space, if it is known that the operands for a program segment will be located within a relatively small memory region, say of length 2^{12} bytes, then the address of such operands can be defined by means of a base register B that points to the start of the relevant area and a displacement D, *which need not be more than 12 bits long.* Assuming that 4 or 5 bits are needed to identify the base register, a total of 16 or 17 bits suffice to reference main store operands—a valuable saving in instruction space.

This completes our general discussion of the "classical" addressing modes— "classical" in the sense that all these modes had been clearly identified by the early-to-mid-1960s; it is important to note, however, that although these are the modes most commonly present in register machines, they are by no means the only ones that are implemented in contemporary computers. Two other important modes are *stack-based* addressing, which is discussed in Chapter 6, and *capability based* addressing, discussed in Chapter 8.

In the rest of this section we will examine in some detail the addressing modes available on the PDP-11/VAX-11 families and conclude by considering some empirical data on the actual uses of addressing modes.

Example 4.17

The PDP-11 (Digital, 1978) is a 16-bit word length minicomputer. Its addressing modes are particularly interesting because of the way they are encoded, their large number, and their semantics.

In the PDP-11 the address modes of an operand is designated by a 6-bit field of which the high-order 3 bits specify the actual modes whereas the low-order 3 bits designate one of the eight general purpose registers. A summary of the eight addressing modes is given in Table 4.7. There are essentially four classes of modes:

1. **Register** In the direct version, mode 0, the operand is in the specified register Rn. This is, then, an instance of simple register addressing. In the indirect or "deferred" version, mode 1, Rn contains the effective main store address of the operand.
2. **Autoincrement** In mode 2, the effective main store address is, once more, in the specified register Rn. The operand in main store may be a byte or a word, depending on the opcode. After the effective address has been computed (or, at least, the value in Rn has been read), Rn is incremented by 1 in the former case or by two in the latter (Fig. 4.20). In the deferred version, mode 3, the effective address is contained in the main memory word pointed at by Rn. Thus, after the original value of Rn has been read for the purpose of effective address computation, Rn is incremented by 2 *only*, since Rn has been pointing to an address rather than to a data item (Fig. 4.21). The autoincrement mode thus allows for a form of indirect addressing with the

TABLE 4.7   Addressing Modes in the PDP-11

Mode Number	Mode Name	Assembler Notation	Semantics
0	Register	Rn	Operand is in Rn
1	Register deferred	(Rn)	Effective address <= Rn
2	Autoincrement	(Rn)+	Effective address <= Rn; Rn <= Rn+1 if operand is byte Rn <= Rn+2 if operand is word
3	Autoincrement deferred	@(Rn)+	Effective address <= Mem[Rn]; Rn <= Rn+2
4	Autodecrement	−(Rn)	Rn <= Rn−1 if operand is byte Rn <= Rn−2 if operand is word; Effective address <= Rn
5	Autodecrement deferred	@−(Rn)	Rn <= Rn−2 Effective address <= Mem[Rn]
6	Index	X(Rn)	Effective address <= Rn+X; PC <= PC+2
7	Index deferred	@X(Rn)	Effective address <= Mem[Rn+X]; PC <= PC+2

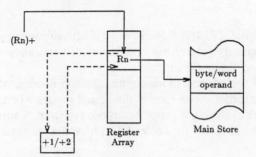

FIGURE 4.20   Autoincrement in the PDP-11.

added capability of automatically incrementing the value of the concerned register. This feature can be used to implement *stack pointers* (see Chapter 6).

3. **Autodecrement**   The autodecrement mode is similar to the autoincrement mode except that the specified register Rn is decremented *before* effective address computation. In mode 4, the stepdown value is 1 or 2, depending on whether the operand is a byte or a word long, whereas in mode 5 Rn is always decremented by 2.

4. **Index**   In these two modes, the word following the instruction contains an immediate operand, X, that serves as an offset. In mode 6, the effective address is computed by adding the offset X to Rn, whereas in mode 7, this addition leads to the main store address that contains the effective address. In the PDP-11 at the time an instruction is being executed the program counter, PC, points to the *next* word — in this case, the word containing X. Thus, when an operand is being accessed in index mode, PC is also incremented by 2 so that it skips the word containing X and points to the word following X.

In the PDP-11, register R7 serves as the program counter (PC). It is of

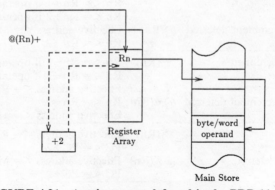

FIGURE 4.21   Autoincrement deferred in the PDP-11.

particular interest to note the effect of using R7 as the specified register, Rn, in some of the addressing modes. These are summarized in Table 4.8.

Given the large set of addressing modes in the PDP-11, the question arises as to the extent to which these are actually used in programs. Several investigators have studied various aspects of the performance of the PDP-11, including the dynamic usage frequencies of the addressing modes. These include measurements obtained by Marathe (1977) and Strecker (1978) and presented in summary form by Baer (1980); additional data have been gathered by Snow and Siewiorek (1978, 1982). Although there are some variations in the data, two interesting general features emerge.

1. Modes 0 (register) and 2 (autoincrement) together show the largest frequency of usage—accounting for between 58 and 73% of all the addressing modes.
2. Mode 5 (autodecrement deferred) is hardly ever used, and the usage of mode 7 (index deferred) is only marginally higher. ∎

Example 4.18

The VAX-11 (Digital, 1981a) is an evolutionary descendant of the PDP-11 with a 32-bit word length. It incorporates a larger and more elaborate set of addressing modes than does the PDP-11 and, having 16 rather than 8 general purpose registers, requires a larger number of bits to encode these modes. An operand is, thus, specified by an 8-bit field with the four high-order bits representing the mode and the four low-order bits encoding the register. Register 15 serves as the program counter, PC.

Compared to the PDP-11, the main features of the VAX-11's addressing modes may be summarized as follows.

TABLE 4.8 Program Counter-based Addressing Modes in the PDP-11

Mode Number	Mode Name	Assembler Notation	Semantics
2	Immediate (Autoincrement)	#n	Effective address <= PC PC <= PC+1 or PC <= PC+2
3	Absolute (Autoincrement deferred)	@#A	Effective address <= Mem[PC]; PC <= PC+2
6	Relative (Index)	A	Effective address <= PC+X; PC <= PC+2
7	Relative Indirect (Index deferred)	@A	Effective address <= Mem[PC+X]; PC <= PC+2

1. Because of its negligible use in the PDP-11, the autodecrement deferred mode was excluded.
2. The register, register deferred, autoincrement, autoincrement deferred, and autodecrement modes are present in the VAX in essentially the same form as in the PDP-11.
3. A number of modes called *displacement* modes were introduced in the VAX-11 in which the displacement — given as a byte, a word, or a longword integer — is added to the specified register, Rn, to obtain the effective operand address. These displacement modes collectively correspond (roughly) to the PDP-11 index mode.
4. The mode called the *indexed* mode in the VAX-11 is both new and powerful. The operand is specified in an instruction by two adjacent bytes: a *primary operand* (PROP) specifier contained in the low-order byte describes the actual mode and the index register, Rx; and the high-order byte encodes a *base operand* (BOP) specifier (Fig. 4.22).

The *primary operand address* (PROP-address) is computed as

PROP-address < = Rx* size of PROP in bytes

where the size may be 1, 2, 4, 8, or 16. The *effective* operand address is then obtained as

PROP-address + address specified by BOP specifier

The base operand (BOP) address may itself be specified in one of the other modes. As a specific example, consider a word instruction containing an operand specified in the *register deferred indexed* mode

(R4) [R5]

and assume that R4 contains the value 4014 and the index register R5 contains the value 6. Then the primary operand address is computed as 6*2 = 12, which is then added to 4014 to obtain the effective address 4026.

The usage frequencies of the VAX-11 addressing modes have been studied empirically by Emer and Clark (1984). Their data may be summarized as follows.

(a) The register mode is the most highly used, accounting for approximately 40% of the total.
(b) The next most highly used modes are the displacement modes (25%).
(c) The autoincrement feature accounted for only 2% of the total.

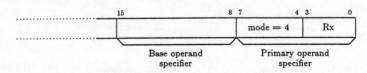

FIGURE 4.22 The indexed mode in the VAX-11.

(d) The autoincrement deferred, autodecrement, and absolute modes were the least used — their usages ranged from 0.3 to 0.9% of the total.

■

4.8   THE OPERATION SET

We have seen, in Section 4.3.4, that a data type is defined as a set of values together with a collection of operations that can be applied to such values. It follows that the kinds of *operations* that may be defined as part of an exo-architecture are almost a natural "fallout" of the data types available on the machine. Thus, in a register machine one may observe the following typical operations.[8]

1. Operations that *load* registers (or parts thereof) with the contents of main store words and *store* the contents of registers in main store words. LOAD and STORE operations are, strictly speaking, operations defined on the intrinsic data type *bit sequence* of well-defined lengths (such as nibbles, bytes, 16-bit words, 32-bit words) since these operations ignore what these bit sequences represent. In a register machine LOADs and STOREs are also viewed as the archetypal *overhead* operations necessary to simply transmit operands and results between main store and the processing unit.
2. The class of *logical* operations such as AND, OR, COMPLEMENT, and EXCLUSIVE-OR. Strictly speaking, of course, logicals should only operate on Boolean types (with values TRUE and FALSE). Because of the binary digit representations of Boolean values, however, the logical operations are generalized in most machines to accept bit sequences as inputs and produce bit sequences as outputs.
3. Another important class of operations defined explicitly on bit sequences are *shift* operations.

Example 4.19

The IBM System/370 (IBM, 1981) supports many different types of SHIFT operations, depending on,

(a) The lengths of the bit sequences involved, that is, whether arguments are SINGLE (32-bit) or DOUBLE (64-bit) words.

---

[8]I will use the word *operation* to refer to the actual functions that are performed on data items during the execution of a program and reserve the word *instruction* to refer to the collective set of items that must be known to the computer in order to execute any given operation; specifically, an instruction is comprised of the operation as encoded in the *opcode field*, the specifications of the locations of all the *operands* needed as input arguments by the operation, and the specification of the location where the result of the operation must be stored. The collection of all operations for a given machine is referred to here as the *operation set*, which, in the architectural literature, is usually referred to as the *instruction set*. In the light of the distinction I make between "operation" and "instruction," I will, for obvious reasons, avoid the term "instruction set."

(b) The direction of shift: LEFT or RIGHT.

(c) Whether the high-order bit is treated as a sign bit (and therefore *not* included among the shifted bits) or not: In the latter case, shifts are said to be of the LOGICAL sort. ∎

4. *Arithmetic* operations that accept and/or produce values of type fixed-point (integer) or floating-point (real). The classes (and consequently, the number) of arithmetic operations may be determined by the varieties of integer and real types that are explicitly supported in the computer, as, for instance, in the VAX-11. (Examples 4.7 and 4.12) or the Intel 432 (Example 4.8).

5. In addition to arithmetic operations, numeric data types may also have operations for *comparing* values associated with them.

Example 4.20

The VAX-11 (Digital, 1981a) architecture includes distinct COMPARE operations for its four different floating-point data types (denoted by the mnemonics CMPF, CMPD, CMPG, and CMPH) and for its byte and word integers (CMPB and CMPW, respectively). The effect of these operations is to record whether one operand is less than another or whether they are equal in specific *condition codes* (see Section 4.10). ∎

Example 4.21

The Intel 432 (Myers, 1982) has distinct *classes* of instructions for distinct types of comparisons: EQUAL, EQUAL-TO-ZERO, NOT-EQUAL, NOT-EQUAL-TO-ZERO, GREATER-THAN, GREATER-THAN-OR-EQUAL, GREATER-THAN-ZERO and NEGATIVE. Each of these classes in turn consist of different instructions, depending on the numeric types involved. ∎

Example 4.22

In contrast, the IBM System/370 (IBM, 1981) has a single numeric type COMPARE operation defined on 32-bit integers. Again, the result is to set a condition code depending on equality of operands, the first being less than the other, or the first being greater than the other. ∎

6. Operations defined on the character and character string data types. These include MOVE operations for transferring a character string from one location to another, LOAD/STORE type operations defined specifically for single characters, COMPARE operations for comparing the lengths of two character strings, and MATCH type operations for determining whether one character string contains another as a substring (see Examples 4.13 and 4.14).

7. In addition to operations that directly and explicitly reflect architectural data types, all machines will have a repertoire of *control operations* (or what Flynn, 1974, termed P-type instructions; see section 4.3.3) that allows for the explicit alteration of the flow of control through a program.

The most obvious and familiar instances of these are the unconditional and conditional BRANCHes. Other control operations vary widely in number and complexity. Thus, for example, many contemporary machines include special operations to CALL subroutines and to RETURN from subroutines, whereas some computers have incorporated "high-level" operations for controlling iterations and multiway branches.[9]

Example 4.23

A specific example of an abundantly rich set of control operations can be seen in the case of the VAX-11 (Digital, 1981a). This architecture includes

(a) A collection of 16 *conditional* branches that test for various relations [EQUAL, NOT EQUAL, EQUAL (unsigned), NOT EQUAL (unsigned), GREATER THAN (signed), GREATER THAN (unsigned)] and previously set condition codes, and transfer control, accordingly.

(b) Three types of *unconditional* branches, each being associated with a distinct way the branch-to address is specified. Thus, the BRB and BRW operations add, respectively, a byte length and a word length displacement to the contents of the program counter (PC) to generate the effective branch-to-address whereas JUMP simply replaces the PC value with the address specified in the instruction.

(c) A set of 10 branches defined on single-bit fields.

(d) A collection of 11 "high-level" *loop control* operations. An example from this set is the class of ACB ("Add Compare and Branch") operations intended for the implementation of such programming language constructs as the FOR or DO statements.

(e) A class of CASE operations that, depending on operand values, allow for the implementation of multiway branches.

(f) Operations for transferring control to, and returning from, subroutines and for passing arguments to, and results from, subroutines. ∎

8. The exo-architecture of most contemporary machines usually contains operations used for specific purposes as needed in operating systems; for example, for the enforcement of security and protection, or for process synchronization in parallel processing systems. Some of these specialized operations will be seen in later chapters.

From the foregoing, it would appear, then, that the architect can design as large or as small, as complex or as simple, an operation set as one wishes. There are, however, some important factors and trade-offs that have to be taken into account in designing and implementing operation sets.

---

[9]We will examine the nature and the power of procedure CALL and RETURN operations later, in the context of *stack* machines (Chapter 6) and the so-called *reduced instruction set computer* (Chapter 7).

4.8.1 Operation Set Size and Instruction Organization

Assuming a constant size operation code (opcode) field for all instructions, the larger the set of operations, the larger will be the size of the opcode field. This will have an impact on the format and size of the overall instructions—possibly by limiting the number of operand fields and the sizes of these fields.

Example 4.24

Assume that instructions are to be 16 bits long and that a total of 64 distinct operations have been identified. The opcode field will be 6 bits, leaving only 10 bits for operand specification. The architect, then, has only a few choices as to how the instructions can be organized. The most obvious choice is to design all instructions with two operands, one of which is also the destination of the result, and specify all operands using direct or indirect register addressing. Branch instructions may also be encoded with a register specifying the branch address. ■

Conversely, if the designer assumes a fixed size instruction and has also fixed the sizes of the operand fields, then this limits the size of the opcode field and, thus, the number of operations. In Example 4.24, if there are 32 programmable registers, then the opcode cannot exceed 6 bits if only 16 bit instructions with a constant size opcode field are to be maintained.

Several heuristic techniques have been devised for the efficient implementation of opcodes. One of these, called the *expanding opcode scheme*, may be described as follows:

Consider, again, a computer in which all instructions are to be 16 bits long. As we have just seen, if we fix the size of the opcode field to some constant value, then there are serious constraints on instruction organizations, the size of the operation set, and the nature of the addressing modes that can be employed.

However, if we are willing to *vary* the size of the opcode field, then these same 16 bits can be used in a number of different ways. Figure 4.23 shows an example where we can encode, in 16 bits, up to 63 2-address instructions, 31 1-address instructions, and 32 0-address instructions.[10]

Note that expanding codes may be used even with variable length instructions.

Example 4.25

Both the PDP-11 and the VAX-11 use expanding opcodes. A sample of the PDP-11 instruction formats follows. Here, the numbers in parentheses denote the length of the fields in bits; "source" and "destination" encode the PDP-11 addressing modes discussed in Section 4.7 (Example 4.17), and "register" denotes one of the eight registers.

[10]0-address instructions, consisting solely of an operation code, are usually associated with *stack machines* (see Chapter 6).

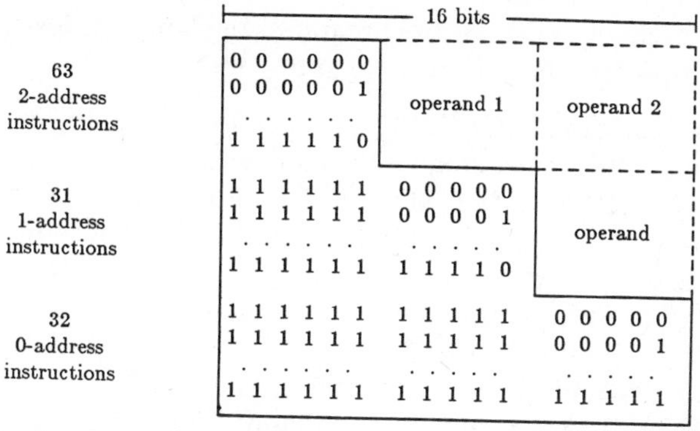

FIGURE 4.23 An expanding opcode scheme (opcodes = 6, 11, 16 bits long; operands = 5 bits long).

(a) 16-bit Instructions
(i)   Opcode (4), Source (6), Destination (6)
(ii)   Opcode (7), Register (3), Source (6)
(iii) Opcode (8), Offset (8)
(iv)   Opcode (16)

(b) 32-bit Instructions
(i)   Opcode (7), Register (3), Source (6), Memory address (16)
(ii)   Opcode (4), Source (6), Destination (6), Memory address (16)
(iii) Opcode (10), Destination (6), Memory address (16)   ∎

4.8.2 The Effect of Operation Frequencies on Instruction Organizations

An important goal in instruction set design is to minimize the amount of memory space required by programs. One of the benefits this would yield is the minimization of the number of *pages* required to hold the program.[11] Another is the minimization of the number of processor or memory cycles required to transfer instructions from memory to processor during the execution of programs (see Chapter 5).

The variability in the use of different types of operations has been widely documented, both at the level of programming languages (Knuth, 1971; Alexander and Wortman, 1975; Elshoff, 1976; Tanenbaum, 1978; Ditzel, 1980; Olafsson, 1981; Patterson and Sequin, 1981) and at the assembly language/machine code level (Alexander and Wortman, 1975; Lunde, 1977; Flynn, 1980; Myers, 1982; Snow and Siewiorek, 1982).

---

[11]The concepts of "pages" and "paging" are central to the topic of *virtual memory*, discussed in Chapter 8, Section 8.4.

When we examine the data at the programming language level, a number of general conclusions can be drawn (Dasgupta, 1984).

1. The ADD (including INCREMENT) operation is usually, and by a considerable margin, the most frequently used arithmetic or logical operation, followed by SUBTRACT, AND, and OR. For example, Olafsson's (1981) static analysis of C programs indicates that the ADD accounts for 53.6% of all arithmetic operations, followed by 12.1% for the SUBTRACT. Ditzel's (1980) data on SPL, the programming language for the Symbol computer (Myers, 1982, Part 3) shows that the ADD and SUBTRACT statements account for 27% and 11.7%, respectively, of all statements. Elshoff (1976), in his analysis of PL/1 programs, shows that 68% of all arithmetic were ADDs and 16% were SUBTRACTs. Tanenbaum's (1978) sample of SAL programs includes 50% ADDs followed by 28.3% SUBTRACTs among the arithmetic operations.

2. Among the relational operations, by far the most frequent is the EQUAL, followed by NOT EQUAL.

    As evidence, Ditzel's (1980) analysis of SPL programs shows that 50% of all relational are EQUAL whereas NOT EQUAL, GREATER THAN, and LESS THAN occur roughly the same number of times (12 to 13%). In Elshoff's (1976) data on PL/1, 66% of the relationals are EQUAL and 18% NOT EQUAL. Tanenbaum (1978) indicates that among the relationals, EQUAL accounts for 48.3% followed by 22.1% of NOT EQUALs. Finally, Olafsson's (1981) analysis of C programs show that EQUAL accounts for 35.2% of all relational operations (including, in this case, the logicals), NOT EQUAL for 13.2%, and AND for 12.6%.

3. The single most important *control* statement is the procedure CALL. It is also the most *time consuming* of high-level language operations.

    The evidence for this statement is perhaps less conclusive than for the foregoing. Olafsson (1981) indicates that 26.4% of all statement types are procedure CALLs and that this is (after the assignment), the second most common statement type. Moreover, in 77% of all procedures the ratio of the number of executable statements to CALL statements is less than 4.5; in only 17% of cases does this ratio exceed 6. This suggests a high level of modularization in Olafsson's sample programs. Tanenbaum's (1978) data shows that 24.6% of all statements were CALLs. However, its dynamic frequency was only 12.4%.

    A revealing analysis of procedure CALLs was performed by Patterson and Sequin (1981). Their dynamic frequencies for Pascal and C CALL statements were, respectively, $12 \pm 1\%$ and $12 \pm 5\%$—data that seem consistent with Tanenbaum's figures. However, to determine which statements *consumed the most time* in executing typical programs, they examined object code produced by compilers for each typical high-level language statement. By multiplying the frequency of occurrence of each source language statement with the corresponding number of machine instructions and memory references, the *weighted frequencies* of CALL/RETURN statements were determined to be $43 \pm 19\%$ for C. Thus, the CALL/RETURN combination was found to be the most time consuming of all the high-level language operations.

It is interesting to note that Elshoff's (1976) static analysis included only 2% of CALL statements. However, this same sample had nearly 12% of GOTOs, suggesting that the programs examined were relatively unstructured and poorly modularized.

There are several implications of data such as the foregoing for the design and implementation of exo-architectures. One of these, suggested by the Patterson-Sequin (1981) data is that the implementation of procedure CALLs and RETURNs should be "optimized" for executional efficiency (see Chapter 7). The other significant implication more relevant to the present discussion is that by constructing instructions the *lengths of which are inversely proportional to the frequencies of the associated operations* one may hope to achieve very efficient use of memory space. This approach can be seen in a number of designs.

Example 4.26

The Burroughs B1700/B1800 series of machines (Wilner, 1972a, 1972b; Organick and Hinds, 1978; Myers, 1982) are a family of *universal host machines*— that is, each such computer is a generalized microprogrammable engine with no specific exo-architecture implemented on it; rather, each engine is intended to support a *range* of exo-architecture. The user realizes any desired exo-architecture by writing his or her own microprogram that *emulates* the target architecture on the B1700/B1800 host processor (see Chapter 5, Section 5.4, for a detailed discussion of universal host machines and emulation).

The B1700 has been used to implement a COBOL/RPG-oriented exo-architecture and an SDL-oriented exo-architecture[12] (Myers, 1982). In both cases, the instruction set design was based on frequencies of operations. In the case of the COBOL/RPG architecture, the seven most frequent operations were encoded in a 3-bit field while the remaining operations used 9-bit opcodes. The SDL architecture contained three classes of opcodes of lengths 4, 6, and 10 bits, respectively, with the most frequent operations encoded in the smallest field and the least frequent ones in the largest.

The results of these encodings were found to be spectacular. For example, Wilner (1972a, 1972b) reported that a sample of 20 COBOL programs occupied 450K bytes on the B1700/COBOL-RPG machine compared to 1490K bytes on the IBM System/360; a set of 31 RPG11 programs required 150K bytes of storage on the B1700/COBOL-RPG machine in contrast to 310K bytes on an IBM System/3. ■

Myers (1982) has studied the effect of operation code encoding on the space-

---

[12]SDL was the language used to write the operating system and the compilers for the B1700. These programs were compiled into code for, and executed by, the SDL-oriented exo-architectures.

efficiency of programs on the B1700/SDL architecture. Using 4-, 6-, and 10-bit encodings of operations, the B1700 operating system required about 180K bits. This compared very favorably with the *optimal* encoding of about 168K bits that obtains if Huffman encoding is used.[13]

Example 4.27

Tanenbaum (1978) has described the design of a "paper machine" called the EM-1 intended for executing code compiled from a language called SAL. The operation set and instruction formats are based on an analysis of the frequencies of various statement types and operations empirically observed in SAL programs. Basically, five classes of instructions were identified, with shorter instruction types being associated with the more frequent operations.

1. 1-byte instructions that reference one or two implicit operands; for example, PUSHZERO and PUSHONE, which place constants 0 and 1, respectively, onto the top of a stack, and zero-addresses ADD, SUB, MUL, DIV, which take two implicit operands from a stack and leave the result on the stack. (See Chapter 6 for a discussion of stack machines.)
2. 2-byte instructions consisting of a 1-byte opcode and a 1-byte offset (relative to an implicit store).
3. 3-byte instructions consisting of a 1-byte opcode and a 2-byte offset.
4. 3-byte instructions with a 2-byte opcode and a 1-byte offset.
5. 4-byte instructions with a 2-byte opcode and a 2-byte offset.

Tanenbaum's design, thus, combines frequency-based encoding of operations with the expanded-opcode scheme. Again, the resulting economy in the use of memory bits is significant. A set of four algorithms were programmed for execution on the EM-1, the PDP-11, and the CDC Cyber (Tanenbaum, 1978). The ratios of PDP-11/EM-1 object code sizes for the benchmarks ranged between 1.5 to 2.8. The ratios of Cyber/EM-1 object code sizes ranged between 2.0 and 6.3. ■

[13]*Huffman encoding*, named after its inventor (Huffman, 1952), is an algorithm that, given an alphabet of symbols $\{S_1, S_2, \ldots S_k\}$ with known probabilities of occurrences $\{P_1, P_2, \ldots, P_{ik}\}$, produces an encoding of the alphabet so as to minimize the number of bits required for a message using the alphabet. In our context, the alphabet is the set of operations, the probabilities are the usage frequencies, and a message is a program composed of the operand. The use of Huffman encoding produces the smallest number of opcode bits for a given program. However, it is rarely possible to actually use Huffman encoding as a means of determining opcodes since the number of different length opcodes may be impractically large: The greater this number, the more complex will be the decoding of the opcode field during instruction execution. Myers (1982) has shown, for instance, how for a given set of seven operations with known probabilities of occurrence, Huffman encoding yields opcodes of four distinct lengths. The value of this algorithm lies in the fact that it establishes the optimum that can be achieved so that the "goodness" of a more heuristic encoding scheme can be assessed by comparing with the optimum. Informal descriptions of the Huffman encoding method are given in Tanenbaum (1984, Chapter 2) and Myers (1982, Chapter 23).

4.9 THE WORD LENGTH

In discussing computers and computer architectures, it is, in a sense, appropriate to say that "in the beginning was the word length." For, the *word length* perhaps more than any other single parameter has been used as a measure of the overall capability of a machine. Yet, when one attempts to define this parameter or at least identify the majority opinion as to what the term denotes, one quickly realizes, to some amazement, how elusive the concept really is.

For our purposes, I will adopt what seems to be the least controversial characterization of word length; in this regard I follow Siewiorek, Bell, and Newell (1982), Blaauw (1976), and Hamachar, Vranesic, and Zaky (1984):

The *word length* of a computer determines the number of bits that can be read (from main store to processor) or written (from processor to main store) in one memory cycle.

Even this definition is somewhat ambiguous. For instance, when we consider a computer with *interleaved memory* (see Chapter 8) involving n distinct memory modules, the number of bits that can be accessed in one memory cycle will be n times that of an otherwise identical, noninterleaved memory. We will, thus, assume that the word length refers to the case of noninterleaved (i.e., single-module) memory: that is, memory that can accept only one read or one write at a time.

As so defined, note that the word length is primarily an *endo-architectural* parameter that reflects characteristics of both the main memory and the processor-memory data path. However, the determinants of a machine's word length may well be, and indeed often are, exo-architectural factors. Furthermore, the decision to adopt a particular word length will, in turn, have significant exo-architectural as well as endo-architectural implications. Some of these correlates are presented next.

4.9.1 Determinants of Word Length

Bell and Newell (1971) have suggested that historically a computer's word length has largely been related to the intended function of the total system: "Scientific" computers that perform predominantly numeric computations have relatively large word lengths — 32 bits and above; "business" computers, being primarily character-string manipulators, have relatively small word lengths — between 8 and 16 bits; finally, "control" computers used in manufacturing, process monitoring, and laboratory environments, though also involved with numeric processing, have very modest arithmetical demands, so moderate word lengths (8 to 18 bits) are used.

The main point being made here is that computer function determines its predominant supported data types, and the word length is established so that one or more variables of these types can be allocated in single words and be transmitted across the processor-memory interface in single memory cycles.

In the context of VLSI technology, quite a different determinant of word length may be seen, namely, the pin limitation issue (see Chapter 2, Section 2.4). More specifically, since in the case of a single-chip processor the actual number of pins on a chip will determine the amount of information that may be transmitted in parallel across the chip boundary, the pin count for the data lines will determine the word length. Thus, the fact that the Intel 8086, Zilog Z8000, and Motorola MC68000 are all regarded as 16-bit processors is a consequence of the width of the data port leaving these processor chips (Toong and Gupta, 1981).

The word length, once determined, has several implications for other architectural decisions. Instructions are designed so as to fit into a word or into multiple words without wasting bits. The widths of exo-architectural registers are made identical to the word length. Data types (other than those that may have contributed to the word length determination in the first place) are designed so as to be encodable in one word or multiple words, again without bits remaining unused. Finally, such endo-architectural characteristics as the widths of the processor data paths, internal registers, and functional units are, usually, determined on the basis of word lengths.

Example 4.28

The PDP-11 series (Digital, 1978) is usually regarded as a family of 16-bit computers. The memory word length for all family members is 16 bits, although memory is byte addressable. Integer data types are 8 or 16 bits long, and Boolean vectors (or binary strings) of 16 bits can be held in a word. Characters, of course, are held in bytes so that a word can hold an integral number of characters. The general purpose registers are all 16 bits long as are the widths of the internal data paths and ALUs for all implementations.

In the case of the VAX-11/780, the first of the VAX-11 successors to the PDP-11 family, the word length was increased to 32 bits with corresponding increases in the sizes of the significant data types (32-bit integers, 32-bit single-precision floating-point numbers, variable length bit strings up to 32 bits long) that can be accommodated in a word or in a multiple number of words (e.g., 64-bit integers and multiple-precision floating-point numbers). The processor's internal data path is 32 bits wide. ∎

(Counter) Example 4.29

Truly notable exceptions to these general principles can be seen in some members of the IBM System/360 and System/370 families of computers (Case and Padegs, 1978). For example, in the case of the 360/85 model, the number of bits transmitted across the memory/processor interface is 128 bits (per memory module) whereas the internal data paths are 64 bits wide. Similarly, in the 370/145, 370/148, and 370/155, the common word length (as we have defined it) is 64 bits, but the common data-path width is 32 bits. In the case of the 370/158, the word length is 128 bits whereas the data path is 32 bits wide.

Indeed, in the case of the IBM 360 and 370 series, the notion of word length as we have defined the term hardly seems valid. This is in part due to the fact that a common exo-architecture (that of the "IBM System/360" or of the "IBM System/370") is realized by implementations involving different endo-architectures and technologies. At the exo-architectural level the width of all interesting entities is 32-bits: the fixed-point and single-precision floating-point data types and three of the five instruction formats (all of the register storage type).

Thus, it appears to make more sense, in the case of the 360 and 370 families where there is a very real distinction between the two architectural levels, to talk of *two* word lengths — those of the exo-architecture and of the endo-architecture, respectively. ∎

(Counter) Example 4.30

We noted previously that the word length of microprocessors is predominantly determined by pin constraints. In the case of the Motorola 68000 this limits the data bus width at the processor-memory interface to 16 bits; it is because of this that the 68000 is regarded as a 16-bit processor (Toong and Gupta, 1981). However, the internal data paths are all 32-bits wide. ∎

4.9.2 The Impact of Word Length on Addressing Capability

Perhaps one of the most profound architectural consequences of the word length is on the *addressing capability* of a machine. In his retrospective assessment of the PDP-11, Bell (1977) (see also Bell and Strecker, 1976) has pointed out that perhaps the biggest mistake that can be made in planning the design of a computer is to unduly limit its addressing capability.

Suppose an *n*-bit *address width* (i.e., the number of bits to specify a memory address) is chosen. This limits the addressable space to 2^n words (or bytes, or whatever is the smallest addressable entity). However, given the well-known exponential growth in memory density (see Chapter 2, Section 2.5.1), the demand for address space (at constant cost) can easily double every 2 to 3 years; thus, the address width may be required to grow at the rate of 1 bit every 2 years. Limiting the address width on a given computer without taking into account the potential expandability of the address space can turn out to be a very costly mistake.

If the address width is correlated to the word length, then the latter may have profound consequences for the machine's addressing capability. This may be particularly observed in the case of the PDP-11, where the different addressing modes (see Section 4.7, Table 4.7) use general registers as an address source. Thus, the 16-bit registers limit the address width to 16 bits and the effective address space to 2^{16} (64K) bytes of memory.

This limitation was partly overcome in later implementations of the PDP-11 where the 16-bit program specified addresses were mapped onto 18-bit physical memory addresses (e.g., in the PDP-11/45) and to 22-bit physical memory addresses (e.g., in the PDP-11/70) (Bell and Mudge, 1978). The problem was solved in a more general way in the VAX-11 design by adopting a 32-bit word length and address width (Strecker, 1978).

4.10 THE PROCESSOR STATE

In designing exo-architectures, the architect must be cognizant of the notion of the *processor state*, which is essentially a measure of the state of the processing unit at any stage of program execution. More precisely, following Siewiorek, Bell, and Newell (1982):

> The *processor state* is the amount of information within the processing unit that must be known (to the processor) at the end of one instruction's execution in order for the processor to execute the next instruction.

For example, consider the execution of a program P on a processor and suppose that for some reason the execution of P is interrupted temporarily on completion of instruction I_j in P. The processor is required to switch to some other program Q. Then the processor state denotes the amount of information stored in the processing unit (reflecting the state of P's computation at the end of I_j's execution) that must be saved (usually in a specially designated area in main store) before the processor is switched from P to Q in order that P may resume execution at instruction I_{j+1} when the processor is switched back to P. This state information must be restored to the processor when P resumes execution.

Note that the execution of Q will also presume a proper processor state to begin with, hence this information must also be placed (from a special area in main store) in the processor before Q can begin execution.[14]

What are the components of a processor state? In a register machine they are, precisely, the processor registers that are explicitly or implicitly visible at the *exo-architectural* level. Typically, the state consists of the arrays of general and special purpose registers, the program counter (PC), and the set of flags or flip-flops that serve to record the condition codes. It is important to note that the processor state does not include other hardware registers that may be visible at the endo- but not at the exo-architectural level since the values of such registers change *during* the interpretation of an instruction; only those registers that transmit information between instructions are contributors to the processor state. Thus, for the original von Neumann machine (Section 4.2, Fig. 4.2) this state consists essentially of the accumulator, the arithmetic register, and the control (or program) counter, CC. The other registers shown in Figure 4.2, namely SR, CR, and FR, are not components of the processor state.

---

[14]The dynamic switching of a processor from the execution of one program P to another Q, with the attendant saving of the processor state of P and loading of the processor state for Q, is called *context switching*.

Example 4.31

In the case of the VAX-11, the processor state [also called the *hardware context* in Digital (1981b)] consists of several components:

1. Sixteen general registers, denoted RO–R15 of which R15 is the program counter (PC), and R14, R13, and R12, called, respectively, the stack pointer (SP), the frame pointer (FP), and argument pointer (AP), are registers used by a program for stack and subroutine management (see Chapter 6 for a discussion of stacks).

2. A 32-bit register called the *processor status long word* (PSL), which consists of (a) condition code bits to record the negative, zero, overflow, and carry conditions resulting from instruction execution; (b) bits that may be set to enable exception conditions; and (c) additional, special purpose bits.

3. A collection of *base* and *length registers* used for the management of a program's memory space (see Chapter 8 for an extensive discussion of memory management).

4. A set of additional *stack pointers* used by the processor for additional stack management functions.

The practical significance of the processor state should be evident from the definition itself. Whenever programs are being executed in a multiprogramming environment[15] and the processor is being dynamically switched from one program to another, the processor state is the amount of information that must be saved and restored during a context switch. The larger the processor state, the longer will be the time incurred in switching contexts.

Bell and Newell (1971) (see also Siewiorek, Bell, and Newell, 1982) have pointed out that there is a correlation between a computer's processor state and the nature and format of its instruction set. In a typical register machine of the type described in this chapter, a significant subset of the instruction set will be of the register-to-storage or register-to-register types:

```
Memory[addr]  < =  Mem[addr] op Register i
Reg i         < =  Mem[addr] op Register i
Register i    < =  Register i op Register j
```

That is, in an obvious sense, general or special purpose registers will hold values that need to be passed between instructions. In contrast, consider a computer involving *only* storage-to-storage type instructions:

```
Memory[addr1] < =  Memory[addr1] op Memory[addr2]
Memory[addr1] < =  op Memory[addr2]
```

---

[15]*Multiprogramming* is the technique used to share, dynamically, a computer's main store and processor between two or more programs so as to simulate (or create the illusion of) concurrent execution of these programs (Brinch Hansen, 1973; Madnick and Donovan, 1974; Habermann, 1976).

Instructions of these types map from one state of the main memory to another; thus, most of the information passed from one instruction to the next is contained in *main memory* rather than in registers. The processor state in such computers will be far less than in register machines—although it cannot be eliminated altogether since there must at least be a program counter in the processor.

In general, then, register machines will have a larger processor state than the so-called *1-address machine* (which has the accumulator as an implied operand and a memory address as the explicit second operand specifier—e.g., the original von Neumann model), whereas the 1-address machine will have more processor state than a computer consisting of only storage-to-storage instructions. Notice that a register machine having storage-to-storage instructions in its instruction set (e.g., as in the IBM System/370) will still have registers as part of its processor state. ∎

PROBLEMS

4.1 One of the important features of the original von Neumann model was the *stored program* concept.
  (a) Define this concept.
  (b) Why was this feature introduced by von Neumann and his associates in their computer design?
  (c) What are the problems associated with this feature?
  (d) Describe ways by which these problems can be avoided or solved.

4.2 State the fundamental characteristics of the von Neumann architectual style.

4.3 At the heart of the register machine style is a storage organization consisting of a slow, large main memory and a fast, small register array.
  (a) Explain *why* such a storage hierarchy came about.
  (b) Describe the main *functions* of the registers in the register array.

4.4 One of the hallmarks of a complex system is that it usually consists of a large number of components that interact in a nontrivial way. This has obvious consequences for the complexity of the design process itself, since the designer must impose some "structure" on the system design so as to render the interactions between components "intellectually manageable."

  By the foregoing criterion, exo-architectures may be regarded as complex systems. Using appropriate examples (such as the computers cited in this chapter), describe the nature of the interactions among the following components of an exo-architecture.
  (a) Storage organization, instruction size, and instruction organizations (formats).
  (b) Storage organization and processor state.
  (c) Addressing modes and storage organization.

    (d) The set of data types, the operation set, and the instruction organizations.

    (e) Word length, data types, and instruction size.

4.5 [This problem is related to Problem 4.4.] One of the abstract tools that designers use for the "management of complexity" is *hierarchic design*. In general, this means that the system is constructed "upward" on a level-by-level basis such that given two adjacent levels L_i, L_{i+1} (where L_i is a "lower" level than L_{i+1}), the decisions made and the features designed at level L_{i+1} can use the features at level L_i but not vice versa.

    Clearly, in such a design process the designer must decide which features to place at what level.

    Consider the application of this principle in the design of exo-architectures. Assuming interaction between architectural components C_i and C_j, a decision to develop the design of C_i before that of C_j (i.e., C_i will appear lower in the hierarchy than C_j) may be rationalized by invoking any one of the following principles.

Principle 1: The design of C_i is determined by independent (or external) factors that have higher priority than mere consideration of the interaction between C_i and C_j.

Principle 2: The component of C_i is more convenient to use in the design of C_j than the converse. That is, C_i is the "more independent" component.

Principle 3: The design of C_i lower in the hierarchy than C_j should not affect the efficient design of C_j.

    (a) Consider, now, the interaction among storage organization, instruction size, and instruction format. Show *how* one or more of the principles can be applied so as to establish an ordering on the design of these components. (That is, construct a plausible scenario in which, by invoking one or more of these principles, the designer can rationalize a particular ordering in the design of these components).

    (b) Consider the interactions among word length, data types, and operation set. Again, how would you apply these principles to order the design of these components?

4.6 Consider the question of architectural *quality*. Certainly, the most obvious factor that determines quality is *efficiency*.

    (a) Identify four distinct measures that can be used by the architect to assess the overall efficiency of an exo-architecture design. Note that these measures should evaluate the efficiency of the exo-architecture *only*; they should not reflect any aspect of how the exo-architecture is implemented.

    (b) Discuss the methods or tools that would have to be used to determine values for these measures.

4.7 A second important property that contributes to architectural quality is *modifiability*. To understand the context of this issue recall from Chapter

3 (Section 3.3.6) that designs may undergo both short-term ("ontogenic") and long-term ("phylogenic") evolution. Thus, after an exo-architecture has been designed, implemented, released, and marketed, certain changes or enhancements may be made to the operational computers "in the field." As a specific example, one of the enhancements made to the VAX-11 exo-architecture after the VAX-11/780 computer had been introduced into the market was the addition of new floating-point data types and several instructions to support these types (Bhandarkar, 1982).

Clearly, such enhancements or modifications should be enforceable with minimum effort and impact on the rest of the design.

For each of the significant components of exo-architecture (i.e., data types, addressing modes, instruction formats, etc.), discuss the issue of modifiability and how the component should be *designed for modifiability*.

4.8 The design of almost every artifact has an *aesthetic* aspect to it. In the case of some — notably, buildings — the aesthetics are obviously of a visual kind. In other artifacts, it assumes a more subtle, technical form. An engineering structure, for instance, may appear commonplace to the eye but may have been designed on a novel principle of structural engineering theory. Its aesthetics lie in the manner in which this principle has been used in this particular structure.

Following these thoughts, we may say that a third important parameter of exo-architectural quality is its aesthetic content.

Discuss the concept of exo-architectural aesthetics and establish, giving appropriate arguments, a set of *aesthetic guidelines* for the design of register-machine style exo-architectures.

[*Hint.* In answering this question take into account the notion of "beauty" as the term is used in mathematics. Mathematicians often talk of a "beautiful theorem" or a "beautiful proof." Similarly physicists are often attracted to one of a set of alternative hypotheses because of its "elegance." Another powerful aesthetic guideline is "Occam's razor," the principle espoused by the fourteenth century English philosopher William of Occam, which states that the hypothesis or explanation involving the fewest assumptions is the best.]

4.9 Supposing you are conducting a preliminary study for the design of a special purpose word processing computer intended to meet the typical word processing needs of students and professors in an academic environment. You are required to establish a "first version" design of the word processor exo-architecture.

(a) Analyze the problem and identify the most important *requirements* that the design must satisfy. [Keep in mind that not all requirements may be evident at this stage — some may be generated in the course of design (see Chapter 3, Problem 3.1].

(b) Because of the interactions among exo-architectural components, some sort of ordering of the design steps for these components must be established (see Problems 4.4 and 4.5).

Identify an ordering of the component design steps, and provide arguments justifying your ordering decisions.

4.10 [Continuation of Problem 4.9.] Perform a thorough analysis of the problem of designing the *data types* to be supported in this computer and the set of associated *operations*. As a result of this analysis, identify the supported data types and operation set for this word processor.

4.11 [Continuation of Problem 4.10.] Design the instruction formats for the word processor. Provide arguments for your design decisions.
[*Note*: In both Problems 4.10 and 4.11, keep in mind that the design of these components will be affected by the relative ordering of their respective design steps (see Problem 4.9). Thus, depending on how this ordering influences the interdependencies between components, you may have to make decisions regarding other components before you even begin the design of these particular ones.]

4.12 [Continuation of Problem 4.11.] In Chapter 3 (Section 3.3.5), it was said that design is mostly a *satisficing* process; and that for most design problems one can rarely produce an optimal solution.

Discuss this issue in the context of your solutions to Problems 4.10 and 4.11. In particular:
(a) Describe at least two aspects of these designs where you were forced to satisfice.
(b) What criteria did you use (or can you use) to judge the "goodness" of the satisficing decisions.
(c) Describe any aspect of these two designs where you were actually able to optimize.

4.13 [Continuation of Problem 4.11; this question is also related to Problems 4.6, 4.7, and 4.8.] Comment on the *quality* of the (possibly) partial exo-architecture design produced from Problems 4.10 and 4.11.

4.14 [This is a fairly extensive design project.] You are required to design an exo-architecture—call it X1—that must satisfy the following given requirements.

(R1)   The word length is to be 16 bits.
(R2)   All instructions are to be 16-bits long or multiples of 16 bits.
(R3)   X1 must provide the arithmetic operations "+" and "−" on integers; "*" and "/" are optional.
(R4)   X1 must provide "+" and "−" operations on real numbers.
(R5)   The data type bit string must be supported.
(R6)   X1 must support the Boolean (logical) data type.
(R7)   It must support operations on characters and character strings.

(R8) There must be "efficient" support for subroutine call and return.

(R9) There must be "adequate" support for branching.

(R10) The number of opcodes should not exceed 32.

(R11) Addressable memory should be at least 2**24 bytes.

Your design will explore one particular architectural style, namely, the register machine style. (Assume that other designers have been entrusted with the exploration of alternative architectures.) Thus, your design will consist of the following components.

(a) *Storage organization*—that is, main memory and one or more programmable registers.

(b) The supported *data types*: the representation and ranges of values for each type.

(c) For each supported data type, the *set of instructions.* The specification of an instruction must include

(i) Its syntax: that is, the components of the instruction and the binary encoding of the opcode.

(ii) Its semantics: what the instruction does. The semantics should be defined informally (in English) and formally (in an algorithmic notation such as Pascal or C).

(iii) Its representation in assembly language notation.

(d) The *addressing modes*: each addressing mode must be specified by

(i) Its syntax: that is, its components and its binary encoding.

(ii) Its semantics: the way the effective address is generated from the addressing mode.

(iii) Its assembly language representation.

(e) The *instruction formats*: for each format, the fields must be specified in terms of their positions and what they represent.

4.15 [Continuation of Problem 4.14.] Discuss thoroughly, the *quality* of the exo-architecture X1 from the perspectives of its *efficiency*, its *modifiability*, and its *aesthetics*.

4.16 [Continuation of Problems 4.14.] A design must be *tested* as thoroughly as possible before it is implemented or refined to a more detailed level. Thus the architect must attempt to confirm that his or her *expectations* about the total design—these being the results of individual decisions made during the design process—are indeed justified.

In particular, testing a design to assess or confirm its efficiency may require constructing appropriate experiments that will be used to test definite *hypotheses* about the design. There are two issues to this:

(i) Stating hypotheses in such a way that they can be meaningfully tested (e.g., a proposition that "the instruction set is efficient" may be adequate as an initial requirement but is hardly a testable hypothesis).

(ii) Devising the right experiments to test the hypotheses.
   (a) For your design of X1, state two testable hypotheses that can be used to ascertain the efficiency of the architecture.
   (b) Describe feasible experiments that can be carried out to test these hypotheses.

4.17 [Continuation of Problem 4.16.] Perform the experiments you describe in Problem 4.16 and describe their results. What are your conclusions concerning the efficiency of your design?

CHAPTER 5

REGISTER MACHINES II: INTERNAL ARCHITECTURE AND MICROPROGRAMMING

5.1 INTRODUCTION

In Section 4.2 the basic aspects of a computer's endo-architecture were described with respect to the original von Neumann model. In general, an endo-architecture consists of two entities:

1. A static or *structural* entity composed of storage devices (e.g., main memory, programmable registers, internal registers), functional units (e.g., arithmetic and logical unit, counters, shifters), and the data paths that connect these components. In the conventional, informal descriptions of endo-architectures, this structural aspect is depicted in the form of block diagrams (see, e.g., Fig. 4.2).

2. A dynamic or *behavioral* aspect that specifies how the resources of the endo-architectural structure are actually used in implementing a given exo-architecture. Endo-architectural behavior is, thus, concerned with the actual flow, transformation, and control of information through the structural entity for the purpose of realizing exo-architectures.

At the very heart of endo-architectural behavior in von Neumann style machines is the *instruction interpretation cycle* (*Icycle*), which, in very general terms, and shorn of all complexities, can be depicted as follows.

Repeat
    FETCH INSTRUCTION: From main store at address specified in program counter to processing unit.
    UPDATE PROGRAM COUNTER: In preparation to fetch next instruction.
    DECODE INSTRUCTION: Determine what the instruction is to do.
    EXECUTE INSTRUCTION: Access the operands, perform the operation, and place the result in the appropriate store.
Until Halt signal is detected.

The vast majority of computers, from the late 1940s to the present, follow this fundamental behavioral logic. The Icycle schematic shown here is the one universal mechanism governing the behavior and functioning of all von Neumann style computers, much as the genetic code and its transcription into proteins is the one universal mechanism governing the structure and functioning of all life on this earth. Distinct computer designs and endo-architectural styles are differentiated by variations in the details and in the complexities of the Icycle steps, in the amount of concurrency or overlap between these steps, and in the number of Icycles that may be active concurrently in any given system.[1]

One further general remark must be made at this stage: Although the structural aspect of an architecture specifies storage and functional components and their interconnections, a proper understanding of an endo-architectural structure requires that the *behavior of the components* be specified and understood. Thus, an adequate structural description must contain the behavioral specification of its components. It is for this reason that the *block diagram* representation of an endo-architectural structure is, except for the simplest of designs, so inadequate as a description mechanism: It does not capture the implied behavior of the components.

Endo-architectures can be designed and described at different levels of abstraction. The choice of a particular level will depend on such factors as the complexity of the architecture as a whole, the underlying design methodology, and where we consider architecture "design" to end and "implementation" to begin.

In many of the chapters comprising this book and Volume 2 I will be discussing many different aspects of endo-architecture, including such topics as instruction pipelining, virtual memory mechanisms, and interconnection networks. In the current chapter, I will focus on the endo-architecture of register machines at a specific abstraction level, namely, as it appears to the microprogrammer. In Chapter 1, this level was termed the *micro-architectural* level. The specific concern of the present chapter, then, is the *micro-architecture of register machines*.

Our treatment of this topic will be as follows: As in Chapter 4, we begin with a relatively simple case study and then gradually add complexity. Thus, using the previous description of the original von Neumann machine (Chapter 4, Section 4.2) I first present, without exploring too deeply the design choices available, a possible micro-architecture and show how the von Neumann exo-architecture

---

[1]A number of architectural styles can be explained in terms of the "variations on the Icycle" theme. For example, Flynn's classification scheme (see Volume 2, Chapter 2, Section 2.4) can be characterized as follows: SISD (or uniprocessor) machines are those in which the endo-architecture behavior is governed by a *single Icycle* composed of *single* Fetch, Update, Decode, and Execute components. In an SIMD machine there is also only one Icycle. However, within a particular iteration of the Icycle there will be single Fetch, Update, and Decode steps but *several Execute steps* (all involving the same operation but different operands) may take place in parallel. In an MIMD machine at any given time *several distinct Icycles* may be iterating concurrently. Finally, in machines that are *pipelined*—and such computers may be SISD, SIMD or MIMD—*several distinct iterations* of the same Icycle may be active in parallel. Thus, we regard all these styles as mutations or variations of the von Neumann style. In Volume 2, Chapter 9, we discuss an architectural style that does not exhibit the Icycle as its essential behavioral trait. Such architectures represent a fundamentally different paradigm.

can be realized on this *micromachine*[2] using the technique of micro-programming.

In subsequent sections I will then explore more complex situations and the range of design choices available to the architect of the micromachine. I will examine alternative styles of designing both the structural component of the micro-architecture and its behavioral component. A substantial part of this discussion will be concerned with the principles of microprogramming.

5.2 A MICRO-ARCHITECTURE FOR THE VON NEUMANN MODEL

Recall from Section 4.2 the basic exo-architecture of the von Neumann machine: a set of (primarily) 1-address instructions with the second operand being implicitly drawn from the accumulator or the arithmetic register; a 40-bit word length; 20-bit instructions with two instructions packed into each memory word; and a 40-bit signed integer data type. The instruction set was summarized in Table 4.1. In the following discussion, the same instruction set, with the exception of the *load accumulator negative absolute* and the *multiply* and *divide* instructions, will be implemented.

Our starting point will be this "reduced" instruction set and the block diagram of the endo-architectural structure previously shown as Figure 4.2. This diagram, however, is not detailed enough to reveal all that must be known of the machine in order to implement the instruction set. For one thing, the functional properties of the *control unit* were not specified, as a result of which the instruction interpretation cycle could only be described in very general and informal terms.

Thus, this endo-architecture must be further *refined* to a level that can be used to specify precisely the functional characteristics of the control unit. In general, the refinement procedure will modify or augment the resources shown in Figure 4.2; make more precise the functional properties of the individual resources, particularly those of the functional units and the control unit; and introduce details of the *timing* characteristics of the resources.

5.2.1 The Data Path

One possible design of the von Neumann machine micro-architecture will now be described.[3] Figure 5.1 shows the structural aspect of the micro-architecture, in particular, the *data path* part of the micromachine. In this figure, the control unit remains a "black box." The legend identifies the principal refinements and modifications to the original endo-architectural structure of Figure 4.2. These refinements may be summarily explained as follows.

[2]A computer, seen at the micro-architectural level, is often called a *micromachine* or a *microengine*.

[3]It should be noted that this design evolved through two iterations of the cycle:

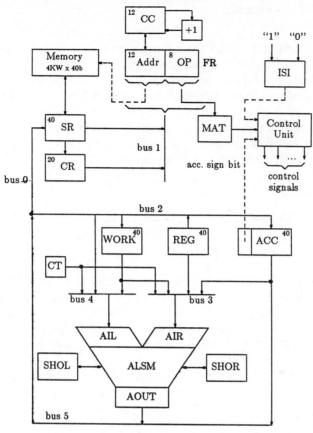

Legend

ALSM:	arithmetic/logical/shift/mask unit
WORK:	working ("scratchpad") register
IŠI:	instruction status indicator
SHOL:	shifted-out left bit
SHOR:	shifted-out right bit

Legend

MAT	microroutine address table
AIL:	left input buffer in ALSM
AIR:	right input buffer in ALSM
AOUT:	output buffer in ALSM
CT:	constant table

FIGURE 5.1   Micro-architecture of the von Neumann model: The data path.

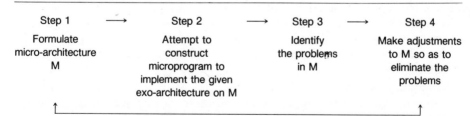

This sequence of steps is an instance of the general evolutionary schema of design discussed in Chapter 3 (Section 3.3.6, Fig. 3.5). The original design (Step 1) corresponds to the "design hypothesis" of Figure 3.5. This was formulated based on the author's knowledge of micro-architecture styles and design principles. Step 2, in which an attempt is made to construct a microprogram to implement the von Neumann machine exo-architecture on this micromachine, corresponds to the "empirical test" stage of Figure 3.5. Step 3 identifies the difficulties observed in developing the microprogram and thus constitutes the "error identification" phase of Figure 3.5. Finally, step 4, where changes to the original design were made to solve the observed problems, corresponds to the "design modification" phase of Figure 3.5. The cycle is completed with a new design.

1. The original arithmetic unit has been generalized into a functional unit (named ALSM) capable of *arithmetic, logical, shift*, and *mask* operations. The precise nature of these operations will be elaborated herein. Associated with the ALSM unit are two input buffers (AIL, AIR) and an output buffer (AOUT).

2. The opcode part of the instruction in the function register (FR) is transmitted to a unit called the *microroutine address table* (MAT), which has one entry per opcode. Each entry in MAT is of the form:

Opcode	Starting address in control memory of corresponding microroutine

When an opcode from FR is presented as an input to this table, the matching circuitry in MAT produces as an output the starting address (in control memory—which is part of the control unit, as will be explained in Section 5.2.2) of the microcode segment (or *microroutine*) that interprets this operation and transmits this address to the control unit. The internal logic of MAT need be of no concern to us.

3. An additional *working* ("scratchpad") *register* (WORK) that is visible and accessible at the micro-architectural level (but not at the exo-architectural level). This register can be used by the microprogrammer to hold temporary or intermediate values.

4. A *constant table* (CT) permanently holds useful constants that may be required by the microprogram. Under the appropriate activation by the control unit, CT can emit the desired constants to the ALSM unit. The two constants that will be required by the microprogram described later are the 40-bit binary strings '00 . . . 0' and '10 . . . 0.'

5. A single-bit register called the *instruction status indicator* (ISI) can be set (to 1) or cleared (to 0) when commanded by the control unit. The purpose of ISI will be made evident when we describe the microprogram in Section 5.2.3.

6. A *bus-oriented* organization of the overall data-path. That is, almost all information transmissions between stores, or between stores and functional units, involve centralized, shared data paths called *buses*. In its essence, a *bus* is a collection of wires that allows for the parallel transmission of information from a source to a destination. By its very purpose, a bus may be connected to several sources and several destinations but at any given time only one of the sources may have access to the bus and, usually, a single source-destination pair uses the bus at a time to communicate.

   Bus-oriented data-path organizations produce a smaller number of interconnections than would be required in a decentralized or *distributed* data-path organization in which there exists a physically distinct path for each source-destination pair that requires to communicate.[4]

---

[4]For a discussion and comparison of bus-oriented and distributed data-path styles, see Tseng and Siewiorek (1982).

Actual information transfers within the data path or the activation of functional units are effected by means of *control signals* issued by the control unit. Viewed abstractly, a control signal *enables* a particular operation to occur in the micromachine. For example, referring to Figure 5.1, the appropriate control signal may cause the contents of SR to be transmitted along buses 0 and 2 to ACC; some other control signal may cause the ALSM unit to perform the AND operation on the values contained in AIL and AIR and place the result in AOUT.

Each distinct operation that can be effected by a control signal issued from the control unit is called a *micro-operation* (MO). At the micro-architectural level, MOs may be viewed as the set of the most primitive (and indivisible) operations that may take place. Of course, if the architecture is refined to the logic design level, then an MO can be defined in terms of more primitive events.

Table 5.1 specifies the set of MOs for the data path shown in Figure 5.1. For the present, the rightmost two columns may be ignored. The MOs have been grouped according to the resources (stores, buses, or functional units) involved in their executions.

The meanings of most of the MOs should be clear with, perhaps, a few exceptions. The MO

AOUT : = AIL **mask** AIR [i_1 . . . i_2]

where $i_1 \geq i_2$, uses a **mask** in AIR to control the transformation of the bit sequence contained in AIL: for bit positions in AIL to the left of bit position i_1 and to the right of i_2, the values are transmitted unchanged from AIL to the corresponding bit positions in AOUT. For the bit positions i_1 through i_2, the values from AIR are transmitted to the corresponding bit positions in AOUT.
The MO

SHOL @ AOUT := **shl** AIR **by** i

left shifts the value of AIR by i bits ($1 \leq i \leq 40$) and leaves the result in AOUT. The last shifted-off bit is also held in SHOL so that effectively a 41-bit result is produced in the concatenated "virtual" store SHOL @ AOUT.
The MO

AOUT @ SHOR := **shr** AIR **by** i

is similar except that it effects a right shift of i bits and the resulting 41-bit quantity is left in the "concatenated" store AOUT @ SHOR.[5]

5.2.2 The Control Unit

As I have noted, each MO is activated by control signals issued by the control unit. From a formal viewpoint, a control unit is a *finite-state machine* (Fig.

---

[5]There is no "magic" involved in the creation of these MOs. They resulted from the evolutionary method used in designing the microarchitecture; the necessity of these MOs became evident when the microprogram to implement the instruction set was being first attempted.

TABLE 5.1 Data Path Micro-operations

Micro-operations	Resources Used	Timing Attribute		Microword Field
1. SR := Mem[FR.addr] 2. Mem[FR.addr] := SR	Memory unit	Mem. cycle	(F1):	00:NOP 01:1 10:2
3. CC := CC+1[a] 4. FR.addr := CC 5. CC := FR.addr	CC	MU.ph1	(F2):	00:NOP 01:3 10:4 11:5
6. ISI := 1[b] 7. ISI := 0	ISI	MU.ph1	(F3):	00:NOP 01:6 10:7
8. FR := SR.high[b,c] 9. CR := SR.low[b,c] 10. FR := CR 11. FR := SR.low	Bus 1	MU.ph1	(F4):	00:NOP 01:8&9 10:10 11:11
12. AIL := SR 13. WORK := SR 14. REG := SR 15. ACC := SR	Bus 2	MU.ph1	(F5):	000:NOP 001:12 010:13 011:14 100:15
16. AIR := REG 17. AIR := ACC 18. AIR := WORK 19. AIR := '00 . . . 0' 20. AIR := '10 . . . 0'	Bus 3	MU.ph1	(F6):	000:NOP 001:16 010:17 011:18 100:19 101:20
21. SR := ACC 22. SR := AOUT	Bus 5 Bus 0	MU.ph3	(F7):	00:NOP 01:21 10:22
23. AIL := ACC 24. REG := ACC 25. WORK := ACC 26. ACC := ACC	Bus 5 Bus 2	MU.ph1	(F8):	000:NOP 001:23 010:24 011:25 100:26
27. AIL := AOUT 28. ACC := AOUT 29. REG := AOUT 30. WORK := AOUT	Bus 5 Bus 2	MU.ph3	(F9):	000:NOP 001:27 010:28 011:29 100:30
31. AIL :=WORK 32. AIL :='00 . . . 0' 33. AIL :='10 . . . 0'	Bus 4	MU.ph1	(F10):	00:NOP 01:31 10:32 11:33

TABLE 5.1 Data Path Micro-operations (Part 2 of 2)

Micro-operations	Resources Used	Timing Attribute	Microword Field
			0000:NOP
34. AOUT := AIL + AIR			0001:34
35. AOUT := AIR − AIL			0010:35
36. AOUT := AIL ∧ AIR			0011:36
37. AOUT := AIL ∨ AIR			0100:37
38. AOUT := AIL + AIR			0101:38
39. AOUT := ∼AIR			0110:39
40. AOUT := AIL			0111:40
41. AOUT := AIR			1000:41
	ALSM	MU.ph2	(F11):
42. AOUT := AIL **mask** AIR[i_1..i_2] ($i_1 \geq i_2$; $0 < i_1, i_2 \leq 39$)[d]			1101:42
43. SHOL @ AOUT := **shl** AIR **by** i[e]			1110:43
44. AOUT @ SHOR := **shr** AIR by i[e] ($1 \leq i \leq 40$)			1111:44

[a] These MOs are only needed for instruction fetch or for the BRL/BRR instructions.
[b] These MOs are only needed during instruction fetch.
[c] These MOs are always executed together.
[d] i_1, i_2 provide the bounds of the mask's bit positions. When this operation is encoded in field F11, i_1 is specified in the concatenated field F2@F3@F4, and i_2 is specified in the concatenated field F8@F9.
[e] i denotes shift amount. When this operation is encoded in field F11, then i is specified by the concatenated field F2@F3@F4.

5.2)—also called a *sequential circuit* in logic design (Hayes, 1984; Kohavi, 1982). At any given time, the device is in one of a finite set of *states*

$$S = \{S_1, S_2, \ldots, S_m\}$$

When in state S_i (i.e., when the "present state" of the control unit is S_i), the device issues one of more control signals that collectively constitute one of the state machine's *output* O_j. Since control signals are specifically associated with MOs, it is practical to view an output O_j as a subset of MOs drawn from the alphabet of MOs:

$$M = \{m_1, m_2, \ldots, m_n\}$$

characterizing the micromachine. Table 5.1 is an instance of such an alphabet. Along with the output (of control signals or, equivalently, MOs) the device switches from its "present state" S_i to a "next state" S_k. The mechanism for determining the output and the next state is shown in Figure 5.2 as the combinational logic box. The state machine must also have some memory device to receive and hold this "next state" information. Once this "next state" has been received by the memory device, it then becomes the "present state."

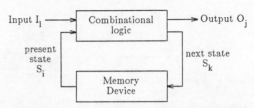

FIGURE 5.2   Structure of a finite state machine.

More generally speaking, the functioning of the control unit may involve *input* signals received by the unit. Such inputs may originate as condition code or other status information within the data path; or they may be components of the previously generated output signal. In any case, the "next state" S_k to be generated will be determined by both the "present state" S_i and the input signal I_l rather than the "present state" alone.[6]

A key decision that the designer of micro-architectures must make is the choice of the control-unit *implementation technique.* The problem that arises may be stated as follows.

First, the control unit is by no means the only finite-state machine or the sole controller present in a computer. Counters, shift registers, and parity generators are other instances of state machines, while components such as a main memory module or a multiplier/divider unit will also have their own local controllers. The problem is that the control unit is usually the most *complex* state machine or controller in a computer. Typically, as I will later show by examples, the control unit may be characterized by several hundreds of unique states—and the number of states is a good measure of the complexity of the state machine.

One choice, then, is to implement a control unit just as one implements other simpler state machines—as a sequential logic circuit. The first computers all had control units implemented in this way, and such control units came to be known as *hardwired.*

Control units implemented in the form of such hardwired logic circuits are inherently irregular, ill-structured, and ad hoc. Consequently, they are difficult to design, understand, debug, and modify. The innate complexity of control units, consisting of possibly several hundreds of states, further exacerbates the problem of ill-structuredness. Such devices, thus, came to be known as *random logic* circuits.

---

[6]In other words, in the terminology of finite-state machine theory (Kohavi, 1982), control units are instances of a *Moore machine* defined formally as the 5-tuple <S,I,O,fs,fo>, where

1. S is a finite nonempty set of states.
2. I is a finite nonempty set of inputs.
3. O is a finite nonempty set of outputs.
4. fs: $S \times I \longrightarrow S$ is the state transition (or next-state) function.
5. fo: $S \longrightarrow O$ is the output function.

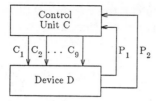

FIGURE 5.3 **The interaction between C and D (see Example 5.1).**

Example 5.1

Consider, as a small example, a control unit C that is to issue control signals to a hardware device D in some specified sequence (Fig. 5.3). The device D, will perform one or more operations at particular times, as determined by the control signals it receives. The role of C, then, is to *sequence* the control signals to D in some desired procedural fashion.

Suppose, in particular, that this sequence of control signals follows the procedure outlined in Figure 5.4. We assume that the control signals are drawn from an alphabet $\{C_1, C_2, \ldots, C_9\}$, say, and each such signal causes some MO to be executed in D. The relations "$P_1 = 1$" and "$P_2 = 1$" represent the testing of status bits that may have been generated within D (Fig. 5.3).

The symbols within "$\{\ \}$" denote the issuance of parallel signals whereas ";" denotes sequencing between (parallel sets of) signals. Assume for simplicity that any two statements separated by a ";" require the same amount of time t. That is, given a sequence of signals C_i; C_j, each of these will require the same amount of time, t, and, consequently, the control signal C_j must be issued t time units after C_i is issued.

```
            begin
[1]             issue control signals {C₁,C₂,C₃}
                if P₁ = 1 then
[2]                     issue control signals {C₁,C₄}
                else
[3]                     issue control signals {C₃,C₆,C₇}
                endif
                if P₂ = 1 then
[4]                     issue control signals {C₁,C₂,C₄};
[5]                     issue control signals {C₅,C₇,C₈,C₉}
                else
[6]                     issue control signals {C₃,C₅,C₇}
                endif
            end
```

FIGURE 5.4 **Sequencing of control signals in C.**

The important point to note in this example is that each of the control signals may have to be activated in different steps and, therefore, at different times. For example, C_1 is issued in step 1, in step 2 (after a delay of time t), and in step 4 (after further delay of time t); C_2 is issued in steps 1 and 4, and so on. The logic circuit implementing this control unit must, then, ensure that these signals are indeed issued at these appropriate times.

There are several ways by which a hardwired implementation of this control unit can be realized (Hayes, 1978, Chapter 4; Ercegovac and Lang, 1985, Chapter 9). For our purposes, the choice of the method is not important, since the main objective in this example is to illustrate the nature of the resulting circuit. Figure 5.5 shows how the control unit C, satisfying the behavior specified by the procedure of Figure 5.4, can be realized in hardwired form using *delays* to sequence the issuance of control signals. ∎

The difficulties posed by hardwired control units prompted Wilkes (1951) to propose a very different technique for the implementation of the control unit. To understand this technique, consider Figure 5.4 once more: It will be seen that the logic of control can be conveniently represented by a *program*. Each step of this program—which corresponds to a distinct state of the state machine—can be encoded in the form of an *instruction*, which, in turn, can consist of several *operations* corresponding to the control signals issued in that step or, equivalently, the micro-operations executed by the control signals. The entire set of instructions can be held in a memory array; each instruction will then be read out from the memory, decoded, and "executed." The result of execution is the issuance of the control signals; this, of course, implements the output function f_0 of the finite-state machine (see footnote 6). The state transition function f_s, which, identifies the next state (or instruction to read out from memory), is realized by a relatively simple hardwired logic circuit called *sequencing* logic.

Because of the obvious analogy to programming, Wilkes invented the term *microprogramming* to denote this technique. The resulting sequence of *microinstructions* came to be known as a *microprogram*. Because of the regularity of the resulting control unit, where all the state information is held in a regular memory array, much of the arbitrariness of random logic could be avoided. The practicality of the microprogramming approach was demonstrated by Wilkes and colleagues at the University of Cambridge in their implementation of the EDSAC-2 computer (Wilkes and Stringer, 1953; Wilkes, Renwick, and Wheeler, 1958).

There are advantages as well as disadvantages to both the hardwired and microprogrammed approaches. However, one should note that with the development of PLAs (see Chapter 2, Section 2.5.4) and other such regular combinational circuit structures, the distinction between hardwired and microprogrammed control units often becomes fuzzy.

In our discussion, however, I will concentrate entirely on *microprogrammed control units* (MCUs) and show the design of one such implementation for the control part of the von Neumann machine.

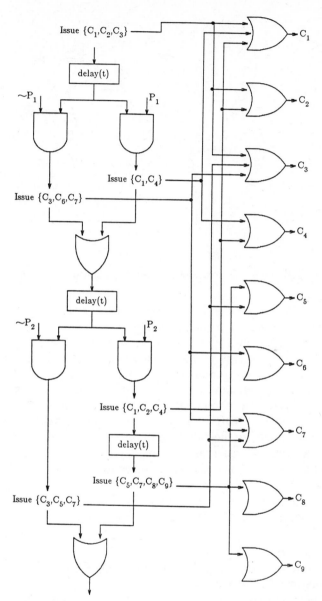

FIGURE 5.5   Hardwired (random logic) control circuit.

5.2.3 A Microprogrammed Control Unit for the von Neumann Model

Figure 5.6 shows the overall structure of a MCU for the von Neumann machine. If you were to ignore such details as the dimensions of the stores and the specific information emanating from the data-path section, Figure 5.6 depicts the archetypal structure of almost all MCUs.

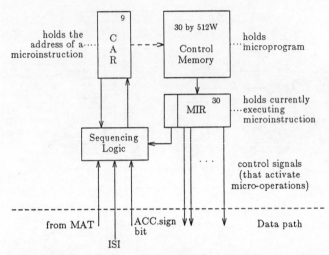

FIGURE 5.6 Structure of a microprogrammed control unit.

A *microinstruction* is an encoded representation of one or more micro-operations. A *microprogram* is a sequence of micro-instructions stored in a set of words (*microwords*) in the *control memory* (or *control store*), which, from an architectural point of view, is similar to the main memory of the computer. A microprogram stored in control memory, beginning at some address, is executed by first loading this address into the *control memory address register* (CAR) and reading out the microinstruction contained in the accessed microword into the *microinstruction register* (MIR). The microinstruction in MIR is decoded, and control signals are issued to the data path in order to activate the MOs that were encoded in that microinstruction. To prepare for the execution of the next microinstruction, the contents of CAR are modified suitably by the *sequencing logic*.

The entire sequence of actions in the *microinstruction interpretation cycle* ("MICycle") can, thus, be depicted as:

repeat
    Update CAR;
    Read microinstruction from control memory into MIR;
    Decode microinstruction;
    Execute microinstruction
until halt[7]

---

[7]The operation and behavior of the control unit itself obeys the essential principles of the von Neumann model of computation. Thus, as first pointed out by Flynn and MacLaren (1967) and then by Rakoczi (1969), one can reasonably view a MCU as an "inner" computer or a "computer-within-a-computer." This is not simply a simile or a fanciful analogy: as discussed in Section 5.4 of this chapter, this concept has been generalized in the form of *universal host machines*—that is, machines that have no intrinsic exo-architecture but can be (micro)programmed by users to create any desired exo-architecture.

This sequence is under the control of a *clock* whose period determines the *microcycle* time—that is, the minimal time interval between two successive activations of the same MO.

The fetching, decoding, and execution of a single microinstruction is usually engineered to complete within a microcycle. However, as will be shown, some microinstructions may need several microcycles to complete in the event that they encode specific "slow" MOs.

The principle parameters affecting the architecture of MCUs are:

Microinstruction organizations Schemes for encoding and representing micro-operations within microinstructions. Referring back to the finite-state machine model of control units, this parameter is related to the problem of representing the states of the state machine and the implementation of the output function.

Microinstruction sequencing The methods for generating the address of the next microinstruction to be executed. With reference to the finite-state machine model, this parameter is related to the problem of implementing the state transition function.

Temporal aspects of microprograms The methods for properly timing the sequence of events involved in the execution of microprograms.

In this section, I will merely provide one set of choices for these three parameters without much explanation. Section 5.3 discusses these issues in a more general and comprehensive setting.

Microinstruction Organizations for the von Neumann Model

Microinstructions for the von Neumann machine are of two types. Type I microinstructions allow for the encoding of all the data-path operations—that is, the MOs shown in Table 5.1. Thus, a type I microinstruction when decoded and executed will cause MOs in the machine's data path to be executed.

Type I microinstructions have the format shown in Figure 5.7(*a*), where each of the 11 *fields* encodes for a specific *group* of MOs. The meanings of each of these fields F1, . . . , F11 are explained in the rightmost column of Table 5.1. The basic rationale for grouping MOs into these particular fields is that the MOs in each group use some common hardware resource (as indicated by the "Resources Used" column in Table 5.1) and, hence, cannot be activated in parallel. Consequently, they can be encoded in one field. Note that given a group of K MOs, the field width will be $\lceil \log_2(K + 1) \rceil$ bits, the extra MO being the "NOP"

The von Neumann model of the MCU has, for 35 years since its inception, remained the dominant style of MCU architecture. The only significant departures have been (1) an *asynchronous* model proposed by Lawson and implemented in a computer called the Datasaab FCPU (Lawson and Malm, 1973), and (2) the very recent style of micro-architecture based on the *data-flow* model developed by Patt and colleagues (1985a, 1985b). Data-flow-based architectural styles are discussed in Volume 2, Chapter 9.

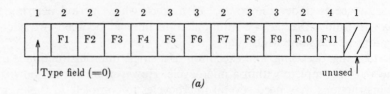

(a)

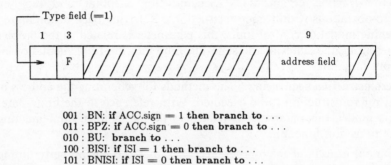

```
001 : BN: if ACC.sign = 1 then branch to . . .
011 : BPZ: if ACC.sign = 0 then branch to . . .
010 : BU: branch to . . .
100 : BISI: if ISI = 1 then branch to . . .
101 : BNISI: if ISI = 0 then branch to . . .
```

FIGURE 5.7 **Microinstruction organizations for the von Neumann model:** *(a)* **Type I microinstructions;** *(b)* **Type II microinstructions.**

operation. This type of microinstruction is often referred to as an example of *minimally encoded* organizations (see Section 5.3).

An important point to note about this instruction format is that in the process of executing a single microinstruction, *several MOs may be activated in parallel* (providing they do not interfere with one another in any way). At the *micro-architectural* level, then, the von Neumann machine is potentially a parallel machine.

As in the case of programs fetched and executed from main memory, when a type I microinstruction is executed, the content of CAR (see Fig. 5.6) is automatically incremented by the sequencing logic so that the next sequential microinstruction is read from control memory into MIR. However, as in the case of ordinary programs, it may be necessary to alter this implicit flow of control explicitly by means of branches within the microprogram.

Type II microinstructions are, then, dedicated to the encoding of MOs that only affect the *flow of control* through a microprogram. Such microinstructions have no influence on the date path. As Figure 5.7(*b*) indicates, type II microinstructions can be used to specify an unconditional branch (BU), a branch on (accumulator sign bit) 0 (BPZ), or a branch on (accumulator sign bit) 1 (BN). The branch address is held in the low-order end of the microinstruction and the "opcode" at the high-order end. Unlike the case of type I microinstructions, only one branch MO can be encoded at a time in a single type II microinstruction.

Microinstruction Sequencing in the von Neumann Model

Recall that the duration of a microcycle is determined by the durations of the individual steps of the MICycle. For the von Neumann machine, I separate these steps into two logically distinct phases: the updating of CAR and the fetching of a microinstruction from the control memory into MIR will constitute the FETCH phase; the decoding and execution of the microinstruction will collectively constitute the EXECUTE phase. Thus, a microinstruction may be said to be processed through a two-stage *pipeline* (Fig. 5.8).[8] Furthermore, and this is why the pipelining concept is so useful, the EXECUTE phase of one microinstruction MI_j (say) is *completely overlapped* with the FETCH phase of the next microinstruction (MI_{j+1}). In terms of the pipeline of Figure 5.8, while the E stage is processing the EXECUTE phase of MI_j, the F stage is executing the FETCH phase of MI_{j+1}. The duration of the microcycle is taken to be the larger of the durations of these two phases.

Figure 5.9 diagrams the resources used and the times consumed by successive microinstructions. This type of diagram, often used to show the schedules of events and the resources used to perform those events, is called a *Gantt chart*.

The situation shown in Figure 5.9 is, in some sense, an ideal state of affairs that may be disrupted by two kinds of events:

1. It assumes that the time for the EXECUTE phase of all microinstructions is the same. In fact, this may not be so, and we will consider this latter situation when we discuss timing issues.
2. From the viewpoint of sequencing, a problem arises when the microinstruction MI_j (say) being executed happens to be a branch and the branch actually takes place. In that case, when microcycle i + 1 completes, a branch address (of microinstruction MI_k, say, where $k \neq j + 1$) is in CAR whereas

---

[8]See Volume 2, Chapter 6, for a detailed examination of the principles of pipelining and pipelined architectures.

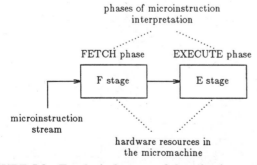

FIGURE 5.8   Two logical stages of the microinstruction pipeline.

Resource	← microcycle i →	← microcycle i+1 →	← microcycle i+2 →
F stage	FETCH MI$_j$	FETCH MI$_{j+1}$	FETCH MI$_{j+2}$
E stage	EXECUTE MI$_{j-1}$	EXECUTE MI$_j$	EXECUTE MI$_{j+1}$

$\longrightarrow$ time

FIGURE 5.9   Gantt chart for the microinstruction pipeline.

MIR will hold MI$_{j+1}$, the microinstruction *following* the (branch) microinstruction MI$_j$ that has just executed (Fig. 5.10).

Obviously, MI$_{j+1}$ should either (1) not be allowed to execute or (2) be such that it can legitimately execute while the new microinstruction MI$_k$ is being fetched.

In this particular design, the second option is chosen since it eliminates the need, in the first option, for the extra hardware required to lock out MI$_{j+1}$. The microinstructions in a microprogram are so ordered that whenever a branch microinstruction appears in the microprogram "text," *it is immediately followed either by a NOP* (no operation) *microinstruction or by a microinstruction that would be executed regardless of whether or not the branch was executed.*

Example 5.2

Thus, one legitimate sequence of microinstructions would be

MI$_j$:   (type II) {**If** ACC.sign = 0 **then branch to** MI$_k$}
MI$_{j+1}$:   (type I) {NOP}

When MI$_k$ is being fetched, MI$_{j+1}$, a NOP, will be executed but with no impact on the state of the machine.   ∎

Example 5.3

Consider the following trio of adjacent microinstructions:

MI$_j$:   (type I) {AIR := REG}
MI$_{j+1}$:   (type II) {**if** ACC.sign = 0 **then branch to** MI$_k$}
MI$_{j+2}$:   (type I) { . . . . . . }

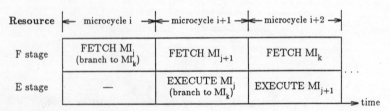

Resource	← microcycle i →	← microcycle i+1 →	← microcycle i+2 →
F stage	FETCH MI$_j$ (branch to MI$_k$)	FETCH MI$_{j+1}$	FETCH MI$_k$
E stage	—	EXECUTE MI$_j$ (branch to MI$_k$)	EXECUTE MI$_{j+1}$

$\longrightarrow$ time

FIGURE 5.10   Gantt chart for the microinstruction pipeline involving a branch.

If this sequence is processed by the pipeline and assuming that the branch takes place, when MI_k is being fetched, MI_{j+2} would be executed (Fig. 5.10)—an incorrect situation if MI_{j+2} is not a NOP. However, if the sequence is *reordered* as follows:

MI_j: (type II) {**if** ACC.sign = 0 **then branch to** MI_k}
MI_{j+1}:   (type I) {AIR := REG}
MI_{j+2}:   (type I) { . . . . . . }

then when MI_j (the branch) is being executed, MI_{j+1} is being fetched. Assume that the branch does not take place. Then in the next microcycle, MI_{j+1} will be executed and MI_{j+2} will be fetched, which is correct. If the branch does take place, then MI_{j+1} will still be executed while MI_k is being fetched; this is perfectly legitimate, as can be seen from the original sequence. This kind of mechanism for correctly executing a branch appearing in an instruction (or microinstruction) pipeline is called *delayed branching* (Gross and Hennessey, 1982; see also Section 5.3 and Chapter 7).   ∎

Temporal Aspects of Microprograms in the von Neumann Model

We have already described one aspect of timing in micro-architectures: the overlapping of FETCH and EXECUTE and the fact that the overall microcycle duration is the larger of these two phases. The other aspect that must be addressed is the temporal attributes of the individual MOs, since this will also determine the extent of potential parallelism in the micro-architecture and the space and execution time requirements of microprograms.

The basic temporal structure of MOs in this design is organized around the following ideas.

1.   During a single microcycle it must be possible to read the contents of micromachine registers into the ALU, perform an ALU operation, and write the result of the operation back into a register (see Fig. 5.1).
2.   It is assumed that all register-to-register MOs (those encoded in fields F2 through F10, see Table 5.1) require the same amount of time and that this is less (being less complex) than the duration of ALU operations (those encoded in field F11).
3.   Because of differences in processor and memory technologies (see Chapter 2), the main memory read/write time will be an integral multiple of the microcyle time. The duration of main memory MOs will be termed a *memory cycle* (see Chapter 2, Section 2.5.1, for further discussion of the memory cycle time) and is assumed to be some multiple of the microcycle.

To satisfy these requirements, the microcycle for the von Neumann machine (denoted as "MU") is structured as a three-phase cycle, the phases being identified as "ph1," "ph2," and "ph3" (Fig. 5.11). Each MO in Table 5.1 (with the exception of the main memory MOs) is executable in a specific phase of MU. This temporal property of an MO is called its *timing attribute*; For the MOs of

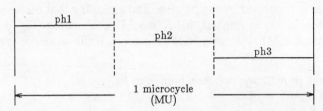

FIGURE 5.11 Structure of the von Neumann machine microcycle.

the von Neumann machine, these timing attributes are listed in the appropriate column of Table 5.1. The timing attributes of main memory read/write are, of course, both defined by the memory cycle. The precise duration of the microcycle and its phases, and of the memory cycle, are left unspecified in this design.

A microcycle of the type shown in Figure 5.11, which is composed of several phases, is termed a *polyphase* microcycle (see Section 5.3 for more on this).

You will notice that the description of the microcycle is an abstraction of the physical clocking system that may, in reality, be required in the implementation of this architecture. As far as the specification of micro-architectures are concerned, such abstract descriptions of the clocks are sufficient.

5.2.4 Microprogramming the von Neumann Micro-Architecture

Thus far (in Sections 5.2.1 and 5.2.3), the micro-architecture of the von Neumann machine has been developed. What now remains is to write the microprogram for this machine and thereby implement the von Neumann instruction set shown in Table 4.1. To simplify and shorten our task slightly, three of these instructions will not be implemented.

As in the case of software design and implementation, it is extremely convenient and desirable to be able to specify microprograms in an abstract, symbolic notation that is, to some extent, independent of the architectural details of the micromachine itself. Indeed, the design and implementation of *microprogramming languages* has been a focus of considerable research since the early 1970s (Dasgupta, 1980; Sint, 1980; Dasgupta and Shriver, 1985; Davidson, 1986). Some of the important results of this research program is described at length in Volume 2, Chapter 5.[9] For our immediate purposes, I introduce, again without any justification or explanation at this time, part of a language called S* (VN), which will be used to describe the microprogram.[10]

---

[9]See also Section 3.2.1 and Table 3.1 in Chapter 3 of Volume 2 for a discussion of microprogramming languages in the broader context of hardware-description languages.

[10]S*(VN) is actually a machine-specific instantiation of a general *microprogramming language schema* called S* (Dasgupta, 1980, 1984; see also Volume 2, Chapter 5, Section 5.3.2). That is, the schema S* has been particularized with respect to the von Neumann machine, thus resulting in the von Neumann machine-specific language S*(VN). S* and the two architecture description languages S*A (Dasgupta, 1983, 1984) and S*M (see Volume 2, Chapter 4, Section 4.3; see also Dasgupta, Wilsey, and Heinanen, 1986; Wilsey, 1985) are members of a family of languages that have been developed by Dasgupta and colleagues over a period of years to investigate various aspects of the architecture design process.

The relevant constructs of S* (VN) may be summarized as follows.

1. There are only two *primitive* statement types in S* (VN), the assignment type and the control type.
2. The only *assignment* statements allowed in an S* (VN) program are those shown in Table 5.1. Thus, the set of legal assignments in S* (VN) are, functionally, exactly identical to the repertoire of data-path MOs in the von Neumann micromachine.
3. The only *control* statements allowed in an S* (VN) program are

    if ISI = 1 then goto L fi
    if ISI = 0 then goto L fi
    if ACC.sign = 1 then goto L fi
    if ACC.sign = 0 then goto L fi
    goto L

    where L is a statement label. The legal control statements in this language, thus, are functionally identical to the branch MOs in the von Neumann micromachine (see Fig. 5.7). The notation "ACC.sign" denotes the sign bit of the variable named "ACC."
4. Because of the restrictions on legal assignments and control statements, the only variables that can appear in an S* (VN) program are those appearing in these primitive statements. These correspond to the stores visible at the micro-architectural level (Fig. 5.1). In a completely specified S* (VN) program, one would have to declare all referenced variables and define their *data types.* We will ignore this aspect for the present.
5. Assignment statements can be *composed* to form more complex statements using either the *sequencing* operator ";" or the *parallel* operator "||." The composite statement

    $$S_1 \; ; \; S_2$$

    means as usual that statement S_2 begins after statement S_1 terminates. The composite statement

    $$S_1 \; || \; S_2$$

    means that statements S_1, S_2 begin together. Note that S_1, S_2 may themselves be composite statements. Where there is any chance of ambiguity in the interpretation of such composites, the delimiters **do** . . . **od** are used as in

    $$\textbf{do } S_1 \; || \; S_2 \textbf{ od; } S_3; \textbf{ do } S_4 \; || \; S_5 \textbf{ od}$$

6. Given a (primitive or composite) statement S, the **cocycle** statement

    cocycle S coend

    indicates that the statement enclosed between the **cocycle** and the **coend** is initiated in a "new" microcycle—the duration of which is defined by the von Neumann machine itself; furthermore, S terminates in the same microcycle in which it is initiated. S can be a composite, so that we may have either of the forms

cocycle $S_1 \,||\, S_2$ coend
cocycle S_1 ; S_2 coend

In the first case S_1, S_2 will be initiated together in a new microcycle. They may not terminate together but will both terminate within the microcycle. In the second form, S_1 will begin and end before S_2 begins, but the statement sequence as a whole will begin and terminate in one microcycle.

7. Whereas a **cocycle** allows the S* (VN) user to specify actions that are completed within a microcycle, the **stcycle** construct allows for the specification of actions requiring two or more microcycles. The general form is

stcycle S **stend**

where S is a primitive, a composite, a **cocycle**, or another **stcycle** statement. It indicates that S is initiated in a new microcycle; however, nothing is stated about when S terminates. This can only be inferred from the specifics of S.

8. Finally, an S* (VN) *program block* is composed of a sequence of **cocycle** and **stcycle** statements interspersed, if necessary, with comments delimited by the symbols "/*" and "*/".

It is assumed that an S* (VN) program will be *compiled* into *object microcode* in a loadable form.

Using S* (VN), we can now describe the microprogram implementing the exo-architecture of the von Neumann machine. This is shown in Figure 5.12. Several explanatory comments must be made about this microprogram.

1. **[General]** Because of the overlapping of microinstruction FETCH and EXECUTE in this micromachine, the compiler must ensure that whenever a control statement is compiled into a branch microinstruction this must be followed by either a legitimate microinstruction (see Example 5.3) or a NOP (see Example 5.2). Thus, the S* (VN) compiler must have some *optimizing capabilities* that will allow it to analyze the microcode and reorder microinstructions as illustrated in Example 5.3, or insert a NOP microinstruction if no satisfactory reordering can be achieved. Microcode optimization and other aspects of the design and implementation of microprogramming languages are further discussed in Volume 2, Chapter 5.

2. **[inst_fetch1]** In this routine, ISI is set to 0 to indicate that the first of the two instructions that have just been fetched is yet to be processed. The first instruction has been loaded into FR and the second into CR. When the last **cocycle** in this microroutine has been executed, the opcode part of the instruction in FR (see Fig. 5.1) is transmitted to MAT and the starting address of the corresponding microroutine (in control memory) is read out from MAT into CAR (see Fig. 5.6). As noted in comment 1., when this S* (VN) routine is compiled into object microcode, the **stcycle** and **cocycle** statements will each be translated into a single microinstruction and an additional NOP microinstruction will be automatically generated to follow the last **cocycle** statement. A Gantt chart for "inst_fetch1" is shown in Figure 5.13.

inst_fetch1: /* this microroutine is responsible for fetching inst. from main memory into processor; it assumes that the next instruction pair to be accessed is contained in memory at address specified in CC */

    cocycle
      FR.addr := CC
    coend;
    stcycle
      SR := Mem[FR.addr] || CC := CC + 1
    stend;
    cocycle
      FR := SR.high || CR := SR.low || ISI := 0
    coend;

inst_fetch2: /* this microroutine is responsible for preparing the second inst. fetched into CR for interpretation */

    cocycle
      ISI := 1 || FR := CR
    coend

load_acc: /* microroutine for LD inst */

    stcycle SR := Mem[FR.addr] **stend**;
    cocycle ACC := SR **coend**;

which_fetch:

    cocycle if ISI = 0 **then goto** inst_fetch2 **fi**
    coend;
    cocycle goto inst_fetch1 **coend**;

load_acc_neg: /* microroutine for LDN inst. */

    stcycle SR := Mem[FR.addr] **stend**;
    cocycle ACC := SR **coend**;
    cocycle
      if ACC.sign = 0 **then goto** acc_pos **fi**
    coend;

    /* ACC.sign = 1; change to 0 by shifting out sign bit and shifting in 0 into sign bit position */

acc_neg: **cocycle**
      AIR := ACC;
      SHOL @ AOUT := **shl** AIR by 1;
      WORK := AOUT

FIGURE 5.12 **Microprogram for the von Neumann machine described in S∗(VN). (Part 1 of 5)** *(Continued)*

```
                      coend;
                      cocycle
                        AIR := WORK;
                        AOUT @ SHOR := shr AIR by 1;
                        ACC := AOUT
                      coend;
                      cocycle goto which_fetch coend

                      /* ACC.sign = 0; change to 1 */
acc_pos:              cocycle
                        do AIL := ACC || AIR := '10...0' od;
                        AOUT := AIL ∨ AIR;
                        ACC := AOUT
                      coend;
                      cocycle goto which_fetch coend

load_reg:             /* microroutine for LDR inst */
                      stcycle SR := Mem[FR.addr] stend;
                      cocycle REG := SR coend;
                      cocycle goto which_fetch coend

load_acc_from_reg:    /* microroutine for LDAR inst */
                      cocycle
                        AIR := REG;
                        AOUT := AIR;
                        ACC := AOUT
                      coend;
                      cocycle goto which_fetch coend

load_acc_abs:         /* microroutine for LDAB inst */
                      stcycle SR := Mem[FR.addr] stend;
                      cocycle ACC := SR coend;
                      /* in order to load the acc. with abs. value of acc., microroutine
                         identical to 'acc_neg' part of 'load_acc_neg' */
                      cocycle goto acc_neg coend

store_acc:            /* microroutine for ST inst. */
                      cocycle SR := ACC coend;
                      stcycle Mem[FR.addr] := SR stend;
                      cocycle goto which_fetch coend

add:                  /* microroutine for ADD inst. */
                      stcycle SR := Mem[FR.addr] stend;
                      cocycle
                        do AIL := SR || AIR := ACC od;
                        AOUT := AIL + AIR;
                        ACC := AOUT
                      coend;
                      cocycle goto which_fetch coend;
```

FIGURE 5.12   Microprogram for the von Neumann machine described in S∗(VN). (Part 2 of 5)

```
sub:                /* microroutine for SUB inst */
                    stcycle SR := Mem[FR.addr] stend;
                    cocycle
                       do AIL := SR || AIR := ACC od;
                       AOUT := AIL - AIR;
                       ACC := AOUT
                    coend;
                    cocycle goto which_fetch coend;


shift_left:         /* microroutine for SHL inst. */
                    cocycle
                       AIR := ACC;
                       SHOL @ AOUT := shl AIR;
                       ACC := AOUT
                    coend;
                    cocycle goto which_fetch coend;


shift_right:        /* microroutine for SHR inst. */
                    cocycle
                       AIR := ACC;
                       AOUT @ SHOR := shr AIR;
                       ACC := AOUT
                    coend;
                    cocycle goto which_fetch coend;


add_abs:            /* microroutine for ADDAB inst */
                    stcycle SR := Mem[FR.addr] stend;
                    cocycle WORK := SR coend;
                    /* find abs. value of fetched operand */
                    cocycle
                       AIR := WORK;
                       SHOL @ AOUT := shl AIR by 1;
                       WORK := AOUT
                    coend;
                    cocycle
                       AIR := WORK;
                       AOUT @ SHOR := shr AIR by 1;
                       WORK := AOUT
                    coend;
                    cocycle
                       do AIL := WORK || AIR := ACC od;
                       AOUT := AIL + AIR;
                       ACC := AOUT
                    coend;
                    cocycle goto which_fetch coend;


sub_abs:            /* microroutine for SUBAB inst. */
                    stcycle SR := Mem[FR.addr] stend;
                    cocycle WORK := SR coend;
```

FIGURE 5.12   **Microprogram for the von Neumann machine described in S*(VN). (Part 3 of 5)** *(Continued)*

```
                /* find abs. value of fetched operand */
                cocycle
                   AIR := WORK;
                   SHOL @ AOUT := shl AIR by 1;
                   WORK := AOUT
                coend;
                cocycle
                   AIR := WORK;
                   AOUT @ SHOR := shr AIR by 1;
                   WORK := AOUT
                coend;
                cocycle
                   do AIL := WORK || AIR := ACC od;
                   AOUT := AIR - AIL;
                   ACC := AOUT
                coend;
                cocycle goto which_fetch coend;
```

```
branch_left:    /* microroutine for BRL inst */
                cocycle CC := FR.addr coend;
                cocycle goto inst_fetch1 coend;
```

```
branch_right:   /* microroutine for BRR inst */
                cocycle CC := FR.addr coend
                stcycle
                   SR := Mem[FR.addr] || CC := CC + 1
                stend;
                cocycle
                   FR := SR.low || ISI := 1
                coend;
```

```
branch_left_pos:  /* microroutine for BRLP inst. */
                  cocycle
                     if ACC.sign = 0 then goto branch_left fi
                  coend;
                  cocycle goto which_fetch coend;
```

```
branch_right_pos: /* microroutine for BRRP inst. */
                  cocycle
                     if ACC.sign = 0 then goto branch_right fi
                  coend;
                  cocycle go to which_fetch coend;
```

```
store_partial_right: /* microroutine for STPRTR inst. */
                     /* first adjust ACC contents till the left hand 12 bits are aligned to
                        bit positions 19..8; while this is being done fetch target inst.
                        from main mem */
```

FIGURE 5.12 **Microprogram for the von Neumann machine described in S∗(VN). (Part 4 of 5)**

```
stcycle
  SR := Mem[FR.addr]
  ‖
cocycle
  AIR := ACC;
  AOUT @ SHOR := shr AIR by 28;
  WORK := AOUT
coend;
cocycle
  AIR := WORK;
  SHOL @ AOUT := shl AIR by 8;
  WORK := AOUT
coend
stend;
/* store 12 ACC bits in target inst. */
cocycle
  do AIL := SR ‖ AIR := WORK od;
  AOUT := AIL mask AIR [19..8];
  SR := AOUT
coend;
stcycle Mem[FR.addr] := SR stend;
cocycle goto which_fetch coend;
```

store_partial_left: /* microroutine for STPRTL inst. */
```
stcycle
  SR := Mem[FR.addr]
stend;
cocycle
  do AIL := SR ‖ AIR := ACC od;
  AOUT := AIL mask AIR [39..28];
  SR := AOUT
coend;
stcycle
  Mem[FR.addr] := SR
stend;
cocycle goto which_fetch coend
```

FIGURE 5.12   Microprogram for the von Neumann machine described in S∗(VN). (Part 5 of 5)

3. **[inst_fetch2]** ISI is set to 1 to indicate that the second instruction, having been transferred from CR to FR, is to be processed. As in "inst_fetch1," on completion of this microroutine CAR is loaded with the starting address of the microroutine for the instruction to be executed.

4. **[which_fetch]** The sequence of two statements at label "which_fetch" will be executed immediately after the execution of all the instruction-executing microroutines (except "branch_left" and "branch_right") in order to determine to which of the instruction fetch microroutines ("inst_fetch1" or "inst

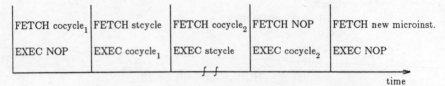

FIGURE 5.13   Gantt chart for *inst_fetch1* microroutine.

fetch2") to branch. If the instruction just executed was the first of the two instructions fetched previously from main memory—and this is indicated by the condition "ISI = 0"—then control must transfer to "inst-fetch2." If the instruction just executed was the second of the two instructions fetched previously from main memory—and this is indicated by the condition "ISI = 1"—then control must transfer to "inst-fetch1."

5. **[branch_right]**   This microroutine both executes the BRR instruction, then fetches the word containing the new target instruction of the branch, and prepares the instruction in FR for execution.

6. **[store partial right]**   In this microroutine the first (memory read) operation is initiated in a new microcycle (as indicated by the **stcycle**). The duration of this operation is a memory cycle that is assumed to be some (unspecified) multiple of the microcycle duration. Thus, rather than wait for the memory operation to complete, additional MOs are executed in succeeding microcycles (as indicated by the two consecutive **cocycle** statements). The third **cocycle** in this routine will only begin when all the operations preceding it in the text have terminated. A timing diagram for the first part of this microroutine is shown in Figure 5.14; this assumes that the memory cycle is more than two microcycles in duration.

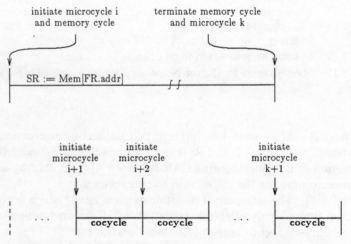

FIGURE 5.14   Timing diagram for part of *store partial right*.

Using the microinstruction formats shown in Figure 5.7 and the field encodings indicated in Table 5.1, it is easy to determine the contents of the control memory when it holds the translated object code form of this microprogram. Each of the **cocycle** and all but one of the **stcycle** statements shown in Figure 5.12 will be translated into a microstruction and will occupy a single microword. The only exception is the first **stcycle** in "store-partial-right", which will occupy three microinstructions, the first holding the "SR := Mem[FR.addr]" MO, the second and third encoding the two enclosed **cocycle** statements. Note that whenever a **cocycle** is of the form

cocycle S_1; S_2; S_3 **coend**

it indicates that S_1, S_2, and S_3 execute sequentially within the microcycle. Such statements are only legal if, in fact, the timing attributes of S_1, S_2, S_3 are, respectively MU.ph1, MU.ph2, and MU.ph3. Similarly, whenever a **cocycle** is of the form

cocycle . . . S_1 || S_2 **coend**

then S_1, S_2 are executed in parallel; such parallelism is only legal if, in fact, S_1, S_2 have identical or overlapping timing attributes.

The total size of the microprogram *as specified* is 68 microwords. When translated into object microcode, some additional NOP microinstructions will be inserted in order for the fetch-execute pipeline to function correctly when branches are executed.

5.3 ARCHITECTURAL ASPECTS OF MICROPROGRAMMING

Having described, more or less completely, a specific microprogrammed machine, we now consider the architectural aspects of microprogramming in a more general setting. As noted in Section 5.2.3, the three principal issues of interest are: *microinstruction sequencing*—the mechanisms for generating the address of the "next microinstruction"; *microinstruction organizations*—the formatting of microinstruction and the ways of encoding the state information (MOs) within them; and the *temporal aspects of microprograms.* It is important to note that these are by no means independent of one another. Design choices along any one of these dimensions will affect the choices at one's disposal along the other dimensions. Nevertheless, in the interest of clarity I will describe them as independently as possible.

Prior to a detailed consideration of these issues, however, one other aspect of microprogramming must be noted and that is the concept of a "control memory," which is, in an obvious sense, the *piece de résistance* of microprogrammed control units. Thus, I begin with this topic.

5.3.1 The Control Memory

A "Working" Definition

From a functional viewpoint, the control memory (Fig. 5.6) is the store *from which microprograms are executed*. Given that a microprogram interprets instructions residing in main memory, and that a MCU must be sufficiently fast so as to be competitive with hardwired control units, you would assume that the control memory is physically distinct from main memory. Most microprogrammed computers, in fact, contain such a two-level memory hierarchy with programs (software) held in main store and microprograms (firmware) held in a relatively smaller but faster control memory (Fig. 5.15).[11,12]

There are, however, some notable exceptions to this archetypal scheme.

Example 5.4

In one model of the Burroughs B1700/B1800 family of *user microprogrammable* computers (Wilner, 1972a, 1972b; Organick and Hinds, 1978),[13] namely the B1710, there is no separate control store. Instead, software and firmware share the same main store (Fig. 5.16). In another model of this same family, the B1726, microprograms reside in main memory or in a separate control memory, and can be executed from either (Fig. 5.17). ∎

Example 5.5

The IBM System/360 Model 25 was one of the low performance members of the IBM System/360 family (Tucker, 1967; Husson, 1970). This was also the only member of the 360 family in which the main store served as a repository of firmware as well as software: control memory, in this case, was the high-order 16K bytes of main store. ∎

Example 5.6

The Nanodata QM-1 (Nanodata, 1979; Salisbury, 1976; Dasgupta, 1984) is, like the Burroughs B1700, a `user microprogrammable (universal-host) machine.

---

[11]We are simplifying matters somewhat here: A computer system has, in general, a much more elaborate memory hierarchy than that shown in Figure 5.15 (see chapter 8). We are only identifying the components of such a hierarchy that are relevant to this discussion.

[12]The word *firmware* appears to be from Opler (1967). It was coined as a synonym for "microprogram" to emphasize the relationship of microprograms with programs (software) and circuits (hardware). *Firmware engineering*, a term first used around 1978 (Davidson and Shriver, 1978), is now a well-established subdiscipline at the intersection of computer architecture, microprogramming, software technology, design automation, and hardware description languages, and is concerned with the development of a scientific foundation for microprogramming (Dasgupta and Shriver, 1985; Dasgupta and Mueller, 1986). It forms the topic of Volume 2, Chapter 5.

[13]More precisely, these computers are regarded as *universal host machines*, which are discussed in Section 5.4.

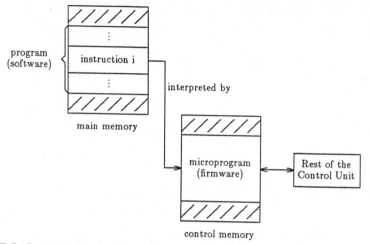

FIGURE 5.15 Archetypal two-level memory hierarchy in microprogrammed computers.

This computer has *two* levels of control (Fig. 5.18). The higher level stores narrow (18-bit wide) microinstructions (also called generically, *vertical* microinstructions—see Section 5.3.3) in a control store. Such control-store resident microprograms can interpret instructions contained in main store. The second and lower level of control allows the user to write very wide (360-bits) "nanoinstructions" (which fall under the generic category of *horizontal* microinstructions—see Section 5.3.3). An ordered sequence of such nanoinstructions, called a "nanoprogram," resides in the QM-1 "nanostore" and interprets microinstructions from the control store.

Main memory instructions may also be interpreted directly by a nanoprogram so that in implementing an exo-architecture, the microprogrammer may choose to write the firmware using the QM-1's (vertical) microinstruction repertoire only, its (horizontal) nanoinstruction repertoire only, or a combination of the two. ∎

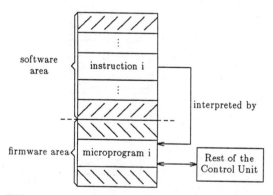

FIGURE 5.16 Memory hierarchy in the B1710.

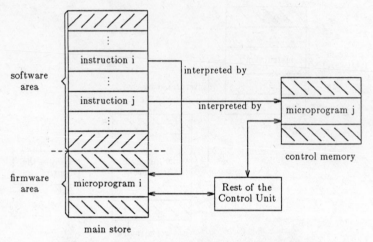

FIGURE 5.17 Memory hierarchy in the B1726.

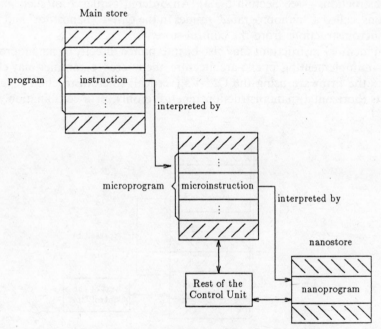

FIGURE 5.18 Two-level control memory in the QM-1.

For our purposes, a *control memory* will be characterized as a store in which microprograms reside and the organization, design, and technology of which is determined solely from the perspective of microprogramming. Furthermore, between the microinstructions in the control memory and the resources that they control in the processor there exists no more than a buffer register (the MIR) and some amount of decoding logic (Manville, 1973; Dasgupta, 1979).

Thus, in the case of the B1710, the fact that microprograms reside in the same store as programs does not pose any real problem. As long as microinstructions are accessed, decoded, and executed directly from it and the internal organization of this memory was determined as much by microprogramming as by programming considerations, the B1710 main store is both control memory and main memory.

By these same characteristics, the QM-1 control store does not qualify as a control memory, since there is an additional level of interpretation between the microinstructions in control store and the hardware resources that they control.

Types of Control Memory

We have already pointed out that the most important performance characteristic of the control memory is its speed — more precisely, its access and cycle times.[14] Because of this, up to the early 1970s control memories were almost invariably implemented in the form of the faster *read only memories* (ROMs), since the speed/cost characteristics of *random access memories* (RAMs) were unacceptable from the viewpoint of implementing control memories (see Sections 2.5.1 through 2.5.3, Chapter 2, for discussions and comparisons of RAMs and ROMs). In the early to mid-1970s, however, memory technology had sufficiently advanced so that *writable control stores* (WCSs) with the desired speed characteristics had become economically viable. Thus, control memories may now be implemented in the form of ROMs, WCSs, or a combination of the two.

The main technological distinction between ROMs and RAMs that is of interest from the microprogramming perspective is, of course, that the contents of a WCS can be altered dynamically — while the machine is in operation — whereas those of a ROM cannot. There are at least two important consequences of this.

1. Microcode should, ideally, be implemented in ROM when it is not likely to be changed (if at all) over a significant period of time.[15] Microcode should also be implemented in ROM when its security is of importance. On the other hand, whenever there is the possibility of relatively frequent changes to

---

[14]These characteristics of memory are discussed in Section 2.5.1, Chapter 2. Briefly stated, the *access time* t_A is the maximum time required to access a word from memory whereas the *cycle time* t_C is the minimum time between the initiation of two successive memory operations. For more on this, see Section 2.5.1.

[15]See Section 2.5.1 for a discussion of how ROMs are programmed.

microcode, or where user-microprogramming is an important objective, then the control memory must, in part at least, be of the writable type.

2. A read-only control memory is not merely a memory device; it is a memory device that already contains (one or more) microprograms. Thus, the internal organization of the ROM microwords will be strongly influenced not only by the nature of the data path that the control unit is to manipulate, but also by the microprogram itself. A ROM organization can, in principle, be determined *after* the microprogram specification has been completed so as to obtain the most economic encoding of the microcode with respect to both space and execution time.

In contrast, a writable control store is an empty memory—a *tabula rasa*: The user will use the available microinstruction repertoire and formats to develop his or her own firmware and load it into the control memory. The control memory exists *before* the microprograms, which, in addition, may vary over time. Thus, the internal organization of WCSs (microinstruction organizations, encoding of MOs in the microinstruction, and the representation of sequencing information) can only be determined on the basis of the data-path structure and such other issues as flexibility and ease of user-microprogramming.

Finally, it should be noted that as a result of developments in LSI/VLSI technologies (see Chapter 2) an alternative to the use of ROMs (wherever, that is, ROMs are preferred to WCSs) is the application of *programmable logic arrays* (PLAs). Section 2.5.4, Chapter 2, gives an overview of PLAs and their relationship to ROMs.

5.3.2 Microinstruction Sequencing

In this section we discuss the mechanisms for sequencing from one microinstruction to the next during the execution of a microprogram. As in almost all facets of microprogramming, the primary concern is to make this mechanism as efficient as possible so as to minimize the delay between the accessing and execution of successive microinstructions.

The sequencing mechanism employed in any particular computer will depend enormously on a number of factors, notably the desired flexibility in changing the flow of control through a microprogram, the amount of hardware the designer is willing to devote to sequencing logic, and the extent to which the events in the processor data path may influence sequencing decisions. Thus, as in so many other aspects of computer architecture, the spectrum of design choices is considerable. I will, however, limit the discussion to a few distinct and significant elements in this spectrum.

In following the discussion below, it is useful to keep in mind that there are really two aspects to the sequencing problem:

1. Where and in what form should the "next microinstruction address" information reside?
2. How can this information be used to access the relevant microinstruction in control memory rapidly and economically?

The Wilkes Model

In Wilkes's original model (Wilkes, 1951; Wilkes and Stringer, 1953; Wilkes, Renwick, and Wheeler, 1958), the next address information is given explicitly in each microinstruction. A slightly abstract version of this scheme is depicted in Figure 5.19. If the next address to be selected depends on some external conditions, then the two alternative next addresses would both have to be explicitly specified. In Figure 5.19 these are shown as belonging to the same microinstruction, which, coupled with the fact that the next addresses are stated in the same word as the MOs, makes the potential width of the microword in any realistic machine considerably large.

During the execution of a microinstruction (enabled by a clock pulse CP_2), the next address information is loaded into an auxiliary register (AUX_CAR). After sufficient time has elapsed for the MOs to execute and the new value in AUX-_CAR to stabilize, a second clock pulse CP_1 transfers the next address from AUX_CAR to CAR. In modern terms, the microinstruction interpretation cycle (see Section 5.2.3) is strictly serial:

```
repeat
    CP₂:   ⎧ Decode CAR;
           ⎨ Read microinstruction from control memory into MIR;
           ⎩ Execute microinstruction;
    CP₁:     Update CAR from AUX_CAR
until halt
```

Since each microinstruction contains the address of its successor, microinstructions can be placed anywhere in memory. The microprogram is effectively a linked list.

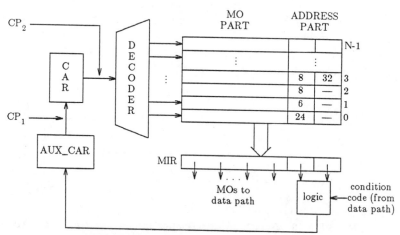

FIGURE 5.19 Sequencing in Wilkes's model.

Implicit Sequencing

If the microinstructions of a microprogram are held in successive words of the control memory, then the only time the next address information needs to be provided explicitly is when a branch is to be specified. During the "normal" sequential flow of control through the microprogram, the control memory address register (CAR) will simply be incremented by 1. However, in the event of a branch within the microprogram, the branch address explicitly specified in the microinstruction will be loaded into CAR.

This was the scheme used in the von Neumann machine in Section 5.2.3. In fact, in this design there were two microinstruction types: one for encoding nonbranch MOs, the other for the specification of branch MOs (Fig. 5.7). One disadvantage of the second format, as can be seen from Figure 5.7 (*b*), is the amount of the microword that is unused. Furthermore, if we examine the microprogram described in Figure 5.12, we note that

1. Three of the microroutines ("which_fetch," "branch_right_positive," "branch_left_positive") end with the sequence

    cocycle if . . . **then goto** . . . **fi coend;**
    cocycle goto . . . **coend**

2. The execution of almost all the instruction-interpreting microroutines involves execution of the sequence:

    cocycle goto which_fetch **coend**
    which_fetch: **cocycle if** ISI = 0 **then goto** inst_fetch2 **coend;**
    cocycle goto inst_fetch1 **coend**

It is possible to make the branching mechanism more efficient in both use of space and executional time — at the cost of some extra hardware — by modifying the type II (branch) format so that up to *two* sequential branch MOs may be represented. This possibility is shown in Figure 5.20. When such a microinstruction is executed, if the condition specified in field F_1 is found to be true, then the next address information is taken from Address field 1; if the condition specified in field F_2 evaluates to true, the next address is extracted from Address field 2.

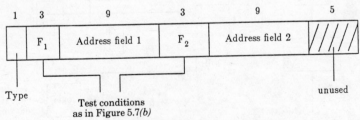

FIGURE 5.20 Branch microinstruction format with two branch MOs.

Only when neither of the conditions is true does control transfer to the next sequential microinstruction.

Nonbranch MOs often use literals as immediate operands. In the von Neumann machine, some such literals were hardwired into the constant table CT. A more flexible arrangement at the possible cost of extra microword bits is to provide one or more *literal fields* in the microword itself. In such cases, a shared next address/literal field may be organized in the microword so that separate formats for nonbranch and branch microinstructions are unnecessary (Fig. 5.21). The contents of the address/literal field is interpreted by the decoding logic as a literal (or one or more literals) or as a branch address, depending on the value of some other field—such as the branch condition (BC) field itself.

As in the Wilkes model, the microinstruction interpretation cycle may be strictly serial. However, a more efficient mechanism—used in the von Neumann machine implementation (see Section 5.2.3)—would overlap the FETCH phase of one microinstruction with the EXECUTE phase of the previous one.[16] As seen in Section 5.2.3, this necessitated the use of *delayed branching* to avoid disrupting the pipeline when branches are executed. An additional issue that must be considered in the hardware implementation of this mechanism is to ensure that the "new" (fetched) microinstruction is not actually loaded into MIR until the control signals from the "current" microinstruction in MIR have been issued for the required time to effect correct executions of the micro-operations.

Multiway Branching

The foregoing discussion of branching within a microprogram has been limited to the possibility of at most two alternative paths of control at any branch point. In actual fact, it is often necessary for control to be transferred to one of *several* control store locations, depending on the value of some field in the microinstruction. In other words, microprograms will contain, not only the equivalent of the statement

if B then goto L₁ else goto L₂ fi

[16]Recall, from Section 5.2.3, that FETCH collectively refers to the updating of the CAR and the fetching of a microinstruction from the control memory into MIR; EXECUTE collectively refers to the decoding and execution of the microinstruction in the MIR.

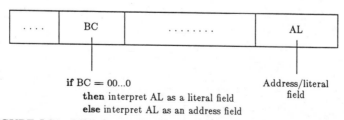

FIGURE 5.21   Microinstruction format with shared address/literal field.

but also the equivalent of **case** statements of the form

case var **of**
   V_1 : **goto** L_1
   V_2 : **goto** L_2
   . . . . . .
   V_n : **goto** L_n
endcase

Thus, it becomes necessary to implement some sort of a *multiway branch* mechanism to deal with such situations.

One possibility, of course, is to generalize the format of Fig. 5.20 to the case of $n > 2$ alternative branch addresses, where n will be determined by the sizes of the address fields and the total width of the microword.

A second possibility is as follows. Suppose it is required to implement an n-way branch where $n = 2^k$ for some positive integer k, and k is the size in bits of a status store SS somewhere in the processor. Depending on the $n = 2^k$ possible values of SS, control must transfer to one of n locations in the microprogram.

In this situation, when executing a branch MO, the k-bit value of SS may be logically appended at the *low-order* end of the branch address field in the MIR in order to generate one of 2^k alternative *consecutive* control memory addresses. Alternatively, supposing that the address field in the microinstruction is M-bits long, the k-bit SS value may be logically attached at the *high-order* end of the branch address field in order to generate one of 2^k alternative control memory addresses *that are 2^M words apart*.

Other possible variations of these basic themes will, no doubt, occur to you.

Example 5.7

Suppose that status store SS is $k = 2$-bits long, and the branch address field in the microinstruction is $M = 8$-bits long. Then Figure 5.22 shows, for a given

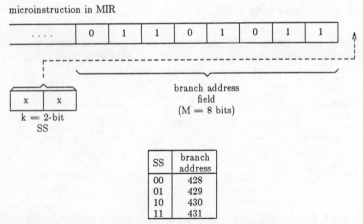

FIGURE 5.22 Appending SS bits at the low-order end of the branch address.

state of the branch address field as may be specified by the microprogrammer, the alternative addresses that may be generated when the SS bits are appended at the low-order end. The scheme effectively conforms to the **case** statement.

    case SS **of**
       0 : **goto** L
       1 : **goto** L + 1
       2 : **goto** L + 2
       3 : **goto** L + 3
    endcase

where L is the effect of concatenating the 8-bit branch address and the bit sequence '00'.

In contrast, Figure 5.23 shows the alternative addresses that would be generated when the SS value is appended at the high-order end of the address field. This scheme effectively conforms to

    case SS **of**
       0 : **goto** L'
       1 : **goto** $L' + 2^8$
       2 : **goto** $L' + 2^9$
       3 : **goto** $L' + 2^8 + 2^9$
    endcase

where L' is the value of the branch address field. ∎

Microsubroutining

Finally, it should be noted that, as in software, microprograms may also contain subroutines. In such a situation, the branch address field specifies the address of the microsubroutine and the MO, rather than being a branch, would be a subroutine CALL. The execution of the CALL MO would cause the value of CAR (possibly incremented by 1, depending on whether or not at the time of the CALL's execution it points to the currently executing microinstruction or the

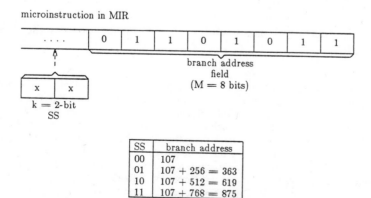

SS	branch address
00	107
01	107 + 256 = 363
10	107 + 512 = 619
11	107 + 768 = 875

FIGURE 5.23 **Appending SS bits at the high-order end of the branch address.**

next sequential microinstruction) to be pushed into a hardware *stack* (see also Chapter 6) before the subroutine address is loaded into CAR. Obviously, there must also be a RETURN type MO, which, when executed, pops the topmost value of the stack back into CAR in order to resume execution of the calling routine. The depth of the hardware stack in the micromachine will determine the allowed levels of nesting of microroutine calls.

5.3.3 Microinstruction Word Organizations

Determination of microinstruction word (or microword) organizations is yet another vital aspect of micro-architecture design; indeed, to such an extent that the two principal styles by which micromachines are characterized are based on categories of microword organizations.

As always in matters of design, microword organizations must take into account several mutually interacting constraints that have to be traded off against one another.

1. Minimization of the *microword length.*
2. Minimization of the number of microwords required to hold a microprogram; that is, the *microprogram size.*
3. Preservation of the data path's *potential parallelism.* That is, if the processor data path is such that two micro-operations can be executed in parallel, then the microword should be so organized as to permit the microprogrammer to exploit this parallelism.
4. Maximization of the *flexibility* of the organization. That is, the effect of a small change in the data-path design or in the microword itself should not necessitate a redesign of the microword organization. It should be possible to absorb such changes into the existing microword structure.

The two principal categories of microword organizations are named, respectively, *horizontal* and *vertical*.[17] It is important to note that there are no precise definitions of these terms; from a taxonomic viewpoint, these are by no means exact concepts. Nonetheless, they serve as very useful approximate categories for classifying microword organizations and, by implication, micro-architectures and microprogramming approaches.

Horizontal microword organizations exhibit one or more of the following characteristics.

[17]It is interesting to try and trace the origins of these terms. The first textbook on microprogramming (Husson, 1970) contains extensive discussions on microword organizations but has no references to these terms. Nor do two influential earlier papers (Flynn and MacLaren, 1967; Wilkes, 1969) contain any mention of them. To our knowledge, the earliest occurrences of "horizontal" and "vertical" appear in Rosin (1969b), in which the author defines the characteristics of *horizontal* and *vertical microprogramming* and suggests that these are the two principal approaches to microprogram control. By 1971, the concepts of horizontal and vertical microword organizations seemed to have become commonly accepted (Flynn and Rosin, 1971; Redfield, 1971). Redfield (1971) also used the terms *hard* and *soft* as synonyms for "horizontal" and "vertical" respectively.

1. They enable different resources (e.g., functional units, data paths) in the micromachine to be controlled independently from the same microinstruction. That is, a horizontal microinstruction may specify several concurrently executable MOs.
2. They lead to relatively large microword lengths—of the order of 64 to a few hundred bits.
3. They allow the microprogrammer to exercise control at the level of individual MOs.

Vertical microword organizations, in contrast, usually exhibit the following characteristics.

1. Microinstructions usually specify one or two MOs. Thus, they do not allow the microprogrammer to exploit to any great extent (if at all) the potential parallelism in the processor.
2. They result in relatively small microword lengths—of the order of 16 to 32 bits.
3. Sometimes, however, the word "vertical" is used to designate short microinstructions that do not allow the microprogrammer to exercise control at the level of individual MOs. Rather, a single vertical microinstruction may cause a particular *set* or *sequence* of MOs to be invoked.

I will describe different instances of these two types of organizations using the von Neumann micro-architecture of Figure 5.1, its associated list of MOs (Table 5.1), and the microprogram of Figure 5.12 to illustrate these ideas. I will ignore for the present the timing attributes of the MOs and assume that (1) a microcycle consists of a single undifferentiated phase—that is, it is a *monophase* microcycle; and (2) all MOs except main memory operations require exactly one microcycle for their execution.

Horizontal Organizations I: Direct Control

With these assumptions we can organize microwords such that there exists a bit in the microword *for every distinct* MO in the machine. For the von Neumann machine, then, the microword would consist of 44 bits, one for each of the nonbranch MOs (Table 5.1); 5 bits, one each for the five branch MOs [see Fig. 5.7(b)]; 9 bits for the address field, and at least 12 extra bits to hold the two mask bounds or the two shift amounts: a total of some 70 bits (Fig. 5.24). This is usually referred to as the method of *direct control*. The main advantage of this scheme is that there is no need to decode the contents of a microinstruction. Furthermore, the organization is quite flexible in that one may later change the microprogram without having to redesign the microword organization. Finally, all the potential parallelism in the data path is retained.

The disadvantages of this scheme are, however, considerable. First, excluding the space required to hold the branch address or the constants, if $M = \{m_1, m_2, \ldots, m_n\}$ is the set of all MOs, then the width of the resulting micro-

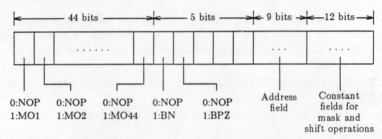

FIGURE 5.24 Direct-control organization.

word is n. For any reasonably sized machine the microword length would be prohibitively large.

Second, as you may easily verify, each microinstruction of a microprogram (such as the one implementing the von Neumann exo-architecture) will not specify more than a very small number of concurrently executable MOs. The resulting set of microwords will, thus, be very sparsely used.

For these reasons, direct control is, to our knowledge, rarely used alone in microword organizations. The scheme is chiefly of historic interest, since it was part of Wilkes's original proposal (Wilkes, 1951; Wilkes and Stringer, 1953) and was used in implementing the EDSAC-2 (Wilkes, Renwick, and Wheeler, 1958).

Horizontal Organizations II: Minimal Encoding

An organization that tries to combine the attractive properties of direct control —namely, its flexibility and its capacity to retain the inherent parallelism in the data path—with a more concise representation of MOs is the method of *minimal encoding*. The idea, here, is to encode within a single *field* a group of MOs that are *mutually exclusive* in the sense that it is known that these MOs are never, or can never be, executed simultaneously.

There are essentially two ways in which mutual exclusion information can be gathered. First, using the list of MOs M, and knowing about their resource requirements, the desired microprogram can be constructed in *control store independent* terms. In general, such a microprogram can be symbolized as a *sequence of parallel sets* of MOs:

$$\begin{aligned}
MI_1 &= \{m_{11}, m_{12}, \ldots, m_{1,n1}\} \\
MI_2 &= \{m_{21}, m_{22}, \ldots, m_{2,n2}\} \\
&\quad \ldots \ldots \ldots \ldots \ldots \ldots \ldots \ldots \ldots \ldots \\
MI_k &= \{m_{k1}, m_{k2}, \ldots, m_{k,nk}\}
\end{aligned} \tag{5.1}$$

where (1) $m_{11}, m_{12}, \ldots, m_{k,nk}$ are not all necessarily distinct and are all elements from the MO set M; and (2) it is desired to place each parallel set

$$MI_p = \{m_{p1}, m_{p2}, \ldots m_{p,np}\}$$

$(1 \leq p \leq k)$ into a distinct microword of the control memory. That is, each MI_p

is to be made a microinstruction. Note that any pair of MOs appearing in a MI_p must be completely disjoint in their resource requirements.

Based on the microprogram so formulated, if there exists an MO pair $m_i,m_j \in$ M that do not appear together in any of the parallel sets $MI_1, \ldots ,MI_k$, m_i,m_j will never be required to execute concurrently; m_i,m_j can then be encoded in the same set of bits.

One problem with this method is that it is not very flexible — in the sense that a change in the microprogram may cause MOs to be added or deleted from one or more of the MI_p's, thus altering the mutual exclusion information. Furthermore, this approach depends on prior construction of the microprogram, which may not always be possible — as in the design of microword organizations for writable control stores where it is the user who will implement the microprogram after the machine has been built.

Thus, an alternative approach is to gather mutual exclusion information from the list of MOs alone and from the knowledge of the resource requirements for these MOs. More specifically, if M is the set of MOs, then one can construct *a set of potentially parallel sets* of MOs:

$$PP_1 = \{m_{11},m_{12}, \ldots ,m_{1n1}\}$$
$$PP_2 = \{m_{21}m_{22}, \ldots ,m_{2n2}\}$$
$$\cdots\cdots\cdots\cdots\cdots\cdots\cdots\cdots\cdots \qquad (5.2)$$
$$PP_q = \{m_{q1},m_{q2}, \ldots ,m_{q,nq}\}$$

such that (1) $m_{11}, \ldots ,m_{q,nq}$ are not necessarily distinct and are all drawn from the MO set M; (2) every MO in M appears in at least one of the PP_k's ($1 \leq k \leq q$); and (3) it is desired that each of the PP_k's is potentially executable as a single microinstruction.

Note that, as in the case of the MI_p's (Equation 5.1), any pair of MOs appearing in a PP_k must be completely disjoint in their resource requirements.[18]

Thus, regardless of whether mutual exclusion information is based on Equation (5.1) or Equation (5.2), any group of r mutually exclusive MOs can be encoded in a single field. The encoding must allow each MO to be uniquely encoded. In addition, the condition where none of the r MOs from the group are to be executed (the NOP condition) must be provided for. A group of r mutually exclusive MOs can thus be encoded in

$$\lceil \log_2(r + 1) \rceil$$

---

[18]More precisely, let I_i,O_i denote the *input* and *output* data stores, respectively, for MO m_i; let U_i denote the set of functional units required to execute m_i. Then, under the assumption that all MOs execute in one (or possibly more) monophase microcycles, two MOs m_i,m_j are *potentially parallel* (i.e., can be executed without conflicts from the same microinstruction) if:

$$(I_i \cap O_j = \emptyset) \wedge (O_i \cap I_j = \emptyset) \wedge (O_i \cap O_j = \emptyset) \wedge (U_i \cap U_j = \emptyset)$$

is true, where $\emptyset$ is the empty set. If any one of these conditions is violated, m_i,m_j can never be executed in parallel.

bits.[19] The complete microword will, then, consist of a collection of such fields each encoded in this fashion (Fig. 5.25).

Example 5.8

The type I microinstruction organization in the von Neumann micromachine [see Table 5.1 and Fig. 5.7(a)] is based on minimal encoding. The basis for identifying mutually exclusive MOs is the list of MOs and the resources used by these MOs. The branch MO field F in the type II microinstruction also encodes the five mutually exclusive branch conditions in one field.

The 44 nonbranch MOs are represented in 29 rather than 44 bits, a 33% saving. Even if a single microword organization was to be adopted instead of two, only 32 bits would be required to represent all 49 MOs instead of the 49 bits needed in the direct-control scheme of Figure 5.24. ∎

Horizontal Organizations III: Optimal Minimal Encoding

It should be obvious that given a sequence (Equation 5.1) or a set (Equation 5.2) of parallel sets of MOs one can arrive at many different minimally encoded organizations, each one of which satisfies the urge to preserve potential parallelism and also achieves economy of encoding. Of all the possible solutions, there will be some that produce the *smallest width* of the microword; that is, there will be one or more *optimal* minimally encoded forms among the possible solutions.

Example 5.9

Consider as a very simple instance the parallel sets of MOs shown in Figure 5.26.

[19]The notation ⌈x⌉ signifies the least integer greater than x.

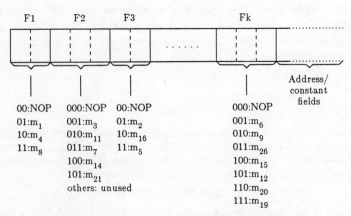

FIGURE 5.25   Minimally encoded organization.

$$PP_1 = \{m_1, m_3, m_5\}$$
$$PP_2 = \{m_2, m_4\}$$
$$PP_3 = \{m_1, m_3, m_8\}$$
$$PP_4 = \{m_1, m_5, m_7\}$$
$$PP_5 = \{m_1, m_4, m_6\}$$

FIGURE 5.26 **Parallel sets of MOs: An example.**

Several possible groupings of MOs and their encodings into minimally encoded fields are possible, for example

1. $F_1 = \{m_1, m_2\}$, $F_2 = \{m_3, m_6, m_7\}$, $F_3 = \{m_4, m_5, m_8\}$
2. $F_1 = \{m_1, m_2\}$, $F_2 = \{m_3, m_6\}$, $F_3 = \{m_4, m_5\}$, $F_4 = \{m_7, m_8\}$
3. $F_1 = \{m_1\}$, $F_2 = \{m_2, m_3, m_7\}$, $F_3 = \{m_4, m_5, m_8\}$, $F_4 = \{m_6\}$

The width of the resulting microwords are, respectively, 6 bits, 8 bits, and 6 bits. The minimal solution to this problem happens to be 6 bits, thus, both (1) and (3) are possible optimal solutions. ∎

Determination of such an optimal minimally encoded form can be formulated as a mathematical optimization problem as follows.

As before, based on the available information regarding the set of MOs, M, let

$$PP_1 = \{m_{11}, m_{12}, \ldots, m_{1n1}\}$$
$$PP_2 = \{m_{21}, m_{22}, \ldots, m_{2n2}\}$$
$$\cdots\cdots\cdots\cdots\cdots\cdots\cdots\cdots\cdots\cdots\cdots\cdots \qquad (5.3)$$
$$PP_q = \{m_{q1}, m_{q2} \ldots, m_{q,nq}\}$$

denote a collection of (potentially) parallel sets of MO.

A pair of MOs $m_i, m_j \in M$ is said to be *compatible* if m_i, m_j *never* appear in the same parallel set. A *compatible class* (CC) is any set of MOs that are pairwise compatible. Intuitively, a CC denotes a set of MOs that are pairwise mutually exclusive—that is, any two MOs in a CC never appear together in a single parallel set; they can, therefore, be encoded within the same microword field.

Example 5.10

Instances of compatible MOs for the parallel sets of Figure 5.26 are $\{m_1, m_2\}$, $\{m_3, m_4\}$, $\{m_6, m_7\}$. Examples of compatible classes are the sets $\{m_4, m_5, m_8\}$, $\{m_2, m_3, m_6, m_7\}$, $\{m_1, m_2\}$, and $\{m_2, m_6\}$

For a given collection of parallel sets (Equation 5.3), let $\{C_1, C_2, \ldots, C_k\}$ be a set of CCs such that each MO appearing in the parallel sets appears in one and exactly one CC. The CCs are, then, mutually exclusive and collectively exhaustive. Each C_i can be encoded in one microword field F_i the length of which B_i is

$$B_i = \lceil \log_2 (|C_i| + 1) \rceil \text{ bits}$$

where $|C_i|$ is the cardinality of the set C_i. The total length of the microword, excluding space for branch address/constants, is

$$B = \sum_{i=1}^{k} B_i$$

Then an *optimal* minimally encoded organization is one where the CCs, $\{C_1, C_2, \ldots, C_k\}$ are such that B is minimized. This is often referred to as the *microword length* or the *control memory width minimization* problem. It was originally formulated and solved by Schwartz (1968) and has subsequently been studied extensively, as reviewed in Dasgupta (1979). The problem has also been shown to be NP-complete (Robertson, 1979).

Note that the solution to the microword length minimization problem is subject to the constraint that each parallel set of MOs must be executed from one microinstruction. Thus, q, the number of parallel sets, and the parallelism in each of the parallel sets are fixed, and B is minimized under these constraints. It is quite possible, though, that this could result in a solution that leaves the majority of the fields unused in most of the microinstructions. If some of the parallelism is allowed to be reduced, a smaller microword length could well be obtained with an attendant improved use of the fields. Of course, the cost is an increase in the number of microinstructions.

Highly Encoded Vertical Organizations

From the perspective of performance—the time required to execute a microprogram—it is highly desirable to do as much of parallel processing as possible within each microinstruction. For this reason, most microprogrammed computers and many user-microprogrammable computers employ horizontal schemes. If, however, reducing the control memory width is a critical objective (if, for example, the control unit is placed on a separate chip from the data path), then horizontal organizations of the kind discussed previously may not produce sufficiently narrow microwords.

Furthermore, in the case of user-microprogrammable computers, *ease of microprogramming* becomes a design goal of considerable importance. Programming a horizontal machine where one has to keep track of, and exploit fully, the available parallelism can be a hazardous, error-prone task, especially when relatively primitive firmware development tools are used.[20]

Under such circumstances, vertical microword organizations may be chosen, the most common form of which is the *highly encoded* format. This organization is very similar to machine-language instruction formats at the exo-architectural level. Its most characteristic features are that the microwords are very narrow—usually in the range of 16 to 32 bits—and that each microinstruction in a microprogram specifies one or two MOs.

Example 5.11

Figures 5.27 through 5.30 show a repertoire of highly encoded microword

---

[20]See Volume 2, Chapter 5, for a detailed discussion of firmware design and implementation tools.

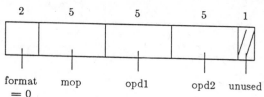

Interpretation Rule:
if format = 0
   then
      mop ∈ {TRANSFER}
      and interpret (opd1 as source, opd2 as result).

FIGURE 5.27   **Format 0 vertical microword for the von Neumann machine.**

organizations for the von Neumann micromachine of Section 5.2. Several aspects of these microwords are worth noting.

1. The length of microwords is 18 bits in contrast to the 30-bit minimally encoded form of Figure 5.7 and the 70-bit direct-control form of Figure 5.24.
2. The formats are very heavily encoded, as can be seen by the interpretation rules. Note that these rules would be implemented by decoding circuitry and the resulting decoding complexity will be somewhat higher than for the minimally encoded form.
3. In all but the format 1 organization, only one MO can be specified per microinstruction. When format 1 is used, up to three distinct MOs can be executed in parallel.
4. Interpretation of one field depends on the value of another field. This kind of a feature is often called *bit steering*. ∎

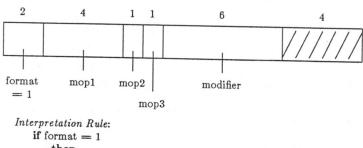

Interpretation Rule:
if format = 1
   then
      mop1 ∈ {ADD,SUB,OR,AND,EXCL_OR,NOT,SHL,SHR}
      mop2 ∈ {READ_MM, WRITE_MM}
      mop3 ∈ {INCR_CC}
   & **if** mop1 ∈ {SHL,SHR}
         then interpret (modifier as shift amount).

FIGURE 5.28   **Format 1 vertical microword for the von Neumann machine.**

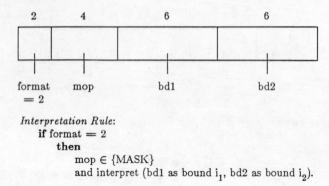

Interpretation Rule:
    if format = 2
        then
            mop ∈ {MASK}
            and interpret (bd1 as bound i_1, bd2 as bound i_2).

FIGURE 5.29   **Format 2 vertical microword for the von Neumann machine.**

Example 5.12

The Microdata 1600 (Microdata, 1970; Banerji and Raymond, 1982) is an example of a user microprogrammable computer where the highly encoded 16-bit wide vertical microword organization greatly enhanced the ease of user microprogramming.   ■

Example 5.13

In the case of the LSI-11, a minimal cost microcoded LSI implementation of the PDP-11 (Snow and Siewiorek, 1978), the data path is placed on one chip whereas the microcode is contained in two separate chips. Only 40 pins were available to carry signals between chips. Because of this, the microword length had to be kept to a minimum, at the sacrifice of parallelism, if necessary. The resulting microwords for the LSI-11 control store were highly encoded 22-bit entities.   ■

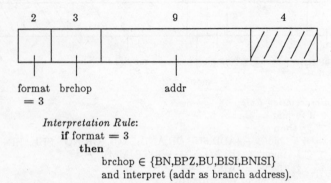

Interpretation Rule:
    if format = 3
        then
            brchop ∈ {BN,BPZ,BU,BISI,BNISI}
            and interpret (addr as branch address).

FIGURE 5.30   **Format 3 vertical microword for the von Neumann machine.**

Hybrid Organizations: Dual-Level Control Store

While discussing types of control memory in Section 5.3.1, mention was made of the QM-1 (Nanodata, 1979; Salisbury, 1976; Dasgupta, 1984), which is characterized by a two-level control store (Fig. 5.18). At the higher level, a repertoire of highly encoded 18-bit-wide microinstructions are defined. Each of these microinstructions is interpreted by low-level *nanoprograms* residing in a 360-bit wide *nanostore*. The microprogrammer may completely ignore this lower level and implement vertical microprograms that will reside in and be executed from the (vertical) control store.[21]

Alternatively, the user may program the machine at the "nanolevel" itself and write (horizontal) nanoprograms that will interpret instructions and operate on data residing either in main store or in the control store. When used in such a way, the QM-1 is a highly horizontal micromachine with an 18-bit wide main store and an 18-bit wide large (8K) local store.

Quite a different motivation underlies the use of a dual-level control store in the Motorola 68000 (Stritter and Tredennick, 1978). The concept used an idea originally proposed 15 years earlier by Grasselli (1962). Recall (from Section 5.2.2) that a microinstruction encodes a *control state*. In a single-level control store, a microprogram residing in the store may consist of W microinstructions, each being B-bits wide (Fig. 5.31). The total area of the control store is then $S_1 = W*B$ bits.

On the other hand, if the microprogram is developed prior to the design of the control-store organization, it may be observed that, although W microinstructions are required, each of these microinstructions is one of only V *distinct and unique control states* — that is, particular microinstructions may have been used several times in the microprogram.

If $V \ll W$, we may take advantage of this observation by encoding the microprogram in a two-level control store in which the higher level *microstore* is W words long but only $|\log_2 V|$ bits wide, and the lower level nanostore is V words long and B bits wide (Fig. 5.32).

---

[21]Of course, as noted in Section 5.3.1, it may be debated whether one is really executing microcode when its source is the QM-1 control store.

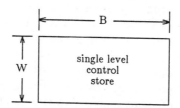

FIGURE 5.31 Dimensions of a single-level control store.

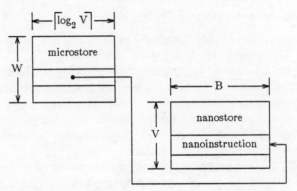

FIGURE 5.32 **Dimensions of a dual-level control store.**

Each machine instruction, residing in main store, is interpreted by a sequence of narrow microinstruction residing in microstore. A microinstruction, however, is nothing but an *address* or a pointer to a wide-word nanoinstruction residing in nanostore. The microinstructions are, thus, vertically organized; However, they are not organized in the way that highly encoded microinstructions normally are as discussed earlier. Rather, they may be viewed as *maximally encoded* representations of unique control states that are stored in the nanostore.

Note that the nanoinstructions (i.e., the unique control states) can be placed randomly in the nanostore, since the sequencing information is actually contained in the microstore. The total size of the two-level control store, then, is

$$S_2 = (W * \lceil \log_2 V \rceil) + (V * B)$$

Clearly, if $S_2 < S_1$, then the dual-level control store turns out to be more economic, especially when chip area conservation is a critical objective. In the case of the MC68000 microprocessor, $S_1 = 52,400$ bits and $S_2 = 30,550$ bits. A 42% saving in control-store area was achieved by adopting the dual-level scheme.

Residual Control

Implicit in the entire discussion thus far is that all the control information required to manipulate the micromachine in a given microcycle is to be encoded in fields of the microinstructions alone. The microinstructions, in a sense, exercise *immediate control* (Kornerup and Shriver, 1975). Furthermore, we have more or less assumed that the control state will change from one microcycle to the next.

It may be the case, however, that during the execution of a microprogram a part of the control-state information *remains invariant* for significant periods, spanning the execution of many microinstructions. Flynn and Rosin (1971) suggested that under such circumstances, instead of holding this same information in successive microinstructions, one can filter it out, place it in special registers, and hold it there for any desired period of time. This was named the principle of *residual control* by Flynn and Rosin, and registers used to hold such control information are called *residual control* or *setup registers*. By reducing the amount of control information that needs to be held in the microinstruction, one can significantly reduce the width of the latter. The state of residual control registers can, of course, be altered, if necessary, by microprogrammed means.

Example 5.14

The Nanodata QM-1 (Nanodata, 1979; Salisbury, 1976; Dasgupta, 1984) features extensive use of the residual control principle. One of the important features of this machine is that specific buses can be connected to specific local store registers under nanoprogram control. For example, the two ALU input buses may be connected to registers 1 and 2, and the ALU output bus to register 3. Such connections may remain unchanged for as long as is required—for the entire duration of a nanoprogram's execution, for instance. The QM-1 contains a set of residual control registers called F registers, each controlling the connection of a specific bus. The programmer may, then, "set up" these F registers with the identifiers of the local store registers that are to be connected to the corresponding buses. ∎

5.3.4   Temporal Aspects of Microprogramming

We have already considered some of the timing aspects of microprogramming earlier in this chapter: Specific timing characteristics of the von Neumann micromachine were described in Section 5.2.3, whereas in Section 5.3.2 we discussed, in more general terms, the nature of microinstruction sequencing and the fact that the fetching of one microinstruction can be overlapped in time with the execution of another.

There are essentially two important issues that determine the overall temporal structure of micromachines:

1. The fact that different MOs may need different amounts of time to execute. In particular, the time to execute main memory read/write operations will usually be much longer than the execution time for data-path MOs.
2. In general, the time required to read a microinstruction from control store into the microinstruction register will be longer than that required to execute the average data-path MO.

Ultimately, it is convenient to construct an abstract interval of time that can be used as a frame of reference to control and describe the timing behavior of micromachines: I will call this the *microcycle*, although other terms such as *CPU cycle* and *processor cycle* are used synonymously.

Physically speaking, it is useful to imagine a *clock* associated with the computer that emits a signal at regular intervals of real time; the microcycle is the time between successive clock signals.

From an architectural perspective, as in so many other aspects of architecture, it is difficult to establish a universally accepted, unambiguous definition of "microcycle." Thus, once more, we adopt a "working definition" as follows:

Let

$$M = \{m_1, m_2, \ldots, m_n\}$$
$$T = \{t_1, t_2, \ldots, t_n\}$$

be, respectively, a set of MOs and the corresponding set of time durations such that m_i executes in time t_i. Let $m_s \in M$ be the "fastest" MO—that is, $t_s \leq t_j$ for all $t_j \in T$. Note that there may be several MOs that are the "fastest." Then, given a micromachine capable of executing the MOs in M, the microcycle is the *shortest* time interval between the successive invocations of the fastest MO m_s.

Thus, if a microcycle is of duration D, and if m_s is executed from two successive microinstructions MI_j, MI_{j+1}, the time between the start of execution of these two instances of m_s will be D time units.

The determination of a microcycle will depend on several factors:

1. In the case where microinstruction FETCH, DECODE, and EXECUTE are performed strictly serially, the microcycle time will be the sum of these events (Fig. 5.33). If the execution times of MOs vary, then the microcycle time may be defined by taking the "fastest" or the "typical" MO into account. Thus, microinstructions encoding longer MOs will require *multiple* microcycles to execute (Fig. 5.34).

2. If the fetching of a microinstruction (including the updating of the CAR) is overlapped with the execution of the previously fetched microinstruction, then the longer of these two phases will dictate the microcycle duration (Fig. 5.35). Again, in the case of executing microinstruction with "slow" MOs, the execution phase may consume several microcycles.

Typically, then, a microcycle will determine the time required to execute "most" microinstructions.

An important characteristic of the microcycle is whether it is "monophase" or "polyphase." Although in the serial FETCH/DECODE/EXECUTE scheme the microcycle will at least consist of two phases (see Fig. 5.33), this issue appears to be mostly related to the *execution* of microinstructions rather than to their fetching. Assume, then, that the FETCH and EXECUTE of microinstructions are completely overlapped, as discussed in Section 5.3.2. A microcycle is, then, the shortest time interval between the beginning of execution of two successive

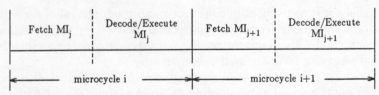

FIGURE 5.33   Serial Fetch/Decode/Execute of a microinstruction.

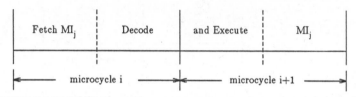

FIGURE 5.34   Serial Fetch/Decode/Execute of a "slow" microinstruction.

microinstructions (this is equivalent to our earlier "working definition" under some obvious assumptions).

A *monophase* microcycle is one in which the microcycle consists of one logically undifferentiated *phase* such that all MOs are assumed to consume at least the entire duration of the microcycle for their execution.

In contrast, a *polyphase* microcycle consists of two or more disjoint *phases* (or *subcycles*) such that each MO is executed in precisely one of these phases or in two or more adjacent phases (Fig. 5.36). Polyphase timing appears advantageous when the control store is slow relative to the data path. For instance, suppose that the time to fetch a microinstruction from control store requires 150 ns, whereas the time to execute each datapath MO is no more than 50 ns. Then a three-phase, 150-ns microcycle

$$C = <\text{phase1, phase2, phase3}>$$

where each phase is of 50-ns duration may be used and the timing attribute of the MOs be defined so that some common, frequently used *sequence* of MOs may be executed in a single microcycle.

Example 5.15

In the von Neumann micromachine of Section 5.2 precisely such a scheme was used, although the actual durations of the phases of the microcycle were left unspecified. The microcycle was three phases long (Fig. 5.11) and the timing attributes of the MOs were so determined that data could be read from a register into ALSM, an arithmetic/logical shift/mask operation performed, and the result written back to a register in a single microcycle.   ■

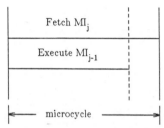

FIGURE 5.35   Overlapped Fetch/Execute phases.

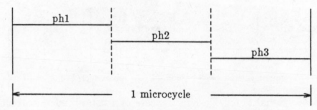

FIGURE 5.36 Polyphase microcycle.

5.4 EMULATION AND UNIVERSAL HOST MACHINES

The "classic" role of microprogramming, as conceived by Wilkes (1951), is as a means for implementing the control unit. However, as I have noted, it may also be viewed as a technique for programming one machine—called the *host*—so that it behaves like another—called the *target*.[22] Furthermore, the host and the target machines are not defined at the same abstraction level: The latter is more abstract than the former. From this perspective, then, microprogramming is a technique for programming a machine at a particular abstraction level to create a machine at another, higher abstraction level (Fig. 5.37). In the foregoing discussions, the host machine is what I have termed the micromachine whereas the target was specified in terms of exo-architectural characteristics.

The technique of using firmware to simulate the behavior of one machine on another is known as *emulation*. Once it was realized that the problem of designing a computer could be factored into the subproblems of designing two distinct types of machines—a target and a host—and that one could emulate the former on the latter, the possibilities of emulation were very quickly realized. Indeed,

[22]Flynn and coworkers (Flynn, 1980; Flynn and Hoevel, 1983; Flynn and Huck, 1984) also refer to the target as the *image* machine. This term has been adopted by others, for example, Mueller (1984).

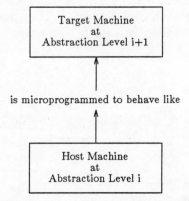

FIGURE 5.37 Creating a multilevel machine by microprogramming.

the commercial and technical success of the IBM System/360 series (Blaauw and Brooks, 1964) owed not a little to the use of microprogramming and the concept of emulation. The 360 series was, in fact, the first large-scale application of microprogramming both in its classic sense and as a machine mapping/emulation technique.

Emulation can be applied in several ways:

1. To make a new computer *software compatible* with another, perhaps older machine. This was first effectively achieved on the IBM System/360 family of processors, each of which, in addition to being able to execute programs written for the 360, contained emulators for predecessors of this series, notably, the IBM 1401, the 1620, and the 7000 series. For instance, when running in the "1401 emulation mode" 360 processor could execute 1401 object code (Fig. 5.38). This capability allowed users of 1401 hardware to upgrade their installation to a 360 computer without having to reprogram their 1401 software; or at least, to effect a smooth transition from the old to the new. Mallach (1975) has pointed out that the objective of achieving compatibility between computers was an important reason for the emergence of emulation in the first place. Many models of the IBM System/370 family appearing between 1971 and 1977 (Case and Padegs, 1978) continued to include emulators for such computers as the IBM 1401/1440/1460, the IBM 1410/7010 series, and the IBM 7070/7074/7080/7090 family of computers (Mallach, 1975)—all products of the 1950s.

2. To implement a common exo-architecture on different micromachines in order to produce a *family* of computers with identical exo-architectures (and, therefore, capable of executing the same software) but different cost-performance characteristics. This was first achieved with the development of the IBM System/360 family (Tucker, 1967). A common abstract target machine, the "IBM System/360," is emulated on several host micromachines, namely the Models 22, 25, 30, 40, 44, 50, 65, 67, and 85 (Fig. 5.39). The hosts span a range of cost and performance characteristics. For example, the CPU cycle (microcycle) times range from 750 to 900 ns for the "smaller" models, through about 200 ns for the "medium-sized" models down to 80 ns for the "largest" model (Case and Padegs, 1978).

As is well known, it was the use of microprogramming that enabled a

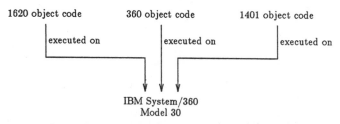

FIGURE 5.38 Emulation for software compatibility.

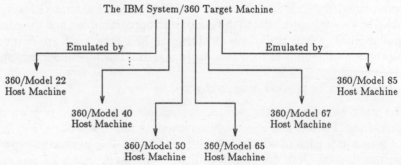

FIGURE 5.39   Emulating a common target machine on different hosts.

family of such computers with varying cost and performance to be implemented with a common, rather complex exo-architecture (Tucker, 1967). This was possible because once the basic cost of the control unit hardware is incurred the cost of implementing a microcoded instruction set or other functions is only marginally dependent on the size of the instruction set: Large instruction sets merely require more firmware development time than do small instruction sets. For this reason, it was possible to implement the same exo-architecture on the "smaller" (i.e., cheaper and slower) models as was provided on the larger ones. This same principle was adopted in developing the IBM System/370 series (Case and Padegs, 1978).

3. In the case of the IBM System 360 (or 370) families, the host micromachines were designed to support the 360 (or 370) exo-architectures: The hosts, in other words, were deliberately *biased* toward a particular target so as to facilitate efficient emulation (in some sense) of the target on each of the host machines. Flynn (1980) termed such a mapping from target to host a *well-mapped* correspondence.

Note, however, in such situations as depicted in Figure 5.38 there may not be a well-mapped correspondence between target and host. Generalizing this to its ultimate form, it is possible to devise a host micromachine that is *not biased* toward any particular target machine but that has sufficiently powerful capabilities to emulate many different targets (Fig. 5.40). This is yet

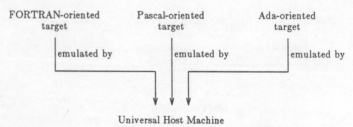

FIGURE 5.40   Emulating different target machine on one host.

another application for emulators; such host machines have come to be known as *universal host machines* (UHMs). Some of the desirable characteristics of UHMs will be discussed in Section 5.4.2.

5.4.1   The Nature of Emulation

Previously, I stated that emulation is the use of microprogramming to simulate the behavior of one machine on another. It is worth examining somewhat more closely what it means for one machine to behave like another.

The emulation process may be described formally as follows.

1. We are given a target machine T. Let $D = \{d_1, d_2, \ldots, d_n\}$ be the set of *stores* in T, and let $OP = \{OP_1, OP_2, \ldots, OP_m\}$ be the set of *operations* (or instructions) that T is capable of performing. Then a particular *state* S_i of T is an n-tuple of values of $d_1, d_2, \ldots, d_n$. The set of all such states constitute the *state space* of T, denoted STATE(T). Each operation $OP_k \in OP$ causes a mapping from one state to another in the state space of T (Fig. 5.41):

$$OP_k : STATE(T) \rightarrow STATE(T)$$

2. We are also given a host machine H. Let $d' = \{d_1', d_2', \ldots, d_r'\}$ be *its* set of data stores such that an r-tuple of values of $d_1', d_2', \ldots, d_r'$ defines a state of H and the set of all such states constitutes the state space of H, STATE (H).

3. Corresponding to each $OP_k \in OP$ of the target machine T, let $proc(OP_k)$ be a microprogrammed procedure (or, simply, microprocedure) defined on STATE (H). That is

$$proc(OP_k) : STATE (H) \rightarrow STATE (H)$$

The set $proc(OP) = \{proc(OP_1), proc(OP_2), \ldots, proc(OP_m)\}$ constitutes a microprogram executing on H.

4. For H to emulate T, there must be a *mapping* of states in T to states in H. More precisely, given STATE (T) and STATE (H), the two state spaces, let MAP be a *relation* between them such that for each $S_i \in STATE (T)$.

$$MAP(S_i) = S_i'$$

and $S_i' \in STATE (H)$.[23]

5. Clearly, a necessary condition that must hold in order for the (microprogrammed) host machine H to *emulate* the target machine T is the commutativity relation shown in Figure 5.41. That is, for each $OP_k \in OP$, $proc(OP_k) \in proc(OP)$, given that $(S_i, S_i') \in MAP$, $(S_j, S_j') \in MAP$, then

$$MAP[OP_k(S_i)] = proc(OP_k) [MAP (S_i)]$$

---

[23]Recall that given two sets S,S', R is a *relation* if $R \subset S \times S'$. We denote an element of R by $(S_i, S_j) \in R$. The relation R is a *function* if there is exactly one $S_j \in S'$ such that $(S_i, S_j) \in R$, in which case we can use the usual notations for functions, namely, R: $S \longrightarrow S'$ or $R(S_i) = S_j$ for $S_i \in S$, $S_j \in S'$. For more on relations, see any textbook on modern algebra, for example, Birkhoff and Bartee (1970).

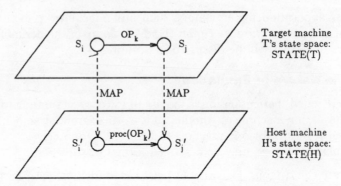

FIGURE 5.41 Desired commutativity relationship in emulation.

In other words, given the relation MAP that maps S_i to S_i' and S_j to S_j', if we assume that we have no way of distinguishing between S_i and S_i' or between S_j and S_j' then, when H emulates T, we should not be able to determine, from a *logical* viewpoint, which of T or H is executing.

It is important to note in the foregoing formulation that each operation OP_k in T is assumed to have a corresponding procedure $proc(OP_k)$ in H. This means that during emulation an operation OP_k is *interpreted* by the procedure $proc(OP_k)$. Indeed, emulation and interpretation are virtually synonymous, except that interpreters, in the conventional use of the word, are taken to be implemented in software rather than in firmware.

One may also note that nothing is said in this model about the *intermediate states* that may be traversed when OP_k maps from S_i to S_j and when $proc(OP_k)$ maps S_i' to S_j'. The commutativity relationship need only hold over the initial and final states (S_i, S_j) and (S_i', S_j').

Finally, although the foregoing model formalizes the concept of emulation, it leaves open the nature or extent of the state spaces STATE (T) and STATE (H) and the extent of the sets OP and proc(OP) that enter into the emulation relationship. Should *every conceivable* type of behavior of the target machine be emulated? Flynn and coworkers (Hoevel and Wallach, 1975; Flynn and Huck, 1984) have proposed an informal classification of emulators based essentially on the extent to which the target machine behavior is to be considered. For example, the strongest class of emulators is one in which the host H not only replicates "correct" behavior of the target machine T but also T's failure modes. A weaker class consists of emulators that transform all "correct" target-machine programs but does not necessarily preserve "incorrect" behavior—for example, those of programs that violate arithmetic overflow conditions or memory protection.

5.4.2 Characteristics of a Universal Host Machine

One of the most interesting aspects of the evolution of microprogramming is the idea of the *universal host machine* (UHM)—that is, machines with micro-architectures that are designed for emulating arbitrary target exo-architectures. The concept of the UHM can be traced back at least to Rosin's (1969b) influential paper, where he raised and discussed the question: "Is there a microprogram environment that can best support the typical environments that a computer system provides?" In this same paper, Rosin described the Standard Computer Corporation IC-9000 computer, designed to support the emulation of a wide variety of machines.

The theoretical idea of UHMs was further developed in the early 1970s in a series of papers by Rosin, Flynn, and their coworkers (Flynn and Rosin, 1971; Rosin, Frieder, and Eckhouse, 1972; Cook and Flynn, 1970; Tucker and Flynn, 1971). During the 1970s and early 1980s several UHMs were implemented both in commercial and academic sectors. Notable among these are the Standard Computer Corporation MLP-900 (Lawson and Smith, 1971), the Burroughs B1700/B1800 series (Wilner, 1972a, 1972b), the Microdata 1600 (Microdata, 1970), the Nanodata QM-1 (Nanodata, 1979), the Stanford EMMY (Neuhauser, 1977; Flynn and Hoevel, 1983), the Aarhus University MATHILDA (Kornerup and Shriver, 1973), the Datasaab FCPU (Lawson and Malm, 1973), the Varian 75 (Varian, 1975), and the QA-1 and QA-2 systems developed at Kyoto University (Hagiwara *et al.*, 1980; Shibayama *et al.*, 1980; Tomita *et al.*, 1983).

When a host machine H is biased toward a particular target T, there will be (one hopes) a well-mapped correspondence between T and H. This means that the stores of T can be allocated economically to those of H such that the emulated stores can be read or written without undue overheads. The same biased host when emulating a target T' that differs visibly from T may, on the other hand, emulate T' inefficiently.

Example 5.16

Ardoin, Linn, and Reynolds (1984) implemented a special-purpose target machine called ARDA—a machine that is tailored to support recursive descent translators—using the VAX-11/780 micro-architecture as the host. They showed that some of the ARDA instructions actually took more time than if the functions had been implemented as VAX-11/780 instructions. The VAX-11/780 micromachine, in other words, was a host designed specifically to emulate the VAX-11 exo-architecture. Ardoin and colleagues concluded that although this computer has user microprogramming capabilities, it is not designed to serve as an unbiased or "universal" host. ∎

The challenge in designing a UHM is to provide a capability for implementing equally efficient emulators for a range of target machines. Precisely what levels of performance are desired or inefficiencies are acceptable, will, of course, depend critically on the uses to which UHMs are put as well as the costs that the designer is willing to incur.

It is clear, though, that the search for universality posits some specific architectural characteristics for UHMs.

Variable Word Length Capability

As discussed in Section 4.9 (Chapter 4), the word length is, in some sense, the most significant single characteristic of an architecture; consequently, the ability to emulate different targets with different word lengths—or a single target with different sizes of data objects, instructions, registers, or data paths—is central to the ideal of universality.

There are essentially two approaches to the attainment of this goal. In one, a standard, sufficiently large word length is provided along with micro-operations and hardware to reduce the word length to the desired size. In others, the standard length can be expanded by iterative microprogramming techniques.

Example 5.17

The Burroughs B1700/B1800 series (Wilner, 1972a, 1972b; Organick and Hinds, 1978) combines both these features. These machines have a "nominal" word length of 24 bits; the microprogrammer can, however, use control facilities to implement word lengths ranging from 1 through 24 bits or, through iterative microprogramming, implement lengths beyond 24 bits. The widths of the registers, data paths, functional units, and main memory can be controlled in this way. As a specific example, the width of the ALU is controlled by setting a (residue control) register. ∎

Shift, Rotate, and Mask Capabilities

A highly desirable feature of a UHM is the ability to extract fields of different sizes and positions from a memory word or register. Such a capability is required, for example, to decode instructions that may vary quite considerably in size and format from one machine to the next. Field extraction can be achieved in several ways:

1. By using MOs that explicitly specify the positions and lengths of fields to be extracted from stores.
2. By shifting off unwanted bits.
3. By using mask registers to mask or filter out unwanted bits from the target register.

Thus, in addition to the more obvious features, such as a large general repertoire of arithmetic and logical operations, powerful shift, rotate, and mask operations are required in UHMs.

Large Local Stores

A UHM should have a reasonably large set of high-speed, read/write, easily accessible registers (or local store). This is needed, first, to map target machine programmable registers directly onto the host; second, to allocate register space for holding the target's condition codes and other state information; and third, to provide a sufficiently large workspace for the emulator to use.

Salisbury (1976) has pointed out that a useful accompanying feature is the *indirect addressability* of registers in the local store. That is, given a local store LS of n registers, say, and a particular register R, then a register in LS can be directly accessed by the microprogram using R as an indirect address. This feature is useful in that it allows the emulator to access target machine register-based operands directly rather than having to program a lengthy decoding procedure.

Example 5.18

The Nanodata QM-1 (Nanodata, 1979) has an extensive set of registers that can provide an extended local store during emulation. Figure 5.42 shows the overall data-path organization for this machine. At its heart is the *local store*, a set of 32 18-bit registers that can be used in a variety of ways: for example, to serve as the target's programmable registers or to hold the target's program counter. In addition, there are a set of 32 6-bit registers called *F registers* of which 20 are used for special purposes (residual control, microprogram counter, etc.), but the remaining 12 are available for general use.

Yet a third group is the *external store* consisting of 32 18-bit registers. These include 12 index registers and 8 that are available for general use.

Finally, the control store (which, in QM-1 terminology is at the higher of the two-level control store) itself can be employed, in addition to its use as a microprogram memory, to hold data. Demco and Marsland (1976; see also Marsland and Demco, 1978) for instance in their emulation of the PDP/11/10 on the QM-1 used the control store to hold, among other things, the instruction decode table.   ■

Dynamic Sharing of Writable Control Store

A writable control store (WCS) is, of course, a *sine qua non* for UHMs. However, additional features are also desirable. The WCS must be sufficiently large so as to hold several target-machine emulators simultaneously. Since an UHM can, in principle, be used to emulate an arbitrarily large set of target machines it should have the capacity to store emulators in a *backup store* and load them *dynamically* into control store when required.[24] The obviously appropriate candidate for the backup store is main memory. Thus, the control memory and (some part of) main store combine to form a *virtual control memory* (see Chapter 8 for discussions of virtual memory principles).

---

[24]This is *dynamic microprogramming* in the true sense of the word "dynamic." The phrase is, however, often used in a much weaker sense to refer to the user's ability to alter the contents of the control store, thereby creating different exo-architectures at different times. For discussions of "real" dynamic microprogramming see Guha (1977), and Winner and Carter (1986).

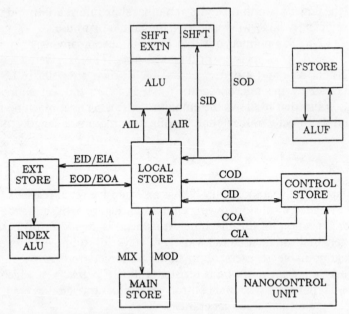

FIGURE 5.42 Data-path organization in the QM-1 (Dasgupta 1984; © 1984, John Wiley & Sons, Inc.; reprinted with permission).

Example 5.19

The Burroughs B1726 model (a member of the B1700/B1800 series) uses a two-level memory hierarchy as shown in Figure 5.43 (Organick and Hinds, 1978). The control store or *M-memory* holds the most frequently used emulators or parts thereof. The remaining microcode is held in main store or *S-memory*. Normally, the B1726 host executes microinstructions from the M-memory; when a microinstruction required to be executed is not in M-memory then the operating system (called the Master Control Program or MCP) will either load the relevant block of microcode from S-memory into M-memory and continue execution of the emulator or (less usually) directly fetch and execute microinstructions from S-memory. Since S-memory is slower than M-memory, the first alternative will be preferred for more frequently used blocks of microcode. ∎

Reconfigurability of the Data Path

A biased host machine generally has a fixed data path. In the case of a universal host, one would *ideally* desire some ability to reconfigure the data-path organization so as to enhance the efficiency of each distinct emulator. Such a capability extends, in an obvious way, the flexibility and generality of the host.

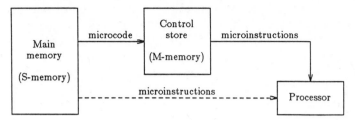

FIGURE 5.43   Control memory hierarchy in the B1726.

Example 5.20

A modest form of reconfigurability is available on the QM-1 (Nanodata, 1979). As Figure 5.42 shows, this host is organized around a set of 10 buses, all of which are connected to the local store. Each bus, in fact, connects one of the other units to the local store. However, which local store register is to be connected to a particular bus is not fixed. Each bus has associated with it a residual register in F store. For example, FAIL and FAIR in F store determines which of the local store registers will be connected to the AIL and AIR buses, respectively, whereas FMOD in F store determines which local store register will be connected to the MOD bus. In effect, by setting these F store registers, the nanoprogrammer can change the ALU path in the QM-1.   ∎

Comprehensive Firmware Development System

It must be remembered that an UHM is a computer defined at one level of abstraction to be *programmed* so as to create a more abstract machine. Micro-programming, in this context, is thus a form of systems or even applications programming. Thus a vital component of a universal host machine *environment* is the availability of software that can be effectively used to design, verify, implement, and test firmware. Indeed, this is considered such an important aspect of microprogramming that it has spawned a whole new subdiscipline of computer science called *firmware engineering* (Dasgupta and Shriver, 1985; Dasgupta and Mueller, 1986). This forms the topic of Volume 2, Chapter 5.

5.5   BIBLIOGRAPHIC REMARKS

Microprogramming has continued to fascinate, in a theoretical sense, both the hardware and software specialist: The former wishes to establish either a clear distinction, or the similarity, between microprogrammed and hardwired control unit; the latter, to identify the relationship between microprogramming and programming. The notion of MCUs as finite-state machines is explored in Mead and Conway (1980, Chapter 6). The relationship between firmware and software has been explored extensively by researchers in firmware engineering, see especially Dasgupta (1980), Mueller (1984), Dasgupta and Shriver (1985), Davidson (1986). Chapter 5 of Volume 2 also describes this relationship at length.

An interesting polemic that, in some sense, *revolts against* microprogramming is Rosin (1974). In this paper, Rosin advances the concept of a "reasonable" machine and contends that the "significance" of microprogramming is that it serves to create a reasonable machine on top of an unreasonable base. An "unreasonable" machine, according to Rosin, is one that requires the programmer to have to grapple with gates, buses, timing hazards, race conditions, and other such hardware features—precisely those features that the microprogrammer traditionally copes with. Thus, Rosin states, if reasonable base machines are built, then microprogramming will lose its raison d'etre, hence will not be necessary. The reduced instruction set computer (RISC) of almost a decade later seems to be such a reasonable machine and, indeed, advocates of the RISC style are claiming that microprogramming is no longer necessary (Patterson, 1985; Hopkins, 1983). Whether this is so remains to be further investigated, and, indeed, the claim has already been challenged (Colwell *et al.*, 1985). RISCs will be discussed in Chapter 7.

Wilkes (1969) is an excellent survey of the early state of the art by the founder of the field, while in Wilkes (1986) the same author has reflected on the origins of microprogramming almost four decades after the birth of the idea. Other early influential papers are Rosin (1969b) and Flynn and MacLaren (1967). Husson (1970), the first textbook on the subject, still remains an outstanding reference on developments in microprogramming in the first two decades.

Several book-length works have appeared since Husson's pioneering treatise. These include Agrawala and Rauscher (1976) and Salisbury (1976), both of which are essentially dedicated to microprogrammable computers; Banerji and Raymond (1982) is a more general text that surveys both architectural and programming matters; Andrews' (1980) volume, somewhat mistitled, has detailed discussions of control unit architecture and some aspects of firmware engineering. Habib (1988) is an up-to-date collection of surveys on practically all aspects of microprogramming and firmware engineering. More specialized monographs on control unit and universal host machine architectures include Organick and Hinds (1978), Dasgupta (1984, Chapter 11), Dasgupta (1979), and Rauscher and Adams (1980). The last two references are included in an anthology of papers on microprogramming and emulation edited by Mallach and Sondak (1983), which includes papers of both great historical interest as well as more recent research contributions.

A significant but almost forgotten paper that has helped to establish the principal parameters of micro-architectures (discussed in Section 5.3) is Redfield (1971). The various microinstruction encoding schemes, the distinction between mono- and polyphase microcycles, and the dichotomy of serial and overlapped sequencing appear to have been first discussed systematically by Redfield.

PROBLEMS

5.1   Recall the concept of processor state (Chapter 4, Section 4.10).
   (a)   Examine the data path shown in Figure 5.1 and identify which of its components contribute to the processor state of the von Neumann *micromachine.*
   (b)   What useful objectives are served by identifying the micromachine's processor state?

5.2   It was pointed out in Section 5.2.2 that a control unit is really a finite-state machine. At any time, the device is in one of a finite set of states. When the "current" state of the control unit is S_i (say), it issues a specific combination of control signals as an "output," and then changes from S_i to some "next" state S_j.
   (a)   Explain how the state of the control unit differs from (or is similar to) the micromachine's processor state.
   (b)   Examine the description of the von Neumann micromachine in Section 5.2 and determine, exactly, how many distinct states the control unit can be in.

5.3   A microprogrammed control unit has been described as the "computer-within-a-computer" because it appears to adhere to the von Neumann model of architecture. Describe the exact points of similarity between the architecture of microprogrammed control units and the general architecture of von Neumann machines.

5.4   [Continuation of Problem 5.3.] If the microprogrammed control unit is indeed significantly similar (architecturally) to von Neumann machines, then microprogramming the micromachine would be as easy (or as difficult) as programming the exo-architecture level machine. This is not exactly the case. In some ways microprogramming is an easier task, in other ways programming is easier. Clearly, there are definite points at which the architectures of microprogrammed control unit and von Neumann machines *differ.*
   (a)   From a (micro) programming point of view, describe significant aspects of the microprogrammed control unit and the micromachine that make microprogramming a more complex task than programming.
   (b)   Describe those aspects of the micromachine that make microprogramming a simpler task than programming.

5.5   By definition (Section 5.1; see also Chapter 1, Section 1.3) the micro-architecture is to the microprogrammer what the exo-architecture is to the assembly language level programmer (or to the compiler writer). In view of this analogy it would be instructive to describe micro-architectures in exo-architectural terms (i.e., in terms of such components as storage organization and addressing modes). Such an exercise might also help in understanding the similarities and distinctions between exo- and micro-architectures.

(a) Describe the following components within a micro-architecture along the lines in which the corresponding components of exo-architectures were described in Chapter 4.
(i) Data types
(ii) Storage organization
(iii) Addressing modes
(iv) Instruction (operation) set

(b) Also, discuss the significance of the word-length concept at the micro-architectural level.

5.6 [This question may be answered in conjunction with Problem 5.5 or independently of it.]
Consider now the problem of the systematic and methodical design of micro-architectures. The first step is to identify the *principal components* that will have to be designed. The next step is to establish the nature of the *interactions* of these components—that is, how design decisions concerning one component affect decisions regarding others (see, for example, Problem 4.4, Chapter 4).

(a) Identify (i.e., name) all the significant components of a micro-architecture and describe briefly the function or role of each component.

(b) Examine and describe the nature of the most significant interactions between these components.

5.7 [Continuation of Problem 5.6.] Based on your solution to Problem 5.6, establish an *ordering* on the design of each of these components and explain the reasoning behind your ordering. [*Hint*: Refer to Problem 4.5, Chapter 4.]

5.8 Consider the question of micro-architectural *quality*. As in the question of exo-architectures (see Problem 4.6, Chapter 4), the most significant factor determining quality is *efficiency*.

(a) Identify three distinct measures that can be used by the architect to assess the efficiency of a micro-architecture design.

(b) Describe the methods, tools, or experiments that would be required to determine each of these measures in the course of design.

5.9 A second important factor determining quality is modifiability (see Problem 4.7, Chapter 4). The issue here is that at any stage of the design process or even after the design has been completed, any modification to the architecture should be achievable with minimum effect on the rest of the design. A change in one component should not "make too many waves"!

(a) What kinds of changes to the data-path part of a micromachine must be anticipated by the architect?

(b) How should the data-path part be *designed for modifiability* in the event of such changes?

(c)   What kinds of changes should the architect anticipate for the control-unit part of the micromachine?

(d)   How should the control unit be designed for modifiability?

5.10   In Problem 4.7 (Chapter 4) an example was given of changes to an exo-architecture after the computer had been introduced into the market. The enhancement was an addition of new floating-point data types and several instructions to support these types. Explain the possible role of microprogramming in such enhancements.

5.11   In the course of designing a 32-bit machine a decision had been made to support 32-bit integers (represented in 2's complement form) with an associated set of four integer arithmetic instructions. The exo-architecture design was "frozen," the micro-architecture was developed, and the microcode to implement the instruction set was written, tested, and debugged.

At this stage, the exo-architecture design was revised to include short, 16-bit integers as a data type and to extend the instruction set with a corresponding set of "short" arithmetic instructions.

Fortunately, the architect's wisdom and experience had caused him to have "designed for modifiability." Thus, these enhancements were absorbed into the micromachine design with only a change to the firmware. The micro-architecture itself was unaffected. Furthermore, the change to the firmware was only in terms of *adding* new microcode. No alteration to the original firmware was required.

(a)   Assuming a fixed-length instruction format (at the exo-architectural level) with a fixed-length opcode field, try to recapitulate this architect's achievement. That is, describe a (partial) micromachine (showing only those parts that are relevant to this problem) that the architect *could* have originally designed so as to absorb the late changes in the manner stated herein — that is, only by adding new microcode and no other change whatsoever.

(b)   Clearly *some* price has to be paid by designing for modifiability. In this particular example what was the price?

5.12   [Continuation of Problem 5.11.] As discussed in Section 5.3.3, it may be the case that in the course of executing a microprogram part of the control state information remains constant for periods spanning the execution of several microinstructions. This relatively constant (or slowly changing) control information may be held in special processor registers rather than in the microinstructions. This is referred to as the principle of *residual control.*

Describe how residual control could have been effectively used by our wise, hypothetical architect in designing the (partial) micromachine of Problem 5.11.

5.13   Develop an alternative architecture for the von Neumann machine's microprogrammed control unit using a *two-level control store.* Comment on whether or not this is preferable to the control unit developed in Sections 5.2.3 and 5.2.4.

5.14 A number of different mechanisms for sequencing in microprogrammed control units was described in Section 5.3.2. The task of the sequencing logic is to select the address of the "next" microinstruction to execute on termination of the "current" microinstruction's execution.

Consider now, a control unit in which there are five possible sources of a next microinstruction address:

(a) A register called TO-ADDR, which holds the fixed (hardwired) starting address of a microroutine for handling microprogram *timeouts*. This is a fault condition arising when a microroutine's execution exceeds some time limit indicating a malfunction or possibly an infinite loop in the microcode. A time-out condition is signaled to the control unit by a 1-bit register TO being set to 1.

(b) A register called INT-ADDR, which holds a fixed starting address of an interrupt-handling microroutine. The interrupt condition is signaled to the control unit by a 1-bit register INT being set to 1.

(c) An address field, F-ADDR, in the "current" microinstruction (held in the microinstruction register, MIR), which specifies either an unconditional branch, a conditional branch, or a subroutine call. A single 2-bit field F-BRCH in the microinstruction indicates which of these operations is to be executed. In the event of a conditional branch, the condition to be tested is held in a 1-bit register COND, which is set to 1 if the condition is true, is zero otherwise.

(d) A RET-ADD register, which holds the return address following the execution of a subroutine call. A return from a subroutine is specified by a 1-bit field, F-RET, in the microinstruction.

(e) The normal next sequential microinstruction address, held in the control store address register, CAR.

The *priorities* of these address sources, from highest to lowest are: TO-ADDR, INT-ADDR, F-ADDR, RET-ADDR, and CAR. Thus, for example, the value in CAR is used to access the next (sequential) microinstruction only if *none* of the higher priority address sources demand attention. On the other hand, if the TO and INT registers are both set to 1, then the CAR will be updated with the value in TO-ADDR, since this has a higher priority than INT-ADDR. Similarly, if a subroutine call is specified in the "current" microinstruction and the INT flag is also set, then the interrupt handler will have higher priority than the subroutine call, since INT is a higher priority address than F-ADDR. CAR will then be updated with the value in INT-ADDR.

You are required to design the micro-architecture of the control unit that selects correctly from these five sources the address of the next microinstruction having the highest priority. [*Hint*: Use a priority encoder.]

5.15 [This is a design project that is a continuation of the project initiated in Problem 4.14, Chapter 4.] Design a microprogrammed implementation of the exo-architecture X1 that you had designed in response to Problem 4.14. Call the resulting micromachine, MX1. Your design will consist of the following components:

(a) The micro-architecture of the data-path part. This will include a structural description of the functional units, the registers and their interconnections, and a specification of all the microoperations (MOs). Each MO will be specified (using an appropriate notation) in terms of its behavior or function and its timing characteristics. The latter will be described in terms of the overall *timing model* for the micromachine.

(b) The architecture of the microprogrammed control unit. This will include a specification of the size of the control store; the microinstruction organizations and the encoding of MOs in these formats; the sequencing logic used to fetch and execute microinstructions and for generating the next microinstruction address.

(c) The overall timing model governing the behavior of the micromachine as a whole.

(d) A description of the microcode routine responsible for the fetch and decode of X1 instructions.

(e) A description of the microcode that implements the ADD instruction for real numbers, the subroutine CALL instruction, and one of the character-string manipulation instructions as these were designed for X1.

[*Note*: The microcode should be written in an assembly language notation or in a "high-level" notation such as a dialect of Pascal or C such that each statement of the microcode maps onto a single microinstruction.]

5.16 [Continuation of Problem 5.15.] Discuss thoroughly the design decisions you made concerning the quality of the micro-architecture from the perspectives of *efficiency* and *modularity*.

5.17 [Continuation of Problem 5.15.] No matter how carefully the design is carried out, it should be *tested* as completely as possible after the design is terminated and before it is implemented or refined to the next level of detail. It was pointed out in Problem 4.16 (Chapter 4) that testing a design is essentially a scientific experiment. It involves stating definite *hypotheses* about the design in such a way that they can be meaningfully tested and then devising the right experiments to test the hypotheses.

(a) For your design of MX1, propose two testable hypotheses that can be used to ascertain the quality of the micro-architecture.

(b) Describe feasible experiments that can be carried out to test these hypotheses.

5.18 [Continuation of Problem 5.17.] Perform the experiments you described in Problem 5.17 and report their results. What are your conclusions concerning the *actual* quality of the architecture compared to the *expected* quality?

5.19 A *universal host machine* (UHM) is a micromachine intended for the emulation of arbitrary target exo-architectures (see Section 5.4.2). One of the essential requirements that a UHM must meet is the ability to extract fields of different sizes and positions from a register or a memory word.

Supposing you are developing a UHM with registers, functional units, and data paths having a maximum width of 32 bits. One of the registers will serve as the instruction register, IR, which may hold instructions of arbitrary formats and lengths up to 32 bits.

The extractions of fields of arbitrary lengths from IR will be performed in the UHM using a combination of hardware and firmware. That is, the UHM architect will have to make some key decisions concerning what capabilities will be provided in the micromachine itself and what will be the responsibility of the microprogrammer.

Design a micro-architecture showing

(a) How the UHM will provide support for the extraction of fields of arbitrary sizes and positions from IR; and

(b) How the microprogrammer can use this capability in decoding the contents of IR during instruction fetch.

[*Note*: Only those aspects of the micro-architecture relevant to this particular issue need be developed.]

5.20 [This is an advanced project based on a problem originally posed by M. V. Wilkes.] Consider a microprogrammed computer that supports *several sets of* (exo-architecture level) *instructions.* One is a *general* instruction set G whereas the others are *special sets* $S_1, S_2, \ldots, S_n$, each set "optimized" for efficient execution of particular applications, programs, or programming language statements. For example, G may be the instruction set for a typical register machine. One special instruction set S_i (say) may have been specifically developed to support the efficient execution of COBOL programs, whereas another set S_j is oriented toward matrix manipulations and computations. New special instruction sets may be implemented as and when required by "the user."

The control memory for this machine is a writable control store (WCS). The microroutines for the general instructions set G reside permanently in a fixed area of the WCS. However, one cannot expect the firmware for all the special instructions sets to be held simultaneously in the WCS. Thus, they are stored in *main memory* and are loaded into the WCS as and when required.

When the computer is executing a program, instructions of this program will, in general, be a mix of instructions from the set G and from one or more of the special sets $S_1, S_2, \ldots$. Since the firmware for G resides permanently in the WCS, a general instruction can be immediately executed. If a special instruction is to be executed and its microcode is not "currently" in the WCS, then *the latter must be located in main memory and loaded into some area of the WCS before execution can begin.* Assume that the loader is itself a microroutine residing in some fixed area of the WCS.

The loading mechanism must also satisfy the following requirements:

(1) Instructions from G should execute as efficiently as if the loading mechanism were not present.

(2) If the microcode for a special instruction is already loaded into the WCS, the instruction should execute as fast as a general instruction.

You are required to design the architecture of the control unit that satisfies these objectives. Your design should include:

(a) A description of the structural aspect of the micro-architecture.

(b) A specification of the behavior of the control unit including descriptions of (i) how it generates the correct address of general or special microroutines already in the control store; (ii) how it correctly accesses special microroutines in main memory; (iii) how it loads the microroutines into the control store; and (iv) how it handles the condition where the WCS is full and a new microroutine has to be loaded in.

[*Note*: You are not required to describe the loading microroutine in detail—only what its functional behavior is.]

CHAPTER 6

THE EXPLOITATION OF STACKS

6.1 INTRODUCTION

In this chapter I describe a class of computers that is characterized by the use of the *stack* as a primary storage component. Such machines may be contrasted with those discussed in Chapters 4 and 5, where the significant storage components are a linear, word-addressable "main" memory and one or more high-speed registers.

The stack as a data structure has long had an honorable and important place in programming (Knuth, 1968). Its interest to the computer architect can be traced back at least to when Samelson and Bauer (1959) described how a stack store could be used to support the translation of programs written in Algol-like programming languages. A detailed discussion of the role of stacks in the celebrated "Whetstone" Algol-60 compiler is given in Randell and Russell (1964).

Precisely how such uses of stacks have influenced the design of architectures is the subject of this chapter. Prior to delving into this topic, however, two important points should be noted.

First, because of the close association of stacks with the implementation of programming languages, architectures that support stack concepts are often viewed as *language-directed architectures*—that is, architectures that have been designed explicitly to support the implementation and execution of high-level language programs. Stack-based machines are certainly the most well-known examples of language-directed architectures, although they are by no means the only examples (see Chapter 7 for another instance).

Second, as we will see, stacks may play a role in architectures that ranges from the nominal to one in which the entire exo-architecture design is informed by the presence of the stack. It would be a travesty of meaningful terminology to embrace the whole spectrum by the term "stack machines." They are all, certainly, *stack-based.* But the architectural style named *stack machines* is usually (and rightfully) reserved for that subclass in which the stack dominates the architecture design and even its implementation. The exemplar *par excellence* of the stack style is the Burroughs family of "Algol machines," beginning with the Burroughs B5000 in the early 1960s and culminating in the B6700/B7700 processors in the early 1970s (Doran, 1979; Organick, 1973).

6.2   THE BASIC OPERATIONS

The fundamental characteristic of a stack is its *last-in, first-out* property. That is, the data item most recently inserted into the stack is also the item that can be most immediately extracted from it. Thus, the most basic stack operations are those that *push* an element into, and *pop* an element out of, the stack.

Figure 6.1 shows the essential structure of a stack system as it may appear as part of some exo-architecture. It consists of an array of storage elements—the stack—together with a counter or register called STKPTR (stack pointer). Whenever a stack operation is not actually taking place, the value of the stack pointer defines the "current" *top of the stack*—that is, it points to the stack word containing the most immediately accessible value. The stack is defined here to "grow upward"; that is, a new element would be added on top of the current top element.

Consider now a 1-address PUSH instruction that uses as an operand the address "opd_addr" of a word in memory. The effect of executing this instruction is such that on its completion STKPTR would point to the *next higher* word of the stack, which would also contain the contents of main memory address opd_addr (Fig. 6.2*a*). Conversely, the effect of executing a 1-address POP instruction with an operand "res_addr" specifying the address of a main memory word would be such that on its completion STKPTR would point to the *next lower* word of the stack whereas the main memory word at address res_addr would contain the value of the "original" top of stack word (Fig. 6.2*b*).

Specification 6.1

For the sake of preciseness, Figure 6.3 shows a formal specification of this basic stack system in the form of an abstract data type.

Some explanation of the notation may be necessary. At the top of the specification, the *stores* that participate in the BASIC_STACK system are declared along with the store *types*. Types are either the primitive *bit* or the composites *bit sequence* and *arrays*. Three of the *bit*-type stores are initialized to 0. In addition, a *bit*-type constant store with the value 1 is also defined.

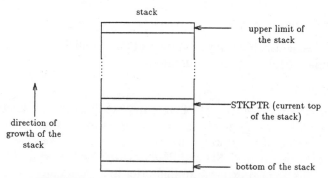

FIGURE 6.1   **Basic structure of a stack system.**

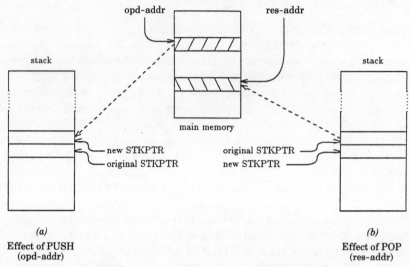

(a)
Effect of PUSH
(opd-addr)

(b)
Effect of POP
(res-addr)

FIGURE 6.2   Effects of basic stack operations.

The operations PUSH and POP are specified as *modules*. For each operation, the *inports* and *outports* describe, respectively, their input and output stores. *Inoutports* obviously serve both roles.

The *functional behavior* of each operation is described in the *effects* section. The basic form of this specification is

if COND **then new** $x_1 = E_1$ & **new** $x_2 = E_2$ & . . .
  else new $x_3 = E_3$ & **new** $x_4 = E_4$ & . . .

where $x_1, x_2, . . . , x_n$ identify stores (or their constituent elements) and E_1, $E_2, . . . , E_n$ are expressions. Thus, if at the start of the module's activation the condition COND holds, then when the module's activation terminates, the equalities

new $x_1 = E_1$, **new** $x_2 = E_2$, . . .

will *all* simultaneously hold. If COND was not true initially, then on completion of the modules' activation, the equalities

new $x_3 = E_3$, **new** $x_4 = E_4$, . . .

will all simultaneously be true. Here, an unprefixed identifier indicates the value of that store at the beginning of the module's activation, whereas the prefix **new** indicates the value of the store at the termination of the module's activation.

Note that the modules PUSH and POP describe the behavior of the two basic stack operations taking into account that prior to a PUSH the stack may already be full (the stack *overflow* condition) whereas prior to a POP the stack may already be empty (the stack *underflow* condition).

system BASIC_STACK
    type mem_array **is array** (..) **of seq**[31..0]**of bit**
    type stk_array **is array** (1..128) **of seq**[31..0]**of bit**
    type mem_space_size **is seq**[31..0]**of bit**
    type stack_space_size **is seq**[7..0]**of bit**
    store
        mem : mem_array;
        add_reg : mem_space_size; —holds address of a mem word
        stkovflow, stkundflow : **bit init** (0);
        stack : stk_array;
        stkptr : stack_space_size **init** (0)
            —minimum and maximum values of stkptr are
            —1 and 128 respectively

constant yes : **bit init** (1);

module PUSH
      inport mem; add_reg
      outport stack; stkovflow
      inoutport stkptr

      effects
          if stkptr >= 128
              then new stkovflow = yes
              else new stack(stkptr+1) = mem(add_reg) &
                  new stkptr = stkptr + 1
          end if
end module

module POP
      inport stack; add_reg
      outport mem; stkundflow
      inoutport stkptr

      effects
          if stkptr = 0
              then new stkundflow = yes
              else new mem(add_reg) = stack(stkptr) &
                  new stkptr = stkptr - 1
          end if
    end module
end system

FIGURE 6.3 Specification of the basic stack system.

6.3 EXPRESSION STACKS

An exo-architecture with minimal hardware stack support would, then, consist of a register serving as the stack pointer and the 1-address instructions PUSH and POP. The stack store may itself be implemented in a number of ways. If it is contained entirely in main memory, for instance, then additional registers may be required to point to the lower and upper limits of the stack (Fig. 6.1).

This basic stack system can be directly used by the assembly language programmer or the compiler to save and recall data items required on a last in, first out basis. Consider, now, the effect of augmenting this basic architecture with *0-address* instructions with the common characteristic that they all take their operands from the top one or two elements of the stack and place the result back into the stack.

Consider, in particular, a set of *binary instructions* $\{BI_1, BI_2, \ldots\}$ and a set of *unary instructions* $\{UI_1, UI_2, \ldots\}$ such that

1. Each BI_i takes the top two elements of the stack as arguments, performs a binary operation "bop_i" on them, and puts the result back on the stack, replacing the original arguments. Typical instances of binary instructions are ADD, SUBTRACT, MULTIPLY, DIVIDE, AND, OR, and EXCLUSIVE OR.
2. Each UI_j takes the top element of the stack as argument, performs a unary operation "uop_j" on it, and puts the result back on the stack, replacing the original argument. Instances of unary instructions are NEGATE (i.e., change the sign of) and NOT.

A stack system consisting of the features described in Section 6.2 augmented with a collection of 0-address binary and unary instructions is called an *expression stack* (or synonymously, *arithmetic stack*), as it provides an elegant method for the evaluation of arithmetic, logical, and relational expressions.

Table 6.1 gives a partial specification for a repertoire of 0-address arithmetic and logical instructions that are useful for evaluating expressions. Also included in this table are 0- and 1-address instructions for placing constants into the stack.

Consider now, the arithmetic expression EXP1:

$$(A + B) * (C - 1/D)$$

typical of the kind encountered in a high-level language program. Taking into account the precedence rules for arithmetic operators, and the effect of parentheses on operator precedence, the order of evaluation of the subexpressions ("A + B," "1/D," "C − 1/D," etc.) leading to the evaluation of the expression as a whole is explicitly defined by traversing the corresponding expression tree (Fig. 6.4) in *postorder* form.[1] For this particular example, this would lead to the following sequence of subexpression evaluations:

Evaluate A + B; call this value T1
Evaluate 1/D; call this value T2
Evaluate C − T2; call this value T3
Evaluate T1*T3

Using a stack supported by the instruction repertoire of Table 6.1, a compiler could generate code for EXP1 as follows:

[1]For a discussion of postorder, preorder, and inorder traversals of binary trees, see Knuth (1968).

CODE 1 : (i) PUSH A
        (ii) PUSH B
       (iii) ADD
       (iv) PUSH C
       (v) PUSHONE
      (vi) PUSH D
     (vii) DIV
    (viii) SUB
     (ix) MPY

TABLE 6.1 Zero-Address Stack Instructions

Arithmetic Instructions

ADD	:	**new** stack[stkptr−1] = stack[stkptr] + stack[stkptr−1] & **new** stkptr = stkptr−1
SUB	:	**new** stack[stkptr−1] = stack[stkptr−1] − stack[stkptr] & **new** stkptr = stkptr−1
MPY	:	**new** stack[stkptr−1] = stack[stkptr] * stack[stkptr−1] & **new** stkptr = stkptr−1
DIV	:	**new** stack[stkptr−1] = stack[stkptr−1] / stack[stkptr] & **new** stkptr = stkptr−1
NEG	:	**new** stack[stkptr] = −stack[stkptr]

Logical Instructions

AND	:	**new** stack[stkptr−1] = stack[stkptr] ∧ stack[stkptr−1] & **new** stkptr = stkptr−1
OR	:	**new** stack[stkptr−1] = stack[stkptr] ∨ stack[stkptr−1] & **new** stkptr = stkptr−1
NOT	:	**new** stack[stkptr] = ~stack[stkptr]

Push Constant Values

PUSHZERO : **new** stack[stkptr+1] = 0 & **new** stkptr = stkptr+1
PUSHONE   : **new** stack[stkptr+1] = 1 & **new** stkptr = stkptr+1
PUSHC "literal" : **new** stack[stkptr+1] = "literal" & **new** stkptr = stkptr+1

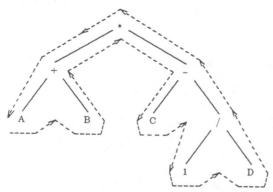

FIGURE 6.4 Expression tree for EXP1 and its traversal.

The successive states of the stack system resulting from the execution of CODE1 is shown at selective points in Figure 6.5.

The generation of CODE1 by the compiler can be greatly facilitated if the original expression EXP1 (which is in the familiar *infix* form) is first mapped into an equivalent parenthesis-free form called *reverse* (or *postfix*) *Polish* notation.[2] Informally stated, a reverse Polish expression is one in which operators follow their operands in the expression. For example, the reverse Polish forms of

1.   A + B is AB+
2.   A + B − C is AB + C−
3.   A + B*C is ABC*+
4.   (A + B)*C is AB + C*

[2]The name "Polish" derives from the fact that this notation was invented by the Polish logician Jan Lukasiewicz. An alternative form of the Polish notation is *prefix* Polish.

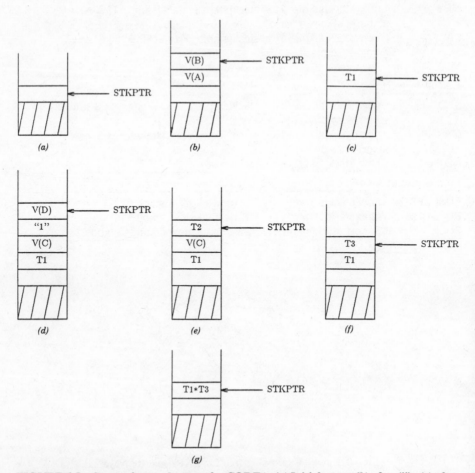

FIGURE 6.5 Successive stack states for CODE1: *(a)* Initial state; *(b)* after (ii); *(c)* after (iii); *(d)* after (vi); *(e)* (vii); *(f)* after (viii); *(g)* after (ix).

More formally, reverse Polish expressions can be obtained from infix expressions according to the following recursive definition (Aho and Ullman, 1973):

Let $B = \{+, -, *, \ldots\}$ be a set of binary operators, and $U = \{-, \ldots\}$ be a set of unary operators. Let OPD be a set of operands. For an infix expression I, denote by I' its reverse Polish form. Then,

1. If an infix expression I is a single operand $a \in OPD$, then the reverse Polish form of I is a.
2. If $I_1 \, b \, I_2$ is an infix expression where $b \in B$ and I_1, I_2 are infix expressions then the corresponding reverse Polish form is $I'_1 I'_2 b$.
3. If uI is an infix expression where $u \in U$ and I is an infix expression of the form (I_1) or is an operand $a \in OPD$, then the reverse Polish form is $I'u$.
4. Finally, if (I) is an infix expression, then its reverse Polish form is I'.

Specification 6.2

As stated before, the instructions in Table 6.1 are only partially defined. A complete specification of these instructions at the exo-architectural level must also indicate any and all side-effects—particularly, condition code settings—that may result from the execution of these instructions.

Let us require, for instance, that in the case of ADD the following side-effects be recorded:

1. A "carry" condition code will be set if there is a carry-out from the high-order (sign) bit of the result.
2. A "sign" condition code will be set if the result sign bit is a "1."
3. A "zero" condition code will be set if the result of addition is zero.

Furthermore, we desire that stack underflow conditions be detected as in the case of the POP instruction.

To meet these requirements with minimal changes to BASIC_STACK, we need to introduce some additional global stores:

carry,sign,zero : **bit init** (0)

Figure 6.6 is a formal specification of the ADD instruction as it would be visible at the exo-architectural level, whereas Figure 6.7 outlines the EXPR _STACK system resulting from augmenting BASIC_STACK with ADD and other modules. Note that a new component in this specification is the definition of a (private) function inside the ADD module and its reference in the *effects* section.

6.4 DATA STACKS FOR BLOCK-STRUCTURED PROGRAMS

The last-in/first-out characteristic of a stack can also be used to advantage in managing storage for *block-structured programs*—that is, programs written in a language like Algol 60 (Naur, 1963; Rutihauser, 1967), PL/1 (Conway, Gries, and Wortman, 1977), or Pascal (Jensen and Wirth, 1975) in which the textual

```
module ADD
    inoutport stack; stkptr
    outport stkundflow; carry; sign; zero

    —private function: width of function value is 1+stack word length
    function result_add: seq[32..0]of bit
        =stack(stkptr) + stack(stkptr-1)
    end function

    effects
        if stkptr = 1 or stkptr = 0
            then new stkundflow = yes
            else
                    new stack(stkptr-1) = result_add[31..0] &
                    new stkptr = stkptr-1 &
                    new carry = result_add[32] &
                    new sign = result_add[31] &
                    if result_add[31..0] = 0
                        then new zero = yes
                        else new zero = no
                    end if
        end if

end module
```

FIGURE 6.6   Specification of the ADD instruction.

structure of a (possibly nested) program determines the scopes of items declared in that program.

In Algol 60, for example, an arbitrary number of consecutive statements enclosed within the symbols **begin** and **end** is called a compound statement. If, in addition, one or more declarations are inserted after the **begin** symbol the resulting structure is called a *block*. Since blocks are themselves statements, it is possible to construct a program with blocks *nested* to any arbitrary depth. An outline of such a program is shown in Figure 6.8.

```
system EXPR_STACK
    —global store declarations as in 'BASIC_STACK'
    . . . . . .
    . . . . . .
    —in addition:
    store carry, sign, zero: bit init (0);

    —constant declaration as in 'BASIC_STACK'
    . . . . . .
    . . . . . .
    module PUSH . . . . end module
    module POP . . . . end module
    module ADD . . . . end module
    . . . . . .
end system
```

FIGURE 6.7   Outline of an expression stack system.

```
a:          begin   comment block at level 0;
                real x, y, z;
                integer n;

                   .
                   .
                   "executable statements"
                   .

b:              begin   comment block at level 1;
                integer m, n;

                   .
                   "executable statements"
                   .

c:              begin   comment block at level 2;
                integer p, q;
                real x;

                x := y - p;
                   .
                   "other executable statements"
                   .
                   .
                end
d:              begin   comment block at level 2;
                real s;
                boolean t;

                   .
                   .
                   "executable statements"
                   .
                   .
                end
                end
            end
```

FIGURE 6.8   Outline of a block-structured Algol 60 program P1.

From our point of view, the interesting properties of such block-structured programs are discussed in the following two sections.

6.4.1   The Scope Rule

By inspection of the program text one can determine the *scope* of declared items. By "scope" is meant the region of the program in which the declared item is accessible and can be referred to by its identifier. The scope rule for Algol 60 is that the scope of a declared item is the block, B, in which it is declared and all the blocks declared inside B unless the same identifier is used for another declared item within an inner block.

Referring to Figure 6.8, the scope of the variables y and z declared in the block labeled "a" is the entire program. The scope of x is the entire program except inside block c, since the identifier x appears there in another declaration. The scopes of variables m, n declared in block b are that block as well as blocks c and d. The scopes of variables p, q are limited to block c.

Blocks defined at the same level (e.g., blocks c and d in Fig. 6.8) also obey this scope rule. Thus, the scopes of p and q do not extend to block d just as those of s, t do not include c.

6.4.2 Dynamic Creation and Destruction of Declared Objects

As a result of the scope rule and the fact that blocks may be nested hierarchically, items are, effectively, created on entry into the block in which they are declared and are destroyed on exiting from that block. Thus, given a block c nested in block b, and b nested in block a, during program execution the variables in a are first created and last destroyed; those in b are created after those in a and destroyed before; and, finally, variables in c are created last but destroyed first.

Herein lies the last-in/first-out property of block-structured programs. Stacks can be advantageously used for storage management during the execution of such programs by allocating storage in the stack for items in a block only when the block is entered and deallocating storage on exit. Items declared in blocks at the same level (e.g., as in c and d in Fig. 6.8) may then share the same stack storage since their existence is mutually exclusive in time. The area allocated to a block is often called a *stack frame*.

6.4.3 Instructions for Storage Allocation and Deallocation

A stack used for the allocation and deallocation of storage in this manner is referred to as a *data stack* or *storage stack*. Figure 6.9 shows the state of such a data stack at various stages of program P1's execution. The hatched elements indicate those variables that, although in the stack, are inaccessible because the corresponding identifiers have been reused.

The code to be generated from a program such as P1 must include two kinds of information: instructions for allocating and deallocating area in the stack on block entry and exit, respectively; and, for each operand referenced in the program, the stack address of that operand.

When the amount of storage to be reserved for a variable is known at compile time, as in the case of the scalars of Figure 6.8, the compiler will know exactly how much storage to allocate for the variable. Furthermore, since the stack pointer ("d_stkptr" in Fig. 6.9) in a data stack will, after storage allocation for the most recently entered block, always point to the "current" top of the data stack, the address of each variable referenced inside a block can be expressed as an offset relative to the stack pointer.

Let us define two instructions

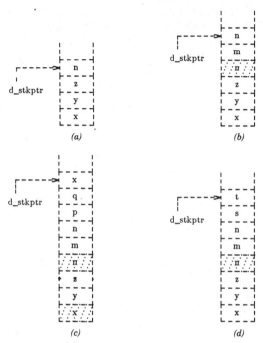

FIGURE 6.9 States of the data stack while executing program P1: *(a)* in Block a; *(b)* in Block b; *(c)* in Block c; *(d)* in Block d.

```
BLOCK      reserved_amount
UNBLOCK    reserved_amount
```

such that a BLOCK instruction with the literal operand "reserved_amount" is generated by the compiler whenever a block is entered; its execution causes the data stack pointer to be incremented so that the appropriate (reserved_amount) number of words are saved in that stack. That is, a stack frame is created. An UNBLOCK instruction is generated by the compiler whenever the flow of control leaves a block. Its execution causes the data stack pointer to be decremented by reserved_amount so that the frame previously reserved in the stack for the block is effectively freed.

Specification 6.3

A formal specification of the BLOCK and UNBLOCK instructions is shown in Figure 6.10. In each case, if there is insufficient space in the stack for storage space allocation (or deallocation), then special flags are set.

As an example of how these instructions would be used by a compiler, Figure 6.11 shows the (partial) code that would be generated from program P1 (Fig. 6.8). It is assumed here that a *separate* expression stack is used to execute assignment statements. The code fragment beginning at L1 refers to variables in the data stack relative to the value of the *data stack pointer* as it would be inside block c (Fig. 6.9c).

```
      . . . . . .
      store dstkptr : seq[..]of bit init (0);
           dstack_ovflow, dstack undflow : bit init (0);
           reserved_area : seq[..]of bit;

      constant yes : bit init (1);
           max_dstack : seq[..]of bit init (..)
      . . . . . .
      module BLOCK
           inport reserved_area
           inoutport dstkptr
           outport dstack_ovflow
           . . . . . .
           effects
               if dstkptr + reserved_area ≥ max_dstack
                   then new dstack_ovflow = yes
                   else new dstkptr = dstkptr + reserved_area
               end if
      end module

      module UNBLOCK
           inport reserved_area
           inoutport dstkptr
           outport dstack_undflow
           . . . . . .
           effects
               if dstkptr < reserved_area
                   then new dstack_undflow = yes
                   else new dstkptr = dstkptr - reserved_area
               end if
      end module
```

FIGURE 6.10   Specification of BLOCK and UNBLOCK.

6.4.4   Displays and Stack Markers

The scheme outlined in the preceding section assumes that the storage requirements for data can be known at compile time. It also assumes that when inside a
block during execution, the stack pointer will remain unchanged, pointing to the
most recent stack word allocated to a variable in the block.

However, consider the program fragment P2 in Figure 6.12 in which the size
of the array A is not known at compile time. In this case, the addresses of the
scalars b, i, or c cannot be generated by the compiler (Fig. 6.13).

Alternatively, suppose we wish to use the same storage as both data and
expression stacks. Once inside a block, the expression stack will sit on top of the
stack area allocated to variables of the "currently" executing block (Fig. 6.14). In
this case, the stack pointer will change in value during expression evaluation;

```
            BLOCK 4
               .
               .
            "other statements in block a"
               .
               .
            BLOCK 2
            "other statements in block b"
               .
               .
            BLOCK 3
        L1: PUSH @-7
            PUSH @-2
            SUB
            POP @
               .
               .
            "other statements in block c"
               .
               .
            UNBLOCK 3
            BLOCK 2
               .
               .
            "other statements in block d"
               .
               .
            UNBLOCK 2
            UNBLOCK 2
            UNBLOCK 4
```

FIGURE 6.11   Code fragment for program P1.

```
(1)  begin
            integer n;
            read(n);
               . . .
(2)         begin
                   integer array A[0:n];
                   integer b, i;
                   read(i);
                      . . .
                   b := A[i]
(3)                begin
                          integer c;
                             . . .
                   end
            end
     end
```

FIGURE 6.12   Code fragment for program P2.

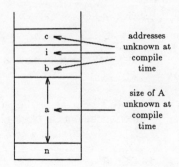

FIGURE 6.13   State of the stack for program P2.

consequently, the compiler can no longer generate addresses of the variables relative to the stack pointer.

Displays

A general solution that resolves both these problems is as follows.

First, each *named* data item in a block (e.g., n, A, b, i, c) is assigned a fixed number of words on the stack. For scalars such as n, b, i, or c, the allocated words serve as a place holder for the variables themselves. For the array A, a *descriptor* of the array is held in the stack.[3] Storage for nonnamed data items (e.g., the elements of A) is assigned elsewhere in memory.

Second, because of the hierarchic nature of block-structured programs, blocks may be assigned *level numbers*, which for program P2 are indicated on the left side of Figure 6.12. Each allocated item in the stack can now be assigned an address in the form of an ordered pair:

VAR_ADDR : <level number, offset>

where "offset" denotes the relative position of the variable in the "level number"-th block.

---

[3]In general, a descriptor D is a data object that specifies the starting address in memory of some structured data object D′, together with other relevant information concerning D′. In particular, an array descriptor may contain the starting address of the array, the number of array dimensions, the type of the array elements, and the size of the array. A descriptor itself occupies a fixed number of words. Array descriptors are also referred to as *dope vectors* (Gries, 1971).

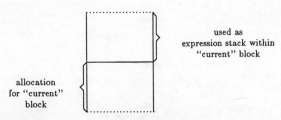

FIGURE 6.14   Combining data and expression stacks.

Third, the starting locations in the stack for data items corresponding to each block-level number is held in a register called a *display* register (Dijkstra, 1960). Because of the last-in/first-out nature of block traversal, the set of display registers may itself be implemented as a stack, although this is not necessary.

With these arrangements all addresses will be generated by the compiler in the form of VAR_ADDR. At run time the actual address ACT_ADDR for an item on the stack may be computed by the hardware or firmware as

ACT_ADDR (<level number, offset>) = display_reg[level number] + offset

For the program P2, the run-time organization and states of the stack, the displays, and the array memory, and the addresses of the variables, are shown in Figure 6.15. Note that with this arrangement the stack pointer can continue to be used for managing the expression stack corresponding to the execution of the "current" block without disturbing the data stack part of the stack store.

Stack Markers

To avoid the use of a separate set of display registers, the displays may themselves be placed on the stack in the form of *stack markers* (or *block markers*) (Doran, 1979). A stack marker is an ordered pair

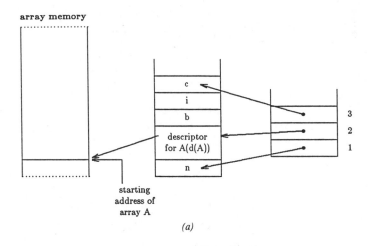

Variables	Addresses
n	< 1,1 >
d(A)	< 2,1 >
b	< 2,2 >
i	< 2,3 >
c	< 3,1 >

(b)

FIGURE 6.15 Descriptor-based addressing: *(a)* Organization of stack, displays, and array memory for program P2; *(b)* ordered-pair addresses for variables in program P2.

STK_MRKR:<block level number, pointer to previous stack marker>.

That is, it records the level number of the block for which it has been created, along with the stack address of the previous stack marker. When a new "topmost" stack marker is placed on the stack, a special register, which we may call "top-stack-marker pointer" must be used and updated to point to the topmost marker.

Figure 6.16 shows the states of the stack and the two associated registers when program P2 is executing the innermost block. Note that now the stack pointer is free to be used as required for pushing and popping elements onto the stack — for the evaluation of expressions, for example. This is because the variables in the stack can be accessed by means of the linked list formed by top-stack-marker pointer and the stack markers themselves.

At any given state of a program's execution, the set of identifiers that are accessible constitute the "current" *addressing environment* (or where there is no confusion, simply *environment*). From Figure 6.16, it will be seen that the linked list starting at the top-stack-number pointer explicitly defines this addressing environment in a block-structured program such as P2; and because this linked list is determined by the textual ordering of the blocks in the program, it is called a *static link*.

Given an operand address in the form

VAR_ADDR : <level number, offset>

the actual stack address, ACT_ADDR, is obtained by following the static link till the address of (or pointer to) the stack marker at "level number" is accessed; this is then added to "Offset."

Specification 6.4

A formal specification of the actual address computation is given in Figure 6.17. There are three new notational features that appear here. The first of these is the *record* store type, which is similar to the Pascal record data type.

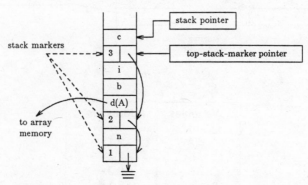

FIGURE 6.16 States of the stack and "top_stk_mrkr_ptr" when inside block 3 of program P2.

```
. . . . . . .
type stack_word is
    overlay data_word : seq[..]of bit;
         stk_mrkr : record
                  level_no : seq[..]of bit
                  ptr_to_prev_mrkr : seq[..]of bit
             end record
         end overlay

constant stacklimit : seq[..]of bit init (..);
    yes : bit init (1);
    no : bit init (0);
. . . . . .
store
    stack : array(1..stacklimit) of stack_word;
    top_stk_mrkr_ptr : seq[..]of bit
    var_addr : record
         level_no : seq[..]of bit;
         offset : seq[..]of bit
    end record;
    actual_addr : seq[..]of bit
. . . . . .
function path(s_index, d_index : seq[..]of bit) : bit
  —determines whether a linked path exists from s_index to d_index;
  =
  if stack(s_index).ptr_to_prev_mrkr  <  d_index then no
    else if stack(s_index).ptr_to_prev_mrkr = d_index then yes
           else path(stack(s_index).ptr_to_prev_mrkr,d_index)
        end if
  end if
end function

function is_stack_marker (j : seq[..]of bit) : bit
  —returns whether stack(j) is a stack marker or not by
  —determining where there is a linked path from top_stk_mrkr_ptr
  —to stack(j)
  =path(top_stk_mrkr_ptr, j)
end function
. . . . . . .
module compute_actual_addr
  inport stack; top_stk_mrkr_ptr; var_addr
  outport actual_addr
  . . . . . . .
  effects
    for first i in {1..top_stk_mrkr_ptr}
      such that
        is_stack_marker(i) = yes   &    stack(i).stk_mrkr.level_no = var_addr.level_no
        +1
      then new actual_addr = stack(i).stk_mrkr.ptr_to_prev_mrkr + var_addr.offset
    end for
end module
```

FIGURE 6.17 Specification of actual stack address computation.

Second, the *overlay . . . end overlay* construct permits us to define two or more alternative structures for a single store type.[4] Thus, the *overlay* declaration states that the store type "stack_word" can be viewed as having either the structure of "data_word" (a specific bit *sequence* type) or the structure of "stk_mrkr" (a specific *record* type). Given that "stack" is declared as an array of elements of type stack_word, a particular element or word of the stack may be referenced either as "stack.data_word" or as "stack.stk_mrkr."

Third, the *effects* section includes a *for first* statement. The general form for this construct is

```
for   first i in {e₁,e₂, . . . ,eₙ}
      such that b
      then s₁
      else s₂
end  for
```

where i is an index variable (whose scope is strictly within the **for** statement) that takes on values in the range of the expressions $e_1, e_2, \ldots, e_n$, b is a Boolean variable dependent on i, and s_1, s_2 are statements.

The meaning of this construct is: For the first value of i in the range $\{e_1, e_2, \ldots, e_n\}$ (provided such a value of i is found) if b is true, then the postcondition satisfies s_1. If there is no i in the range such that b is true, then the postcondition satisfies s_2. The **else** clause is optional as in the **if** statement.

Clearly, when stack markers are employed, the instructions to be executed on entry to, and exit from, a block will have to be somewhat more powerful than the BLOCK and UNBLOCK instructions of Figure 6.10. On entry to a block, a stack marker must be created, assigned proper values, and placed on the stack; the top-stack-marker pointer must be updated so that it points to the newly created stack marker. On exit from a block, the pointer must be reset to the value it had prior to the entry to this block.

Specification 6.5

Figure 6.18 describes the extended versions of the BLOCK and UNBLOCK instructions. The former is a 1-operand instruction where the operand specifies the number of data words to be reserved; this operand is assumed to be in "reserved_area" at the time BLOCK is activated. The UNBLOCK instruction is a 0-operand instruction. The specification as a whole assumes that the stack marker and all named data items require only one stack word each.

Example 6.1

As an example of the use of the extended versions of the BLOCK and UN-BLOCK instructions, Figure 6.19(*a*) shows an Algol-like fragment P3. The corresponding code that may typically be generated by a compiler is shown in

---

[4]The total bit-string lengths of the alternative structures in an *overlay* declaration must be the same.

```
. . . . . .
type stack_word is . . . . . .        —as in Fig. 6.17
constant max_dstack . . . . . .       —as in Fig. 6.10
     yes . . . . . .                   —as in Fig. 6.17
store reserved_area . . . . . .        —as in Fig. 6.10
     stack . . . . . .                 —as in Fig. 6.17
     dstkptr . . . . . .               —as in Fig. 6.10
     top_stk_mrkr_ptr . . . . . .      —as in Fig. 6.17
     stkovflow, stkundflow : bit init (0);
module BLOCK —extended form
     inport reserved_area
     inoutport dstkptr; top_stk_mrkr_ptr; stack
     outport stkovflow
     . . . . . .
     effects
          if dstkptr + reserved_area + 1≥max_dstack
          then new stkovflow = yes
          else —create & write values into new stack marker on top of stack
               new stack(dstkptr+1).level = stack(top_stk_mrkr_ptr).level + 1 &
               new stack(dstkptr+1).ptr_to_prev_mrkr = top_stk_mrkr_ptr &
               —update top_stk_mrkr_ptr to point to new marker
               new top_stk_mrkr_ptr = dstkptr + 1 &
               —allocate storage for data stack
               new dstkptr = dstkptr + reserved_area + 1
          end if
end module


module UNBLOCK —extended form
     inport stack
     inoutport dstkptr; top_stk_mrkr_ptr
     outport stkundflow
     . . . . . .
     effects
          if top_stk_mrkr_ptr = 0 then new stkundflow = yes
          else
               new top_stk_mrkr_ptr = stack(top_stk_mrkr_ptr).ptr_to_prev_mrkr &
               new dstkptr = top_stk_mrkr_ptr - 1
          end if
end module
```

FIGURE 6.18 **Description of extended BLOCK/UNBLOCK instructions.**

Figure 6.19(*b*). In this code fragment, the format of the PUSH and POP instructions symbolizes operations involving array elements. For instance, the execution of PUSH (1,2; 1,4) involves access of the descriptor at stack location (1,2), the extraction from this descriptor of the starting address of the array B, and the computation of an actual address by adding the value of index variable j [which is at address (1,4)] to B's starting address. ∎

```
begin
    integer n,m;
    read(n,m)

    begin
        integer array A[0:n];
        integer array B[0:n];
        integer i,j;

        read(i);
        read(j);
        A[i] := B[j];
        . . . . . .
    end
end
```

(a)

```
BLOCK 2
READ (0,1)
READ (0,2)
BLOCK 4

[Code to allocate memory
 to array A based on value
 in (0,1) and to insert
 starting address of A in
 descriptor at location (1,1)]
[Code to allocate memory
 to array B based on value
 in (0,2) and to insert
 starting address of B in
 descriptor at location (1,2)]

READ (1,3)
READ (1,4)
PUSH (1,2; 1,4)
POP (1,1; 1,3)

. . . . . . . .
UNBLOCK
UNBLOCK
```

(b)

FIGURE 6.19   Algol 60 program fragment P3 *(a)* and corresponding object code *(b)*.

6.5 CONTROL STACKS

Consider the program skeleton P4 shown in Figure 6.20. At the time procedure A is called from inside the main program W, the address to which control must return when A terminates must be saved in some memory location. Similarly, at the time procedure B is invoked from within A, the address in A to which B must return control has to be saved. Since the call to A precedes that to B and the return from B precedes the return from A, the saving and recalling of return addresses exhibit a last-in/first-out characteristic. Return addresses can, thus, be saved on, and retrieved from, a stack by means of appropriate instructions such as CALL and RETURN, defined as follows:

```
CALL add_reg:   new stack(stk_ptr + 1) = prog_ctr
              & new stk_ptr = stk_ptr + 1
              & new prog_ctr = add_reg
RETURN     :    new prog_ctr = stack(stk_ptr)
              & new stk_ptr = stk_ptr − 1
```

Here, "prog_ctr" symbolizes the program counter whereas "add_reg" designates a storage location holding the effective address of the procedure to which control is to be transferred.

A stack used to control procedure calls and returns is often referred to as a *control stack*.

A control stack may also be used to hold the *parameters* passed between procedures. Thus, for example, the state of the stack just after the *call* B statement in Figure 6.20 has been executed would appear as shown in Figure 6.21.

```
            program W

                .
                .
                .
            call A (X1, X2)
                .
                .
                .
            end

            proc A(x1, x2)
                .
                .
                .
            call B(Y1, Y2)
                .
                .
                .
            end

            proc B(y1, y2)
                .
                .
                .
            end
```

FIGURE 6.20 Program fragment P4.

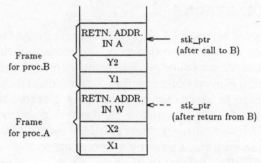

FIGURE 6.21 **State of the control stack after B's call.**

The placement of the parameters (which may be values or addresses) in the stack may be done either by standard stack instructions such as PUSH or PUSHADDR[5] or by a CALL instruction somewhat more powerful than the one defined herein. The RETURN instruction must correspondingly restore the stack pointer so that it points to the previous return address on the stack (Fig. 6.21); hence, the number of parameters placed on the stack during a CALL must either appear as an operand in the RETURN instruction or be itself saved on the stack during the execution of CALL.

Notice that with the arrangement shown in Figure 6.21 the parameters may be addressed relative to the stack pointer that points to the most recently saved return address.

6.5.1 Combining Control and Expression Stacks

Just as the same store can be used for data and expression stack management, one can also combine control and expression stacks. For this to be effected, the stack pointer must serve its usual function of always pointing to the "current" top of the stack so that it can be used for managing the expression stack. Obviously, in this situation, the parameters cannot be addressed relative to the stack pointer.

The solution is very similar to the use of the stack markers described in Section 6.4.4, except that instead of stack markers, a data structure termed a *return constant* (Doran, 1979) of the form

RTN_CONST:<return address, pointer to previous return constant>

can be created when a procedure is called and placed on top of the stack; and, analogous to a top-stack-marker pointer (see Section 6.4.4 and Fig. 6.16) a *top-return-constant pointer* will be needed so as to point at all times to the topmost return constant.

---

[5]The 1-operand "PUSHADDR x" instruction pushes the *address* of operand x onto the stack rather than its value.

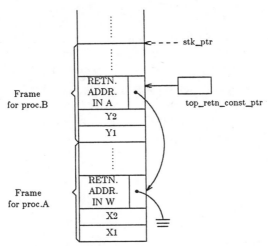

FIGURE 6.22   Combined control/expression stack: Stack state inside procedure B.

Figure 6.22 shows the overall organization of a combined control/expression stack. Parameters in the currently activated procedure will be addressed relative to "top_retn_const_ptr"; note that this pointer, together with all the return constants present in the stack form a linked list, which is often called a *dynamic link* since it explicitly defines the history of procedure calls during program execution.

6.6 BIBLIOGRAPHIC REMARKS

For an authoritative discussion of the Burroughs 6700/7700 exo-architecture, refer to Doran (1979). Organick's earlier book (1973) is also recommended, although the emphasis there is more on operating systems aspects.

Several other systems that employ variations on the stack themes described in this chapter have been developed commercially. One of these, the Hewlett Packard HP 3000 minicomputer is discussed by Baer (1980). Another example is the ICL 2900 mainframe, developed in Britain. This system is described by Buckle (1978).

Randell and Russell (1964) provide a detailed discussion of an early Algol 60 compiler for the English Electric KDF-9. This compiler came to be known as the "Whetstone compiler." Randell and Russell's account of the development of a virtual stack machine architecture as the run-time environment for Algol 60 still remains fascinating reading.

The notation used in this chapter for the formal specifications is based on the architecture description language S*M (Dasgupta, Wilsey, and Heinanen, 1986). This language is described in more detail in Volume 2, Chapter 4.

PROBLEMS

6.1 Despite the elegance with which stacks may be used to evaluate expressions and execute assignments, in reality they offer mixed blessings. Describe the advantages and disadvantages of using expression stacks.

6.2 Extend the instruction set shown in Table 6.1 with a repertoire of stack based *branch* instructions and instructions for the evaluation of *relational expressions*. Using the extended instruction set, write object code for the following Pascal-style program:

```
program
    var   x : array [1..64] of char;
    var   low, high, max : integer;
    var   temp : char;

    max : = 64;
    while max > 1 do
        low : = 1 ; high : = 2;
        while low < max do
            if x [low]  >  x [high]
                then do temp : = x [low];
                        x [low] : = x [high];
                        x [high] : = temp
                    od
            fi
            low : = low + 1 ; high : = high + 1
        od
    od
end program
```

6.3 An expression stack—that is, a stack dedicated to the execution of assignments and the evaluation of expressions—can be implemented by an array of processor registers.

(a) Why is this a reasonable proposition? What would be a reasonable bound on the number of registers that would be needed in such an implementation?

(b) Design the *micro-architecture* of such a register-based expression stack, assuming that:

(i) All zero-address instructions can be executed in a single micro-cycle of 150 ns.

(ii) PUSH and POP instructions can be executed in a memory cycle of 600 ns.

Call the micro-architecture MSTK. Your design of MSTK should include (1) a description of the data-path part of the micro-architecture; (2) its timing structure; (3) a specification of the micro-operations (MOs) required to control the stack; the specification should define both the behavior and the timing of these MOs; (4) the microinstruction formats showing the fields encoding the relevant stack control MOs; and (5) the microcode for implementing a PUSH (or a POP) type instruction, and one of the arithmetic instructions.

6.4   Consider the implementation (at the endo-architectural level) of an expression stack which satisfies the following property: *The top two stack elements are always contained in two fixed processor registers whereas the rest of the stack is held in main memory.*

The two registers (which are *not* visible at the exo-architectural level) may be called TOP and NEXT-TOP. The execution of all stack-based instructions (PUSH, POP, and the 0-address operations such as ADD and SUB) will be such that they take their operands either from TOP only (in the case of a unary operation) or from TOP and NEXT-TOP (in the case of a binary operation).

(a)   Design the endo-architecture of such a system, including details of how the stack systems is accessed and controlled during the execution of the object code CODE1 shown in Section 6.3.

(b)   Describe the advantages and disadvantages of this system compared to those where the stack is implemented entirely (i) in main memory or (ii) in a register array.

6.5   An *accumulator-stack* system is a system (visible at the exo-architectural level) with the following properties:

(i)   There is a single programmable arithmetic register—the accumulator.

(ii)   Execution of assignments and the evaluation of expressions use the accumulator in conjunction with a stack (which may or may not be implemented in main memory).

(iii)   In executing instructions, the system behaves as a *register machine* (where the accumulator serves as the sole register) but uses the stack *if and only if it is absolutely necessary*. In other words, the stack is only used to hold temporary, intermediate values of subexpressions.

(a)   Design, and give a formal specification of, an instruction set for such an accumulator-stack machine.

(b)   Show the object code corresponding to the assignment statement

$$A := (A + B) * (C - 1/D)$$

(c)   Discuss the advantages and disadvantages of this type of a system in contrast to (1) a "pure" register machine, and (2) a "pure" expression stack.

6.6   As part of the design of a stack-based language-directed architecture you are required to develop a subroutine CALL instructions satisfying the following conditions.

Assume, to begin with, that the stack "grows" from the high address end of main memory toward the low address end.

Suppose now, that procedure A is about to call procedure B. Prior to the execution of the CALL instruction, it is assumed that the parameters to be passed from A to B have already been placed in the stack at the beginning of a new stack frame corresponding to procedure B.

The function of the CALL instruction is fourfold: (i) To save the contents of a set of *up to* 16 general registers (numbered 0 through 15) on the stack. (The actual number to be saved depends on how many of the registers are being used by procedure A.) (ii) To save the return address. (iii) To allocate space for the local variables of the called procedure B; and finally (iv) to transfer control to B. The format of the CALL instruction is

CALL reg-no, size

where "reg-no" is the number of the lowest of the general registers that B will use (i.e., B will use registers 15 through "reg-no"), and "size" is the size of the stack space for the local variables of B. When inside a procedure the top of the "current" stack frame is also used to evaluate expressions.

(a) Give a complete formal specification of the CALL instruction (use, if you like, the specification notation used in this chapter or any other convenient specification language).

(b) To illuminate this specification, show the relevant state of the stack at the beginning of the CALL instruction.

(c) Describe also the relevant state of the stack just after the CALL has been executed.

(d) Explain how the called procedure's parameters and local variables will be addressed from within B.

6.7 Construct and specify formally a RETURN instruction that matches the CALL of Problem 6.6, such that on executing the RETURN the state of the stack and other relevant registers is restored to what it was prior to the CALL's execution.

6.8 In Section 6.4.4, schemes for combining data and expression stacks were described. Section 6.5.1 showed how control and expression stacks could be combined. Describe in detail, the architecture of a system that combines data, expression, and control stacks in a single, uniform, consistent stack held in main memory. Your description should include the relevant instructions, registers, and the data structures (to be held in the stack) and should be supported by "snapshots" showing the state of the stack when executing programs involving block entry/exit, statement execution, and procedure call/return.

CHAPTER 7

LANGUAGE-DIRECTED ARCHITECTURES: THE "RISC" STYLE

7.1 INTRODUCTION

I noted in Chapter 1 that architectures are abstract characterizations of physical computers. It was further suggested (in Chapter 3, Section 3.4) that the role of such a characterization is to provide a *specification* of structural, functional, and performance constraints that has to be met by some physical computer.

Accordingly, the architect's principle role—indeed, obligation—is to translate the requirements established by the *environment* into a specification of constraints that the implemented machine must satisfy.[1] At the same time, this translation process must not be uncritical; the architect should use his or her knowledge of the relevant technological issues to produce an *economically realizable* specification. The similarity between the roles of the computer and the building architect (see, e.g., Broadbent, 1973) in this respect is striking!

If one accepts this viewpoint, it follows that architectural design should be, fundamentally, "driven" by environmental needs; that the design process should be top down. Furthermore, when the environment changes over time, architectures should change accordingly. The development and evolution of computer architectures over any given period of time should, according to this line of reasoning, reflect the evolution of environments.

Unfortunately, history belies such expectations. The register machine style as conceived in the 1940s has essentially prevailed over the years: The *exo-architectures* of most computers are not very different from that of the original von Neumann design, although they have certainly grown in complexity; and yet the environments—the classes of problems requiring computational solutions and the methods for describing and implementing such solutions—have changed enormously over the course of these four decades. Most of the developments, in

---

[1]In the present context the environment is the universe within which the computer, as a system, must function. The environment may be defined in terms of a particular user community or the class of problems that this community is interested in solving (e.g., image-processing computations or problems in numeric analysis) or it may be defined in terms of the programming languages in which the users will do most of their programming. From the opposite viewpoint, a computer system also defines an environment; that is, the universe in which the *user* is constrained to perform computation.

fact, have taken place at the endo-architectural level and have been driven, not by the environment, but by developments in technology.

This mismatch between architectural ideals and architectural reality has, of course, been noted by many. The first significant attempt at developing an exo-architecture that reflected "current" environmental needs was the exploitation of stacks (see Chapter 6). In the early 1960s, the Burroughs Corporation produced the first members of the B5000/B6000 series (Organick 1973; Doran, 1979); these were the earliest commercial systems with architectures consciously designed for the representation and execution of programs compiled from Algol-like languages. During the 1960s and early 1970s, some of the theoretical ideas underlying such *language-directed architectures* were outlined by Iliffe (1968), Lawson (1968), and Barton (1970). The universal host machines of the early 1970s—especially the Burroughs B1700 and the Nanodata QM-1—were also commercial computers designed with such architectural ideals in mind (see Chapter 5, Section 5.4).

It is only since the mid-1970s, however, that a truly determined attempt to cast off the shackles of the classical von Neumann style began. Myers (1982) was, if not the first, one of the most influential in developing a systematic and thorough critique of the classical style, in formulating the requirements of language-directed architectures, and in describing a collection of exo-architectures that were designed to meet the needs of contemporary high-level programming environments.[2]

However, even though some agreement may have been tacitly reached among architects that exo-architecture design should be environment-driven, it was far less clear as to how one should try to achieve this ideal. Very different types of solutions have been proposed, which differ in both the architectural concepts that they embody as well as the design process and reasoning used in arriving at the architecture. This chapter will examine one of the approaches that seems particularly attractive, largely because of its underlying principles, the extent of research that has been invested in these principles, the empirical data that supports their validities, and, lastly, but by no means the least, because of their aesthetic appeal. This is the *reduced instruction set computer* (RISC) philosophy, developed by Patterson, Hennessy, Cocke, and their coworkers (Patterson and Sequin, 1981, 1982; Patterson, 1985; Hennessy, 1984; Hennessy *et al.*, 1982; Katevenis, 1985).

7.2 REDUCED INSTRUCTION SET COMPUTERS: THE INITIAL POSTULATES

Although reduced instruction set computers (RISCs) conform to the broad principles of classic register machines and the von Neumann style, the ideas

[2]For other bibliographic aspects of language-directed architectures, see the section on Bibliographic Remarks at the end of this chapter.

underlying RISCs have sufficiently broken with certain evolutionary trends in computer architecture to constitute a significant and distinct architectural style.

The RISC argument, stripped to its essence, can be stated in terms of three postulates:

1. Over the years, computer architectures have evolved toward progressively greater complexity, where the "complexity" of an architecture is characterized by such exo-architectural factors as the size of the instruction set, the computational power of the individual instructions, the types of addressing modes, and so forth. Patterson and Ditzel (1980) termed recent machines falling within such evolutionary trends, *complex instruction set computers* (CISCs).

2. Given present technologies and computational environments, there are neither theoretical nor practical justifications for this trend to continue.

3. Rather, more cost-effective computers can be realized with simpler architectures. Such computers were termed, by Patterson and Ditzel (1980), *reduced instruction set computers* (RISCs).

One must mention here that in the original RISC manifesto of Patterson and Ditzel (1980) neither CISCs nor RISCs were precisely defined. Even the thorny notion of complexity was not satisfactorily characterized. It was only later that a more definite set of RISC architectural characteristics were formulated, and even these have been subject to debate. CISCs would then constitute machines with architectures *not* satisfying RISC characteristics.

7.2.1   The Causes of Increased Architectural Complexity

Concerning the first of these postulates, one has only to examine particular lines of computers (e.g., the IBM System/360 and System/370 families, the Burroughs B5000/B6000/B7000 series, the PDP-11/VAX-11 succession, the Motorola 6800/68000 machines, and the Intel 8080/8086/iAPX-432 series) to see that it is well supported by the empirical evidence.

Of much greater interest are the causes for this observable trend toward greater complexity. One may identify several such causes.

Changing Environments

To anyone even moderately familiar with evolutionary phenomenon, it is clear that a rather fundamental reason why an artifact may be more complex than its predecessor is that the *environment* itself has shifted and, in some sense, become more complex. Consequently, the artifact must necessarily become richer in its capability in order to function efficiently in the new environment.

The environmental change of most relevance to the growth in exo-architectural complexity was the emergence of high-level programming languages as the principal medium of programming rather than assembly languages. Its consequence was the introduction of new instructions intended to "support" the efficient implementation of high-level language programs. Such instructions not only added to the size of the instruction set but were often quite complex because of their relatively high functional power.

Increased Performance within a Given Environment

Second, again following evolutionary arguments, even within an essentially unchanging environment, competition between artifacts will act as a *selection pressure* so that only those artifacts will "survive" that perform best in the given environment.

In practical terms, this puts pressure on the designer to design computers that are more cost-effective than their predecessors or rivals. More on the notion of cost-effectiveness later, but certainly one aspect of this is to make machines *faster* than their predecessors or rivals at constant or only moderately increased cost.

This has also directly affected the architectural complexity of computers. Because of the traditional disparity between the speeds of memory and logic, a given function realized by a sequence of several instructions is expected to require more time to execute (because of a larger number of memory accesses) than when it is implemented by means of a single instruction. Thus, one observes the phenomenon of *vertical migration* of functions from software to firmware and from firmware to hardware (Stankovic, 1981) in order to accelerate the processing speed of computers. Migrating functions across the exo-architectural boundary (i.e., from the software domain into the hardware/firmware domain) will naturally increase the size of the instruction set with an attendant increase in the overall complexity of the computer.

Nonrational Reasons

Increases in architectural complexity have also been ascribed to what are essentially nonrational reasons. One of these, partly dictated by marketing considerations, is the policy of *upward compatibility*: that is, the notion that a new computer should have all the functional capabilities of its predecessor *and more*. Thus, a new instruction set is designed as a superset of its predecessor.

Patterson and Ditzel (1980) have pointed out that the availability and use of microprogramming have also aggravated this situation. One well-known advantage of microprogramming (see Chapter 5, Section 5.3) is that if spare words in the control store are available, then adding microroutines (in order to implement new instructions or addressing modes, say) can be done at virtually no extra hardware cost. Ironically, this very same feature may well be abused: instructions, addressing modes, or other exo-architectural features can be added simply because the control store space "is there"!

7.2.2 The Problem with CISCs

According to the second of the RISC postulates, even if the trend toward complexity had been justified in the past — for instance, because of the rapid enlargement of the computational environment during the 1950s and 1960s — there are powerful grounds to believe that this is no longer so under present assumptions about the environment and the available technologies. Rather, new concerns have arisen that (again, in evolutionary terms) have exerted on architects and computer designers a kind of selection pressure to shift toward simpler and more regular architectures.

The Influence of Compilation Issues

Since a very large part of contemporary computing is done using high-level programming languages, the "goodness" of an exo-architecture is largely determined by (1) how efficiently programs can be compiled into object code and (2) how efficient the resulting code is.

Recall that increased architectural complexity has been motivated in part by the desire for supporting high-level language features. However, the empirical evidence (Alexander and Wortman, 1975; Lunde, 1977; Peuto and Shustek, 1977; Shustek, 1978) indicates that adding instructions that are functionally powerful and semantically close to high-level language functions has not made it easier to compile programs into object code. Rather, it has been observed that compilers very frequently use only a small fraction of the total instruction set.

Example 7.1

Alexander and Wortman (1975) analyzed the characteristics of programs written in a dialect of PL/1 called XPL, and compiled into IBM System/360 code. They observed that only 10 instructions in the 360 instruction set accounted for 80% of all instructions executed, 21 instructions accounted for 95% of executed instructions, and only 30 instructions accounted for 99% of executed code. ■

The main reason for this general phenomenon has been explained by Wulf (1981). He pointed out that a compiler essentially performs a large case analysis; the complexity of an exo-architecture is determined by such factors as the number of different instructions and addressing modes and their respective functional power; and the number of different sizes and formats of instructions. Thus, from the compilation viewpoint, the more complex the exo-architecture, the more ways there are available for realizing some given high-level language function, the larger will be the case analysis, and the greater the resulting compilation time.

Although the production of efficient code is of paramount importance, this must be balanced with the need for compilation speed. If the full complexity of CISC architectures (such as the IBM System/370 or VAX 11/780 exo-architectures) were to be exploited, the compiler might become unbearably slow and complex. As in almost all spheres of design, compiler writing is a satisficing process (see Chapter 3). Thus compiler writers prefer simpler architectures where the number of choices available are fewer and more uniform: Ease of compilation is consequently enhanced with simpler and more uniform exo-architectures.

In Chapter 1 (section 1.7.2) I described more precisely the kinds of desirable exo-architectural properties as enumerated by Wulf (1981) that help ease the compiler writer's burden.

The Effect of VLSI: The Use of Scarce Resources

The impact of VLSI technology on computer architecture has been described in several places in this book (see, in particular, Chapter 1, Section 1.9, and Chapter 2). In the context of the RISC/CISC debate, the effects of VLSI may be summarized as follows (Patterson and Ditzel, 1980; Patterson and Sequin, 1982):

1. The full exploitation of contemporary VLSI technology demands that an entire processor be realized on a single chip.
2. Complex exo-architectures require complex implementations. The larger and more varied the instruction set, addressing modes, instruction sizes, and instruction formats, the more elaborate will be the instruction fetch, decode, and execution logic. In the case of microprogrammed processors, this is directly manifested in large, complex microprograms requiring large amounts of control store.[3]
3. Thus, when CISC architectures are implemented using VLSI technology, a substantial part of the chip area may be consumed in realizing the control unit.

Example 7.2

Patterson and Sequin (1982) provide data on several VLSI-based processor implementations, notably, the Zilog Z8000, the Motorola M68000, and the Intel iAPX 432. The amount of chip area given to control range from 40% for one model of the 432, through 50% for the 68000, up to 65% for another model of the 432. ■

4. A given amount of chip area can be used in many different ways. If part of the chip area given over to control logic could be released, this may be used to implement other functions—such as pipelining or large register banks—by which the processor's performance can be improved.
5. A simple exo-architecture can be expected to require less control logic than a more complex exo-architecture. Thus, an implementation of the former

---

[3]Indeed, the effect of evolving architectural complexity on control-store size is strikingly shown when one examines a particular line of computers.

would make available more of the chip area for other purposes. Consequently, one may expect to improve the speed of the processor. One can, therefore, hope to realize VLSI RISCs that are faster than VLSI CISCs.

6. Furthermore, because simpler exo-architectures imply less control logic, the latter (whether hardwired or microprogrammed) can be expected to be simpler and faster. Thus, quite irrespective of the expected gains due to chip area availability, one may expect an inherent gain in processor speed in RISCs over CISCs, simply because of the former's relative simplicity.

7.2.3 Overall Cost Effectiveness of RISCs

Based on the foregoing arguments, we are led to the third postulate: That RISCs can be expected to be more *cost effective* than CISCs, where the factors contributing to cost effectiveness include not only (1) the speed of the resulting processor—that is, the execution time of individual instructions and the throughput time of instruction streams—and (2) the ease of compilation, but also (3) the time to design, verify, and implement the architecture, and (4) the time to test and debug the resulting hardware.

Traditional discussions of computer architectures rarely (if at all) raise the issues of design time or the effort expended in verifying the architecture or its implementation. Usually, the only explicit recognition of these important facets of computer design is in the use of microprogramming—because of its advantages in implementing, modifying, or augmenting an architecture (see Chapter 5).

In a purely theoretical sense, it is obvious that an architecture that can be designed, implemented, and verified in less time than another is more appealing: This is due to the aesthetic appeal that stems from economy of resource use. In the VLSI context, there are also very sound practical reasons for desiring such characteristics. For one thing, given the rapid development of the technology, longer times for design, implementation, and verification may well lead to a situation where the implementation technology is obsolete by the time the processor is in production; for another, the inherent complexity of VLSI chips—measured in terms of the number of transistors—places formidable demands on the testability of the circuits (Frank and Sproull, 1981). Hence, simple-structured and regular implementations become virtually imperative.

7.3 REDUCED INSTRUCTION SET COMPUTERS: DEFINING CHARACTERISTICS

Thus far, we have avoided giving an actual definition of a RISC. This cannot be postponed any longer.

As in so many other aspects of computer architecture, any attempt to define a RISC rigorously is self-defeating. The designers of each of the first experimental

RISCs [namely, the IBM 801 (Radin, 1982), the Berkeley RISC I (Patterson and Sequin, 1982) and RISC II (Katevenis, 1985), and the Stanford MIPs (Hennessy, 1984; Hennessy et al., 1982)] refined the intuitive notion of a small, simple instruction set into a collection of more precise characteristics for their particular machines. These characteristics did not all coincide. The designers also made certain key decisions about hardware/software trade-offs and the effective use of chip areas that also varied from one project to another.

Based on these machines, a small set of common properties can be identified *post facto* and can serve to "define" a RISC (Patterson, 1985; Colwell et al., 1985).

1. All instructions (operations) are register-register type with the exceptions of LOAD and STORE, which access main memory.
2. All instructions (operations) consume a single processor cycle with the possible exceptions of LOAD and STORE.
3. Fixed length, and simple, fixed format instructions that do not cross main memory word boundaries.
4. Relatively few operations and addressing modes.
5. The use of hardwired rather than microcoded control.
6. The use of instruction pipelining and the concomitant use of compilation and delayed branch techniques (see Chapter 5, Section 5.3.2, and Volume 2, Chapter 6, Section 6.3.7) to eliminate pipeline disruption due to branches.

The implications of each of these features for the overall goal of cost-effectiveness can be thought out by the reader. There are, however, two aspects of this definition that need further discussion.

7.3.1 Implication of RISCs for Microprogramming

One significant aspect of the RISC approach is that the designers of all three experimental machines have eschewed microprogrammed in favor of hardwired control, largely because of speed considerations (characteristic 2). Thus, the emergence of the RISC style has been interpreted by some as sounding the death knell of microprogramming as an architectural implementation technique (Hopkins, 1983). Even its inventor has expressed some doubts about the future of microprogramming (Wilkes, 1982).

Resisting the temptation to offer my own prognosis on this issue, I do, however, make the following observation.

If one examines the defining characteristics of a RISC as just listed, one sees a striking resemblance between these characteristics and those of *micro-architectures* (see Chapter 5, Section 5.3). The notable difference is that micro-architectures usually include horizontal microinstructions with some potential parallelism between micro-operations.

Thus, it seems reasonable to view RISCs as a class of *universal host machines* (UHMs; see Chapter 5, Section 5.4.2) with vertically encoded instructions. The fact that the technique of delayed branching has been borrowed from microprogramming, and that RISC instructions were intended to have the same order of speed as conventional microinstructions (Patterson, 1985) appears to strengthen this view. Stated differently, RISC exo-architectures may be said to constitute a class of micro-architectures raised to a higher level of abstraction than their traditional counterparts. The originality of the RISC approach—by virtue of which it may achieve the technical and commercial success that eluded UHMs —lies in the fact that the exo-architecture of a RISC need not be visible at all to the user.

7.3.2 RISCs as Integrated High-Level Language Machines

This last statement re-emphasizes what is perhaps the most important practical aspect of the RISC style: that RISCs are intended to support *high-level language computer systems*. Such a system has been defined by Ditzel and Patterson (1980) as possessing the following characteristics:

1. All programming and user interaction with the computer system will be done using high-level languages.
2. All error messages reported back by the system will be in terms of the high-level language source program.
3. Any transformations of source programs into internal or machine-language representations will be completely invisible to the user.

Because of the desired invisibility of the underlying RISC exo-architecture, the burden of producing and executing efficient object code rests entirely on the compiler on one hand and the architectural implementation on the other. The RISC approach, thus, encourages *the integration and cooperation of compilation techniques, architectural principles, and architectural implementation techniques* in the design of a system. It encourages the careful analysis of software/architecture/hardware trade-offs as an integral part of the design process. This is a substantial departure from the approaches taken in designing computer families such as the IBM Systems/360 and 370 or the DEC PDP-11/VAX-11, where a clear separation exists between exo-architecture and lower levels; and the same exo-architecture is implemented in different family members by using different endo-architectures and implementation techniques.

7.4 THE BERKELEY RISC

Thus far, we have tried to capture the ideology and spirit of the RISC style. Each of the three prototypal RISCs, however, has specific and distinctive characteristics that are worthy of further study. Thus it is important for at least one of these to be discussed here in more detail.

For this purpose, we will consider the RISC-I developed at the University of California at Berkeley by Patterson and Sequin and their associates. This choice is only dictated by the fact that it has been documented in the published literature more extensively than the MIPs or the IBM 801; consequently, the RISC-1 architecture and design has been more widely disseminated, studied, and criticized than its fellow RISCs.[4]

7.4.1 The "Shape" of the Environment

An important—perhaps the most important—aspect of the RISC-I architecture is a methodological one, namely the empirical basis for deriving the exo-architecture. In keeping with the philosophy underlying the RISC style, the intent of the RISC-I designers was to create a VLSI-implemented architecture; and because of the presence of a large, local community of C users, C was chosen as the particular language to be supported by the RISC-I architecture. Thus it was necessary to gather data on the "shape" of characteristic C programs.

In actual fact, data were collected for both Pascal and C programs. The relevant results of this phase of the design are summarized in Table 7.1.

Several remarks need to be made about this table.

1. A set of four Pascal and four C programs were analyzed at the source level to obtain the figures shown in parts (*a*) and (*b*). The Pascal programs were, respectively, a Pascal compiler, the macro expansion phase of a design automation system, a Pascal prettyprinter, and a program for comparing files. The C programs were, respectively: the portable C compiler for the VAX, a VLSI mask layout program, a text formatter, and a sorting program.

2. The figures for loops in part (*b*) were based on loops being counted once per execution of the loop as a whole rather than one per iteration of the loop body. The statements within a loop body were, of course, counted as many times as they were executed.

3. Part (*b*) does not indicate the *amount of time* taken to execute each of the statement types. To extract this information, "typical" machine code sequences for each of the statement types were generated and used to count both the number of machine instructions and the number of memory references per statement type, weighted by their respective frequencies of occurrences. Part (*c*) of Table 7.1 shows the resulting data.

4. In part (*c*), the figures for the call/return include the overhead of parameter passing and the saving and restoring of registers. For the loop statement, the count includes all machine instructions executed during each iteration.

The two most significant features of this data are: first, that more than 80% of all scalar references were to local variables (of procedures) and more than 90% of all array/structure references were to global variables; and second, that proce-

---

[4]The Berkeley RISC project has involved the development of several RISC style processors. These include RISC-I and RISC-II, both designed to support imperative programming languages such as C and Pascal (Patterson, 1985; Patterson and Sequin, 1982; Katevenis, 1985), and a processor to support the object-oriented language SMALLTALK (Ungar *et al.*, 1984). Of these, RISC-I is the first and most well known. RISC-II has essentially the same exo-architecture but a slightly different endo-architecture and implementation.

TABLE 7.1 Characteristics of Pascal and C Programs

(a)

Dynamic Frequency of Operands	Pascal & C	Remarks
Integer constants	20 ± 7%	
Scalars	55 ± 11%	>80% refer to local variables
Arrays/structures	25 ± 14%	>90% refer to global variables

(b)

Dynamic Frequency of Statement Types	Pascal	C
Assignment	45 ± 8%	38 ± 15%
If	29 ± 8%	43 ± 17%
Call/Return	15 ± 1%	12 ± 5%
With	5 ± 5%	3 ± 1%
Loop	5 ± 0%	3 ± 4%
Case	1 ± 1%	<1 ± 1%

(c)

Weighted Dynamic Frequency of Statement Types	Machine Instructions		Memory References	
	Pascal	C	Pascal	C
Call/Return	31 ± 3%	33 ± 14%	44 ± 4%	45 ± 19%
Loop	42 ± 3%	32 ± 6%	33 ± 2%	26 ± 5%
Assignment	13 ± 2%	13 ± 5%	14 ± 2%	15 ± 6%
If	11 ± 3%	21 ± 8%	7 ± 2%	13 ± 5%

Source: Patterson and Sequin (1982).

dure calls/returns are the most time-consuming of the high-level language statement types.

The studies reported by Patterson and Sequin (1982) were, of course, neither the first nor the only experiments of this kind. Dasgupta (1984, Chapter 13) summarizes several such experiments and some of the general qualitative conclusions that could be extracted from them (see also Chapter 4, Section 4.5, of this book). In the specific context of the RISC project, Katevenis (1985, Chapter 2) has also described some of these same experiments and others, including Knuth's (1971) study of Fortran programs and his own additional experiments with C programs. One can do no better than to quote his overall summary of these studies (Katevenis, 1985, p. 41):

In all cases we saw that programs are organized in procedures and that procedure calls are frequent and costly in terms of execution time. Procedures usually have a few arguments and local variables most of which are scalars and are heavily used. The nesting depth fluctuates within narrow ranges for long periods of time.

As we will see in Sections 7.4.2 and 7.4.3, the design of the RISC-I was based on this profile of the computing environment. In particular, it has an architecture designed for the efficient storage of local variables and procedure arguments and for the fast execution of procedure calls/returns. The instruction set supports the most frequent and time-consuming high-level language operations. Less time-consuming operations would have to be synthesized by the compiler or in the form of subroutines. It is fundamentally in terms of these characteristics that the RISC-I is viewed as a language-directed computer.

7.4.2 The RISC-I Exo-architecture

The RISC-I is, perhaps, one of the purest forms of the register machine in the sense that all instructions except LOADs and STOREs are of the register-to-register type. It is also a 32-bit machine in that instructions, addresses and registers, as well as the word length, are all 32-bits long.

Each program has available to it, a file of 32 general purpose registers identified as R0 through R31. Of these, register R0 permanently holds the hardwired constant '0'. A powerful and highly distinctive characteristic of the register file is that it is organized according to a scheme called *overlapped windows*. As we will see later (in Section 7.4.3), this scheme was invented expressly to provide efficient support for procedure activations and deactivations.

The processor cycle time is determined by the time taken to gate the contents of two registers into the ALU, add the values, and store the result back into a register. The LOAD and STORE instructions require two processor cycles.[5]

Let us now consider some of the specific features of the RISC-I exo-architecture.

Data Types and Memory

There are only two types of supported data types in the RISC-I: *signed integers* in 2's complement notation and *unsigned logicals*.[6] Each of these supported

---

[5]At the time of designing and evaluating a simulated version of the RISC-I, the cycle time had been expected to be 400 ns (Patterson and Sequin, 1982). However, the first VLSI (NMOS) implementation yielded a speed of 2 μs per instruction — a fivefold decrease in cycle time (Foderado, van Dyke, and Patterson, 1982). An NMOS version of RISC-II ran at 330 ns per instruction (Patterson, 1985) whereas an NMOS version of MIPS ran at 500 ns per instruction.

[6]Or, more strictly speaking, *bit sequences*, since both Boolean and shift operations are defined on this data type.

types can, in turn, be implemented as a 32-bit *word*, a 16-bit *halfword*, or an 8-bit *byte*. These latter three-bit sequences, then, constitute RISC-I's intrinsic data types (see Chapter 4, Section 4.6).

Main memory is organized in terms of 32-bit "slices," where each slice can hold a word, two halfwords, or four bytes. Data cannot cross slice boundaries. Memory is byte addressable and has a capacity of 2^{32} bytes. Words and half-words are referenced by the address of their least-significant (rightmost) byte. If a word or a halfword is addressed at an illegal position, an alignment error occurs.

The Instruction Set

The 31 instructions fall into four categories, namely arithmetic/logical, memory access, control transfer, and miscellaneous.

The general action performed by the 12 *arithmetic/logical* instructions can be depicted as

$$R_d := R_{S1} \text{ OP } S_2$$

where R_d is a *destination register*; R_{S1} is the *first source register*; S_2 is either the *second source register* R_{S2} or an *immediate constant* Imm; and OP is one of the following operations:

1. Integer addition or subtraction (with or without carry).
2. Integer inverse subtraction (i.e., $S_2 - R_{S1}$), with or without carry.
3. Bitwise AND, OR, EXCLUSIVE OR.
4. Shift left or right logical or shift right arithmetic by amount specified by S_2.

The general actions performed by the eight *memory access* instructions can be depicted as:

LOADs   : **new** $R_d = \text{Mem}[R_{S1} + S_2]$
STOREs : **new** $\text{Mem}[R_{S1} + S_2] = R_d$

where R_{S1} serves as an index register and S_2, *always* a constant Imm, serves as the displacement or offset.

Thus, the index/displacement scheme is one main addressing mode in the RISC-I. The compiler may use this to *synthesize* a variety of other modes.

Example 7.3

Some of the VAX-11 addressing modes (see Chapter 4, Section 4.7, Example 4.16) may be synthesized as follows (Patterson and Sequin, 1982):

1. Register : R_{S1}
2. Register indirect : $R_{S1} + 0$
3. Immediate : Imm
4. Direct : $R_0(=0) + \text{Imm}$ ∎

There are five *control transfer* instructions. These consist of JMP (jumps) procedure CALLs and RETs (returns). The branch-to address of a conventional JMP or CALL may be specified using the index/displacement mode

R_{S1} + Imm

In the case of a CALLR (call relative) or JMPR (jump relative), the branch-to address is specified as an offset relative to the *program counter*, PC. Since the PC is not part of the RISC-I general register file, a separate *PC-relative* addressing mode, of the form

PC + Imm

is used in the CALLR and JMPR instructions.

The procedure call/return instructions are certainly the most interesting of the RISC-I instruction set. These are discussed further in Section 7.4.3.

The remaining *miscellaneous* category includes instructions to load and set the process status word and to enable and disable interrupts and a "load immediate high" (LDHI) instruction, which loads the high-order 19 bits of R_d with a 19-bit constant, at the same time setting the remaining low-order 13 bits to 0. This, seemingly arbitrary, instruction can be used in conjunction with an immediately following instruction that uses its 13-bit Imm field to load any 32-bit constant into a register.

Instruction Formats

All instructions are 32-bits wide and are encoded according to one of the two basic formats.

The *short-immediate* format is shown in Figure 7.1. Here:

1. OP designates the opcode.
2. SCC is the (optional) "set condition code" bit, which when "1" causes condition codes to be set in the process status word according to the result of the instruction.
3. DEST may specify one of two items depending on OP. For conditional jump instructions its four low-order bits specify the branch condition. For all other instructions it specifies R_d, the destination register.
4. R_{S1} is the first source register.
5. The high-order bit of S_2 signifies whether the rest of the field should be interpreted as a 13-bit, signed 2's complement immediate operand, Imm, or whether its low-order 5 bits is to be taken as identifying R_{S2}, the second source register. In the latter case, the remaining 8 bits of S_2 are ignored.

31	25 24	23	19 18	14 13	0
OP	SCC	DEST	R_{S1}	S_2	

FIGURE 7.1 Short-immediate instruction format.

31		25	24	23		19	18			0

OP	SCC	DEST	Imm

FIGURE 7.2 Long-immediate instruction format.

The *long-immediate* format (Fig. 7.2) is used for all instructions that use PC-relative addressing and for the LDHI instruction. All other instructions are encoded in the short-immediate format.

7.4.3 Overlapping Register Windows

As previously noted, procedure calls and returns were found to be the most time consuming of the high-level language operations. In a conventional register machine containing a small set of general registers the reasons for this are twofold: first, the need to save registers on a call and restore them on return; second, the need to pass parameters to, and results from, the called procedure.

This time-consuming aspect of procedure invocation is likely to be further aggravated in RISCs since other relatively complex operations have to be synthesized in subroutines from the available instructions. Thus, an important, indeed essential, objective in the RISC-I design was to provide an efficient (i.e., fast) procedure call/return mechanism. As Patterson and Sequin (1982) note, the procedure call should not be slower than a "few" jumps.

The approach to this problem is a good example of how both architectural and physical implementation considerations can be used cooperatively to effect a solution. It rested on the following points:

1. The obvious fact that calls and returns can be speeded up by minimizing the physical transfer of information required to save/restore registers and pass parameters/results.
2. The necessity of such transfers in conventional register machines arises because of the very small number of fast registers (typically between 8 and 32) that have to be shared between procedures.
3. One of the attractive benefits of the simpler control logic required by a RISC is that a larger part of the chip area can be dedicated to registers; that is, a larger number of registers can be placed on the processor chip itself.
4. The observation by the RISC-I designers (see Table 7.1 and Section 7.4.1) that a high proportion (> 80%) of all scalars referenced in a procedure are local variables and that a high proportion (> 90%) of all array/structure references are to global variables.
5. Furthermore, although some 55% of referenced operands are scalars and 25% arrays/structures (Table 7.1), each reference (at the source program level) to an array or structure also requires reference (at the machine instruction level) to a scalar, namely, an index variable or a pointer. Thus, the ratio of scalar reference to nonscalar references is more of the order of 80 to 25. And since about 80% of scalar references are to locals, some 60% of all

variable references are to local scalars and the remaining 40% account for nonlocal scalars and nonscalars (Katevenis, 1985, Chapter 3).

6. The observation, in a separate and earlier study by Tanenbaum (1978), that some 98% of dynamically invoked procedures in a sample of highly structured and modularized programs had less than 6 arguments and that some 92% of them had less than 6 scalar variables.[7]

Thus, it was argued, since only a few words (of the order of 12) are referenced so heavily during a procedure call, these can be allocated automatically to registers. Furthermore, if sufficient registers can be accommodated on the processor chip (see point 3), then by *overlapping* some of the registers of the calling and the called procedures it is possible to (a) allocate variables and parameters of procedures almost entirely in registers, and (b) avoid the physical transfer of information that such a call logically entails (see points 1 and 2).

This was the basis of the overlapping register window scheme first suggested by Halbert and Kessler (1980). The basic mechanism is as follows.

At the endo-architectural level, the RISC-I contains a file of 138 registers. Of these, registers 0 through 9 are used as *global* registers for all procedures.

At the exo-architectural level, these registers are not all visible to all procedures. Rather, when a procedure call is executed (from inside a procedure A, say) a new *window* of 32 registers from this large file is assigned to the called procedure B. These include the 10 global registers, which become registers R0 through R9 for B (as they also were for A).

The remaining 22 registers in B's window are partitioned into three groups (Fig. 7.3). Registers R10 through R15 are termed the *low* registers and are used to hold parameters that are to be passed by B to some other procedure, say C that B may call. Registers R16 through R25 serve as *local* registers and are allocated to hold B's local scalar variables. Registers R26 through R31 are B's *high* registers and are used to hold parameters that were passed by A to B.

Thus, both procedures A and B have their own windows of 32 registers of which R0 through R9 are common. The remaining 22 registers are *logically* distinct for the two procedures. However, when A calls B, A's low registers are

---

[7]Tanenbaum's (1978) experiment was based on a typeless language called SAL [see also, Dasgupta (1984, Chapter 13) for further details of this experiment]. Similar figures were observed by Halbert and Kessler (1980) as cited in Katevenis (1985).

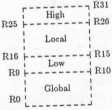

FIGURE 7.3 A procedure's register window.

also allocated as B's high registers. Similarly, when B calls C, the former's low registers become the latter's high registers. It is in this sense that the register windows are said to be overlapped (Fig. 7.4). Thus, one can pass parameters between procedures without *actually* having to pass parameters. Rather, a hardware pointer can be used to switch from A's window to B's, thus identifying the new "current" window. On returning to A, a pointer switch would reestablish A's window as the new current procedure.

Up to eight windows can be held in the register file. If the nesting of procedure calls exceeds eight, then the register file overflows into main memory. Halbert and Kessler's (1980) studies had indicated that with eight such banks, overflow into memory would occur on less than 1% of the calls.

It is instructive, at this stage, to examine the semantics of the procedure call/return instructions. These are specified (in the notation used in Chapter 6) in Table 7.2 and are self-explanatory.

7.4.4   Corroboration of the RISC Hypothesis

Recall (from Section 7.2) that the fundamental hypothesis of the RISC argument is that RISCs can be expected to be more cost effective than CISCs, where cost effectiveness is measured not only by performance but also by such factors as ease of compilation and the time to design, test, and debug the resulting hardware. In this section we present some of the data produced by the RISC-I designers that seem to corroborate this hypothesis.

Design Time

Partly because of the reduced instruction set itself and partly owing to the use of an excellent collection of computer-aided design (CAD) tools, the design effort

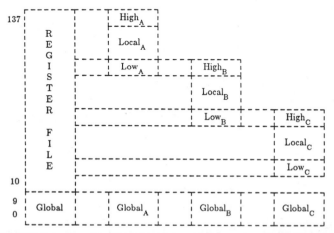

FIGURE 7.4   Overlapping of register windows: A calls B, B calls C.

TABLE 7.2 RISC-I Call/Return Instructions

Instruction Form	Semantics
CALL R_d, $S_2(R_{S1})$ (call)	**new** Rd = PC & **new** PC = R_{S1}+S_2 & **new** curr_wdw_ptr = curr_wdw_ptr−1
CALLR R_d, Y (call relative)	**new** R_d = PC & **new** PC = PC+Y & **new** curr_wdw_ptr = curr_wdw_ptr−1
RET R_{S1}, S_2 (return)	**new** PC = R_{S1}+S_2 & **new** curr_wdw_ptr = curr_wdw_ptr+1

Notes: (1) curr_wdw_ptr is a register that points to the "current" register window. It is visible at the exo-architectural level only by virtue of these control transfer instructions and their effects. (2) Y denotes the 19-bit immediate operand in the long immediate format.

for the RISC-I was considerably less than for several other more complex 32-bit microprocessors. The times for design and layout for several machines are shown in Table 7.3.[8]

Processor Performance

Two measures were used to evaluate the performance of the RISC-I processor. The first is the *execution time* required to run a collection of benchmark programs. This, of course, was a straightforward measure of the computer's processing power. The second metric is termed the *high-level language execution*

[8]The CAD system used in the Berkeley RISC project consisted of tools for all significant levels of abstraction: exo-architectural, micro-architectural, logic, and layout. Of relevance to our domain of interest were the following (Katevenis, 1985):

(a) The use of ISPS (Barbacci *et al.*, 1978) to describe, test and simulate the exo-architecture. However, because the ISPS simulator was too slow for large programs, a more specialized RISC simulator was developed and used for running benchmark programs during the performance evaluation of the RISC-I.

(b) A hardware description language called SLANG was used to describe and simulate the processor at the micro-architectural level.

TABLE 7.3 Design Metrics for the RISC I and Some Other Microprocessors

Processor	Transistor Count (× 1000)	Design Effort (Man-months)	Layout Effort (Man-months)
RISC I	44	15	12
MC68000	68	100	70
Z8000	17.5	60	70
iAPX-432/01	110	170	90
iAPX-432/02	49	170	100

Source: Patterson and Sequin (1982); Katevenis (1985).

support factor (HLLESF), first proposed by Ditzel and Patterson (1980) and defined as:

$$\text{HLLESF} = \frac{\text{speed of a program written in assembly language}}{\text{speed of the "same" program written in a HLL}}$$

The smaller this ratio (i.e., the nearer it is to 0), the greater the penalty of using the computer as a high-level language machine. The closer the ratio is to 1, the more appropriate is the computer as a high-level language system.

Using these two measures, Patterson and Piepho (1982) have presented the details of an experiment to evaluate and compare the RISC-I with several other minicomputers and microprocessors. The principle features of the experiment may be summarized as follows.

1. In addition to the RISC-I, the following processors were also considered: three minicomputers, namely, the VAX-11/780, the PDP-11/70, and the BBN C/70, all of which are Schottky TTL machines; and two microprocessors, namely, the Zilog Z8002 and the Motorola MC68000.
2. The benchmarks consisted of a set of 11 algorithms and included algorithms for searching a character string for a substring match; testing, setting, and resetting bits within a bit string; inserting a new element within a linked list; transposing a square-bit matrix; computing Ackermann's function; and solving the Towers of Hanoi problem. The benchmark set also included both the recursive and the nonrecursive versions of Quicksort, a bin-packing algorithm, and a stream-oriented text editor.
3. The benchmarks were programmed both in the assembly languages of each computer and in a common high-level language and, in the latter case, compiled into object code for the different target exo-architectures using a common compiler technology.

    The high-level languages used was C; the Portable C compiler (Johnson, 1978) was used to compile the C benchmark programs into the various target object codes.
4. Since at the time of the experiment the RISC-I prototype was not operational, a simulated version of the RISC-I (assuming a 400 ns cycle time) was used.

Table 7.4 summarizes the results of this experiment. Note that the figures given are the averages across all benchmarks. The first row shows the average HLLESF values whereas the second lists the average ratios of the execution time of each processor to the execution time on the RISC-I. According to both these measures, the RISC-I is found to outperform the other microprocessors and minicomputers.

7.4.5 Refutation of the RISC Hypothesis

Over the years, the von Neumann style has often been severely criticized and radically different approaches to programming and architecture have been pro-

TABLE 7.4—Comparative Performances

Measure (Average ± Standard Deviation)	RISC-I	68000	Z8002	VAX 11/780	PDP-11/70
HLLESF	0.90 ± 0.1	0.34 ± 0.3	0.46 ± 0.3	0.45 ± 0.2	0.50 ± 0.2
Performance ratio (times slower than RISC-I)	1	3.5 ± 1.8	4.1 ± 1.6	2.1 ± 1.1	2.6 ± 1.5

Source: Patterson and Piepho (1982).

posed as alternatives (see, e.g., Volume 2, Chapter 9). The striking feature of the RISC approach is that it is an attack from *within* the von Neumann camp, so to speak. The RISC style is viewed as a means of reforming the architecture of uniprocessor computers that is more in keeping with current technological and computational environments. As such, the RISC hypothesis directly confronts the received wisdom as embodied in most of the commercially successful register machines in contemporary use.

This has given rise to much controversy since 1980 in the form of the so-called "RISC/CISC debate." However, the most significant challenge to the RISC hypothesis—the counterreformation as it were—has undoubtedly been the work of Colwell and associates (1985) and Hitchcock and Sprunt (1985). Their refutation of the RISC hypothesis has both qualitative and quantitative components. We may summarize their thesis as follows.

Design Time

It is misleading, even meaningless, to compare the design efforts for a processor such as the RISC-I, produced within an academic research environment, with those for the products of a commercial environment (see Table 7.3). In the latter case, such issues as profitability and investments in software and other forms of support (such as documentation and training) must be taken into account and it is quite unclear as to their impact on design time, cost, and effort.

High-Level Language Support

As we have seen in the preceding sections, the RISC-I is fundamentally a C machine. Thus, it is to be expected that the RISC-I will outperform such machines as the 68000 or the VAX 11/780 in terms of the HLLESF measure (see Table 7.4). The question is, how effective is the RISC-I in contrast to, say, the VAX 11/780, in its support of a *multiple-language* environment? This has yet to be answered.

Performance Metrics

The execution times for the benchmark programs are but one index of performance. For instance, Colwell and associates (1985) point out that in *safety-critical* applications such performance goals as reliability and availability are more crucial than execution time. In such systems, considerable overheads for error checking may be incurred, thereby slowing down the processing speed.

The Effect of Multiple Register Sets

Finally and most importantly, Colwell's group (1985) pointed out that the execution time characteristics of the RISC-I cannot be entirely attributed to its *RISC* characteristics. A substantial debt is owed to the presence of the overlapping window scheme involving multiple register sets. This is *not* a defining characteristic of RISC architectures (see Section 7.3); rather, multiple register sets is an independent architectural feature that might be as well present in CISCs as in RISCs.

Thus, a hypothesis that the performance effects of multiple-register sets are comparable for RISCs and for CISCs was formulated and tested experimentally as follows (Hitchcock and Sprunt, 1985; Colwell *et al.*, 1985).

For each of the two CISCs—the VAX-11 and the MC68000—architectures with nonoverlapping and overlapping register sets were simulated. The RISC-I was simulated with a single register set and with nonoverlapping multiple register sets. Thus, for each of the three computers (the VAX-11, the 68000, and the RISC-I) three architectural versions were available (either in actual or simulated form):

- Single register set version (which is the standard version for the VAX-11 and the 68000).
- Nonoverlapping multiple register set version.
- Overlapping multiple register set version (which is the standard version for the RISC-I).

The benchmarks used were identical to those used in the RISC-I evaluation studies. However, instead of using execution time as the performance measure —this being implementation dependent—the amount of *processor/memory traffic* (in bytes) was selected.[9]

Table 7.5 summarizes the data for three of the benchmarks, which, because of their recursive nature, are particularly procedure-intensive. As can be seen, the introduction of multiple register sets reduces the processor/memory traffic considerably for both the VAX-11 and the 68000 whereas the removal of the multiple register sets from the RISC-11 increases this traffic dramatically.

A more complete description of the experiment and its results are given in Hitchcock and Sprunt (1985). The importance of this experiment lies in its basic challenge to, and partial refutation of, the RISC hypothesis when the influence of multiple register sets is taken into account.

---

[9]This, of course, is the M measure, originally proposed by the computer family architecture (CFA) committee (Fuller, Stone, and Burr, 1977) as a purely exo-architectural measure (see also Chapter 2, Table 2.4).

TABLE 7.5 Performances of the VAX, the 68000, and the RISC-I with Variable Register Set Configuration

Architectures	Processor/Memory Traffic (in 10^6 bytes)		
	Towers of Hanoi	Fibonacci	Ackermann
VAX with single register set[a]	~ 60	~ 2.3	~ 19
VAX with multiple register sets	~ 45	~ 1.5	~ 16
VAX with overlapping multiple register sets	~ 28	~ 1.1	~ 13
68000 with single register set[a]	~ 78	~ 2.0	~ 17.5
68000 with multiple register sets	~ 50	~ 1.5	~ 14
68000 with overlapping multiple register sets	~ 20	~ 1.2	~ 10
RISC-I with single register set	~ 200	~ 9	~ 68
RISC-I with multiple register sets	~ 50	~ 2	~ 43
RISC-I with overlapping multiple register sets[a]	~ 23	~ 1.6	~ 42

Source: Colwell *et al.* (1985).

[a]Denotes "standard" architecture.

7.5 BIBLIOGRAPHIC AND OTHER REMARKS

The concept of the reduced instruction set computer was first developed in Patterson and Ditzel (1980). The same issue of *Computer Architecture News* included a rebuttal by Strecker and Clark (1980) of some of Patterson and Ditzel's comments, especially with regard to the VAX. A retrospective view of the whole RISC philosophy, with the benefit of the implementations of the Berkeley RISCs, the Standford MIPS, and the IBM 801 to look back on, is provided by Patterson (1985).

The RISC-I was first described in Patterson and Sequin (1981) and then again in Patterson and Sequin (1982). The performance aspects of this processor are discussed in Patterson and Piepho (1982). Katevenis (1985) is a book-length monograph that discusses all aspects of the Berkeley RISC project and, especially, the RISC-II processor.

The first discussions of the MIPS in the open literature appear to be in Hennessey and associates (1982). Hennessy (1984) is a comprehensive survey of microprocessor architecture in which RISCs, including, of course, the MIPs, are discussed. Various aspects of the MIPS micro-architecture are discussed in Hennessey and associates (1983) whereas Hennessy and Gross (1983) is a detailed exposition of the MIPS compiler, in particular, the postprocessing part that reorganizes the compiled code so as to make it fit for pipelined execution.

Although the IBM 801 project was apparently initiated in the mid-1970s, the first published description is in Radin (1982).

As was noted in Section 7.1, several pathways to the development of language-directed architectures (within the von Neumann framework) have been explored. The RISC style is the most recent and, perhaps, the most widely discussed among these.

Myers (1982) gives a detailed view of some of these approaches. These include the design of language-specific exo-architectures that are implemented by microcoding the Burroughs B1700, the SYMBOL system in which a single hardware/architecture/programming language/compiler complex is created; Myers' own SWARD machine, which is organized around a complex storage structure and rejects the concept of registers altogether; and the Intel iAPX 432, an object-oriented architecture that has come to be associated closely with the Ada programming language.[10]

Over the past decade, Flynn and colleagues have identified and developed a class of architectures called *directly executable language* (DEL) machines (Flynn, 1977; Hoevel, 1974; Flynn, 1980; Neuhauser, 1980; Flynn and Hoevel, 1983). At the heart of the DEL approach is the idea that corresponding to each target programming language L (say) to be supported, there is an exo-architecture E (or, in Flynn's terminology, an *image machine*). E is closely related to L to the extent that there is a one-to-one correspondence between identifiers and statements of a source program written in L and the identifiers and instructions of the object program for E. These exo-architectures are termed DELs. Thus, for example, there are DELs for Fortran and Pascal (called DELTRAN and Adept, respectively).

Given the close correspondence between a programming language and its DEL, the compilation process is rendered relatively easy. Each DEL representation of a source program is then *interpreted* (by microcode) on a *universal host machine* (see Chapter 5, Section 5.4). Thus, there will exist a microprogrammed emulator for each DEL on a common host. The host developed by Flynn and colleagues specifically for their DEL machine studies was the Emmy (Flynn, 1980).

PROBLEMS

7.1 The first of the three RISC "postulates" (Section 7.2) states that over the years, architectures have evolved toward progressively greater complexity.

  (a) Characterize the "complexity" of exo-architectures.

  (b) Using any family or series of computers that you are familiar with (e.g., the PDP-11/VAX-11, the Intel 8080/8086/80286, or the IBM System 360/370 series) give detailed evidence of the validity of this postulate.

7.2 Stack and RISC machines represent two approaches to the development of language-directed architectures. Identify and compare the similarities and differences between the two approaches.

---

[10]Ada is a registered trademark of the U.S. Department of Defense.

7.3 The RISC style has a general *aesthetic* appeal that the more well known CISCs appears to lack. Using, as a frame of reference, both the general characteristics of the RISC style and the specific characteristics of the Berkeley machine, discuss the factors that make this architectural style aesthetically satisfying.

7.4 [A design project.] PIE is a small programming language consisting of the following main features.

(a) The primitive data types are *integer, real, Boolean, character*.

(b) The structured data types are *array, record*, and character *string*.

(c) The set of integer arithmetic operations are $\{+,-,*,\ quot,\ rem\}$ where *quot* is the quotient and *rem*, the remainder, of integer division. The set of real arithmetic operations are $\{+,-,*,/\}$

(d) The set of Boolean operations are $\{\wedge,\vee,\neg,\oplus\}$.

(e) The set of relational operations are $\{<,>,\leq,\geq,=,\neq\}$.

(f) The following operations are defined on character strings: the *length* of a string, *concatenation* of two strings, *extracting* a substring of given length and starting position from a larger string, and *comparing* two strings for equality.

(g) Arithmetic, logical, and relational expressions are of the usual form, namely, infix, partially or fully parenthesized, or without parenthesis.

(h) The primitive statements in PIE are the assignment, the procedure *call*, and the *return* (from procedure).

(i) Input parameters to procedures are passed by value and output parameters by reference.

(j) Composite statements in PIE are

    [i] Sequential Composition: $S_1; S_2; \ldots$

    [ii] Conditional: **if . . . then . . . fi** or
    if . . . then . . . else . . . fi.

    [iii] Iteration: **while . . . do . . . od** or **return . . . until . . .**

(k) A procedure is of the general form

```
proc x ( parameter list ) ;
    local variables ;
    procedure body
return
```

where the "body" references only parameters or locals.

(l) A program has the form

```
prog Y ;
    local variables ;
    begin . . . end
end prog
```

You are required to design on exo-architecture in the RISC style for the efficient support of object programs compiled from PIE. The defining characteristics of a RISC are as given in Section 7.3. Pay particular attention to the first four characteristics stated there.

Call this machine RISC-X2. The form and content of its design should follow the directions and guidelines stated in Problem 4.14 (Chapter 4). Your design report should include a thorough analysis and discussion of the key design decisions made concerning each of the significant exo-architectural components in RISC-X2.

7.5 [Continuation of Problem 7.4.] Design a "pure" *stack machine exo-architecture* (see Chapter 6) for the efficient support of object code compiled from PIE. As defined in Chapter 6, in a stack machine, the machine design (at the exo-architectural level) should be dominated and dictated by the use of a stack for holding local variables, controlling procedure invocations, and executing statements. Call this machine Stack-X2.

[*Note*: There is nothing to prevent you from adopting the spirit and some of the characteristics of the RISC style even in this design project. See, particularly properties 2, 3, and 4 as stated in Section 7.3].

7.6 [Continuation of Problems 7.4 and 7.5.] As in all design projects it is vital to evaluate and test your architectural design as objectively and thoroughly as possible before committing it to further refinement or implementation. Thus, one needs to devise *experiments* for this purpose.

(a) Construct a set of four *benchmark programs* in PIE that collectively (i) use all the principal features of the programming languages; and (ii) are typical applications for which PIE might be used.

(b) Hand compile these benchmarks into object code for both RISC-X2 and Stack-X2. Determine and compare their efficiencies in terms of the *memory space* required to store the compiled code and the *number of processor cycles* required to execute them.

(c) Based on this experiment, what are your conclusions concerning the relative performances of the two architectures?

7.7 [Continuation of Problem 7.6.] An assumption underlying the development of both stack and RISC architectures is that both styles — in possibly different ways — address the issue of *compilability*. That is, both approaches make claims about *easing the compilation task*.

Clearly, to test hypotheses regarding compilability properly requires the design and implementation of compilers. Compilability could, then, be measured in terms of either the HLLESF metric (see Section 7.4.4) or the size of the compiler. Note that to *compare* compilabilities for two or more exo-architectures demands even more stringent experimental conditions since the compilers should differ only in their code-generation routines.

In the absence of such protracted experiments, we can attempt to *speculate* rationally on this matter by comparing the *relative complexities* of corresponding exo-architectural components with respect to the programming language PIE.

(a) Identify the complexity characteristics of exo-architectures from the perspective of compilability. That is, identify those aspects of an exo-architectural design that are likely to ease or aggravate the compilation task.

(b) Based on these characteristics, compare the complexities of RISC-X2 and Stack-X2 with reference to PIE.

(c) Based on these comparisons, draw "speculative" conclusions about the respective merits of the two architectures from the viewpoint of compilability.

[*Note*: Refer also, to Problem 7.1a].

7.8 Another face of exo-architectural complexity relates to the *implementability* of exo-architectures. Again, in the absence of actual implementations, or without further refinement of the machine design to lower levels, one must try to draw conclusions based on the evidence at hand.

(a) Identify the complexity characteristics of exo-architectures from the perspective of implementability at the micro-architectural level.

(b) Based on these characteristics, compare the complexities of RISC-X2 and Stack-X2. On the basis of these comparisons, speculate about their respective merits from the viewpoint of implementability.

CHAPTER 8

ASPECTS OF MEMORY

8.1 INTRODUCTION

In a very obvious sense, memory issues inform every facet of computer architecture. They influenced the development of the register machine style, both in respect to its exo- and endo-architectures (see Chapters 4 and 5). They have controlled the extent to which, and the manner in which, microprogramming was gradually adopted for the implementation of the control unit (see Chapter 5). Memory considerations played a powerful role in the emergence of the RISC philosophy (Chapter 7). And, of course, many of the design considerations for high-performance systems are dictated by memory-related concerns (see Volume 2, Part 3). In fact, memory considerations are integral to the development of every architectural style considered in this text.

There are, however, certain aspects of the memory subsystem that are independent of, and common to, all architectural styles. It is the purpose of this chapter to discuss some of these aspects. In particular, I will describe the principles of *virtual memory*, the use and efficacy of *cache memory*, aspects of *memory interleaving*, and the problem of *memory protection*.

8.2 THE LATENCY PROBLEM

At the heart of any discussion of memory issues is the problem of *memory latency*. Latency is the time that elapses between a request by a processor to memory and the receipt of the requested item of data by the processor. Several factors contribute to latency; Some of these are architectural factors—that is, they are induced by specific architectural design decisions. For instance, as discussed in Volume 2, Chapter 8, the latency problem in multiprocessors is aggravated because several processors may contend simultaneously for access to the same memory module and because of the presence of the processor-memory interconnection network.

Leaving aside such architectural causes, there is a rather fundamental technological aspect to the matter. This is the fact that there has almost always been a disparity between logic speed (and therefore, processor speed) and the speed of memory.

Matick (1977) has pointed out that this was not always the case. In the very earliest days of computer design, the technologies were such that memory and processor speeds were very close to one another. For instance, the 36-bit IBM 704—the first large scientific computer of the mid-1960s—had main memory and processor cycle times of 12 μsec each. Its successor, the IBM 7090 (delivered in 1960) had a 2-μsec cycle time for both processor and memory.[1] However, subsequent advances in logic technology proceeded at a rate somewhat ahead of progress in memory technology, thus resulting in a very substantial gap between memory and processor speeds. Technology, then, was a basic contributor to the latency problem.

Example 8.1 (Matick, 1980)

The memory and processor cycle times for the CDC 6600 (delivered in 1964) were 1 μsec and 100 nsec, respectively. Its successor, the 7600 (delivered in 1969) had a memory cycle time of 275 nsec and a processor cycle time of 27.5 nsec. ∎

Example 8.2 (Siewiorek, Bell, and Newell, 1982)

Table 8.1 presents memory and processor cycle times for selected models of the IBM System/360 and the IBM System/370. ∎

One must keep in mind, however, that despite the gap between memory and

---

[1] The IBM 704 was one of the first commercial computers to use ferrite core technology for its main memory (Matick, 1977; Chapter 1). Its processor logic was based on vaccum-tube technology (Bell and Newell, 1971, p. 515). The 7090 used core for memory and discrete transistors for logic.

TABLE 8.1 Memory and Processor Cycle Times for Selected Models of the IBM System/360 and System/370 Families

Architectural Family	Model	Year Introduced	Memory Cycle (nsec)	Processor Cycle (nsec)
360	40	1964	2500	625
	67	1965	750	200
	85	1965	960	80
	91	1965	750	60
370	145	1970	540 (R) 608 (W)	203–315
	155	1970	2070	115
	168	1972	320	80
	195	1971	756	54

Source: Siewiorek, Bell, and Newell, 1982, Chapter 52.

processor speeds, the actual speed of main memory has improved vastly over the years (see Fig. 2.8). Furthermore, the density of memory chips has tended to follow Moore's law (see Section 2.2, Chapter 2), increasing at the rate of about 1.66 per year. Although the actual speeds of memory chips will depend on the size (in bits) of the chip, typical speeds of recent semiconductor memories are listed in Table 2.5.

Because of the inherent technology induced latency characteristic just noted, computer systems usually include some variation of the *memory hierarchy* scheme shown in Figure 8.1.

1. The function of the *local store* has been discussed extensively in Chapters 4, 5, and 7. To recall briefly, the speed of local store is of the same order as that of processor logic and, in fact, local store is logically and physically considered part of the processor itself. The capacity of local store is usually between 8 and 64 registers, although recently local stores of more than 100 registers have been implemented (see Chapter 7).

2. The *cache memory* is larger and perhaps (though not necessarily) slower than local store and is used to hold relatively large segments of instructions or data. Unlike local store, caches are usually hidden from view at the exo-architectural level. That is, the cache is an endo-architectural component. Cache memory capacities are of the order of kilobytes (Kbytes). Examples of cache sizes are 4 Kbytes for the VAX 11/750 and the IBM 4331; 16 Kbytes for the VAX-11/780, the Amdahl 470v/6, and the IBM 4341; 32 Kbytes for the IBM System/370, Model 168-3, and the Amdahl 470v/7; and 64 Kbytes for the IBM 3033 and the Amdahl 470v/8. Even larger cache sizes have been used.[2]

3. A much larger and slower *main memory* has capacities of the order of megabytes (Mbytes). Examples of main memory sizes in some recently marketed systems are the Encore Multimax multiprocessor with 32 Mbytes of shared memory (Encore, 1986); the CRAY X-MP/48 with 64 Mbytes of

[2]The cache sizes cited here are taken from Smith (1982).

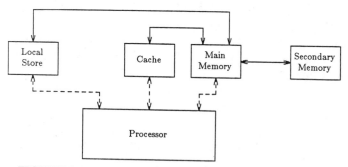

FIGURE 8.1   The "standard" memory hierarchy scheme.

memory (Cray, 1984); and the CRAY-2, which contains 2048 Mbytes (i.e., 2 Gigabytes) of common memory (Cray, 1986).

4. A very large and (relatively) very slow secondary memory typically consists of disks and tapes with capacities in the gigabytes (Gbyte) range.

The objective of a memory hierarchy is to establish, through architectural means, a memory subsystem that appears to the user to have the (virtually unlimited) capacity of secondary store and the speed of the fastest component —the local store or, perhaps, cache. These goals can be achieved using a combination of the following ways.

1. The use of *interleaved* memories in which a body of related information is distributed across several memory modules that can then be accessed in parallel or overlapped fashion. The basic principles of memory interleaving are explained in Section 8.3, where the effectiveness of such schemes is analyzed.
2. Efficient management of the main memory/cache memory subsystem so that most processor requests for instructions or data can be resolved by accessing the faster cache memory.
3. The design and implementation of a *virtual memory* mechanism that provides the user with the illusion of unlimited main memory with a minimal attending speed penalty.

Historically, the development of virtual memory principles preceded the emergence of cache memories.[3] Thus, after completing the discussion of memory interleaving, I will first consider virtual memory (in Section 8.4), then caches (in Section 8.5).

8.3 INTERLEAVED MEMORY

The basic idea in an N-way *interleaved memory scheme* is to organized a set of N memory modules such that N sequential addresses, $a_0, a_1, \ldots, a_{N-1}$ are distributed across the modules according to the rule

Address a_i is assigned to module M_j if $j = i \bmod N$

Thus, if an instruction at address a_0 is requested, then not only that instruction but also those at $a_1, a_2, \ldots, a_{N-1}$ can be accessed in parallel, read into N distinct memory buffer registers, and then stored in an instruction buffer (Fig. 8.2). As an example, suppose that the *degree of interleaving* is $N = 2^n$ and that

---

[3]The genesis of virtual memory is the "one-level storage system" proposed by Kilburn and colleagues (1962) and implemented on the Atlas computer at the University of Manchester. The cache memory was first implemented on the IBM System 360/85 (Conti, Gibson, and Pitkowski, 1968; Liptay, 1968). However, an earlier exposition of the idea under the name of "slave memories" appears in Wilkes (1965).

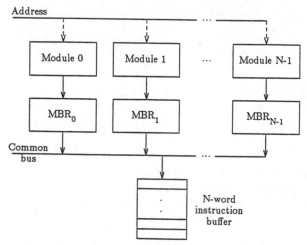

FIGURE 8.2 **N-way interleaved memory scheme.**

the capacity of each memory module is $M = 2^m$ for some pair of integers m,n. Then an (m + n)-bit address will be delivered to the memory system with the high-order m-bits used to access a word in each module, whereas the low-order n bits will determine which of the accessed words is to be placed first in the instruction buffer. Once this instruction has been transmitted to the processor for decoding, the remaining instructions will be advanced one step down the buffer so that the time lag between successive instructions delivered to the processor will essentially be the time for the instructions to be shifted down the buffer.

You will realize that an interleaved memory generalizes to an N-module *parallel memory* organization that can be accessed concurrently by multiple-processing units—as may be necessary in array computers or multiprocessors.

For interleaving to be effective, the memory requests produced by a processor must also distribute as uniformly as possible across the memory modules. If two or more concurrent requests address the same module, we have a case of memory *interference* or *contention* in which case all but one of the requests to the module must be deferred. The question, then, is how bad can one expect the average memory contention to be?

Clearly, it is of great interest to probe further into the effectiveness of inter-leaved memory schemes, in particular, to determine the effective memory band-width (or degree of parallelism in memory access) as a function of N, the number of modules. Several studies of this problem have been carried out; we will review a few of the results that were obtained. As is common in the modeling and analysis of system performance, these studies differ essentially in the assumptions and parameters underlying their respective models.

8.3.1 Hellerman's Model

The earliest analysis of memory interleaving appears to be that of Hellerman (1967), which is based on the following assumptions:

1. The bank of N modules are numbered 1, 2, . . . , N.
2. The stream of requests on these modules consists of elements each of which is an integer in the range (1,N). More precisely, it is assumed that each element in the request stream is a uniformly distributed random variable taking on values in the range (1,N).
3. There are always sufficient elements in the request stream so that the system is never held up for paucity of requests.
4. The time to inspect the request stream is overlapped with memory accesses.
5. Finally, there is no queuing of requests on busy modules. That is, there are no buffers associated with the modules.

Under these assumptions, the memory bandwidth Bm—that is the average number of modules accessed in each memory cycle—is given by the *average length of a sequence of integers in the request stream until a repetition is encountered.* This is computed as follows:

The first integer in the request stream may be any one of N.

The probability of the second integer not equaling the first integer $= 1 - 1/N$.

The probability of the third integer not equaling the first or second integer $= 1 - 2/N$.

. . .

The probability of the k-th integer not equaling the first or second or . . . or $(k - 1)$-th integer $= 1 - (k - 1)/N$.

The probability of the $(k + 1)$-th integer being one of the preceding k integers $= k/N$.

Thus, the probability of encountering a stream of exactly k distinct integers with the $(k + 1)$-th being a repetition of these k others is

$$(1 - 1/N)(1 - 2/N) \cdots [1 - (k - 1)/N)(k/N]$$
$$= \left(\frac{N-1}{N}\right)\left(\frac{N-2}{N}\right) \cdots \left(\frac{N-k+1}{N}\right)\left(\frac{k}{N}\right)$$
$$= \frac{(N-1)!k}{(N-k)!N^k}$$

Thus, the average length of a nonrepetitive input sequence is

$$Bm = \sum_{k=1}^{n} \frac{(N-1)!k^2}{(N-k)!N^k} \tag{8.1}$$

This formula was evaluated by Hellerman (1967) for the range $1 \leq N \leq 45$. The results indicate that in this range, a fairly good approximation is

$$Bm \simeq N^{0.56} \tag{8.2}$$

Thus, for example, in a 16-way interleaved memory, given the assumptions stated earlier, one can expect at least four of the modules to be always active at any given time.[4]

8.3.2 The Burnett-Coffman Model

In a series of papers that extended and generalized Hellerman's earlier work. Burnett and Coffman (1970, 1973, 1975) described analytic and simulation studies of the performance of interleaved memories. Here, we will consider one aspect of their studies where the interleaved memory is used to hold programs only, so that the memory requests generated by the processor are instruction addresses produced during instruction fetch.

The analysis is based on the following model:

1. Given a set of N memory modules numbered $0, 1, \ldots, N - 1$, the system maintains a *memory request queue* $r_1, r_2, r_3, \ldots$, where each element r_i of the queue (representing an instruction address) is an integer in the range $(0, N - 1)$.
2. Prior to the start of a memory cycle, that is, during the previous memory cycle, the request queue is scanned and a *maximum length sequence* of requests

$$r_1', r_2', \ldots, r_k', \quad k \leq N, \quad 0 \leq r_j' \leq N - 1$$

to distinct modules is selected. That is, the request queue is scanned from the head of the queue and requests are selected up to the first repetition of a request.
3. Given the selection of such a maximum length sequence, r_k' is assumed to be a branch.

Let $P(k)$ be the probability that the maximum length sequence selected is of length k ($1 \leq k \leq N$). Then the average bandwidth of the N-way, interleaved memory is

$$Bm = \sum_{k=1}^{N} k.P(k) \tag{8.3}$$

$P(k)$ can be derived as follows. Let L, termed the *branching probability*, be the probability that a given instruction is a branch instruction — that is, its execution results in a transfer of control to a nonsuccessive address. Consider, now, a maximum length request sequence $r_1', r_2', \ldots, r_k'$. Then

---

[4]In a much later paper, Knuth and Rao (1975) derived a closed-form solution to the expression (8.1). The first two terms of their solution are

$$\frac{\pi N^{0.5}}{2} - \frac{1}{3}$$

which, when evaluated for different values of N up to 64, yield values that are very close to those produced by Hellerman's approximation to Bm (Equation 8.2).

P(1) = probability that r_1' is a branch = L

P(2) = probability that r_1' is a nonbranch and r_2' is a branch = $(1 - L)L$

. . .

P(k) (where k < N)

= probability that $r_1', r_2', \ldots, r_{k-1}'$ are nonbranches and r_k' is a branch

= $(1 - L)^{k-1} \cdot L$ (8.4)

P(N) = probability that $r_1', r_2', \ldots, r_{N-1}'$ are nonbranches and r_N' is a branch

= $(1 - L)^{N-1}$ (8.5)

Substituting Equations (8.4) and (8.5) into Equation (8.3) we obtain

$$Bm = \sum_{k=1}^{N-1} [k(1 - L)^{k-1}L] + N(1 - L)^{N-1} \quad (8.6)$$

Burnett and Coffman (1970) show that a closed-form solution to Equation (8.6) is

$$Bm = \frac{1 - (1 - L)^N}{L} \quad (8.7)$$

Table 8.2 lists values of Bm against L for N = 8. It can be seen that when L = 1, Bm = 1 and that as L approaches 0, Bm approaches 8.

TABLE 8.2 BM against L for N = 8 Based on Equation 8.7

L	Bm
0.005	7.8
0.2	4.16
0.4	2.46
0.6	1.67
0.8	1.25
1	1

8.4 VIRTUAL MEMORY

As stated in Section 8.2, virtual memory is one of the mechanisms used to exploit a memory hierarchy so as to maximize the availability of memory space without having to pay an excessive penalty in memory latency. The specific role played by virtual memory mechanisms to achieve this overall objective is to provide the user with the illusion of a much larger, directly addressable memory than there actually is.[5]

[5]The historical factors that led to the emergence of the virtual memory concept in the early 1960s were many and were intertwined. These included not only the objective stated in the text but also the development of high-level programming languages on the one hand—FORTRAN had been implemented and Algol 58 had been designed by the end of the 1950s (Wexelblat, 1981)—and the advent

The implementation of virtual memory involves at least two storage levels — main and secondary — and cooperative action of the processor and the operating system. From a more formal viewpoint, however, the function of virtual memory may be characterized as follows (Denning, 1970).

Definition 8.1

An address used by a programmer is referred to as a *virtual address* (or a *name*) and the set of such addresses is called a *virtual address space* or a *name space*.

Definition 8.2

An address of a word (or a byte) in physical memory is referred to as a *memory address* (or a *real* address), and the set of all such addresses is called the *memory space* (or the *real address* space).

I will denote the name space by $N = \{0, 1, \ldots n - 1\}$ and the memory space by $M = \{0, 1, \ldots, m - 1\}$. In general, $n >> m$. That is, the name space available to a user is very much larger than the memory space actually present in main memory.

The purpose of a virtual memory *mechanism* is to realize an *address mapping function*

$$\text{MAP} : N \longrightarrow M \cup \{\phi\}$$

(where ϕ is a special symbol) such that for a ϵ N.

MAP (a) = a' if the item in virtual address a is present in memory address
  $a' \epsilon$ M
  $= \phi$ if the item in virtual address a is not present in M

Figure 8.3 depicts, in a highly schematic way, the structure of a virtual memory mechanism. In the course of executing a program, memory requests produced by a processor are actually virtual addresses that refer to the name space. An address translation mechanism performs the necessary mapping, either generating a memory address a' or generating a *missing item fault* otherwise. In the former case, main memory can be accessed; in the case of the latter, the program that generated address a is temporarily suspended till the required word is located in secondary memory and brought into main memory.

---

of multiprogramming and time sharing on the other (Rosin, 1969a). The first of these promoted the idea of an abstract space of variables that was independent of the linearly addressed memory space available in the actual computer. The second led to the situation where the same program may occupy quite different areas of main memory when executed at different times. The necessity of *automatic storage allocation* and the notion that the user's set of addressable locations must be distinct from the actual set of physical locations thus emerged, leading eventually to the concept of virtual memory. For a scintillating and more detailed account of these various historical issues, refer to Denning (1970).

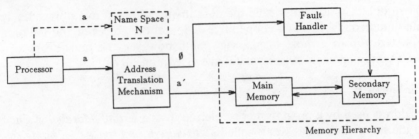

FIGURE 8.3   General schematic of a virtual memory system.

8.4.1   The Principle of Locality

From the discussion so far, you will realize that the efficiency of a virtual memory system relies on the assumption that the frequency of faults will be kept to a minimum. This follows from the given characteristic of a memory hierarchy where the latency of secondary memory will be considerably higher than that of main memory; excessive faults will then result in excessive time being spent in transferring the missing items to main memory.

To minimize fault frequency, it would be necessary to transfer an entire block of information from secondary memory in response to a fault. The block would contain not only the missing item but also items that are *expected to be referenced in the immediate future.* However, this anticipation of future references requires that the address generation pattern be predictable to some extent.

The assumption that the pattern of memory references are predictable is based on an important empirical property of programs called the *principle of locality* (Denning, 1970). Informally, this states that over a given interval of time

1. The addresses generated by a program tend to be restricted to a small region of the virtual address space. This is referred to as the phenomenon of *spatial* locality.
2. The set of such "favored" addresses changes slowly over time. This is also referred to as *temporal* locality.

Further implications of the locality principle will be presented later. For the present, we note that the causes for the locality principle to hold are mainly twofold. First, the fact that the components of a program or a data structure are usually stored in adjacent words of memory; and second, the presence of program loops and the fact that the execution of loops confines references to a localized region of the address space for, often, extended periods of time.

8.4.2   The Basic Issues in Virtual Memory System Design

The implementation of a virtual memory system involves, in addition to a physical memory hierarchy, the cooperative action of the processor and the operating system. Regardless, however, of the precise allocation of responsibilities between hardware and software, and independent of such matters, the design of virtual memory involves decisions concerning four key issues. These are as follows:

1. The *size and nature of information blocks* that are to be transferred from secondary to main memory.
2. When a block of information is brought into memory space M and M is full, then some region of M must be released so as to make room for the new block. The policy governing which part of M is to be released is called the *replacement rule.*
3. Similarly, one must elect a policy governing which region of M is to be used to hold the new block. Such a policy is called the *placement rule.* As will be seen, the placement rule may be determined by the replacement rule but not necessarily so.
4. Implicit in the foregoing discussion is that a missing item is fetched from secondary memory only on the occurrence of a fault. This need not be necessarily true. Thus a fourth design issue is the choice of the *fetch* (or *load*) *rule*, which determines when a missing item (or its encapsulating block) is to be brought into M.

Each of these issues are discussed in the sections that follow.

8.4.3 Paging

Considering the first of the foregoing issues, the size and nature of information blocks, there are essentially two broad choices available to the designer of a virtual memory system. In the first choice, which I describe here, both the name and the memory space are partitioned into blocks of identical sizes. In the former case, these blocks are called *pages*, and in the latter case the blocks are termed *page frames.* For a given program occupying some name space N, some subset of its constituent pages will be mapped onto a subset of the page frames in M (Fig. 8.4). The page, thus, serves both as the unit that is logically mapped from N to M and as the unit of transfer between secondary and main memory.

Figure 8.5 shows the structure of the address translation mechanism in a paged virtual memory system. In general, each process P running on a processor will have a *page table* PT(P) located in main memory. There is one entry in the page table for each page in P's name space. The starting address of PT(P) is held in BR, one of a set of *page table base registers.*

The actual format of the page table entries will depend on the specific system being implemented. In the particular scheme shown here, each entry consists of a *presence* field (PR) indicating whether or not the referenced page (pm) is present in main memory. If it is, the corresponding *address* field (ADDR) denotes the starting address of the page frame in main memory containing the page. Otherwise, ADDR signifies the address of the page in secondary memory. Finally, an *access right* field (AR) specifies the valid access right the running process P has for this particular page. Again, the number and types of access

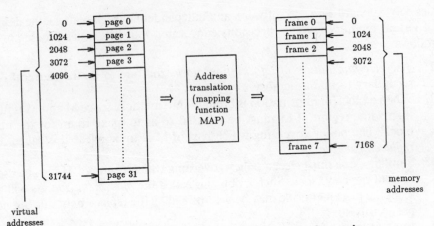

FIGURE 8.4   Paging scheme with 1K page/page-frame size.

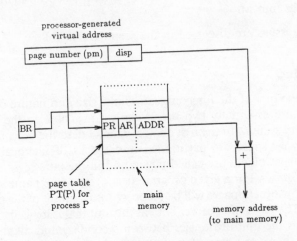

Legend
(a) if PR = 1 **then** page is in main memory at frame address ADDR
                    else page is in secondary memory at address ADDR
(b) AR: access right: R = read only; W = read/write
                    X = execute only

Address Translation

if is_valid(PT(P).AR)
       then if PT(P).PR = 1 **then new** memory address = PT(P).ADDR + disp
                               else trap page_fault
       else trap protection_violation_fault

FIGURE 8.5   Address translation in paged virtual memory system.

rights may vary from one system to another; in this particular example, a page may be of the "read only" type, may be of the "read/write" type, or may only be "executed." The AR field, thus, serves to enforce *memory protection.*[6]

The address translation algorithm is also shown in Figure 8.5. When the access right is found to be violated, a *protection fault* is said to occur and causes the system to *trap* to a hardware, firmware, or software fault handler. Similarly, when the page is not present in main memory, a *page fault* occurs, causing a trap to the fault handler. The process that generated the virtual address is suspended till the missing page is located in secondary memory, loaded into main memory (according to the placement/replacement rules), and the page table is updated. While the page fault is being serviced, a *context switch* is effected so that the processor can be assigned to some other process waiting to run.

Paged virtual memory systems may be such that each process may be assigned a distinct virtual address space or they may be designed so that all processes reside in a single, systemwide address space.

Example 8.3

In the VAX-11/780 (Digital, 1981a; Strecker, 1978) each process sees a 4 Gbyte (2^{32} bytes) virtual address space. Half of this is assigned uniquely to the process (and is composed of two regions) whereas the other half is a systemwide name space shared by all processes (Fig. 8.6). Page size is 512 bytes. ■

The main advantage of paging systems is that because the unit of transfer is a fixed-size entity—the page—the *placement rule* can be very simple: Assign a page to any available page frame or to the frame released by the replacement rule. Paging does, however, pose a number of problems.

Table Fragmentation

The term "fragmentation" refers to areas of the memory space becoming unavailable (for storing programs or their data) for some reason. An instance of this, called *table fragmentation* (Randell, 1969) occurs when, owing to very large name spaces, the page tables (organized according to the mapping scheme depicted in Fig. 8.5) become extremely large. Thus, a significant part of main memory may become unavailable for assigning to pages.

[6]The issue of memory protection is further discussed in Section 8.6.

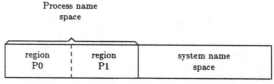

FIGURE 8.6 **Virtual name space/process in the VAX-11/780 (based on Digital, 1981a).**

Example 8.4

Referring to the VAX-11/780 again (Digital, 1981a), its virtual address is 32 bits wide and includes a 21-bit page number and a 9-bit displacement. The remaining (high-order) 2 bits of the virtual address determines whether the address belongs to the system name space or to one of the two regions of the process's unique name space (Fig. 8.7). Thus, a page table can have up to 2^{21} entries! ■

One way to reduce the size of the page table is not to use *direct mapping* of page numbers to page frame addresses (as shown in Fig. 8.5) but *associative mapping*. In this latter scheme, the maximum size of a page table is given by |M|, the number of frames in the memory space M rather than by |N|, the number of pages in a name space. Each entry in the table contains both the page number (PN) and the page frame address (ADDR). Given a virtual address, the table is searched associatively, matching pn against the PN field (Fig. 8.8)

However, as in all cases of associative mapping, the implementation cost may be prohibitive.[7]

Internal Fragmentation

A second form of fragmentation is called *internal fragmentation* (Randell, 1969). This happens when the size of a program is not an integral number of pages. Thus, if the program is brought into main memory (in its entirety or in part), a portion of the last page frame used to hold the program may be wasted (Fig. 8.9).

Despite these disadvantages, paging, either in the "pure" form just discussed or in combination with segmentation (see following) is the most common form of virtual memory.

Example 8.5

The IBM 370/168, the VAX-11/780, the Honeywell 68/80 Multics system, the PDP-10, and the Amdahl 470v/6 and 470v/7 are all examples of systems that use paging.   ■

[7]For further discussions of direct and associative mapping and the implementation of associative mapping schemes, see Section 8.5.

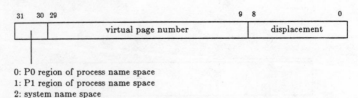

0: P0 region of process name space
1: P1 region of process name space
2: system name space

FIGURE 8.7 Virtual address in the VAX-11/780 (based on Digital, 1981a).

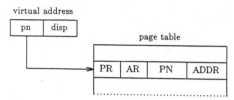

FIGURE 8.8 **Associative mapping.**

8.4.4 Segmentation

The second method of transferring information between secondary and main memory is *segmentation*. This takes advantage of the way that programs are partitioned into named modules or *segments*. Examples of segments are procedures or specific structured data objects.

In a segmented virtual memory system, a user's virtual address space is viewed as a collection of such segments, which, unlike pages, may differ in their sizes. In a *pure* segmented system the unit of transfer from secondary to main memory is an entire segment.

The basic structure of such a segmented scheme is shown in Figure 8.10. A virtual address generated by the processor is composed of a *segment number* (sn) and a *displacement* (disp) within the segment. Each process P, has a *segment table* ST(P) located in memory beginning at an address specified by the *segment table base register* (BR). Segment tables themselves may constitute segments.

Each entry in ST(P), called a *segment descriptor*, corresponds to one of P's segments and contains a *starting address* (ADDR) of the segment in main memory, the *length* (LGTH) of the segment, and [as in the case of page table entries in paging systems (Fig. 8.5)] access right (AR) and presence (PR) fields.

The address translation algorithm may generate three kinds of faults: a *missing segment* fault, which would cause the process to be suspended till the segment is located in secondary memory and transferred into main memory; an *overflow* fault, triggered whenever the specified displacement in the virtual address exceeds the length (LGTH) bound for the segment in question; and a *protection violation* fault.

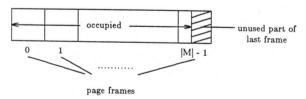

FIGURE 8.9 **Internal fragmentation.**

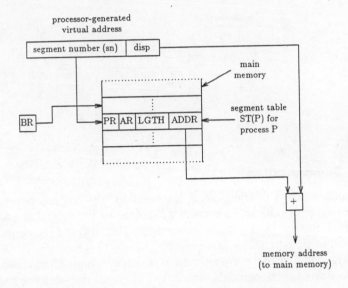

Legend
(a) AR: access right to segment
(b) LGTH: segment length
(c) **if** PR = 1 **then** segment is in main memory at address ADDR
     else segment is in secondary memory at address ADDR

Address Translation

if ST(P)[sn].PR = 0 **then trap** segment_fault
     else if if_valid(ST(P)[sn].AR)
          then if ST(P)[sn].LGTH < disp
               then trap overflow_fault
               else new memory_address = ST(P)[sn].ADDR + disp
          else trap protection_violation_fault

FIGURE 8.10   Address translation in segmented virtual memory system.

Example 8.6

"Pure" segmented schemes of the foregoing form were first proposed for the experimental Rice University computer in the late 1950s (Iliffe, 1968) and first implemented commercially in Burroughs B5500 System (Organick, 1973). An experimental successor to the Rice computer designed by Iliffe and built at International Computers Limited (ICL), called the Basic Language Machine (BLM), also used a segmented scheme (Iliffe, 1968; Levy, 1984). In recent years, the segmented scheme has been generalized into the concept of *capability-based addressing* (see Section 8.6). A recent computer using this form of segmentation is the Cambridge CAP Computer (Wilkes and Needham, 1979). In the Rice and

BLM computers, segment descriptors are called *code words*. In the CAP computers, the (extended) segment descriptors are referred to as *capabilities*. ■

The idea of segmented virtual memory was the direct outgrowth of programming languages and program structuring concepts that began emerging from the late 1950s. Unfortunately, there are two rather serious problems associated with this scheme.

The Placement Problem

Unlike pages, segments may vary considerably in size. Thus, whereas the placement issue is trivial in paging systems, it becomes a serious issue in segmented systems since an area of memory large enough to hold the entire segment must be found.

In a segmented system the state of main memory at any given point of time may appear as shown in Figure 8.11: Segments are interspersed with "holes" of unused fragments producing what Denning (1970) termed a "checkerboard" memory.

Several placement algorithms have been proposed (Knuth, 1968; Denning, 1970; Habermann, 1976) of which the most widely studied are described as follows.

Let $l_1, l_2, \ldots, l_n$ be the lengths (in bytes or words as the case may be) and $a_1, a_2, \ldots, a_n$ be the addresses, respectively, of holes $h_1, h_2, \ldots, h_n$.

1. **The best-fit algorithm** In this algorithm, if the holes are ordered such that $l_1 \le l_2 \le \ldots \le l_n$, then a new segment S with size L is allocated to the hole h_i such that l_i is the smallest size and $L \le l_i$.
2. **The first-fit algorithm** If the holes are ordered such that $a_1 < a_2 < \ldots < a_n$, then a new segment S with size L is placed in the hole h_i with the smallest address such that $L \le l_i$.
3. **The buddy algorithm** Each segment S_i is assumed to be of length $L_i = 2^{k_i}$ for some integer k_i. This algorithm maintains separate *hole lists* for each size of hole, $2^1, 2^2, \ldots, 2^q$. A hole of size 2^i can be taken from the i-list and split into two "buddies" of size 2^{i-1}, which can then be entered into the $(i-1)$-list. Conversely two buddies from the i-list can be fused into a new hole of size 2^{i+1} and added to the $(i + 1)$-list. The buddy algorithm finds a hole of size 2^i for a new segment S of length 2^p by simply selecting a hole from the p-list if available. Otherwise, it selects a hole from the $(p + 1)$-list, splits it into two, places one of the buddies in the p-list, and allocates S to the other.

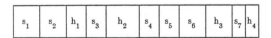

FIGURE 8.11 Interspersed segments and holes in memory.

Simulation studies of these and other placement rules were reported by Knuth (1968). These indicated that the first-fit algorithm is superior to the best-fit (in the sense that the former continues to allocate segments to holes for a longer duration before running out of available holes) and that the buddy algorithm performs slightly better than the first fit.

For placement policies of the first-fit and best-fit types, Knuth (1968) also derived the following interesting relationship.

The Fifty Percent Rule Consider a memory system in which the basic transactions on memory are *inserting* and *deleting* segments. Furthermore, assume that the system is in equilibrium — that is, the number of insertions equals the number of deletions over an extended period of time. If N_s denotes the number of segments and N_h denotes the number of holes, then $N_h \approx N_s/2$.

To derive this, let p be the probability that a segment has a hole on its "right" side (see Fig. 8.11). In the course of the segment's existence in memory, half the transactions on the immediate region to its right are insertions and half are deletions. Thus $p = 1/2$. Thus, the number of segments with holes as right neighbors is $N_s/2$. That is, $N_h \approx N_s/2$.

External Fragmentation

Regardless of the placement rule used, a situation may eventually arise when the available holes in memory are too small to hold any segment. This is yet another form of fragmentation, called *external fragmentation*; when this occurs, a *memory compaction* procedure must be invoked to collect together the holes and create a single large block of unused memory (Fig. 8.12). The process of memory compaction (also called "garbage collection") is extremely time-consuming.[8]

8.4.5 Paged Segmentation Schemes

The designer may enjoy the best of all possible worlds by implementing a scheme that combines segmentation with paging. In such a system, the virtual address space is composed of segments and each segment is partitioned into pages. The virtual address is, thus, a 3-tuple, consisting of a segment number, a

[8]For further discussion of placement algorithms and compaction strategies, refer to Habermann (1976, Chapter 5).

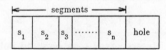

FIGURE 8.12 State of memory after compaction.

page number, and a displacement. The overall structure of the address translation algorithm will be obvious to you. In such systems, a missing-segment fault will be generated whenever no page of the referenced segment is present in main memory. A missing-page fault will occur if the desired page is absent (although other pages for the segment may be present).

Example 8.7

The MULTICS system, implemented on the Honeywell 6000 series (Organick, 1972) is a well-known example of a paged segmentation scheme. Each program can have up to 2^{18} segments, with up to 64k words/segment. The page size is 1024 words.

The IBM System/370 series (IBM, 1981) also used a paged segmentation virtual memory, where the page sizes can be 2048 or 4096 bytes. The number of segments per program and the maximum segment size can be either (1) 16 segments of up to 1 Mbytes/segment, or (2) 256 segments of up to 64k bytes/segment. ■

8.4.6 Optimal Page Size

An obvious issue in designing a paged virtual memory system (with or without segmentation) is the selection of page size. One would clearly like to choose a page size that minimizes fragmentation. Note that as the page size increases the extent of internal fragmentation is likely to increase. However, decreasing page size increases the number of pages/name space (or pages/segment) and thus increases the extent of table fragmentation. An *optimal* page size is one that minimizes the total loss of memory space due to both kinds of fragmentation.

The following approximate analysis of the problem is from Denning (1970). Let n be the expected size (in words) of a process's name space (or a segment) S, and let p be the page size. Then S would be expected to occupy approximately n/p pages, each requiring an entry in the page table. Assume that an entry requires one memory word.

The loss of memory due to table fragmentation is n/p. If $p \ll n$, the expected amount of internal fragmentation in the last page is p/2. The total loss due to fragmentation is then,

$$C = n/p + p/2.$$

To minimize C,

$$\frac{dC}{dp} = \frac{-n}{p^2} + \frac{1}{2} = 0$$

That is,

$$P_{opt} = (2n)^{1/2} \tag{8.8}$$

Assuming a paged segmentation scheme, Table 8.3 shows the values of opti-

TABLE 8.3 Optimal Page Sizes for
Various Segment Sizes (Based on Equation 8.8)

Segment Size (n)	Optimal Page Size P_{opt}
32	8
128	16
512	32
2k	64
32k	256
512k	1k

mal page size for various segment sizes. The question arises as to the expected size of segments. One response to this question is provided by Batson and Brundage (1977), who studied the segment sizes for a sample of Algol 60 programs running on the Burroughs B5500. Three types of segments were identified: *executable code*, data local to a procedure (termed *contour data* segments by Batson and Brundage), and *array* segments.

Both static and dynamic measures were taken, where the former refers to the sizes of segments and the latter denotes segment sizes weighted by the frequency of entry and exit of the segments during execution.

At the risk of simplifying matters somewhat, we may summarize their results as follows: Regardless of segmentation, most segment sizes were very small. In particular:

1. For code segments, the static and dynamic means were, respectively, 93 and 39 words, and the medians were 33 and 23, respectively.
2. For contour data segments, the static mean was 13 words and the median was 6 words. More significantly, 90% of all contour data segments contained less than 30 words.
3. For array segments, 80% of array allocations were for less than 50 words and 90% for less than 125 words.

On the basis of this data and Table 8.3, then, the page size should be in the range of 16 to 32 words. In actual fact, however, the time to transfer pages between secondary and primary memory must also be considered and, in general, the nature of secondary stores (such as moving head disks) is such that large blocks of information may be more economically transferred than small blocks.[9] Taking into account both storage loss and page transfer time, most virtual memory systems use page sizes in the range of 512 to 4k bytes.

[9]I do not intend to discuss the organization of secondary-store devices such as disks, drums, or tapes in this book. For an elementary discussion of these devices, see Foster and Iberall (1985). For detailed descriptions, refer to Matick (1977).

8.4.7 Page Replacement Algorithms

When a new page is brought into main memory and there are no empty page frames available, the selection of a page to be removed is determined by a *replacement* policy.

Much research has gone into the theory of replacement algorithms, since the efficiency and behavior of virtual memory systems depends quite critically on the replacement strategy. Earlier work on this problem is discussed by Denning (1970), whereas developments after 1970 are reviewed by Coffman and Denning (1973), Spirn (1977), and Denning (1980). In this discussion, I will present only the principal ideas and policies.

In discussing page replacement algorithms, it is convenient to represent the behavior of a program in terms of the pages that are referenced during program execution. More precisely, we define a *reference string*

$$R = r_1 r_2 \ldots r_k \ldots$$

as the sequence of successive pages referenced in the course of a program's execution. We also denote by $t(r_i)$ the time at which a reference r_i produces a missing-page fault.

If a replacement algorithm requires precise knowledge of the future page references $r_{i+1}, r_{i+2}, \ldots$, at the time of a page fault $t(r_i)$ the algorithm is said to be *unrealizable* (Denning, 1970). If the algorithm is based on *assumptions* about future references, it is said to be *realizable*.

The central objective in selecting a replacement policy is to minimize the *page fault rate*—that is, to minimize the times when a referenced page is not found in main memory. One way to achieve this is to maximize the time between page faults. This leads to the following.

Principle of Optimality (Denning, 1970)   Let $\{1, 2, \ldots, n\}$ denote the set of pages in memory at the time $t(r_i)$ of a page fault and let $t'(j) \geq t(r_i)$ be the earliest *subsequent* reference to page j. Define

$$T(j) = t(j) - t(r_i)$$

for all pages in $\{1, 2, \ldots, n\}$. Then that page j is selected for replacement for which $T(j)$ is the maximum.

The principle of optimality thus represents an optimal replacement policy, which will be called OPT. The algorithm was originally proposed by Belady (1966) and was later shown by Mattson and colleagues (1970) to exhibit optimal behavior; that is, it minimized the number of page faults generated by any reference string.

Clearly, however, OPT is not a practical replacement algorithm since it requires exact knowledge of future references at the time of a page fault. It is, in fact, an instance of an unrealizable policy. Because of its optimal performance, however, OPT provides a basis against which other algorithms may be compared.

Several realizable replacement algorithms have been proposed, and many of these are described in Coffman and Denning (1973) and Spirn (1977). Here I will describe five of these algorithms that, for reasons indicated, have certain appealing features.

First-In, First-Out (FIFO) Policy

At time $t(r_i)$ of a page fault, replace the page that has been in memory for the longest period of time. More formally, define a *paging-in record* PIR(t) at time t as an ordering of the pages in memory (at time t) as $<1',2', \ldots ,n'>$ such that $i'<j'$ implies that page i' was brought into memory after page j'. At time $t(r_i)$ of the page fault if reference r_i is to page k, and $k \notin$ PIR $[t(r_i)]$, then page n' is replaced and the paging-in record at time $[t(r_i) + 1]$ is updated to

$$PIR [t(r_i) + 1] = <k,1',2', \ldots ,n' - 1>$$

Note that FIFO pays absolutely no homage to the principle of locality (Section 8.4.1) that is assumed to govern program behavior. A page that at page fault time $t(r_i)$ is being frequently referenced may be replaced simply because it is the "oldest" page in memory. Indeed, FIFO appears to exhibit the poorest performance of the various replacement algorithms (Spirn, 1977), and Belady, Nelson, and Shedler (1969) have shown that it exhibits *anomalous behavior* in the sense that it violates the following desirable property of a replacement policy:

(PRP) The page fault rate should be a nonincreasing function of the mean memory allocation.[10]

The principle advantage of FIFO lies in its ease of implementation, since the paging-in record can be very easily maintained and no data regarding past references need be maintained.

Least-Recently-Used (LRU) Algorithm

The LRU algorithm selects the page that was least recently referenced. More formally, at time t, let $d(t) (j')$ be the *backward distance* (in time) to the most recent reference to page j'. Define a *page reference record* PRR(t) at time t as an ordering of the pages in memory $<1',2', \ldots ,n'>$ such that $i'<j'$ if $d(t)(i') < d(t)(j')$. Then at page fault time $t(r_i)$ if r_i refers to page k and $k \notin$ PRR $[t(r_i)]$, then replace page n' and update the page reference record to

$$PRR(t(r_i) + 1) = <k,1',2', \ldots , n' - 1>.$$

Like FIFO, LRU is a *nonlookahead* policy; its enforcement does not require knowledge or assumptions about future references. Unlike FIFO, it does require knowledge about past references and is, thus, more difficult to implement than FIFO. However, it takes into account the locality principle and is, thus, a more "reasonable" algorithm in the sense that pages that have been more recently

[10]This statement of PRP is from Franklin, Graham, and Gupta (1978).

referenced are expected to be referenced in the immediate future and should, therefore, be retained in memory.

The Page-Fault-Frequency (PFF) Algorithm

The PFF algorithm (Opderbeck and Chu, 1974; Chu and Opderbeck, 1976) attempts to maintain the page-fault rate below some defined maximum. For this purpose, a *page-fault frequency* parameter P is used. At the time $t(r_k)$ of a fault, the time distance D_f since the previous fault is compared to $1/P$. If $D_f \le 1/P$, no page is replaced; instead, memory allocation is increased by a page. If $D_f > 1/P$ those pages not referenced in the interval D_f (if there are any) are removed from memory.

Note that PFF is an instance of a *variable partition* algorithm in the sense that the memory allocated to pages may vary during a program's execution. In contrast, FIFO and LRU are examples of *fixed partition* algorithms.

PFF has also been shown, by Franklin, Graham, and Gupta (1978) to exhibit anomalous behavior in that it violates the PRP principle.

The Not-Recently-Used (NRU) Algorithm

Associated with each page j in memory, is a *reference flag* ref(j) such that

$$\text{ref}(j) = 1 \text{ if page j has been referenced in the recent past}$$
$$= 0 \text{ otherwise}$$

At the time $t(r_i)$ of a page fault, replace a page j such that ref(j) = 0. That is, this algorithm replaces a page that has not been referenced in the recent past on the expectation that such a page is unlikely to be used in the near future. What constitutes "recent past" is defined during implementation. For example, the reference flags for all the resident pages may be reset to 0 at fixed time intervals so that in this case, "recent past" is defined as the time since the last of such resets.

The NRU algorithm is a popular approximation to the LRU algorithm because of the ease with which it can be implemented.

The Working Set (WS) Algorithm

In Section 8.4.1 we presented the principle of locality. The idea of a "working set" was developed by Denning (1968) as a direct extension of this principle. Let $N = \{1, 2, \ldots, n\}$ be the set of pages constituting a program. Given a reference string $R = r_1 r_2 \ldots r_k \ldots$, the *working set of* a program at the k-th reference, r_k, is defined as

$$WS(k,h) = \{i \in N \mid i \in \{r_{k-h}, r_{k-h+1}, \ldots, r_k\}\}$$

That is, the working set WS(k,h) is the set of all *distinct pages* appearing in a *window* h references long, looking "back" at the reference string from reference r_k.

Example 8.8

Let R* = <4,4,5,4,5,5,6,20,20,21,4,5,5,6,20> be a reference string. Then Table 8.4 shows the working sets WS(k,2), WS(k,4), and WS(k,6) for three different window sizes (h) 2,4, and 6, and at different points of reference r_k. ∎

The working set (WS) algorithm, then, retains exactly the working set WS(k,h) (for some given window size h) at all times. On a page fault $t(r_k)$, a page is removed only if it has not been referenced in the previous h references.

Like PFF, WS is a variable partitioning algorithm. If the number of page frames allocated to a program does not satisfy the working set requirements, then other page frames are released to accommodate the additional page(s) required to complete the working set. One may also note that WS is a generalization of LRU in that *any* page that has not been referenced in the window of size h can be replaced rather than a specific "least recently used" page as in LRU.

When their respective parameters are properly adjusted, WS and PFF appear to give performances that are close to one another and superior to LRU. As I have indicated, however, PFF exhibits anomalous behavior in that it violates PRP.[11] Furthermore, WS has been economically implemented in hardware on the MANIAC II experimental computer at Los Alamos National Laboratory (Morris, 1972). Based on these considerations, WS is generally regarded as a better replacement algorithm.

8.4.8 Thrashing

As defined previously, the working set WS(k,h) is a function of both the window size h and the reference point r_k in the reference string R. Let S(R) and S[WS(k,h)] denote, respectively, the *size* of R and WS(k,h). For a window size h, the *average working set size* is defined as

$$AWS(h) = \frac{\sum_{k=1}^{S(R)} S[WS(k,h)]}{S(R)}$$

[11]Franklin, Graham, and Gupta (1978) have, however, shown that WS exhibits other forms of anomalous behavior, the discussion of which is beyond the scope of this chapter.

TABLE 8.4 Examples of Working Sets for the Reference String R*

k	WS(k,2)	WS(k,4)	WS(k,6)
3	{4,5}	{4,5}	{4,5}
6	{5}	{4,5}	{4,5}
9	{20}	{5,6,20}	{4,5,6,20}
12	{4,5}	{4,5,20,21}	{4,5,6,20,21}
15	{6,20}	{5,6,20}	{4,5,6,20,21}

Example 8.9

For the reference string R* in Example 8.8, it can be verified that
AWS(4) = 40/15 = 2.67. ∎

Intuitively, the average working set size reflects the expected number of a program's pages that must reside in main memory to keep the rate of page fault at a reasonably low level. If the total number of page frames in a multiprogrammed memory system is significantly below the sum of the average working set sizes for the programs sharing memory space, one effectively has a large number of referenced pages competing for a (relatively) small number of page frames. Thus, a page fault generated in the course of executing a program P_1 (say) may cause a page belonging to some other program P_2 to be replaced. The replaced page may, however, be required very soon after when P_2 executes this in turn precipitating another page fault.

Under such conditions, a phenomenon called *thrashing* (Denning, 1968, 1970) arises in which most of the processor time is given to servicing page faults and very little to actual productive computation. The performance of the system, thus, degrades drastically.

8.4.9 Demand Paging and Prepaging

Recall from Section 8.4.2 that one of the design issues in virtual memory systems is the fetch policy, which determines *when* a page is to be brought into main memory. Our entire discussion in the foregoing sections has been based on the view that pages are loaded into page frames at the time of page fault occurrence—that is, when they are required (but not present in memory space). Such a fetch policy is referred to as *demand paging*.

We conclude our discussion of virtual memory by noting that an alternative to demand paging is *prepaging*, which attempts to anticipate future references to pages and loads them prior to their actual use. This may help to reduce the overhead incurred in transferring pages. Note, however, that prepaging implies that pages already in page frames may have to be removed to make space for the prefetched pages. In the event that a replaced page is referenced before the prefetched page, the potential advantage of prepaging would be lost.

In the case of arbitrary programs (or segments), predicting future references is generally difficult so that most virtual memory systems adopt demand paging.

8.5 CACHE MEMORIES

If virtual memory provides the illusion of almost unlimited main memory, the aim of cache memory is to render that other great illusion—that memory references can be serviced almost at processor speed. In this sense there is a pleasing symmetry between these two facets of the memory hierarchy.

Recall from Section 8.2 that a cache is a fast store of capacity usually in the range of 4 to 64 Kbytes used to hold segments of program and data. The speed of a cache memory is typically in the range of 50 to 100 nsec, and the ratio of main memory/cache speeds is approximately 5/1. A cache must be distinguished from a processor's local store in that the latter (or part of it) is defined as a component of the exo-architecture. They are programmable registers visible to the typical user, whereas a cache is fundamentally an endo-architectural feature.

In very general terms, the structural relationship between cache, main memory, and processor is depicted in Figure 8.13. Information paths exist between main memory and cache, cache and processor, and main memory and processor. The operation and behavior of a cache system is shown, in general terms, in Figure 8.14.

Assume that the processor (perhaps in conjunction with a virtual memory address translation mechanism) has generated a real address to fetch a word from main memory. Each word in the cache corresponds to some main memory address and the information contained in that address. The precise mapping of main memory words to cache words depends on the *placement policy* (see Section 8.5.2).

A search procedure (which again depends on the placement policy in effect) determines whether the cache contains the information corresponding to the processor-generated address. If so, the information is read out from the cache and transmitted to the processor. Access to main memory is thereby avoided. Otherwise, the real address is transmitted to the main memory. The accessed word is sent to the processor and is also loaded into the cache according to the placement policy for future reference.

Although there are important differences between virtual and cache memories, some obvious analogies prevail, giving rise to parallel design issues. The most important of the cache design issues are the following.

1. The *placement policy*, which determines how main memory words are mapped onto cache memory words.
2. The success of a cache system obviously relies on the assumption that most memory requests will be serviced by the cache rather than by main memory. Thus, when a new item of information is fetched into cache memory, the principle of locality will demand that immediate future references will be to words in the neighborhood of the fetched words. Thus, the cache system designer must be concerned with the *size and nature of blocks* transferred from main to cache memory.
3. In the event a block is to be loaded into cache and the latter is full, some block must be removed to make room for the newcomer. Which block is to

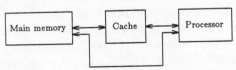

FIGURE 8.13 The cache/main memory hierarchy.

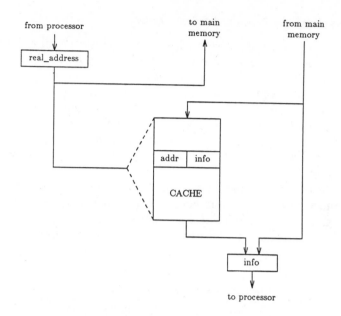

Address Translation

if there is some k such that cache[k].addr = real_address
    then new info = cache[k].info
    else new info = memory[real_address] &
        there is some l such that
        new cache[l].addr = real_address &
        new cach[l].info = memory[real_address]

FIGURE 8.14 **Fetching information in a cache-based system.**

be removed is determined by the *replacement policy.*

4. The *size of the cache.*
5. When a processor executes a store instruction on a word in cache, the corresponding word in main memory must also be modified. The *memory update policy* determines when this is to be done.
6. In a multiprocessor system, each processor may have its own cache and a common block of main memory words may be present in two or more of the caches. The store problem is further aggrevated here since, if a processor executes a store to the shared word in its own store in addition to main memory update, all the other caches containing that word must also be updated. This is referred to as the *cache coherence* problem, associated with multiple cache systems. It is further discussed in the context of multiprocessors in Volume 2, Chapter 8 (Section 8.5.3).

All but the last of these design issues will be discussed herein. Prior to that, I identify the principal measure used to evaluate the performance of cache systems.

8.5.1 Evaluating Cache Performance

The performance of cache systems has been extensively studied using *trace-driven simulation*. A detailed and comprehensive review of these experiments is presented in Smith (1982), which provides the source of the results that I will describe here. By executing a program interpretively and recording every memory address referenced, a *trace* (or memory reference profile) of the program can be obtained. Additional information, such as whether a reference was for fetching an instruction, fetching an operand, or to store a result, can also be associated with each trace element. Such traces are then used to drive a simulation of a cache system.

The results of such simulation experiments indicate that the effectiveness of a cache memory depends on a number of key parameters, namely, the block size, the cache size, and the nature of the placement policy. The performance of a cache memory is usually denoted by a metric called the "miss ratio," which is analogous to the "page fault rate" metric used to evaluate paging systems.

Define, first, the *hit ratio* as

$$HR = \frac{\text{Number of memory references found in cache}}{\text{Total number of memory references}}$$

Then the *miss ratio* is defined as

$$MR = 1 - H$$

The profiles of the miss ratio curve against various parameters will be discussed in the next section.

8.5.2 Placement Policies and Cache Organizations

The placement policy, which determines the address mapping between main memory and cache, is closely related to the internal organization of the cache. The most popular placement policy is called *set associative* mapping. This is, in fact, a generalization of two other algorithms called, respectively, *direct* mapping and *fully associative* mapping. For the sake of clarity, I will describe each of these separately.

Direct Mapping

Suppose that main memory is organized in the form of $B = 2^{k_2}$ *blocks* where the *block size* $b = 2^w$ words, for some pair of integers k_2 and w. The size of main memory, then is 2^{k_2+w} words and the size (in bits) of a real address will be $k_2 + w$.

Suppose also that cache memory consists of $F = 2^{k_1}$ *block frames* where the *block frame size* is also $b = 2^w$ words. The cache size, then is 2^{k_1+w} words.

In the method of *direct mapping*, block i is mapped onto block frame j where

$$j = i \ (\text{modulo } F)$$

Example 8.10

Figure 8.15 shows a direct mapping scheme for the following parameter values:

$$F = 4, \quad k_1 = 2$$
$$B = 8, \quad k_2 = 3$$
$$b = 4, \quad W = 2$$

The main memory size is 32 words, and the cache size is 16 words. ■

Note that main memory blocks mapping onto the same block frame form an equivalence class.[12] Note also that in direct mapping the address of the block or the word-within-a-block need not be explicitly stored in the cache. A processor-generated *real address* will be $(k_2 + w)$-bits long, of which the high-order k_2-bits identify the *block address* and the low-order w-bits locate the word within the block. A word can be located in cache according to the relations:

1. Block frame address = low-order k_1-bits of block address.
2. Word location with the block frame = low-order w-bits of the total real address.

Fully Associative Mapping

In this policy, any block of main memory can be placed in any block frame of the cache. As before, a real address is specified in $(k_2 + w)$-bits. Each block frame in the cache is associated with an *address tag* field (Fig. 8.16). When a memory reference is to be made, the high-order k_2-bits of the real address are compared against the address tag fields of all the block frames. Thus, the search is *associative*. When (and if) a match is found, the low-order w-bits of the real address identify the word within the block frame.

---

[12]That is, viewing main memory (MM) as a set of B blocks, the "modulo F" *relation* partitions the blocks of memory into F subsets $f_1, \ldots, f_F$ such that $f_1 \cup f_2 \cup \ldots \cup f_F = MM$ and for $i \neq j$, $f_i \cap f_j = \emptyset$, where $\emptyset$ is the empty set. For more on equivalence classes, see any text on modern algebra, for example, Birkhoff and Bartee (1970).

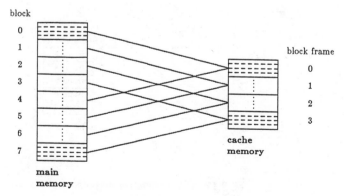

FIGURE 8.15 Direct mapping.

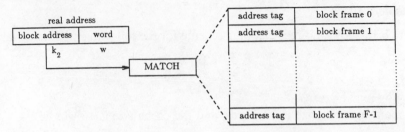

FIGURE 8.16 **Fully associative mapping.**

Set Associative Mapping

As noted earlier, direct and fully associative mappings are, in fact, both special cases of a placement policy called *set associative* mapping. In this scheme, the cache is organized into $S = 2^{k_0}$ *sets*, each of which consists of $F = 2^{k_1}$ block frames. Main memory, as before, consists of $B = 2^{k_2}$ blocks. Both blocks and block frames hold $b = 2^w$ words.

A block i in main memory is mapped onto the *set* j where

$$j = i \ (\text{modulo } S).$$

Within a set a block may be mapped fully associatively in any one of the F frames.

Example 8.11

Figure 8.17 shows a set associative mapping for the following parameter values:

$$S = 4, \quad k_0 = 2 \qquad B = 16, \quad k_2 = 4$$
$$F = 2, \quad k_1 = 1 \qquad b = 4, \quad w = 2$$ ∎

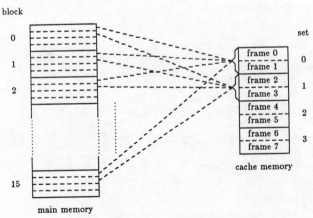

FIGURE 8.17 **Set associative mapping.**

Note that set associative mapping reduced to direct mapping when the *set size* F = 1 and that it reduces to fully associative mapping when the *number of sets* S = 1.

By varying the values of some of the key parameters such as the set size F, the number of sets S, and the block size b, the performance of set_associative_mapped cache memories can be studied and evaluated using trace-driven simulation. However, it must be kept in mind that the miss ratios observed will depend on the benchmarks that are used to drive the traces and on the specifics of the machine architecture.

Smith (1982) presents details of many such experiments on the performance of cache memories. We can summarize these results as follows.

1. For a given cache size z, and a given block size b, lowering the number of sets S tends to reduce the miss ratio MR. However, the experiments showed consistently, that quite substantial reductions in S reduces M by only a very modest amount.

Example 8.12

In one set of experiments cited by Smith (1982) given a cache capacity of about 40 Kbytes, reducing S from 256 to 32 lowered MR from about 0.8% to about 0.6%. ■

2. Keeping in mind that for a given cache size z, S*F = z, a smaller S implies a larger F. However, Smith (1982) points out than an "acceptable" miss ratio is obtained with a value of F between 4 and 8.[13] Above 8, the miss ratio does not decrease to any significant extent.
3. For cache sizes z in the range 32 to 64 Kbytes, the block size b that produced the minimum MR was in the range of 128 to 256 bytes. For z in the range 8 to 16 Kbytes, a value of b in the range of 64 to 128 bytes produced a minimum MR. For z in the range of 4 Kbytes, a minimum MR was obtained with a value of b = 32 bytes.
4. In general, keeping other parameters constant, increasing the cache size z is likely to decrease MR. Although the precise relationship between z and MR will depend on the program workload and the architecture, one set of experiments conducted at Amdahl Corporation for the Amdahl series of machines and cited in Smith (1982) indicates an approximate empiric relationship of the form

$$MR = az^b$$

where a, b are constants and b < 0. In another set of experiments involving the PDP-11/70, Strecker (1976) reported that the miss ratio decreased rap-

---

[13]What constitutes an "acceptable" miss ratio will, of course, depend on the performance goals of the target system. Based on the range of miss ratios presented by Smith (1982) and discussions of miss ratio targets by other designers such as Strecker (1976), a miss ratio of about 5% or below appears to be an "average acceptable" figure.

idly (to about 10%) with increasing cache size up to about 2K bytes, but the subsequent decrease in MR with increase in z fell far less rapidly thereafter.[14]

Of course, in deciding on a cache size the designer must take into account not only the issue of cache performance but also the cost of the high-speed cache memory.

Table 8.5 summarizes values of S, F, b, and z for a variety of machines. The right-most column will be discussed later.

8.5.3 Replacement Policy

In a cache organized according to the set associative mapping policy, the flexibility of placement is confined to a choice of frames within a set. Consequently, the *replacement policy*—determining which block to remove—will also be restricted to the particular set in which the new block is to be placed. In the terminology of paging systems (Section 8.4), the choice of a replacement algorithm is confined to the class of *fixed-partition* algorithms such as FIFO and LRU. In the experiments cited by Smith (1982), FIFO is found to yield, on the average, a miss ratio that is about 12% higher than that generated by LRU. From the perspective of performance, the LRU algorithm is preferable, although its implementation will be costlier than that of FIFO.

8.5.4 Main Memory Update Policy

I conclude this section (8.5) on cache memories with a brief discussion of the policy for updating main memory. The issue is, when to update a word in

[14]Strecker's (1976) experiments assumed a block size of b = 4 bytes and a set size of F = 1.

TABLE 8.5 Cache System Parameter Values for a Range of Machines

Machines	Number of Sets S	Set Size F	Block Size b	Cache Size z	Update Policy
Amdahl 470 v/6	256	2	32 bytes	16 Kbytes	Copy-back
Amdahl 470 v/7	128	8	32 bytes	32 Kbytes	Copy-back
Amdahl 470 v/8	512	4	32 bytes	64 Kbytes	Copy-back
IBM 370/168-3	128	8	32 bytes	32 Kbytes	Write-through
IBM 3033	64	16	64 bytes	64 Kbytes	Write-through
DEC PDP-11/70	256	2	8 bytes	1 Kbyte	Write-through
DEC VAX-11/780	512	2	4 bytes	16 Kbytes	Write-through
Honeywell 66/80	128	4	16 bytes	8 Kbytes	Write-through

Source: Smith (1982).

memory in the event that a word in cache has been modified by the execution of a store instruction. There are essentially two possibilities.

1. In the *copy-back* policy, when a word in the cache is modified a special flag in that word (sometimes referred to as the *dirty bit*) is set to indicate this fact. The corresponding word in main memory is only updated when the block containing the modified word (the "dirty block") is to be replaced in cache and the dirty bit is found to be set.
2. In the *write-through* (or *store-through*) policy, the word in main memory is updated whenever the corresponding word in the cache is updated. Thus, main memory never contains obsolete data.

Apart from the cache coherence problem present in multiprocessors (see Volume 2, Chapter 8, Section 8.5.3), the following principal trade-offs prevail between the two policies.

1. Write-through is *easier to implement* than copy-back since some additional logic must be present in the latter to test the dirty bit. Furthermore, write-through is more conducive to *reliability* since in the event of a processor (and therefore, cache) failure the main memory contains up-to-date information, thus rendering it easier to restore the cache.
2. On the other hand, write-through may generate *more processor-memory traffic* since it necessitates an actual main memory reference for every store instruction executed whereas copy-back generates memory reference only at block replacement time. Furthermore, unless some buffering capability is provided to hold the data to be written into main memory the processor will be blocked more often in write-through, since it must wait for each write-to-memory to be completed.

The right-most column of Table 8.4 shows the memory update policy for each of the machines listed. In general, there does not appear to be any consensus about the relative performance of the two policies.

8.6 MEMORY PROTECTION USING CAPABILITIES

When discussing segmented virtual memories (Section 8.4.4), I noted that segmentation takes advantage of the natural way in which programs and their data are organized. In segmented systems—either of the "pure" or of the paged varieties—the segment is also the *unit of protection* in the sense that all the words of a segment share a common *access right* that determines what kinds of access processes can have to the segment. A segment descriptor—an entry in a segment table—thus includes a field signifying the access rights to that segment (Fig. 8.10).

Clearly, if segment descriptors are used to establish the access rights to segments, not all processes should have access to segment tables. Only routines that execute in privileged mode—that is, certain routines that are part of the operating system—can actually manufacture segment descriptors and place them in segment tables.[15]

The notion of segment descriptors as a basis for both addressing a segment and defining the access rights to it is further generalized into the idea of *capability-based* protection and addressing.

A *capability* is basically identical *in format* to a segment descriptor. It consists of a segment identifier (or a base address and a length field that collectively identify the segment in memory) and an access right that establishes the modes of access to the segment. However, a capability is a more substantial entity, as is next explained.

To begin with, in a conventional segment descriptor-based scheme, the access rights to a segment (as defined by the segment's descriptor) are a property of the segment regardless of who uses the segment. In a capability-based system, a process P_1 must *possess a capability* for a segment S_1 in order to access S_1, and the scope of P_1's access to S_1 is defined by the access rights AR_{11} in that *particular* capability for S_1 possessed by P_1 (Fig. 8.18). A different process P_2 may have a different access right to S_1, as defined by its possession of a capability for S_1 with access right AR_{12}. In general, a process may possess a whole set of capabilities for

---

[15]A feature shared by many computer systems is the presence of instructions that are only available for use by the operating system. These instructions are referred to as *privileged* instructions. Correspondly, such computers will have two states of execution—a *problem* or *user* state in which only nonprivileged instructions can execute and a *supervisor, executive,* or *privileged* state (or mode) in which all, including privileged, instructions can execute. The operating system (or significant parts of it) will execute in the privileged mode. If, for example, the hardware/firmware supports a special instruction that makes segment descriptors, such an instruction would be privileged. For more on this topic, see any text on operating systems, for example, Madnick and Donovan (1974) or Habermann (1976), or an architectural manual, for example, IBM (1981).

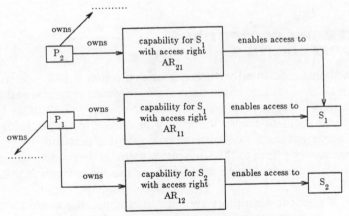

FIGURE 8.18 Capability-based access to segments.

the different segments to which it needs access. Note that unlike the case of descriptor-based systems, a capability is, in fact, a relation between a process and a segment.

The basic principles of a capability-based protection scheme are as follows.[16]

Memory words are of two types: *data words* (which hold both data and instructions) and *capability words* (which hold only capabilities). A capability, as stated before, consists of a segment identifier (or information about its location in memory) and a specification of the access rights afforded to that segment. A capability for a data word is termed a *D-type* capability whereas that for a capability word is termed a *C-type* capability.

For a process P to access a segment S in a particular way during the former's execution, it is necessary for P to own a capability for S with valid access rights. In general, P will have, in one or more segments called *capability segments*, a collection of capabilities that identifies both the segments to which P has access and the specifics of these access rights.

Consider a processor designed specifically to support capability-based protection. It may contain a set of high-speed *capability registers*, collectively forming a *capability store* such that at any given time each register holds a capability belonging to some active process for some segment in memory (Fig. 8.19). Note that this implies that several distinct capabilities possessed by distinct processes for the same segment may reside simultaneously in the capability store.

The address translation mechanism will be rather similar to that for other segmented virtual memory systems (see, e.g., Fig. 8.10); I will not repeat the details here. Briefly stated, when a process P is running on the processor, in the course of executing each instruction the capability store is checked to determine whether the instruction's opcode is consistent with the access right for the referenced segment. If not, a trap to a protection-fault handling routine will be precipitated.

---

[16]The terminology used to describe capability-based systems is not especially standardized. The particular terms used here are from Wilkes and Needham (1979).

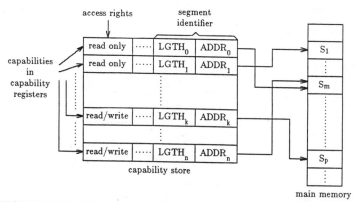

FIGURE 8.19   **The state of a capability store during machine operation.**

In a scheme of this sort, protection depends on the assumption that *an arbitrary process* cannot create a capability for a segment and load it into a capability register. This capacity must only be available to procedures specifically designed to do this. The reason for having data words and capability words is that only those processes owning capabilities for capability words—that is, owning C-type capabilities—may load them into a capability register. A process owning only D-type capabilities can merely access and/or modify data words.

A routine (in the operating system) responsible for creating capabilities must, therefore, possess both C- and D-type capabilities for the same segment. It is then possible for the routine to create a capability (on behalf of a user process P) and place it in one of P's capability segment using its D-type capability, and then load the capability into a capability register using its C-type capability.[17]

The origins of capability-based architectures and protection systems can be traced back to the earliest segment descriptor-based schemes of the late 1950s and early 1960s (see Example 8.6). However, the concept of capabilities as "tickets" owned by processes in order to access segments was developed by Dennis and Van Horn (1966). The first commercial implementation of capabilities was Plessey Corporation's System 250 (England, 1972), which was developed in the early 1970s. Key subsequent developments include the Cambridge CAP computer (Wilkes and Needham, 1979), which became operational in 1976, and the Hydra operating system kernel for the C.mmp multiprocessor implemented in the mid-1970s (Cohen and Jefferson, 1975)—both of which were experimental systems intended to further explore capability-based system design—and the IBM System/38, delivered in 1980; this was the first significant commercial capability-based system (Bertsis, 1980).

Example 8.13

Operations for the manipulation of capabilities can be, of course, implemented in hardware, firmware, or software. In the Cambridge CAP computer (Wilkes and Needham, 1979) protection is effected by a symbiotic combination of all three system levels.

At the exo-architectural level, the CAP is a 32-bit register machine with 16 general purpose registers. Instructions are 32-bits long and are essentially of the register-storage type:

reg$_j$:= reg$_i$ **op** memory [addr]

From the perspective of protection, the features of most interest at the endo-architectural level are the *microprogram unit* (MU) and the *capability unit* (CU), which work cooperatively (in a manner to be explained) to provide the architectural environment for enforcing protection.

The microprogram residing in the control store of the MU includes, in addi-

---

[17]There is no need to have a privileged state for the processor nor the need for privileged instructions. It is the possession of particular capabilities that, in some sense, makes a *process* privileged.

tion to routines that implement the CAP's general and special instruction sets, routines responsible for manipulating capabilities. The principal component of the CU is the capability store, consisting of 64 capability registers (Fig. 8.20).

A capability residing in any one of these registers consists of the base address of the segment, the segment length, an access right, and a *tag*, which uniquely identifies the capability from the others held in the capability store. Possible access rights in the CAP are *read data, write data, read capability, write capability*, and *execute*.

During instruction execution, a memory access is performed in essentially three steps.

Step 1: The microcode loads an address in the form of a capability specifier and an offset into the P register, and the type of access requested into the PAR register (Fig. 8.20).

Step 2: The capability unit is then activated and proceeds on its own to check that the requested access is permitted. It does this by a partially associative search of the capability store for the capability specified in the P register using the tag field in each capability register and comparing this against the specifier contained in P.

In the event a match occurs, the value of the access rights field in the matched capability is used by the CU to validate the requested access previously loaded into PAR. If a match does not occur, then a fault condition is set for further action in the next step.

Step 3: This step is performed by the MU. If the access request in PAR was found to be valid in Step 2, microcode is executed to read to, or write from, memory, as determined by the access request. If, however, a fault condition had been set in Step 2, the microprogram enters and executes a routine for performing a *capability load cycle.* This "cycle" loads the required capability (contained in some capability segment for the process in question) into a capability register, using some appropriate replacement algorithm (e.g., LRU) if necessary, to select which register to write into.

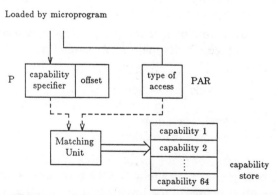

FIGURE 8.20 Validating memory reference in the CAP.

This is a necessarily simplified account of the hardware/firmware support provided in the CAP for manipulating capabilities. In addition, the CAP operating system is responsible for the management of user processes within this environment and, in particular, capability segments. It does so by means of a set of instructions (also implemented in microcode) especially provided for the manipulation of capabilities. ∎

8.7 BIBLIOGRAPHIC REMARKS

Almost two decades after it was published, Denning (1970) remains worthy of study and a pleasure to read. This paper is truly seminal in that it defined the topic and what was known about virtual memories, circa 1970. A more recent paper by Denning (1980) is a highly technical retrospective account of the development of working set principles, by its originator.

At this time, Smith (1982) is probably the most detailed, up-to-date discussion of the various design issues and parameters affecting the performance of cache memories.

Capability-based systems are discussed in a number of recent publications. Levy (1984) is devoted exclusively to such systems and contains valuable descriptions of the most important capability-based systems designed and implemented over the years. Myers (1982) also discusses capabilities and other related notions such as *tagged* and *object-oriented* architectures. Wilkes (1975) is an earlier, concise discussion of virtual memories and capabilities, whereas the monograph by Wilkes and Needham (1979) provides extensive details about the CAP system.

PROBLEMS

8.1 How can memory interleaving be *empirically* justified? That is, what are the grounds for believing that an interleaved memory scheme may actually increase the memory bandwidth?

8.2 Consider the instruction interpretation cycle (Icycle) in a conventional von Neumann style processor. Its main phases are:

IFETCH :   fetch instruction
IDECODE :   decode instruction
EADDR :   calculate effective addresses of operands
OPDFETCH :   fetch operands
IEXEC :   execute instruction

Since IFETCH accesses main memory, this is certainly the most critical bottleneck because no matter how fast the processor is, that is, no matter how fast the other phases of the Icycle are, the overall speed of instruction processing will be limited by IFETCH.

(a)   Describe how memory interleaving can be effectively used to minimize the IFETCH-induced bottleneck.

(b)   What other factor(s) will influence or limit the effectiveness of memory interleaving as a means for speeding up IFETCH?

8.3   [Refer to Problem 8.2.] Even in the "purest" of register machines main memory has to be referenced during OPDFETCH at least during the execution of LOAD/STORE type instructions. In less "pure" register machines, memory will be accessed possibly more frequently during OPD-FETCH, in order to execute register-storage type instructions. Thus, OPD-FETCH may frequently pose an additional bottleneck during Icycle.

Describe how, and under what assumptions, memory interleaving can be used to minimize the OPDFETCH-induced bottleneck.

8.4   It has often been said that the advent of virtual memory has liberated the programmer from having to worry about the size of his or her program. In one sense this is certainly true: the programmer need not worry about whether or not the program will fit into main memory or, in the event that it does not, about such matters as memory management or program overlays. However, this does not imply that virtual memory provides a ready excuse for sloppy programming.

Explain why, despite virtual memory, the programmer and the compiler writer must remain concerned about program size.

8.5   (a) Design an "implementation" of the least-recently-used (LRU) page replacement policy. This implementation should include descriptions of any tables or data structures required and a description of the procedure that would be invoked at page fault time.

(b)   Design an implementation of the not-recently-used (NRU) page replacement policy.

(c)   What are your conclusions regarding the relative merits of these two implementations?

8.6   In Section 8.5, it was noted that a cache is basically an endo-architectural feature, that is, it is not visible to the "typical" user. Consider, however, a *programmable cache*. This would be cache memory that is defined as part of a machine's exo-architecture. Thus, the actual loading of the cache and the subsequent access to it, would be under program control.

Identify at least one class of programming applications that would be well suited for execution on such a system and, using a specific example, show *how* the programmable cache can be effectively used.

8.7   [A design and simulation project.] In the initial stages of a small computer design project it has been determined that the computer's main memory will consist of 2^{16}, 32-bit words. It has also been decided that the system will include a cache memory and that the placement policy to be used is set associative mapping. Furthermore, for reasons having to do with the implementation technology, the total cache size has been fixed at 1K, 32-bit words.

The important parameters that remain to be determined are

1. The set size, S.
2. The number of sets, S.
3. The block size, b.

You are required to design and implement a *software-simulated* cache subsystem to be called SOFT-CACHE. The requirements to be met by SOFT-CACHE are the following:

(a) The input to the simulator will be a stream of (main memory) *addresses* (as they would be generated by the processor during the instruction interpretation cycle). Each address will have attached to it a *tag* indicating a "read" or a "write" (to that address).

(b) SOFT-CACHE will determine whether or not the referenced word is in the cache. If it is, and if the address tag is a "read," the contents of the cache word is transferred to a register called BUFFER. If the address tag is a "write" then a "write" into the cache is simulated.

(c) If the addressed word is absent from the cache, a simulated "loading" of the cache from main memory must be performed. Furthermore, if the address tag is a "read," then a loading of the word into BUFFER must also be simulated, whereas, in the event that the tag is a "write," a simulated "write" into the cache is performed.

The replacement policy to be used will be least-recently-used. (*Note*: Since SOFT-CACHE is not simulating MAIN memory operations, the problem of updating main memory during replacement may be ignored.)

(d) In implementing SOFT-CACHE, the parameters F, S, and b will be maintained as variables that can be assigned specific values during a particular simulation run.

(e) SOFT-CACHE must also keep a record of the number of hits (or misses) during a simulation run.

As in any programming project you are required to demonstrate the correctness of your simulator.

8.8 [Continuation of Problem 8.7.] Construct a set of two or three *address traces* that will be used to drive the SOFT-CACHE simulator.

(a) Using these traces as inputs to the simulator, vary the parameters F, S, and b and measure the miss ratios that are obtained from each simulation run.

(b) Describe the results of your experiments and, in particular, your final choice of values for these three parameters.

8.9 A small library of very special and rare books is being established. A user, U_j, of this library may have two types of *library cards* for a *particular* book B_i. One type of card will permit him to read B_i *inside the library only*. The other type of card will permit him to *take out* B_i from the library (for a specified time period). A user, U_j, may thus own one or both types of cards for each distinct book he is interested in.

A library card not only establishes the user's access right to a book. It also indicates the *location* of the book in the library shelves.

The library rules must be such as to satisfy the following conditions:

1. A user U_j who has a particular card C_k for a particular book B_j must be *guaranteed* (eventual) access to B_i in the manner specified by C_k. ("Eventual" access because B_i may have been borrowed by some other user at the time the request is made).

2. A user U_j who does *not* possess a type of library card C_k for a particular book B_i must be *prevented* access to B_i in the manner that would be specified by C_k.

3. It must be guaranteed that a user U_i can never access a book B_i by false means—that is, by borrowing or stealing a library card from some other user.

4. A book B_i for which *no* user has a library card of either type, or for which all library cards have been lost or destroyed, is "officially" said to be LOST and is forever inaccessible to the world.

(a) Design a "capability-based" system of procedures or rules for this library such that conditions 1 through 3 are always satisfied and no books will ever be LOST.

(b) *Prove* that your system is correct.

APPENDIXES

APPENDIX A

THE ASCII CODE
(PARTIAL)

Bit Positions 3210	Bit Positions 654					
	010	011	100	101	110	111
0000		0	@	P	´	p
0001	!	1	A	Q	a	q
0010	"	2	B	R	b	r
0011	#	3	C	S	c	s
0100	$	4	D	T	d	t
0101	%	5	E	U	e	u
0110	&	6	F	V	f	v
0111	'	7	G	W	g	w
1000	(	8	H	X	h	x
1001	)	9	I	Y	i	y
1010	*	:	J	Z	j	z
1011	+	;	K	[	k	{
1100	,	<	L	\	l	|
1101	-	=	M	]	m	}
1110	.	>	N	^	n	~
1111	/	?	O	—	o	

THE EBCDIC CODE
(PARTIAL)

Bit Positions 3210	Bit Positions 7654										
	0100	0101	0110	0111	1000	1001	1010	1100	1101	1110	1111
0000											0
0001					a	j		A	J		1
0010					b	k	s	B	K	S	2
0011					c	l	t	C	L	T	3
0100					d	m	u	D	M	U	4
0101					e	n	v	E	N	V	5
0110					f	o	w	F	O	W	6
0111					g	p	x	G	P	X	7
1000					h	q	y	H	Q	Y	8
1001					i	r	z	I	R	Z	9
1010		!		:							
1011	.	$	,	#							
1100	<	*	%	@							
1101	(	)	—	'							
1110	+	;	>	=							
1111	|	¬	?	"							

REFERENCES

Ackerman, W. B. (1982) "Data Flow Languages." *Computer* 15(2), 15–25.

Adams, D. A. (1968) "A Computational Model with Data Flow Sequencing." Technical Report TR-CS 117, Department of Computer Science, Stanford University, Stanford, Calif.

Advanced Micro Devices (1983) *Bipolar Microprocessor Logic and Interface Data Book*. Advanced Micro Devices, Sunnyvale, Calif.

Agerwala, T., and Arvind (1982) "Data Flow Systems: Guest Editors' Introduction." *Computer* 15(2), 10–14.

Agrawala, A. K., and Rauscher, T. G. (1976) *Foundations of Microprogramming*. Academic Press, New York.

Agüero, U. (1978) "A Theory of Plausibility for Computer Architecture Designs." Ph.D. Dissertation, Center for Advanced Computer Studies, University of Southwestern Louisiana, Lafayette.

Agüero, U., and Dasgupta, S. (1978) "A Plausibility-Driven Approach to Computer Architecture Design." *Comm ACM* 30(11), 922–932.

Aho, A. V., Hopcroft, J. E., and Ullman, J. D. (1974) *The Design and Analysis of Algorithms*. Addison–Wesley, Reading, Mass.

Aho, A. V., and Ullman, J. D. (1973) *The Theory of Parsing, Translation and Compiling, Vol. 1: Parsing*. Prentice–Hall, Englewood-Cliffs, N.J.

Aho, A. V., and Ullman, J. D. (1977) *Principles of Compiler Design*. Addison–Wesley, Reading, Mass.

Alagic, S., and Arbib, M. A. (1978) *The Design of Well-Structured and Correct Programs*. Springer-Verlag, Berlin.

Alexander, C. (1964) *Notes on the Synthesis of Form*. Harvard University Press, Cambridge, Mass.

Alexander, W. G., and Wortman, D. B. (1975) "Static and Dynamic Characteristics of XPL Programs." *IEEE Computer* 8(11), 41–46.

Allan, V. (1986) "A Critical Analysis of the Global Optimization Problem for Horizontal Microcode." Technical Report MAD.86.20, Department of Computer Science, Colorado State University, Fort Collins, Colo.

Amamiya, M., Hakozaki, K., Yokoi, T., *et al.* (1982) "New Architecture for Knowledge Base Mechanisms." in Moto-oka (1982), 179–188.

Amamiya, M., Takesue, M., Hasegawa, R., *et al.* (1986) "Implementation and Evaluation of a List-Processing-Oriented Data Flow Machine," *Proceedings of the 13th International Symposium on Computer Architecture*, IEEE Computer Society Press, Los Alamitos, Calif., 10–19.

Amdahl, G. M., Blaauw, G. A., and Brooks, F. P. Jr. (1964) "Architecture of the IBM System/360." *IBM J Res Dev* 8(2), 87–101.

Anderson, D. W., Sparacio, F. J., and Tomasulo, R. M. (1976) "IBM System 360 Model 91, Machine Philosophy and Instruction Handling." *IBM J Res Develop* 11(1), 8–24.

Anderson, G. A., and Jensen, E. D. (1975) "Computer Interconnection Structures: Taxonomy, Characteristics and Examples." *ACM Comp Surv* 9(4), 197–214.

Andrews, G. R., and Schneider, F. B. (1983) "Concepts and Notations for Concurrent Programming," *ACM Comp Surv* 15(1), 3–44.

Andrews, M. (1980) *Principles of Firmware Engineering in Microprogram Control.* Computer Science Press, Potomac, Md.

Apt, K. R. (1981) "Ten Years of Hoare Logics. Part I." *ACM Trans Prog Lang Systems* 3(4), 431–483.

Ardoin, C. D. (1988) "Phase Coupled Resource Allocation in Instruction Pipelines." Ph.D. Dissertation, Center for Advanced Computer Studies, University of Southwestern Louisiana, Lafayette.

Ardoin, C. D., Linn, J. L., and Reynolds, B. W. (1984) "The Implementation of the Attributed Recursive Descent Architecture in VAX-11/780 Microcode." *Proceedings of the 17th Annual Workshop on Microprogramming* IEEE Computer Society Press, Silver Spring, Md. 179–190.

Armstrong, R. A. (1981) "Applying CAD to Gate Arrays Speeds 32-bit Minicomputer Design." *Electronics* (Jan. 13), 167–173.

Arvind, and Culler, D. E. (1986) "Dataflow Architectures." Laboratory for Computer Science, MIT, Cambridge, Mass., LCS/TM-294 (Feb.).

Arvind, and Gostelow, K. P. (1982) "The U-Interpreter," *Computer* 15(2), 42–50.

Arvind, Gostelow, K. P., and Plouffe, W. (1978) "An Asynchronous Programming Language and Computing Machine." Department of Information and Computer Science, University of California, Irvine, Technical Report 114a (Feb.).

Arvind, and Ianucci, R. A. (1983) "A Critique of Multiprocessing von Neumann Style." *Proceedings of the 10th International Symposium on Computer Architecture.* IEEE Computer Society Press, Los Alamitos, Calif., 426–436.

Arvind, and Ianucci, R. A. (1986) "Two Fundamental Issues in Multiprocessing." Laboratory for Computer Science MIT, Cambridge, Mass., CSG Memo 226-5.

Arvind, and Thomas, R. E. (1981) "I-Structures: An Efficient Data Structure for Functional Languages." Laboratory for Computer Science, MIT, Cambridge, Mass. LCS/TM-178 (Oct.).

Ashcroft, E. A., and Wadge, W. W. (1982) "Rx for Semantics." *ACM Trans Prog Lang Systems* 4(2), 283–294.

Avizienis, A. (1983) "A Framework for a Taxonomy of Fault Tolerant Attributes in Computer Systems." *Proceedings of the 10th Annual International Symposium on Computer Architecture.* IEEE Computer Society Press, New York, 16–21.

Ayres, R. F. (1983) *VLSI Silicon Compilation and the Art of Automatic Microchip Design,* Prentice–Hall, Englewood-Cliffs, N.J.

Baba, T., and Hagiwara, H. (1981) "The MPG System: A Machine Independent Efficient Microprogram Generator." *IEEE Trans Comput*, C-30(6), 373–395.

Backus, J. (1978) "Can Programming be Liberated from the von Neumann Style? A Functional Style and its Algebra of Programs." *Comm ACM* 21(8), 613–641.

Baer, J.-L. (1973) "A Survey of Some Theoretical Aspects of Multiprocessing." *ACM Comp Surv* 5(1), 31–80.

Baer, J.-L. (1980) *Computer Systems Architecture.* Computer Science Press, Potomac, Md.

Baer, J.-L. (1983) "Wither a Taxonomy of Computer Architecture?" *Proceedings of the IEEE International Workshop on Computer System Organization,* IEEE Computer Society Press, New York, 3–9.

Balzer, R., and Goldman, N. (1979) "Principles of Good Software Specification and their Implications for Specification Languages." *Proceedings of the IEEE Conference on Specifications of Reliable Software.* 58–67. Reprinted in Gehani and McGettrick (1986).

Banerjee, U., Chen, S.-C., Kuck, D. J., *et al.* (1979) "Time and Parallel Processor Bounds for Fortran-like Loops." *IEEE Trans Comput,* C-28(9), 660–670.

Banerji D. K., and Raymond, J. (1982) *Elements of Microprogramming.* Prentice–Hall, Englewood-Cliffs, N.J.

Banham, R. (1982) *Theory and Design in the First Machine Age.* MIT Press, Cambridge, Mass.

Barahona, P. M., and Gurd, J. R. (1986) "Processor Allocation in a Multi-ring Dataflow Machine." *J. Parall Dist Comp* 3(3), 305–327.

Barbacci, M. R. (1981) "Instruction Set Processor Specification (ISPS): The Notation and its Application." *IEEE Trans Comput* C-30(1), 26–40.

Barbacci, M. R., Barnes, G. E., Cattell, R. G., *et al.* (1978) "The ISPS Computer Description Language." Department of Computer Science, Carnegie Mellon University, Pittsburgh, Pa.

Barbacci, M. R., Grout, S., Lindstrom, G., *et al.* (1985) "Ada as a Hardware Description Language." In C. J. Koomen and T. Moto-oka (Eds), *Computer Hardware Description Languages and their Applications,* North-Holland, Amsterdam, 272–302.

Barbacci, M. R., and Northcutt, J. D. (1980) "Application of ISPS, An Architecture Description Language." *J Digital Systems* 4(3), 221–239.

Barbacci, M. R., and Parker, A. (1980) "Using Emulation to Verify Formal Architecture Descriptions." *Computer* 13(5), 51–56.

Barbacci, M. R., and Siewiorek, D. P. (1982) *The Design and Analysis of Instruction Set Processors.* McGraw–Hill, New York.

Barbacci, M. R., and Uehara, T. (1985) "Computer Hardware Description Languages: The Bridge Between Software and Hardware." *Computer* 18(2), 6–8.

Barnes, G. H., Brown, R. M., Kato, M., *et al.* (1968) "The ILLIAC IV Computer." *IEEE Trans Comput* 18(8), 746–757.

Barton, R. S. (1961) "A New Approach to the Functional Design of a Digital

Computer." *Proceedings of the Westerns Joint Computer Conference.* AFIPS Press, Montvale, N.J., 393–396.

Barton, R. S. (1970) "Ideas for Computer Systems Organization—A Personal Survey." J. T. Tou, (Ed.). *In Software Engineering.* Academic Press, New York, 7–16.

Baskett, F., and Keller, T. W. (1977) "An Evaluation of the CRAY-1 Computer." In Kuck, Lawrie, and Sameh (1977), 71–84.

Baskett, F., and Smith, A. (1976) "Interference in Multiprocessor Computer Systems with Interleaved Memory." *Comm ACM,* 19(6), 327–334.

Batcher, K. E. (1974) "STARAN Parallel Processor System Hardware." *Proceedings of the National Computer Conference,* Vol. 43, AFIPS Press, Montvale, N.J., 405–410.

Batcher, K. E. (1977) "The Multidimensional Access Memory in STARAN." *IEEE Trans Comput* C-26(2), 174–177.

Batcher, K. E. (1980) "Design of a Massively Parallel Processor." *IEEE Trans Comput* C-29(9), 836–840.

Batson, A. P., and Brundage, R. E. (1977) "Segment Sizes and Lifetimes in Algol 60 Programs." *Comm ACM* 20(1), 36–44.

Belady, L. A. (1966) "A Study of Replacement Algorithms for Virtual Storage Computers." *IBM Sys J* 5(2), 78–101.

Belady, L., and Lehman, M. M. (1976) "A Model of Large Program Developments." *IBM Sys J* 15(3), 225–252.

Belady, L., and Lehman, M. M. (1979) "The Characteristics of Large Systems." In Wegner (1979), 106–141.

Belady, L. A., Nelson, R. A., and Shedler, G. S. (1969) "An Anomaly in the Space Time Characteristics of Certain Programs Running in Paging Machines." *Comm ACM* 12(6), 349–353.

Bell, C. G. (1977) "What Have We Learned from the PDP-11?" In G. G. Boulaye and D. W. Lewin (Eds.) *Computer Architecture.* D. Reidel, Boston, Mass., 1–38.

Bell, C. G. (1985) "Multis: A New Class of Multiprocessor Computers." *Science* 228 (April 26), 462–467.

Bell, C. G., and Mudge, J. C. (1978) "The Evolution of the PDP-11." In Bell, Mudge, and McNamara (1978), 379–408.

Bell, C. G., Mudge, J. C. and McNamara, J. E. (Eds.) (1978) *Computer Engineering: A DEC View of Hardware Systems Designs.* Digital Press, Bedford, Mass.

Bell, C. G., and Newell, A. (1971) *Computer Structures: Readings and Examples.* McGraw–Hill, New York.

Bell, C. G., Newell, A., Reich, M., *et al.* (1982) "The IBM System/360, System/ 370, 3030 and 4300: A Series of Planned Machines that Span a Wide Performance Range." In Siewiorek, Bell, and Newell (1982), 856–892.

Bell, C. G., and Strecker, W. D. (1976) "Computer Structures: What Have We Learned from the PDP-11?" *Proceedings of the 3rd Annual Symposium on Computer Architecture.* ACM/IEEE, New York, 1–14.

Benes, V. E. (1965) *Mathematical Theory of Connecting Networks and Telephone Traffic.* Academic Press, New York.

Berg, H. K., Boebert, W. E., Franta, W. R., and Moher, T. G. (1982) *Formal Methods of Program Verification and Specification.* Prentice–Hall, Englewood-Cliffs, N.J.

Bertsis, V. (1980) "Security and Protection of Data in the IBM System/38." *Proceedings of the 7th Annual Symposium on Computer Architecture* ACM/IEEE, New York, 245–252.

Bhandarkar, D. P. (1975) "Analysis of Memory Interference in Multiprocessors." *IEEE Trans Comput* C-24(9), 897–908.

Bhandarkar, D. P. (1982) "Architecture Management for Ensuring Software Compatibility in the VAX Family of Computers" *Computer,* 15(2), 87–93.

Bhuyan L. N. (1987) "Guest Editor's Introduction: Interconnection Networks for Parallel and Distributed Processing." *Computer* 20(6), 9–13.

Bhuyan, L. N., Agrawal, D. P. (1983) "Design and Performance of Generalized Interconnection Networks." *IEEE Trans Comput* C-32(12), 1081–1090.

Bilardi, G., Pracchi, M., and Preparata, F. P. (1981) "A Critique and an Appraisal of VLSI Models of Computation." In Kung, Sproull, and Steele (1981).

Birkhoff, G., and Bartee, T. C. (1970) *Modern Applied Algebra,* McGraw–Hill, New York.

Blaauw, G. A. (1976) *Digital System Implementation.* Prentice–Hall, Englewood-Cliffs, N.J.

Blaauw, G. A., and Brooks, F. P. (1964) "The Structure of System/360 Part I: Outline of Logical Structure." *IBM Syst J* 3(2 & 3), 119–135.

Blaauw, G. A., and Händler, W. (Eds.) (1981) *Workshop on Taxonomy in Computer Architecture.* Friedrich Alexander Universität Erlangen-Nürnberg, Nuremberg, West Germany.

Blakeslee, T. R. (1979) *Digital Design with Standard MSI and LSI,* 2nd ed. Wiley, New York.

Borgerson, B. R., Tjaden, G. S., and Hanson, M. L. (1978) "Mainframe Implementation with Off-the-Shelf LSI Modules." *Computer* 11(7) 42–48.

Bouknight, W. Denenberg, S. A., McIntyre, D. E., *et al.* (1972) "The ILLIAC IV System." *Proc IEEE* 60(4), 369–388.

Boyer, R. S., and Moore, J. S. (Eds.) (1981a) *The Correctness Problem in Computer Science.* Academic Press, New York.

Boyer, R. S., and Moore, J. S. (1981b) "A Verification Condition Generator for FORTRAN." In Boyer and Moore (1981a) 9–102.

Breuer, M. A. (Ed.) (1975) *Digital System Design Automation.* Computer Science Press, Potomac, Md.

Bridgeman, P. W. (1927) *The Logic of Modern Physics.* Macmillan, New York.

Brinch Hansen, P. (1973) *Operating Systems Principles.* Prentice–Hall, Englewood-Cliffs, N.J.

Brinch Hansen, P. (1977) *The Architecture of Concurrent Programs.* Prentice–Hall, Englewood-Cliffs, N.J.

Broadbent, G. (1973) *Design in Architecture.* Wiley, New York.

Brown, J. F., III, and Sites, R. L. (1984) "A Chip Set Microarchitecture for a High Performance VAX Implementation." *Proceedings of the 14th Annual Microprogramming Workshop.* IEEE Computer Society Press, New York, 48–54.

Buckle, J. K. (1978) *The ICL 2900 Series.* Macmillan, London.

Budnick, P. P., and Kuck, D. J. (1971) "The Organization and Use of Parallel Memories." *IEEE Trans Comput* 20(12), 1566–1569.

Burger, R. M., Calvin, R. K., Holton, W. C. *et al.* (1984) "The Impact of ICs on Computer Technology." *Computer* 17(10), 88–96.

Burks, A. W., Goldstine, H. H., and von Neumann, J. (1946) "Preliminary Discussion of the Logical Design of a Electronic Computing Instrument." Institute for Advanced Study, Princeton, N.J. Reprinted in Bell and Newell (1971), 92–119.

Burnett, G. J., and Coffman, E. G. (1970) "A Study of Interleaved Memory Systems." *Proceedings of the Spring Joint Computer Conference,* Vol. 36, AFIPS Press, Montvale, N.J., 467–474.

Burnett, G. J., and Coffman, E. G. (1973) "A Combinatorial Problem Related to Interleaved Memory Systems." *J ACM* 20 (Jan.), 39–45.

Burnett, G. J., and Coffman, E. G. (1975) "Analysis of Interleaved Memory Systems Using Blockage Buffers." *Comm ACM* 18(2), 91–95.

Burstall, R., and Goguen, J. A. (1981) "An Informal Introduction to Specifications Using CLEAR." In Boyer and Moore (1981a) 185–213.

Case R. P., and Padegs, A. (1978) "Architecture of the IBM System/370." *Comm ACM* 21(1), 73–95.

Cattell, R. G. G. (1980) "Automatic Derivation of Code Generators from Machine Description." *ACM Trans. Prog Lang* 2(2), 173–190.

Censier, L. M., and Feautrier, P. (1978) "A New Solution to the Coherence Problems in Multicache Systems." *IEEE Trans Comput* C-27(12), 1112–1118.

Chang D., Kuck, D. J., and Lawrie, D. H. (1977) "On the Effective Bandwidth of Parallel Memories." *IEEE Trans Comput* C-26(5), 480–490.

Charlesworth, A. E. (1981) "An Approach to Scientific Array Processing: The Architectural Design of the AP-120B/FPS-164 Family." *Computer* 14(9), 18–27.

Chen, T. C. (1971) "Parallelism, Pipelining and Computer Efficiency." *Computer Design* (Jan.), 69–74.

Chu, W. W., and Opderbeck, H. (1976). "Program Behavior and the Page Fault Frequency Algorithm." *Computer* 9(11), 29–38.

Chu, Y. (1965) "An Algol-like Computer Design Language." *Comm ACM* 8, 607–615.

Chu, Y. (1972) *Computer Organization and Microprogramming.* Prentice–Hall, Englewood-Cliffs, N.J.

Clark, W. A. (1980) "From Electron Mobility to Logical Structure: A View of Integrated Circuits." *ACM Comp Surv* 12(3), 325–356.

Coffman, E. G., and Denning, P. J. (1973) *Operating Systems Theory,* Prentice – Hall, Englewood-Cliffs, N.J.

Cohen, E., and Jefferson D. (1975). "Protection in the Hydra Operating System." *Proceedings of the 5th Symposium on Operating System Principles.* ACM, New York, 141 – 160.

Colclaser, R. A. (1980) *Microtelectronics: Processing and Device Design.* Wiley, New York.

Colwell, R. P., Hitchcock, C. Y., Jensen, E. D. *et al.* (1985) "Computers, Complexity, and Controversy." *Computer,* 18(9), 8 – 20.

Conti, C. J., Gibson, D. H., and Pitkowski, S. H. (1968) "Structural Aspects of the System 360/85: General Organization." *IBM Sys J* 7, 2 – 14.

Conway, R. W., Gries, D. G., and Wortman, D. B. (1977) *Introduction to Structured Programming.* Winthrop, Cambridge, Mass.

Conway, R. W., Maxwell, W. L., and Miller L. W. (1967) *Theory of Scheduling.* Addison – Wesley, Reading, Mass.

Cook, R. W., and Flynn, M. J. (1970) "System Design of a Dynamic Microprocessor." *IEEE Trans Comput,* C-19(3), 213 – 222.

Courtois, P. J. (1977) *Decomposability.* Academic Press, New York.

Cragon, H. G. (1980) "The Elements of Single Chip Microcomputer Architecture." *Computer* 13(10), 24 – 41.

Cray (1984) *CRAY X-MP Series Model 48 Mainframe Reference Manual.* HR-0097, Cray Research, Inc., Mendota Heights, Minn.

Cray (1986) *CRAY-2 Computer System Functional Description.* HR-2000, Cray Research Inc., Mendota Heights, Minn.

Crocker, S. D., Marcus, L., and van Mierop, D. (1980) "The ISI Microcode Verification System." In G. Chroust and J. Mulbacher (Eds.) *Firmware, Microprogramming and Restructurable Hardware.* North-Holland, Amsterdam.

Damm, W. (1984) "A Microprogramming Logic," Ber. No. 94, Schriften Zur Informatik und Angewandten Mathematik, Technische Hochschule Aachen, Aachen, West Germany.

Damm, W. (1985) "Design and Specification of Microprogrammed Computer Architectures." *Proceeding of the 18th Annual Workshop on Microprogramming* IEEE Computer Society Press, Los Alamitos, Calif., 3 – 10.

Damm, W., and Doehmen, G. (1985) "Verification of Microprogrammed Computer Architectures in the S*-System: A Case Study," *Proceedings at the 18th Annual Microprogramming Workshop.* IEEE Computer Society Press, Los Alamitos, Calif., 61 – 73.

Damm, W., Doehmen, G., Merkel, K., *et al.* (1986) "The AADL/S* Approach to Firmware Design Verification," *IEEE Software.* 3(4), 27 – 37.

Darringer, J., Brand, D., Joyner, W. H., *et al.* (1984) "LSS: A System for Production Logic Synthesis," *IBM J. Res. Dev* 28(4), 537 – 545.

Darringer, J. (1985) "Production Logic Synthesis." *Proceedings of the 13th Annual ACM Computer Science Conference.* ACM, New York, 13 – 16.

Das, C. R., and Bhuyan, L. N. (1985) "Bandwidth Availability of Multiple-Bus Multiprocessors," *IEEE Trans Comput,* C-34(10), 918–926.

Dasgupta, S. (1977) "Parallelism in Loop Free Microprograms." In B. Gilchrist (Ed.), *Information Processing 77* (Proc. IFIP Congress), North-Holland, Amsterdam, 745–750.

Dasgupta, S. (1979) "The Organization of Microprogram Stores." *ACM Comp Surv* 11(1), 39–66.

Dasgupta, S. (1980) "Some Aspects of High Level Microprogramming." *ACM Comp Surv* 12(3), 295–324.

Dasgupta, S. (1981) "S*A: A Language for Describing Computer Architectures." In M. A. Breuer and R. Hartenstein (Eds.), *Proceedings of the 5th International Symposium on Computer Hardware Description Languages and their Applications.* North-Holland, Amsterdam, 65–78.

Dasgupta, S. (1982) "Computer Design and Description Languages." In M. C. Yovits (Ed.) *Advances in Computers,* Vol. 21. Academic Press, New York, 91–155.

Dasgupta, S. (1983) "An Early Paper on Program Verification by Alan Turing." Unpublished manuscript, Center for Advanced Computer Studies, University of Southwestern Louisiana, Lafayette, La.

Dasgupta, S. (1984) *The Design and Description of Computer Architectures.* Wiley, New York.

Dasgupta, S. (1985) "Hardware Description Languages in Microprogramming Systems." *Computer* 18(2), 67–76.

Dasgupta, S. (1987) "Principles of Firmware Verification." In Habib (1988).

Dasgupta, S., and Mueller, R. A. (1986) "Firmware Engineering: The Interaction of Microprogramming and Software Technology." *IEEE Software,* 3(4), 4–5.

Dasgupta, S., and Olafsson, M. (1982) "Towards a Family of Languages for the Design and Implementation of Machine Architectures." *Proceedings of the 9th Annual International Symposium on Computer Architecture,* IEEE Computer Society Press, New York, 158–167.

Dasgupta, S., and Shriver, B. D. (1985) "Developments in Firmware Engineering." In M. C. Yovits, (Ed.) *Advances in Computers,* Vol. 24. Academic Press, New York, 101–176.

Dasgupta, S., and Tartar, J. (1976) "The Identification of Maximal Parallelism in Straight Line Microprograms." *IEEE Trans Comput.* C-25(10), 986–992.

Dasgupta, S., and Wagner, A. (1984) "The Use of Hoare Logic in the Verification of Horizontal Microprograms." *Int J Comp Info Sc* 13(6), 461–490.

Dasgupta S., Wilsey, P. A., and Heinanen, J. (1986) "Axiomatic Specifications in Firmware Development Systems." *IEEE Software,* 3(4), 49–58.

Davidson, E. S. (1971) "The Design and Control of Pipelined Function Generators." *Proceedings of the IEEE International Conference on Systems, Networks and Computers,* 19–21.

Davidson, S. (1986) "Progress in High Level Microprogramming." *IEEE Software* 3(4), 18–26.

Davidson, S., Landskov, D., Shriver, B. D., *et al.* (1981) "Some Experiments in Local Microcode Compaction for Horizontal Machines." *IEEE Trans Comput* C-30(7), 460–477.

Davidson, S., and Shriver, B. D. (1978) "Firmware Engineering: A Survey," *Computer* 11(5), 21–33.

Davidson, S., and Shriver, B. D. (1980) "MARBLE: A High-Level Machine-Independent Language for Microprogramming." In G. Chroust and J. Mulbacher (Eds.) *Firmware, Microprogramming and Restructurable Hardware.* North-Holland, Amsterdam, 1–40.

Davis, A. L. (1978) "The Architecture and System Method of DDM1: A Recursively Structured Data Driven Machine." *Proceedings of the 5th Annual Symposium on Computer Architecture.* ACM/IEEE, New York, 210–215.

Davis, C., Maley, G., Simmons, R., *et al.* (1980) "Gate Array Embodies System/370 Processor." *Electronics* (October 9), 140–143.

de Bakker, J. (1980) *Mathematical Theory of Program Correctness.* Prentice-Hall International, Englewood-Cliffs, N.J.

Demco, J., and Marsland, T. A. (1976) "An Insight into PDP-11 Emulation." *Proceedings of the 9th Annual Workshop on Microprogramming.* ACM/IEEE, New York, 20–26.

de Millo, R., Lipton, R. J., and Perlis, A. (1979) "Social Processes and Proofs of Theorems and Programs." *Comm ACM* 22(5), 271–280.

Denning, P. J. (1968a) "The Working Set Model for Program Behavior." *Comm ACM* 11(5), 323–333.

Denning, P. J. (1968b) "Thrashing: Its Causes and Prevention," *Proceedings of the Fall Joint Computer Conference,* Vol. 33, AFIPS Press, Montvale, N.J., 915–922.

Denning, P. J. (1970) "Virtual Memory." *ACM Comp Surv* 2 (Sept.), 153–189.

Denning, P. J. (1978) "A Question of Semantics." *Comp Arch News* (SIGARCH) 6(8), 16–18.

Denning, P. J. (1980) "Working Sets Past and Present." *IEEE Trans Soft Eng* SE-6(1), 64–84.

Dennis, J. B. (1974) "First Version of a Data Flow Procedural Language." *Proc Colloque sur la Programmation* (Lecture Notes in Computer Science Vol. 19), Springer-Verlag, Berlin, 362–376.

Dennis, J. B. (1980) "Dataflow Supercomputers." *Computer* 13(11), 48–56.

Dennis, J. B., Fuller, S. H., Ackerman, W. B., *et al.* (1979) "Research Directions in Computer Architecture." In Wegner (1979), 514–556.

Dennis, J. B., and Misunas, D. P. (1974) "A Preliminary Architecture for a Basic Data Flow Processor." Laboratory for Computer Science, MIT, Cambridge, Mass., CSG Memo 102.

Dennis, J. B., and Misunas, D. P. (1975) "A Preliminary Architecture for a Basic Data Flow Processor." *Proceedings of the 2nd Annual Symposium on Computer Architecture.* ACM/IEEE, New York, 126–132.

Dennis, J. B., and Van Horn, E. C. (1966) "Programming Semantics for Multiprogrammed Computations." *Comm ACM* 9(3), 143–155.

DeWitt, D. J. (1976) "A Machine Independent Approach to the Production of Horizontal Microcode." Ph.D. Thesis, Department of Computer and Communication Science, University of Michigan, Ann Arbor.

Dietmeyer, D. L., and Duley, J. R. (1975) "Register-Transfer Languages and Their Translations." In Breuer (1975), 117–218.

Digital (1978) *The PDP-11 Processor Handbook*. Digital Equipment Corporation, Maynard, Mass.

Digital (1979) *The KA780 Central Processor Technical Description*. Digital Equipment Corporation, Maynard, Mass.

Digital (1981a) *The VAX Architecture Handbook;*. Digital Equipment Corporation, Maynard, Mass.

Digital (1981b) *The VAX Hardware Handbook*. Digital Equipment Corporation, Maynard, Mass.

Digital (1985) "The VAX 8600 Processor." *Digital Technical Journal*. Digital Equipment Corporation, Hudson, Mass.

Dijkstra, E. W. (1960) "Recursive Programming." *Num Math* 2(5), 312–318.

Dijkstra, E. W. (1968) "Cooperating Sequential Processes." In F. Genuys (Ed.), *Programming Languages*. Academic Press, New York, 43–112.

Dijkstra, E. W. (1972) "Notes on Structured Programming." In O. J. Dahl, E. W. Dijkstra, and C. A. R. Hoare. *Structured Programming*. Academic Press, New York, 1–82.

Dijkstra. E. W. (1976) *A Discipline of Programming*. Prentice–Hall, Englewood Cliffs, N.J.

Director, S., Parker, A. C., Siewiorek, D. P., *et al.* (1981) "A Design Methodology and Computer Aids for Digital VLSI Systems." *IEEE Trans Circuits Systems* CAS-28(7), 634–645.

Ditzel, D. R. (1980) "Program Measurements on a High Level Language Computer." *Computer* 13(8), 62–72.

Ditzel, D. R., and Patterson, D. A. (1980) "Retrospective on High Level Language Computer Architecture." *Proceedings of the 7th Annual Symposium on Computer Architecture*. ACM/IEEE, New York, 97–104.

Djordjevic, J., Ibbett, R. N., and Barbacci, M. R. (1980) "Evaluation of Computer Architecture Using ISPS," *Proc IEE*(U.K.) 127(4), Part E, 126–135.

Doehmen, G. (1985) "Verifikation eines Emulators: Eine Fallstudie zur Verifikation Mikroprogrammierter Rechnerarchitekturen." Schriften zur Informatik und Angewandten Mathematik, Technische Hochschule Aachen, Aachen, West Germany.

Donahue, J. E. (1976) *Complementary Definitions of Programming Language Semantics*. Springer-Verlag, Berlin.

Doran, R. W. (1979) *Computer Architecture: A Structured Approach*. Academic Press, New York.

Dubois, M., and Briggs, F. A. (1982) "Effects of Cache Coherency in Multiprocessors." *IEEE Trans Comput* C-31(11), 1083–1099.

Duda, M. R., and Mueller, R. A. (1984) "μ-C Microprogramming Language Specification." Technical Report CS-84-11, Department of Computer Science, Colorado State University, Fort Collins, Colo.

Dudani, S., and Stabler, E. (1983) "Types of Hardware Description." In T. Uehara and M. R. Barbacci (Eds.) *Computer Hardware Description Languages and Their Applications* (Proceedings of the 6th International Symposium), North-Holland, Amsterdam, 127–136.

Duley, J. R., and Dietmeyer, D. L. (1968) "A Digital System Design Language (DDL)." *IEEE Trans Comput* C-17(9), 850–861.

Dunn, G., and Everitt, B. S. (1982) *An Introduction to Mathematical Taxonomy,* Cambridge University Press, Cambridge, England.

Eckhouse, R. H. Jr. (1971) "A High Level Microprogramming Language (MPL)." Ph.D. Thesis, Department of Computer Science, State University of New York, Buffalo.

Elshoff, J. L. (1976) "An Analysis of Some Commercial PL/1 Programs." *IEEE Trans Soft Eng* (June), 113–120.

Emer, J. S. and Clark, D. W. (1984), "A Characterization of Processor Performance in the VAX-II/780," *Proc. 11th Annual Symposium on Computer Architecture,* IEEE Comp. Soc. Press, Los Angeles, CA, 301–310.

Encore (1986) *Multimax Technical Summary.* Encore Computer Corp., Marlboro, Mass.

England, D. M. (1972) "Architectural Features of System 250." *Infotech State of The Art Report on Operating Systems.* Infotech, Maidenhead, U.K.

Enslow, P. H. (1977) "Multiprocessor Organization." *ACM Comp Surv* 9(1), 103–129.

Ercegovac, M. D., and Lang, T. (1985) *Digital Systems and Hardware/Firmware Algorithms.* Wiley, New York

Estrin, G. (1978) "A Methodology for Design of Digital Systems—Supported by SARA at the Age of One." *Proceedings of the AFIPS National Computer Conference.* Vol. 47, AFIPS Press, Arlington, Va., 313–324.

Estrin, G. (1985a) "SARA in the Design Room." *Proceedings of the 13th Annual ACM Computer Science Conference.* ACM, New York, 1–12.

Estrin, G. (1985b) "The Story of SARA." In Giloi and Shriver (1985), 29–46.

Falkoff, A. D., Iverson, K. E., and Sussenguth, E. H. (1964) "A Formal Description of the System/360." *IBM Sys J* 3, 198–262.

Feng, T. Y. (1981) "A Survey of Interconnection Networks." *Computer* (Dec) 12–27.

Feuer, M., Khokhani, K. H., and Mehta, D. (1980) "Computer Aided Design Wires 5000-Circuit Chip." *Electronics* (October 9), 144–145.

Filman, R. E., and Friedman, D. P. (1984) *Coordinated Computing.* McGraw-Hill, New York.

Fisher, A. L., and Kung, H. T. (1983) "Synchronizing Large VLSI Processor Arrays." *Proceedings of the 10th Symposium on Computer Architecture,* IEEE Computer Society Press, Los Alamitos, Calif., 59–66.

Fisher, J. A. (1981) "Trace Scheduling: A Technique for Global Microcode Compaction." *IEEE Trans Comput* C-30(7), 478–490.

Fisher, J. A. (1983) "Very Long Instruction Word Architectures and the ELI-512." *Proceedings of the 10th Annual International Symposium on Computer Architecture* IEEE Computer Society Press, 140–150.

Fisher, J. A., Landskov, D., and Shriver, B. D. (1981) "Microcode Compaction: Looking Backward and Looking Forward." *Proceedings of the National Computer Conference* AFIPS Press, Montvale, N.J., 95–102.

Fitzpatrick, D., Foderaro, J. K., Katevenis, M. G. H., *et al.* (1981) "VLSI Implementations of a Reduced Instruction Set Computer." In Kung, Sproull, and Steele (1981), 327–336.

Floyd, R. W. (1967) "Assigning Meanings to Programs." *Mathematical Aspects of Computer Science,* 19. American Mathematical Society, Providence, R.I.

Floyd, R. W. (1979) "The Paradigms of Programming." (ACM Turing Award Lecture). *Comm ACM* 22(8), 455–460.

Flynn, M. J. (1966) "Very High Speed Computing Systems." *Proc IEEE* 54 (Dec.), 1901–1909.

Flynn, M. J. (1974) "Trends and Problems in Computer Organization." *Information Processing 74* (Proceeding of the 1974 IFIP Congress) North-Holland, Amsterdam, 3–10.

Flynn, M. J. (1977) "The Interpretive Interface: Resources and Program Representation in Computer Organization." In Kuck, Lawrie, and Sameh (1977), 41–70.

Flynn, M. J. (1980) "Directions and Issues in Architecture and Language." *Computer,* 13(10), 5–22.

Flynn, M. J. (1981) "Customized Microcomputers." In M. J. Flynn, N. R. Harris, and D. P. McCarthy (Eds.) *Microcomputer System Design,* Lecture Notes in Computer Science 126, Springer-Verlag, Berlin, 182–222.

Flynn, M. J., and Hoevel, L. W. (1983) "Execution Architecture: The DELTRAN Experiment." *IEEE Trans Comput* C-32(2), 156–174.

Flynn M. J., and Huck, J. C. (1984) "Emulation." In C. R. Vick and C. V. Ramamoorthy (Eds.) *Handbook of Software Engineering.* Van Nostrand–Rheinhold, New York, 134–148.

Flynn, M. J., and MacLaren, M. D. (1967) "Microprogramming Revisited." *Proceedings of the ACM 22nd National Conference* ACM, New York, 457–464.

Flynn, M. J., and Rosin, R. F. (1971) "Microprogramming: An Introduction and Viewpoint." *IEEE Trans Comp.* C-20(7), 727–731.

Foderaro, J., van Dyke, K., and Patterson, D. A. (1982) "Running RISCs." *VLSI Design,* 3(5), 27–32.

Fossum, T., McElroy, J. B., and English, W. (1985) "An Overview of the VAX 8600 System." *Digital Tech J.* Digital Equipment Corporation, Hudson, Mass, 8–23.

Foster, C. C., and Iberall, T. (1985) *Computer Architecture,* 3rd ed. Van Nostrand–Rheinhold, New York.

Foster, M. J., and Kung, H. T. (1980) "The Design of Special Purpose VLSI Chips." *Computer* 13(1), 26–40.

Frank, E. H., and Sproull, R. F. (1981) "Testing and Debugging Custom Integrated Circuits." *ACM Comp Surv* 13(4), 425–451.

Franklin, M. A., Graham, G. S., and Gupta, R. K. (1978) "Anomalies with Variable Partition Paging Algorithms." *Comm ACM* 21(3), 232–236.

Freeman, P. (1980a) "The Context of Design." In Freeman and Wasserman (1980), 2–4.

Freeman P. (1980b) "The Central Role of Design in Software Engineering: Implications for Research." In H. Freeman and P. M. Lewis (Eds.) *Software Engineering.* Academic Press, New York, 121–132.

Freeman, P., and Wasserman, A. (1980) *Tutorial on Software Design Techniques,* IEEE Computer Society Press, Los Alamitos, Calif.

Fuller, S. H., Ousterhout, J. K., Raskin, L., *et al.* (1977a) "Multi-Microprocessors: An Overview and Working Example," *Proc IEEE* 61(2), 216–228.

Fuller, S. H. Shamon, P., Lamb, D., *et al.* (1977b) "Evaluation of Computer Architectures via Test Programs." *Proc AFIPS Nat Comp Conf* Vol. 46, 147–160.

Fuller, S. H., Stone, H. S., and Burr, W. E. (1977c). "Initial Selection and Screening of the CFA Candidate Computer Architectures." *Proc. AFIPS Nat Comp Conf,* 46, 139–146.

Gajski, D. D. *et al.* (1982) "A Second Opinion on Dataflow Machines and Languages." *Computer* 15(2), 58–70.

Gajski, D. D., and Peir, J-K. (1985) "Essential Issues in Multiprocessor Systems." *Computer* 18(6), 9–28.

Ganapathi, M., Fischer, C. N., and Hennessy, J. (1982) "Retargetable Compiler Code Generation." *ACM Comp Surv* 14(4), 573–592.

Gehani, N., and McGettrick, A. D. (Eds.) (1986) *Software Specification Techniques,* Addison–Wesley, Reading, Mass.

German, S. M., and Leiberherr, K. J. (1985) "Zeus: A Language for Expressing Algorithms in Hardware." *Computer* 18(2), 55–65.

Ghoshal, D., and Bhuyan, L. N. (1987) "Analytical Modeling and Architectural Modifications of a Dataflow Computer." *Proceedings of the 14th International Symposium on Computer Architecture,* IEEE Computer Society Press, Los Alamitos, Calif., 81–89

Giloi, W. K. (1981) "A Complete Taxonomy of Computer Architecture Based on the Abstract Data Type View." In Blaauw and Händler (1981), 19–38.

Giloi, W. K. (1983) "Towards a Taxonomy of Computer Architecture Based on the Machine Data Type View." *Proceedings of the 10th Annual International Symposium on Computer Architecture.* IEEE Computer Society Press, New York, pp 6–15.

Giloi, W. K., and Gueth, R. (1982) "Concepts and Realization of a High Performance Data Type Architecture." *Int J Comp Info Sc* 11(1), 25–54.

Giloi, W. K., and Shriver, B. D. (Eds.) (1985) *Methodologies for Computer System Design.* North-Holland, Amsterdam.

Goke, R., and Lipovski, G. J. (1973) "Banyon Networks for Partitioning on Multiprocessor Systems." *Proceedings of the 1st Annual Symposium on Computer Architecture* ACM/IEEE, New York, 21–30.

Goldstine, H. H. (1972) *The Computer from Pascal to von Neuman,* Princeton University Press, Princeton, N.J.

Gonzalez, M. J. (1977) "Deterministic Processor Scheduling." *ACM Comp Surv* 9(3), 173–204.

Gordon, M. J. (1979) *The Denotational Description of Programming Languages.* Springer-Verlag, Berlin.

Gottlieb, A., *et al.* (1983) "The NYU Ultracomputer—Designing an MIMD Shared Memory Parallel Computer." *IEEE Trans Comput* C-32(2), 175–189.

Gottlieb, A. (1986) "The New York University Ultracomputer." In Metropolis *et al.* (1986), 66–77.

Gottlieb, A., Lubachevsky, B., Rudolph, L. (1983) "Basic Techniques for the Efficient Coordination of Large Numbers of Cooperating Sequential Processors," *ACM Trans Prog Lang Sys* April (5) 2.

Gould, S. J. (1977) *Ontogeny and Phylogeny.* The Belknap Press of the Harvard University Press, Cambridge, Mass.

Grasselli, A. (1962) "The Design of Program-Modifiable Microprogrammed Control Units." *IRE Trans Elect Comp* (June), 336–339.

Gries, D. G. (1971) *Compiler Construction for Digital Computers.* Wiley, New York.

Gries, D. G. (Ed.) (1978) *Programming Methodology.* Springer-Verlag, New York.

Gries, D. G. (1981) *The Science of Programming.* Springer-Verlag, New York.

Gries, R., and Woodward, J. A. (1984) "Software Tools Used in the Development of a VLSI VAX Microcomputer." *Proceedings of the 17th Annual Workshop on Microprogramming.* IEEE Computer Society Press, Silver Spring, Md., 55–58.

Grishman, R., and Su, B. (1983) "A Preliminary Evaluation of Trace Scheduling for Global Microcode Compaction." *IEEE Trans Comput* C-32(12), 1191–1193.

Gross, T. R., and Hennessy, J. L. (1982) "Optimizing Delayed Branches." *Proceedings of the 15th Annual Workshop on Microprogramming.* IEEE Computer Society Press, Los Angeles, Calif., 114–120.

Guffin, R. M. (1982) "A Microprogramming-Language-Directed Microarchitecture." *Proceedings of the 15th Annual Workshop on Microprogramming.* IEEE Computer Society Press, Los Angeles, Calif., 42–49.

Guha, R. K. (1977) "Dynamic Microprogramming in a Time Sharing Environment." *Proceedings of the 10th Annual Workshop on Microprogramming.* ACM/IEEE, New York, 55–60.

Gupta, A., and Toong, H. D. (1983) "An Architectural Comparison of 32-bit Microprocessors." *IEEE Micro* (Feb.), 9–22.

Gurd, J., and Bohm, W. (1986) "Implicit Parallel Processing: SISAL on the Manchester Dataflow Computer." *Proceedings of the IBM Europe Institute on Parallel Processing.* Oberlach, Austria.

Gurd, J., and Kirkham, C. C. (1986) "Data Flow: Achievements and Prospects." In H.-J. Kugler (ED.), *Information Processing 86* (Proceedings of the IFIP Congress, 1986). North-Holland, Amsterdam, 61–68.

Gurd, J., Kirkham, C. C., and Watson, I. (1985) "The Manchester Prototype Dataflow Computer." *Comm ACM* 28(1), 34–52.

Gurd, J., and Watson, I. (1983) "Preliminary Evaluation of a Prototype Dataflow Computer." In R. E. A. Mason (Ed.) *Information Processing 83* (Proceedings of the IFIP Congress, 1983). Elsevier North-Holland, Amsterdam, 545–551.

Gurd, J. R., Watson, I., and Glauert, J. R. (1978) "A Multilayered Data Flow Computer Architecture." Internal Report of the Department of Computer Science, University of Manchester, U.K.

Gurd, R. P. (1983) "Experience Developing Microcode Using a High Level Language," *Proceedings of the 16th Annual Workshop on Microprogramming.* IEEE Computer Society Press, Los Angeles, Calif., 179–184.

Guttag, J. V. (1979) "Notes on Type Abstraction." *Proceedings of the Conference on Specification of Reliable Software* 36–46. Reprinted in Gehani and McGettrick (1986).

Guttag, J. V., and Horning, J. J. (1980) "Formal Specification as a Design Tool." *Proceedings of the 7th Annual ACM Symposium on Principles of Programming Languages.* 251–261. Reprinted in Gehani and McGettrick (1986).

Guttag, J. V., Horning, J. J., and Wing, J. M. (1982) "Some Notes on Putting Formal Specifications to Productive Use." *Sc Comp Prog* 2 (Dec.), 53–68.

Guttag, J. V., Horning, J. J., and Wing, J. M. (1985) "The Larch Family of Specification Languages." *IEEE Software* 2(5), 24–36.

Habermann, N. (1976) *Introduction to Operating System Design.* SRA, Chicago.

Habib, S. (Ed.) (1988) *Microprogramming and Firmware Engineering,* Van Nostrand-Rheinhold, New York.

Hack, J. J. (1986) "Peak vs. Sustained Performance in Highly Concurrent Vector Machines." *Computer,* 19(9), 11–19.

Hagiwara, H., Tomita, S., Oyanagi, S., *et al.* (1980) "A Dynamically Microprogrammable Computer with Low-Level Parallelism." *IEEE Trans Comput* C-29(7), 577–595.

Haken, W., Appel, K., and Koch, J. (1977) "Every Planar Map is Four Colorable." *Illinois J Math* 21(84), 429–567.

Halbert, D., and Kessler, P. (1980) "Windows of Overlapping Register Frames." Computer Science Division, Department of Electrical Engineering and Computer Science, University of California, Berkeley.

Hamacher, V. C., Vranesic, Z. G., and Zaky, S. G. (1984) *Computer Organization,* 2nd ed. McGraw–Hill, New York.

Hammerstrom, D. (1983) "The Migration of Functions into Silicon." Tutorial presented at the 10th International Symposium on Computer Architecture, Stockholm (June).

Händler, W. (1977) "The Impact of Classification Schemes on Computer Architecture." *Proceedings of the 1977 International Conference on Parallel Processing.* 7–15.

Händler, W. (1981) "Standards, Classification and Taxonomy: Experiences with ECS." In Blaauw and Händler (1981), 39–75.

Hayes, J. P. (1978) *Computer Architecture and Organization.* McGraw–Hill, New York.

Hayes, J. P. (1984) *Digital Systems and Microprocessors.* McGraw–Hill, New York.

Hellerman, H. (1967) *Digital Computer System Principles*. McGraw-Hill, New York.

Hennessy, J. L. (1984) "VLSI Processor Architecture." *IEEE Trans Comput* C-33(12), 1221-1246.

Hennessy, J. L., and Gross, T. (1983) "Postpass Code Optimization of Pipeline Constraints." *ACM Trans Prog Lang System* 5(3), 422-448.

Hennessy, J. L., Jouppi, N., Przybylski, S., *et al.* (1982) "MIPS: A Microprocessor Architecture." *Proceedings of the 15th Annual Workshop on Microprogramming*. IEEE Computer Society Press, Los Angeles, Calif., 17-22.

Hennessy, J. L., Jouppi, N., Przybylski, S., *et al.* (1983) "Design of a High Performance VLSI Processor." *Proceedings of the 3rd Caltech Conference on VLSI*, California Institute of Technology, Pasadena, Calif., 33-54.

Hill, F. J., and Peterson, G. R. (1978) *Digital Systems: Hardware Organization and Design*. Wiley, New York.

Hillis, D. (1985) *The Connection Machine*. MIT Press, Cambridge, Mass.

Hitchcock, C. Y., and Sprunt, H. M. B. (1985) "Analyzing Multiple Register Sets." *Proceedings of the 12th Annual International Symposium on Computer Architecture*. IEEE Computer Society Press, Silver Spring, Md., 55-63.

Hoare, C. A. R. (1969) "An Axiomatic Approach to Computer Programming." *Comm ACM* 12(10), 576-580, 583.

Hoare, C. A. R. (1972) "Towards a Theory of Parallel Programming" in C. A. R. Hoare, R. H. Perrot (Eds.) *Operating Systems Techniques*, Academic Press, New York, 61-71.

Hoare, C. A. R. (1978) "Communicating Sequential Processes." *Comm ACM* 21(8), 666-677.

Hoare, C. A. R. (1985) *Communicating Sequential Processes*. Prentice-Hall, Englewood-Cliffs, N.J.

Hoare, C. A. R., and Shepherdson, J. C. (Eds.) (1985) *Mathematical Logic and Programming Languages*. Prentice-Hall, Englewood-Cliffs, N.J.

Hoare, C. A. R., and Wirth, N. (1973) "An Axiomatic Definition of the Programming Language Pascal." *Acta Inf* 2, 335-355.

Hockney, R. W. (1981) "A Structural Taxonomy of Computers." In Blaauw and Händler (1981), 77-92.

Hoevel, L. W. (1974) "Ideal Directly Executed Languages: An Analytical Argument for Emulation." *IEEE Trans Comput* C-23(8), 759-767.

Hoevel, L. W., and Wallach, W. A. (1975) "A Tale of Three Emulators." Computer Systems Laboratory, Technical Report TR-98, Stanford University, Stanford, Calif.

Hopcroft, J. E., and Ullman, J. D. (1969) *Formal Languages and their Relation to Automata*. Addison-Wesley, Reading, Mass.

Hopkins, M. (1983). "A Perspective on Microcode." *Proceedings of COMPCON 83* (Spring), IEEE, New York, 108-110.

Hopkins, W. C., Horton, M. J., and Arnold, C. S. (1985) "Target-Independent High-Level Microprogramming." *Proceedings of the 18th Annual Workshop on Microprogramming*. IEEE Computer Society Press, Los Angeles, 137-144.

Hord, R. M. (1982) *ILLIAC IV: The First Supercomputer.* Computer Science Press, Rockville, Md.

Horning, J. J., and Randell, B. (1973) "Process Structuring," *ACM Comp Surv* 5(1), 5–30.

Horowitz, E., and Sahni, S. (1978) *Fundamentals of Computer Algorithms.* Computer Science Press, Rockville, Md.

Huffman, D. A. (1952) "A Method for the Construction of Minimum Redundancy Codes." *Proc IRE* 40 (Sept.), 1098–1101.

Husson, S. S. (1970) *Microprogramming: Principles and Practices.* Prentice–Hall, Englewood-Cliffs, N.J.

Hwang, K. (Ed.) (1984) *Tutorial on Supercomputers: Design and Applications.* IEEE Computer Society Press, Los Alamitos, Calif.

Hwang, K., and Briggs, F. (1984) *Computer Architecture and Parallel Processing.* McGraw–Hill, New York.

Hwang, K., Su, S.-P., and Ni, L. M. (1981) "Vector Computer Architecture and Processing Techniques." In M. C. Yovits (Ed.) *Advances in Computers,* Vol. 20, Academic Press, New York, 116–199.

Ibbett, R. (1982) *High Performance Computer Systems.* Springer-Verlag, Heidelberg.

IBM (1981) *IBM System/370 Principles of Operation.* GA 22-7000-8, IBM Corp., White Plains, N.Y.

Iliffe, J. K. (1968) *Basic Machine Principles,* McDonald/American Elsevier, London, (2nd edition, 1972).

INMOS Ltd. (1984) *Occam Programming Manual.* Prentice–Hall, Englewood-Cliffs, N.J.

Intel Corporation (1981) *The iAPX-432 GDP Architecture Reference Manual.* Santa Clara, Calif.

Intermetrics (1984a) *VHDL Language Requirements.* Technical Report IR-MD-020-1, Intermetrics, Bethesda, Md.

Intermetrics (1984b) *VHDL User's Manual.* Vols. 1–3. Technical Report IR-MD-029, Intermetrics, Bethesda, Md.

Intermetrics (1984c) *VHDL Language Reference Manual.* Technical Report IR-MD-025-1, Intermetrics, Bethesda, Md.

Isoda, S., Kobayashi, Y., and Ishida, T. (1983) "Global Compaction of Horizontal Microprograms Based on the Generalized Data Dependency Graph." *IEEE Trans Comput* C-32(10), 922–931.

Iverson, K. E. (1962) *A Programming Language.* Wiley, New York.

Jensen, K., and Wirth, N. (1975) *Pascal: User Manual and Report,* 2nd ed. Springer-Verlag, Berlin.

Johnson, D., *et al.* (1980) "Automatic Partitioning of Programs in Multiprocessor Systems." *Proceedings of IEEE COMPCON,* IEEE Press, New York, 175–178.

Johnson, P. M. (1978) "An Introduction to Vector Processing." *Computer Design* (Feb.), 89–97.

Johnson, S. C. (1978) "A Portable C Compiler: Theory and Practice." *Proceed-*

ings of the 5th Annual Symposium on Programming Language, ACM, New York, 97–104.

Jones, A. K., and Schwarz, P. (1980) "Experience Using Multiprocessor Systems—A Status Report." *ACM Comp Surv* 12(2), 121–165.

Jones, C. B. (1980) *Software Development: A Rigorous Approach.* Prentice–Hall, Englewood-Cliffs, N.J.

Jones, J. C. (1980) *Design Methods: Seeds of Human Future,* 2nd ed. Wiley, New York.

Jones, J. C. (1984) *Essays in Design.* Wiley, New York.

Jordan, H. F. (1985) "HEP Architecture, Programming and Performance." In Kowalik (1985) 1–40.

Jordan, T. L. (1982) "A Guide to Parallel Computation and Some Cray-1 Experiences." In Rodrigue (1982) 1–50.

Karp, R. M., and Miller, R. E. (1966) "Properties of a Model for Parallel Computations: Determinacy, Termination, Queueing," *SIAM J Appl Math* 14(6), 1390–1411.

Katevenis, M. G. H. (1985) *Reduced Instruction Set Computer Architectures for VLSI.* MIT Press, Cambridge, Mass.

Katz, D. (1983) "VLSI Gate Arrays and CAD Methods." In Rabbat (1983) 139–151.

Katzman, J. A. (1977) "The Tandem 16: A Fault Tolerant Computing System." Tandem Computers Inc., Cupertino, Calif. Reprinted in Siewiorek, Bell, and Newell (1982) 470–480.

Kautz, W. H. (1971) "Programmable Cellular Logic." In Mukhopadhay (1971), 369–421.

Kavi, K., and Cragon, H. G. (1983) "A Conceptual Framework for the Description and Classification of Computer Architectures." *Proceedings of the IEEE International Workshop on Computer Systems Organization* IEEE Computer Society Press, New York, 10–19.

Kawakami, K., and Gurd, J. R. (1986) "A Scalable Dataflow Storage." *Proceedings of the 13th International Symposium on Computer Architectural.* IEEE Computer Society Press, Los Alamitos, Calif., 243–250.

Keedy, J. L. (1978a) "On the Use of Stacks in the Evaluation of Expressions." *SIGARCH Comp Arch News* 6(6), 22–28.

Keedy, J. L. (1978b) "On the Evaluation of Expressions Using Accumulators, Stacks, and Store-Store Instructions." *SIGARCH Comp Arch News* 7(4), 24–28.

Keedy, J. L. (1979) "More on the Use of Stacks in the Evaluation of Expressions." *SIGARCH Comp Arch News* 7(8), 18–23.

Keller, R. M. (1975) "Lookahead Processors." *ACM Comp Surv* 7(4), 177–196.

Kernighan, B. W., and Ritchie, D. M. (1978) *The C Programming Language.* Prentice–Hall, Englewood-Cliffs, N.J.

Kershew, D. (1982) "Solution of Single Tridiagonal Linear Systems and Vectorization of the ICCG Algorithm on the CRAY-1." In Rodrigue (1982) 85–100.

Kilburn, T., Edwards, D. B. G., Lanigan, M. J., *et al.* (1962) "One Level Storage System." *Trans IRE* EC-11(2), 223–235. Reprinted in Bell and Newell (1971) 276–290.

Kilburn, T., Morris, D., Rohl, J. S., and Summer, F. H. (1969) "A System Design Proposal." *Information Processing 68* (Proceedings of the IFIP Congress, 1968), North-Holland, Amsterdam, 806–811.

Klassen, A., and Dasgupta, S. (1981) "S*(QM-1): An Instantiation of the High Level Language Schema S* for the Nanodata QM-1." *Proceedings of the 14th Annual Workshop on Microprogramming.* ACM/IEEE, New York, 126–130.

Kleir, R. L., and Ramamoorthy, C. V. (1971) "Optimization Strategies for Microprograms." *IEEE Trans Comput* C-20(7), 783–795.

Knuth, D. E. (1968) *The Art of Computer Programming: Volume 1: Fundamental Algorithms.* Addison–Wesley, Reading, Mass.

Knuth, D. E. (1971) "An Empirical Study of FORTRAN Programs." *Software — Practice and Experience.* 1, 105–133.

Knuth, D. E., and Rao, G. S. (1975) "Activity in Interleaved Memory." *IEEE Trans Comput* C-24(9), 943–944.

Kogge, P. M. (1981) *The Architecture of Pipelined Computers.* McGraw–Hill, New York.

Kohavi, Z. (1982) *Switching and Finite Automata Theory,* 2nd ed. McGraw–Hill, New York.

Kornerup, P., and Shriver, B. D. (1975) "An Overview of the MATHILDA System." *ACM SIGMICRO Newsletter,* 5(4), 25–53.

Kowalik, J. S. (Ed.) (1985) *Parallel MIMD Computations: HEP Supercomputer and Its Applications.* MIT Press, Cambridge, Mass.

Kuck, D. J. (1968) "ILLIAC IV Software and Application Programming." *IEEE Trans Comput* C-17, 758–770.

Kuck, D. J. (1976) "Parallel Processing of Ordinary Programs." In M. Rubinoff and M. C. Yovits (Eds.) *Advances in Computers,* Vol. 15. Academic Press, New York, 119–179.

Kuck, D. J. (1977) "A Survey of Parallel Machine Organization and Programming." *ACM Comp Surv* 9(1), 29–60.

Kuck, D. J. (1978) *The Structure of Computers and Computation,* Vol. 1. Wiley, New York.

Kuck, D. J., Kuhn, R. H., Leasure, B., *et al.* (1980) "The Structure of an Advanced Retargetable Vectorizer." *Proceedings of COMPSAC 80.,* IEEE Computer Society.

Kuck, D. J., Kuhn, R. H., Padua, D., *et al.* (1981) "Dependence Graphs and Compiler Organization." *Proceedings of the 8th Annual ACM Symposium on Principles of Programming Languages.* Williamsburg, Va., 207–218.

Kuck, D. J., Lawrie, D., Cytron, R., *et al.* (1986) "Cedar Project." In Metropolis *et al.* (1986) 97–123.

Kuck, D. J., Lawrie, D. H., and Sameh, A. (Eds.) (1977) *High Speed Computer and Algorithm Organization.* Academic Press, New York.

Kuck, D. J. and Stokes, R. A. (1982) "The Burroughs Scientific Processor (BSP)." *IEEE Trans Comput* C-31(5), 363–376.

Kuhn, T. S. (1970) *The Structure of Scientific Revolutions,* 2nd ed. University of Chicago Press, Chicago.

Kung, H. T. (1979) "Let's Design Algorithms for VLSI Systems." Technical Report, Department of Computer Science, Carnegie-Mellon University, Pittsburgh.

Kung, H. T. (1982) "Why Systolic Architectures?" *Computer* 15(1), 37–46.

Kung, H. T., and Leiserson, C. E. (1980) "Highly Concurrent Systems." Mead and Conway (1980) Chapter 8.

Kung, H. T., Sproull, R., and Steele, G. (1981) *VLSI Systems and Computations.* Computer Science Press, Rockville, Md.

Kunkel, S. R., and Smith, J. E. (1986) "Optimal Pipelining in Supercomputers." *Proceedings of the 13th International Symposium on Computer Architecture* IEEE Computer Society Press, Washington, D.C. 404–411.

Lah, J., and Atkins, D. E. (1983) "Tree Compaction of Microprograms." *Proceedings of the 16th Annual Workshop on Microprogramming.* IEEE Computer Society Press, Los Angeles, Calif. 23–33.

Landskov, D., Davidson, S., Shriver, B. D., *et al.* (1980) "Local Microcode Compaction Techniques." *ACM Comp Surv* 12(3), 261–294.

Lang, T., Valero, M., and Alegre, J. (1982) "Bandwidth of Crossbar and Multiple-Bus Connections for Multiprocessors." *IEEE Trans Comput* C-31(12), 1227–1233.

Lattin, W. W., Bayliss, J. A., Budde, D. L., *et al.* (1981) "A 32b VLSI Micromainframe Computer System." *Proceedings of the 1981 IEEE International Solid State Circuits Conference,* 110–111.

Lavington, S. H. (1978) "The Manchester Mark I and Atlas: A Historical Perspective." *Comm ACM* 21(1), 4–12.

Lawrie, D. H. (1975) "Access and Alignment of Data in an Array Processor." *IEEE Trans Comput* C-24(12), 1145–1155.

Lawrie, D. H., Layman, T., Baer, D., *et al.* (1975) "Glypnir—A Programming Language for ILLIAC IV." *Comm ACM* 18(3), 157–164.

Lawson, B. (1980) *How Designers Think: The Design Process Demystified.* Architectural Press, London.

Lawson, H. W. (1968) "Programming Language Oriented Instruction Streams." *IEEE Trans Comput* C-17, 476–485.

Lawson, H. W., and Malm, B. (1973) "A Flexible Asynchronous Microprocessor." *BIT* 13, 165–176.

Lawson, H. W., and Smith, B. K. (1971) "Functional Characteristics of a Multilingual Processor." *IEEE Trans Comput* C-20(7), 732–742.

Lee, F. S., Long, S. I., Zucca, R., *et al.* (1983) "VLSI Gallium Arsenide Technology." In Rabbat (1983) 257–295.

Lehman, M. M. (1974) "Programs, Cities, Students—Limits to Growth." Inaugural Lecture Series, Vol. 9., Imperial College of Science and Technology, London. Also in D. G. Gries (1978), 42–69.

Lehman, M. M. (1984) "Program Evolution." *Info Proc Mgmt* 20(1–2, 19–36.

Leiserson, C. E. (1983) *Area-Efficient VLSI Computation.* MIT Press, Cambridge, Mass.

Leung, C. K. C. (1979) "ADL: An Architecture Description Language for Packet Communication Systems." *Proceedings of the 4th International Symposium on Computer Hardware Description Languages.* IEEE Computer Society, New York, 6–13.

Leung, C. K. C. (1981) "On a Topdown Design Methodology for Packet Systems." In M. A. Breuer and R. Hartenstein (Eds.) *Computer Hardware Description Languages and their Applications.* North Holland, Amsterdam, 171–184.

Levitt, K., Robinson, L., and Silverberg, B. A. (1979) *The HDM Handbook,* SRI International, Menlo Park, Calif.

Levy, H. M. (1984) *Capability-Based Computer Systems.* Digital Press, Bedford, Mass.

Lewis, T. G., Malik, K., and Ma, P.-Y. (1980) "Firmware Engineering Using a High Level Microprogramming System to Implement Virtual Instruction Set Processors." In G. Chroust and J. Mulbacher (Eds.) *Firmware, Microprogramming, and Restructurable Hardware,* North-Holland, Amsterdam, 65–88.

Lieberherr, K. J. (1984) "Towards a Standard Hardware Description Language." *Proceedings of the 21st ACM/IEEE Design Automation Conference.* Albuquerque, N.M., (June), 265–272.

Lim, W. Y-P. (1982) "HISDL—A Structure Description Language." *Comm ACM* 25(11), 823–830.

Lim, Y-P., and Leung, C. K. C. (1983) "PADL—A Packet Architecture Description Language," In T. Uehara and M. R. Barbacci (eds.) *Computer Hardware Description Languages and their Applications* (Proceedings of the 6th International Symposium). North-Holland, Amsterdam, 233–242.

Lincoln, N. R. (1986) "Great Gigaflops and Giddy Guarantees." In Metropolis, *et al.* (1986) 16–24.

Linger, R. C., Mills, H. D., and Witt, B. I. (1979) *Structured Programming.* Addison–Wesley, Reading, Mass.

Linn, J. L. (1983) "SRDAG Compaction: A Generalization of Trace Scheduling." *Proceedings of the 16th Annual Workshop on Microprogramming.* IEEE Computer Society Press, Los Angeles, Calif., 11–22.

Liptay, J. S. (1968) "Structural Aspects of System 360/85: The Cache." *IBM Sys J* 7, 15–21.

Liskov, B. (1980) "Modular Program Construction Using Abstractions." In D. Bjorner (Ed.) *Abstract Software Specifications.* Springer-Verlag, Berlin, 354–389.

Liskov, B., and Berzins, V. (1979) "An Appraisal of Program Specifications." In Wegner (1979) 276–301.

Lonergan, W., and King, P. (1961) "Design of the B5000 System." *Datamation* 7(5), 28–32.

Lubeck, O., Moore, J., and Mendez, R. (1985) "A Benchmark Comparison of Three Supercomputers: Fujitsu VP-2000, Hitachi 5810/20, CRAY X-MP/2." *Computer* 18(12), 10–24.

Lucas, P., and Walk, K. (1969) "On the Formal Description of PL/1." *Ann Rev Autom Prog* 6(3), 105–181.

Lunde, A. (1977) "Empirical Evaluation of Some Features of Instruction Set Processor Architectures." *Comm ACM* 20(3), 143–152.

Ma, P.-Y., and Lewis, T. G. (1980) "Design of a Machine Independent Optimizing System for Emulator Development." *ACM Trans Prog Lang Syst* 2(2), 239–262.

Ma, P.-Y., and Lewis, T. G. (1981) "On the Design of a Microcode Compiler for a Machine Independent High Level Language." *IEEE Trans Soft Eng* (May), 261–274.

Madnick, S. E., and Donovan, J. J. (1974) *Operating Systems.* McGraw–Hill, New York.

Mallach, E. (1975) "Emulation Architecture." *Computer* 8(8), 24–32.

Mallach, E., and Sondak, N. (Eds.) (1983) *Advances in Microprogramming.* Artech House, Dedham, Mass.

Manville, W. D. (1973) "Microprogramming Support for Programming Languages." Ph.D. Thesis, Computer Laboratory, University of Cambridge, U.K.

Marathe, M. (1977) "Performance Evaluation at the Hardware Architecture Level and the Operating System Kernel Design Level." Ph.D. Dissertation, Department of Computer Science, Carnegie-Mellon University, Pittsburgh, Pa.

March, L. (Ed.) (1976) *The Architecture of Form.* Cambridge University Press, Cambridge, England.

Marcus, L., Crocker, S. D. and Landauer, J. R. (1984) "SDVS: A System for Verifying Microcode Correctness." *Proceedings of the 17th Annual Microprogramming Workshop.* IEEE Computer Society Press, Los Alamitos, Calif. 246–256.

Marsland, T. A., and Demco, J. (1978) "A Case Study of Computer Emulation." *INFOR* (Canada) 16(2), 112–131.

Maruyama, F., and Fujita, M. (1985) "Hardware Verification." *Computer* 18(2), 22–32.

Marwedel, P. (1984) "A Retargetable Compiler for a High Level Microprogramming Language." *Proceedings of the 17th Annual Microprogramming Workshop.* IEEE Computer Society Press, Los Alamitos, Calif. 267–274.

Marwedel, P. (1985) "The MIMOLA Design System: A System Which Spans Several Levels." In Giloi and Shriver (1985) 223–238.

Masson, G. M., Gingher, G. C., and Nakamura, S. (1979) "A Sampler of Circuit Switching Networks." *Computer* 12(6), 32–48.

Matick, R. E. (1977) *Computer Storage Systems and Technology.* Wiley, New York.

Matick, R. E. (1980) "Memory and Storage." In Stone (1980) 205–274.

Mattson, R. L., Gecsei, J., Slutz, D. L., *et al.* (1970) "Evaluation Techniques for Storage Hierarchies." *IBM Sys J* 9(2), 78–117.

Mayr, E. (1969) *Principles of Systematic Zoology.* McGraw–Hill, New York.

Mayr, E. (1982) *The Growth of Biological Thought: Diversity, Evolution, and Inheritance.* Harvard University Press, Cambridge, Mass.

McGraw, J. R. (1982) "The VAL Language: Description and Analysis." *ACM Trans Prog Lang Syst* 4(1), 44–82.

McGraw, J. R., *et al.* (1983) "SISAL—Streams and Iterations in a Single

Assignment Language: Language Reference Manual." Lawrence Livermore National Laboratory, Livermore, Calif.

Mead, C. A., and Conway, L. (1980) *Introduction to VLSI Systems.* Addison–Wesley, Reading, Mass.

Melliar-Smith, P. M. (1979) "System Specification." In T. Anderson and B. Randell (Eds.) *Computing Systems Reliability.* Cambridge University Press, Cambridge, U.K.

Mendez, R. (1984) "Benchmarks on Japanese and American Supercomputers —Preliminary Results." *IEEE Trans Comput* C-33(4), 374.

Merrifield, C. W. (1879) "Report of the Committee Appointed to Consider the Advisability and to Estimate the Expense of Constructing Mr. Babbage's Analytical Machine and of Printing Tables by its Means." Reprinted in Randell (1975).

Metropolis, N., Sharp, D. H., Worlton, W. J., *et al.* (Eds.) (1986) *Frontiers of Supercomputing.* University of California Press, Berkeley, Calif.

Metropolis, N., and Worlton, J. (1980) "A Trilogy on Errors in the History of Computing" *Annals Hist Comp* 2(1), 49–59

Microdata (1970) *Microprogramming Handbook,* 2nd ed. Microdata Corporation, Santa Ana, Calif.

Millman, J., and Halkias, C. C. (1972) *Integrated Electronics.* McGraw–Hill, New York.

Mills, H. D. (1972) "Mathematical Foundations for Structured Programming." Internal Report, IBM Corporation. Reprinted in H. D. Mills, *Software Productivity.* Little, Brown & Co., Boston, 1983.

Millstein, R. E. (1973) "Control Structures in ILLIAC IV FORTRAN." *Comm ACM* 16(10), 622–627.

Minnick, R. C. (1967) "A Survey of Microcellular Research." *J ACM* 14, 203–241.

Monolithic Memories (1982) *Bipolar LSI Data Book,* 4th ed. Monolithic Memories, Sunnyvale, Calif.

Moore, G. E. (1979) "VLSI: Some Fundamental Challenges." *IEEE Spectrum* (April), 30–37.

Morris, D., and Ibbett, R. (1979) *The MU5 Computer Systems.* Macmillan, London.

Morris, F. L., and Jones, C. B. (1984) "An Early Program Proof by Alan Turing." *Annals Hist Comp* 6(2), 139–143.

Morris, J. B. (1972) "Demand Paging through Utilization of Working Sets on the MANIAC II." *Comm ACM* 15(10), 867–872.

Morse, S. P., Ravenal, B. W., Mazor, S., *et al.* (1978) "Intel Microprocessors: 8008 to 8086," Intel Corporation, Aloha, Or. Reprinted in Siewiorek, Bell, and Newell (1982), 615–642.

Mostow, J. (1985) "Models of the Design Process." *AI Magazine* (Spring), 44–57.

Moszkowski, B. (1985) "A Temporal Logic for Multilevel Reasoning about Hardware." *Computer* 18(2), 10–19.

Moszkowski, B. (1986) *Executing Temporal Logic Programs,* Cambridge University Press, Cambridge, England.

Moto-oka, T. (Ed.) (1982) *Fifth Generation Computer Systems,* North-Holland, Amsterdam.

Mudge, T. N., Hayes, J. P., Buzzard, G. D., *et al.* (1984) "Analysis of Multiple-bus Interconnection Networks." *Proceedings of the International Conference on Parallel Processing.* IEEE, August, 228–232.

Mudge, T. N., Hayes, J. P., Buzzard, G. D., *et al.* (1986) "Analysis of Multiple Bus Interconnection Networks." *J Parall Dist Comp* 3(3), 328–343.

Mudge, T. N., Hayes, J. P., and Winsor, D. C. (1987) "Multiple Bus Architectures." *Computer,* 20(6), 42–48.

Mueller, R. A. (1984) *Automated Microcode Synthesis.* UMI Research Press, Ann Arbor, Mi.

Mueller, R. A., and Duda, M. R. (1986) "Formal Methods of Microcode Verification and Synthesis." *IEEE Software* 3(4), 38–48.

Mueller, R. A., and Varghese, J. (1985) "Knowledge Based Code Selection Methods in Retargetable Microcode Synthesis." *IEEE Design Test* 2(3), 44–55.

Mukhopadhay, A. (Ed.) (1971) *Recent Developments in Switching Theory.* Academic Press, New York.

Mukhopadhay, A., and Stone, H. S. (1971) "Programmable Cellular Logic." In Mukhopadhay (1971), 256–315.

Muroga, S. (1982) *VLSI System Design.* Wiley, New York.

Myers, G. J. (1977) "The Case Against Stack-Oriented Instruction Sets." *SIGARCH Comp Arch News* 6(3), 7–10.

Myers, G. J. (1978a) Letter to the Editor. *SIGARCH Comp Arch News* 6(8), 25–26.

Myers, G. J. (1978b) "The Evaluation of Expressions in a Storage-Storage Architecture." *SIGARCH Comp Arch News* 6(9), 20–23.

Myers, G. J. (1980) *Digital System Design with LSI Bit-Slice Logic.* Wiley, New York.

Myers, G. J. (1982) *Advances in Computer Architecture.* Wiley, New York.

Nagle, A., Cloutier, R., and Parker, A. C. (1982) "Synthesis of Hardware for the Control of Digital Systems." *IEEE Trans CAD,* CAD-1(4), 201–212.

Nanodata (1979) *The QM-1 Hardware Level User's Manual.* Nanodata Corporation, Williamsburg, N.Y.

Naur, P. (Ed.) (1963) "Revised Report on the Algorithmic Language Algol 60." *Numerische Mathematik* 4, 420–453.

Neuhauser, C. J. (1977) "Emmy System Processor—Principles of Operation." Computer System Laboratory Technical Note TN-114, Stanford University, Stanford, Calif.

Neuhauser, C. J. (1980) "Analysis of the PDP-11 Instruction Stream." Technical Report 183, Computer System Laboratory, Stanford University, Stanford, Calif.

Northcutt, J. D. (1980) "High Level Fault Insertion and Simulation with ISPS."

Proceedings of the 17th Design Automation Conference. ACM/IEEE, Minneapolis, June.

Noyce, R., and Hoff, M. (1981) "A History of Microprocessor Development at Intel." *IEEE Micro* 1(1), 8–22.

Oakley, J. D. (1979) "Symbolic Execution of Formal Machine Descriptions." Technical Report Department of Computer Science, Carnegie-Mellon University, Pittsburgh, Pa.

Olafsson, M. (1981) "The QM-C: A C-Oriented Instruction Set Architecture for the Nanodata QM-1." Technical Report TR81-11, Department of Computer Science University of Alberta, Edmonton, Alberta, Canada.

Opderbeck, H., and Chu, W. W. (1974) "Performance of the Page Fault Frequency Replacement Algorithm in a Multiprogramming Environment." *Information Processing 74* (Proceedings of the IFIP Congress, 1974), North-Holland, Amsterdam, 235–241.

Opler, A. (1967) "Fourth Generation Software." *Datamation* 13(1), 22–24.

Organick, E. I. (1972) *The Multics System: An Examination of Its Structure.* MIT Press, Cambridge, Mass.

Organick, E. I. (1973) *Computer Systems Organization: The B5700/B6700 Series.* Academic Press, New York.

Organick, E. I., and Hinds, J. A. (1978) *Interpreting Machines: Architecture and Programming of the B1700/B1800 Series.* North-Holland, New York.

Owicki, S., and Gries, D. G. (1976) "An Axiomatic Proof Technique for Parallel Programs." *Acta Informatica* 6, 319–340.

Papamarcos, M. S., and Patel, J. H. (1984) "A Low Overhead Solution for Multiprocessors with Private Cache Memories." *Proceedings of the 11th International Symposium on Computer Architecture,* IEEE Computer Society Press, Los Alamitos, Calif. 348–354.

Parke, F. I. (1979) "An Introduction to the N.mPC Design Environment." *Proceedings of the 16th Design Automation Conference.* (June), 513–519.

Parker, A. C. (1984) "Automated Synthesis of Digital Systems." *IEEE Design and Test of Computers.* 1(4), 75–81.

Parker, A. C., Thomas, D. E., Crocker, S. D., *et al.* (1979) "ISPS: A Retrospective View." *Proceedings of the 4th International Symposium on Computer Hardware Description Languages and Their Applications.* IEEE, New York, 21–27.

Parker, A. C., and Wallace, J. J. (1981) "An I/O Hardware Description Language." *IEEE Trans Comput* C-30(6), 423–428.

Parnas, D. L. (1972) "On the Criteria to be Used in Decomposing Systems into Modules." *Comm ACM* 5(12), 1053–1058.

Parnas, D. L. (1977) "The Use of Precise Specifications in the Development of Software." In B. Gilchrist (Ed.) *Information Processing 77* (Proceedings of the IFIP Congress). North-Holland, Amsterdam, 861–868.

Parnas, D. L., and Darringer, J. A. (1967) "SODAS and a Methodology for System Design." AFIPS Fall Joint Computer Conference. AFIPS Press, Montvale, N.J., Vol. 31, 449–474.

Patel, J. H. (1981) "Performance of Processor-Memory Interconnections for Multiprocessors." *IEEE Trans Comput* C-30(10), 771–780.

Patnaik, L. M., Govindarajan, R., and Ramadoss, N. S. (1986) "Design and Performance Evaluation of EXMAN: An Extended MANchester Data Flow Computer." *IEEE Trans Comput* C-35(3), 229–244.

Patt, Y. N., Hwu, W-M., and Shebanow, M. (1985a) "HPS: A New Microarchitecture: Rationale and Introduction." *Proceedings of the 18th Annual Workshop on Microprogramming.* IEEE Computer Society Press, Washington, D.C., 103–108.

Patt, Y. N., Melvin, S. W., Hwu, W-M., *et al.* (1985b) "Critical Issues Regarding HPS, A High Performance Microarchitecture." *Proceedings of the 18th Annual Workshop on Microprogramming.* IEEE Computer Society Press, Washington, D.C., 109–116.

Patterson, D. A. (1976) "STRUM: Structured Programming System for Correct Firmware." *IEEE Trans Comput* C-25(10), 974–985.

Patterson, D. A. (1981) "An Experiment in High Level Language Microprogramming and Verification." *Comm ACM* 24(10), 699–709.

Patterson, D. A. (1985) "Reduced Instruction Set Computers." *Comm ACM* 28(1), 8–21.

Patterson, D. A., and Dietzel, D. (1980) "The Case for the Reduced Instruction Set Computer." *Computer Architecture News (SIGARCH)* 8(6), 25–33.

Patterson, D. A., Lew, K., and Tuck, R. (1979) "Towards an Efficient Machine Independent Language for Microprogramming." *Proceedings of the 12th Annual Workshop on Microprogramming.* ACM/IEEE, New York, 22–35.

Patterson, D. A., and Piepho, R. (1982) "RISC Assessment: A High Level Language Experiment." *Proceedings of the 9th Annual Symposium on Computer Architecture* IEEE Computer Society Press, Los Angeles, Calif., 3–8.

Patterson, D. A., and Sequin, C. (1980) "Design Considerations for Single-Chip Computers of the Future." *IEEE Trans Comput* C-29(2), 108–116.

Patterson, D. A., and Sequin, C. (1981) "RISC I: A Reduced Instruction Set Computer." *Proceedings of the 8th Annual International Symposium on Computer Architecture* IEEE Computer Society Press, 443–458.

Patterson, D. A., and Sequin, C. (1982) "A VLSI RISC." *Computer* 15(9), 8–21.

Perrott, R. H. (1979) "A Language for Array and Vector Processors." *ACM Trans Prog Lang Syst* 1(2), 177–195.

Perrott, R. H., and Zarea-Aliabadi, A. (1986) "Supercomputer Languages." *ACM Comp Surv* 18(1), 5–22.

Petri, C. A. (1962) "Kommunikation mit Automaten," Ph.D. Dissertation, University of Bonn, Bonn, West Germany.

Peuto, B., and Shustek, L. J. (1977) "An Instruction Timing Model of CPU Performance." *Proceedings of the 4th Annual Symposium on Computer Architecture.* ACM/IEEE, New York, 165–178.

Pevsner, N. (1963) *An Outline of European Architecture.* Penguin Books, London.

Pfister, G. F., Brantley, W. C., George, D. A., *et al.* (1985) "The IBM Research

Parallel Processor Prototype (RP3): Introduction and Architecture." *Proceedings of the 1985 International Conference on Parallel Processing* (Aug.), 764–771.

Piloty, R., Barbacci, M. R., Borrione, D., *et al.* (1983) *CONLAN Report,* Lecture Notes in Computer Science, No. 151, Springer-Verlag, Berlin.

Pohm, A. V. (1984) "High Speed Memory Systems." *Computer* 18(10), 162–172.

Popper, K. R. (1965) *Conjectures and Refutations: The Growth of Scientific Knowledge.* Harper & Row, New York.

Popper, K. R. (1968) *The Logic of Scientific Discovery.* Harper & Row, New York.

Popper, K. R. (1972) *Objective Knowledge: An Evolutionary Approach.* Clarendon Press, Oxford, U.K.

Rabbat, G. (Ed.) (1983) *Hardware and Software Concepts in VLSI.* Van Nostrand-Rheinhold, New York.

Radin, G. (1982) "The 801 Minicomputer." *Proceedings of the ACM Symposium on Architectural Support for Programming Languages and Operating Systems.* ACM, New York, 39–47.

Rakoczi, L. L. (1969) "The Computer-Within-a-Computer, A Fourth Generation Concept." *IEEE Comp Group News.* 3(2), 14.

Ramamoorthy, C. V., and Li, H. F. (1977) "Pipeline Architecture." *ACM Comp Surv* 9(1), 61–102.

Randell, B. (1969) "A Note on Storage Fragmentation and Program Segmentation." *Comm ACM* 12(7), 365–369.

Randell, B. (Ed.) (1975) *Origins of Digital Computers.* Springer-Verlag, New York.

Randell, B., and Russell, L. J. (1964). *Algol 60 Implementation.* Academic Press, New York.

Rau, B. R. (1979) "Interleaved Memory Bandwidth in a Model of a Multiprocessor System." *IEEE Trans Comput* C-28(9), 678–681.

Rauscher, T. G., and Adams, P. N. (1980) "Microprogramming: A Tutorial and Survey of Recent Developments." *IEEE Trans Comput* C-29(1), 2–19.

Reddaway, S. F. (1973) "DAP—A Distributed Array Processor." *Proceedings of the 1st Annual Symposium on Computer Architecture.* ACM/IEEE, New York.

Redfield, S. R. (1971) "A Study in Microprogrammed Processors: A Medium Sized Microprogrammed Processor." *IEEE Trans Comput* C-20(7), 743–750.

Rennels, D. A. (1978) "Reconfigurable Modular Computer Networks for Spacecraft On-Board Processing." *Computer* 11(7), 49–59.

Rice, R. (Ed.) (1980) *VLSI: The Coming Revolution in Applications and Design.* IEEE Computer Society, New York.

Rice, R. (Ed.) (1982) *VLSI Support Technologies: Computer-Aided Design, Testing, and Packaging.* IEEE Computer Society Press, Los Alamitos, Calif.

Rideout, D. J. (1981) "Considerations for Local Compaction of Nanocode for the Nanodata QM-1." *Proceedings of the 14th Annual Workshop on Microprogramming.* ACM/IEEE, New York, 205–214.

Riganati, J. P., and Schneck, P. B. (1984) "Supercomputing." *Computer* 17(10), 97–113.

Robertson, E. L. (1979) "Microcode Bit Optimization is NP-Complete." *IEEE Trans Comp,* C-28(4), 316–319.

Robinson, L., Levitt, K. N., Neumann, P. G., *et al.* (1977) "A Formal Methodology for the Design of Operating System Software." In R. T. Yeh (Ed.) *Current Trends in Programming Methodology, Vol. I, Software Specification and Design.* Prentice–Hall, Englewood-Cliffs, N.J., 61–110.

Rodrigue, G. (Ed.) (1982) *Parallel Computations.* Academic Press, New York.

Rodriguez, J. E. (1969) "A Graph Model for Parallel Computation." Report MAC-TR-64, Project MAC, Massachusetts Institute of Technology, Cambridge, Mass.

Rose, C. W., Ordy, G. M., and Drongowski, P. (1984) "N.mPC: A Study in University-Industry Technology Transfer." *IEEE Design Test* 1(1), 44–56.

Rosenberg, A. L. (1981) "Three Dimensional Integrated Circuitry." In Kung, Sproull, and Steele (1981), 69–80.

Rosin, R. F. (1969a) "Supervisory and Monitor Systems." *ACM Comp Surv* 1(1), 37–54.

Rosin, R. F. (1969b) "Contemporary Concepts of Microprogramming and Emulation." *ACM Comp Surv* 1(4), 197–212.

Rosin, R. F. (1974) "The Significance of Microprogramming." *Proceedings of the International Computer Symposium 1973.* North-Holland, Amsterdam.

Rosin, R. F., Frieder, G., and Eckhouse, R. H. (1972) "An Environment for Research in Microprogramming and Emulation." *Comm ACM* 15(8), 748–760.

Ross, D. T. (1977) "Structured Analysis (SA): A Language for Communicating Ideas." *IEEE Trans Soft Eng,* SE-3(1), 16–34.

Ross, H. H. (1974) *Biological Systematics.* Addison–Wesley, Reading, Mass.

Rumbaugh, J. (1977) "A Dataflow Multiprocessor." *IEEE Trans Comput* C-26(2), 138–146.

Ruse, M. (1973) *The Philosophy of Biology.* Hutchinson University Library, London.

Russell, R. M. (1978) "The CRAY-1 Computer System." *Comm ACM* 21(1), 63–72.

Rutihauser, H. (1967) *Description of Algol 60.* Springer-Verlag, Berlin.

Rymarczyk, J. (1982) "Coding Guidelines for Pipelined Processors." *Proceedings of the ACM Symposium on Architectural Support for Programming Languages and Operating Systems,* ACM, New York, 12–19.

Salisbury, A. B. (1976) *Microprogrammable Computer Architectures.* Elsevier, New York.

Sameh, A. H. (1977) "Numerical Parallel Algorithms—A Survey." In Kuck, Lawrie, and Sameh (1977) 207–228.

Samelson, K., and Bauer, F. L. (1959) "Sequential Formula Translation." *Comm ACM* 3(2), 76–83.

Samudrala, S., Lo, C., Brown, J, F. III, *et al.* (1984) "Design Verification of a VLSI VAX Microcomputer." *Proceedings of the 17th Annual Workshop on Microprogramming.* IEEE Computer Society Press, Silver Spring, Md, 59–63.

Sargeant, J., and Kirkham, C. C. (1986) "Stored Data Structures on the Manchester Dataflow Machine." *Proceedings of the 13th International Symposium on Computer Architecture.* IEEE Computer Society Press, Los Alamitos, Calif., 235–242.

Satyanarayanan, M. (1980) *Multiprocessors: A Comparative Survey.* Prentice–Hall, Englewood-Cliffs, N.J.

Scherlis, W. L. and Scott, D. S. (1983) "First Steps Towards Inferential Programming." In R. E. A. Mason (Ed.) *Information Processing 83* (Proceedings of the IFIP Congress), North-Holland, Amsterdam, 199–212.

Schlaeppi, H. P. (1964) "A Formal Language for Describing Machine Logic, Timing and Sequencing (LOTIS)." *IEEE Trans Comput* C-13(8), 439–448.

Schön, D. A. (1983) *The Reflective Practitioner.* Basic Books, New York.

Schwartz, S. J. (1968) "An Algorithm for Minimizing Read-Only Memories for Machine Control." *Proceedings of the IEEE 10th Annual Symposium on Switching and Automata Theory.* IEEE, New York, 28–33.

Seewaldt, T., and Estrin, G. (1985) "A Multilevel Design Procedure to Foster Functional and Informational Strength." In Giloi and Shriver (1985), 11–28.

Seitz, C. L. (1985) "The Cosmic Cube." *Comm ACM* 28(1), 22–33.

Severn, M. J. (1976) "A Minicomputer Compatible Microcomputer System: The DEC LSI-11." *Proceedings of the IEEE,* 64(6). Reprinted in Bell, Mudge, and McNamara (1978) 301–315.

Shahdad, M., Lipsett, R., Marschner, E., *et al.* (1985) "VHSIC Hardware Description Language." *Computer* 18(2), 94–104.

Sheraga, R. J., and Gieser, J. L. (1983) "Experiments in Automatic Microcode Generation." *IEEE Trans Comput* C-32(6), 557–568.

Shibayama, K., Tomita, S., Hagiwara, H., *et al.* (1980) "Performance Evaluation and Improvement of a Dynamically Microprogrammable Computer with Low Level Parallelism." *Information Processing 80* (Proceedings of the IFIP Congress). North-Holland, Amsterdam, 181–186.

Shima, M. (1979) "Demystifying Microprocessor Design." *IEEE Spectrum* (July). Reprinted in Rice (1980) 274–282.

Shostak, R. E. (1983) "Formal Verification of VLSI Designs." *Proc COMPCON* (Spring) IEEE Computer Society Press, Silver Spring, Md.

Shriver, B. D. (1978) "Firmware: The Lessons of Software Engineering." *Computer* 11(5), 19–20.

Shriver, B. D., and Kornerup, P. (1980) "A Description of the MATHILDA Processor." Technical Report DAIMI PB-52, Computer Science Department, Aarhus University, Aarhus, Denmark.

Shustek, L. J. (1978) "Analysis and Performance of Computer Instruction Sets."

Ph.D. Dissertation, Computer Systems Laboratory, Stanford University, Stanford, Calif.

Siegel, H. J. (1979) "Interconnection Networks for SIMD Machines." *Computer* 12(6), 57–65.

Siegel, H. J. (1984) *Interconnection Networks for Large Scale Parallel Processing: Theory and Case Studies.* Lexington Books, Lexington, Mass.

Siewiorek, D. P., Bell, C. G., and Newell, A. (1982) *Computer Structures: Principles and Examples.* McGraw–Hill, New York.

Siewiorek, D. P., Thomas, D. E., and Schanfeller, D. L. (1978) "The Use of LSI Modules in Computer Structures: Trends and Limitations. *Computer* 11(7), 16–25.

Simon, H. A. (1975) "Style in Design." In C. Eastman (Ed.) *Spatial Synthesis in Computer Aided Building Design.* Wiley, New York, 287–309.

Simon, H. A. (1976) *Administrative Behavior.* Free Press, New York.

Simon, H. A. (1981) *The Sciences of the Artificial,* 2nd ed. MIT Press, Cambridge, Mass.

Simon, H. A. (1982) *Models of Bounded Rationality,* Vol. 2. MIT Press, Cambridge, Mass.

Sint, M. (1980) "A Survey of High Level Microprogramming Languages." *Proceedings of the 13th Annual Workshop on Microprogramming.* IEEE Computer Society Press, New York, 141–153.

Sint, M. (1981) "MIDL—A Microinstruction Description Language." *Proceedings of the 14th Annual Microprogramming Workshop.* IEEE Computer Society Press, Los Alamitos, Calif., 95–107.

Skinner, B. F. (1974) *About Behaviorism,* Knopf, New York.

Smith, A. J. (1982) "Cache Memories." *ACM Comp Surv* 14(3), 473–529.

Snow, E. A., and Siewiorek, D. P. (1978) "Impact of Implementation Design Tradeoffs on Performance: The PDP-11, A Case Study." In Bell, Mudge, and McNamara (1978) 327–364.

Snow, E. A., and Siewiorek, D. P. (1982) "Implementation and Performance Evaluation of the PDP-11 Family." In Siewiorek, Bell, and Newell (1982) 666–679.

Snyder, L. (1982) "An Introduction to the Configurable Highly Parallel Computer." *Computer* 15(1), 47–56.

Snyder, L. (1984) "Supercomputers and VLSI: The Effect of Large Scale Integration on Computer Architecture." In M. C. Yovits (Ed.) *Advances in Computers* Vol. 23. Academic Press, New York, 1–33.

Sokal, R. R. and Sneath, P. H. A. (1963) *Principles of Numerical Taxonomy.* Freeman, San Francisco.

Sommerville, I. (1985) *Software Engineering,* 2nd ed. Addison–Wesley, Reading, Mass.

Spirn, J. R. (1977) *Program Behavior: Models and Measurements.* Elsevier, New York.

Srini, V. P., and Asenjo, J. F. (1983) "Analysis of CRAY-1 Architecture." *Proceedings of the 10th International Symposium on Computer Architecture* IEEE Computer Society Press, Los Alamitos, Calif., 194–206.

Stankovic, J. A. (1981) "The Types and Interactions of Vertical Migrations of Functions in a Multilevel Interpretive System." *IEEE Trans Comput* C-30(7), 505–513.

Steadman, P. (1979) *The Evolution of Designs.* Cambridge University Press, Cambridge, England.

Stern, N. (1980) "John von Neumann's Influence on Electronic Digital Computing, 1944–1946." *Annals Hist Comp* 2(4), 349–362.

Stern, N. (1981) *From ENIAC to EDVAC: A Case Study in the History of Technology.* Digital Press, Bedford, Mass.

Stevens, K. (1975) "CFD—A Fortran-like Language for the ILLIAC IV." *SIGPLAN Notices* (March), 72–80.

Stone, H. S. (1971) "Parallel Processing with a Perfect Shuffle." *IEEE Trans Comp.* C-20(2), 153–161.

Stone, H. S. (Ed.) (1980) *Introduction to Computer Architecture.* SRA, Chicago.

Stoy, J. E. (1977) *Denotational Semantics: The Scott-Strachey Approach to Programming Language Theory.* MIT Press, Cambridge, Mass.

Strecker, W. D. (1976) "Cache Memories for the PDP-11 Family Computers." *Proceedings of the 3rd Annual Symposium on Computer Architecture* ACM/IEEE, New York, 155–158.

Strecker, W. D. (1978) "VAX-11/780: A Virtual Address Extension to the DEC PDP-11 Family." *Proceedings of the National Computer Conference,* AFIPS Press, Montvale, N.J., 967–980.

Strecker, W. D. and Clark, D. W. (1980) "Comments on 'The Case for the Reduced Instruction Set Computer' by Patterson and Ditzel." *Comp Arch News (SIGARCH)* 8(6), 34–38.

Stritter, S., and Tredennick, N. (1978) "Microprogrammed Implementation of a Single Chip Microprocessor." *Proceedings of the 11th Annual Workshop on Microprogramming.* ACM/IEEE, New York, 8–16.

Su, B., and Ding, S. (1985) "Some Experiments in Global Microcode Compaction." *Proceedings of the 18th Annual Workshop on Microprogramming.* IEEE Computer Society Press, Los Angeles, Calif. 175–180.

Su, B., Ding, S., and Jin, L. (1984) "An Improvement of Trace Scheduling for Global Microcode Compaction." *Proceedings of the 17th Annual Workshop on Microprogramming.* IEEE Computer Society Press, Los Angeles, Calif. 78–85.

Swan, R. J., Bechtholsheim, A., Lai, K. W., *et al.* (1977) "Implementation of the Cm* Multi-Microprocessor." *Proceedings National Computer Conference.* Vol. 46, AFIPS Press, Montvale, N.J., 645–655.

Swan, R. J., Fuller, S. H., and Siewiorek, D. P. (1977) "Cm*—A Modular Multi-Microprocessor." *Proceedings of NCC* Vol. 46, AFIPS Press, Montvale, N.J., 637–644.

Swartout, W., and Balzer, R. (1982) "On the Inevitable Intertwining of Specification and Implementation." *Comm ACM* 25(7), 438–440.

Swartzlander, E. E. (Ed.) (1976) *Computer Design Development: Principal Papers.* Hayden, Rochelle Park, N.J.

Syre, J. C., Comte, D., Durrieu, G., *et al.* (1977) "LAU System—A Parallel

Data-Driven Software/Hardware System Based on Single Assignment." In M. Feilmeier (Ed.) *Parallel Computers–Parallel Mathematics.* North-Holland, Amsterdam, 347–351.

Tanaka, H., Amamiya, M., Tanaka, Y., *et al.* (1982) "The Preliminary Research of Data Flow Machine and Data Base Machine as the Basic Architecture of Fifth Generation Computer Systems." In Moto-oka (1982) 209–219.

Tanenbaum, A. S. (1978) "Implications of Structured Programming for Machine Architectures." *Comm ACM* 21(3), 237–246.

Tanenbaum, A. S. (1984) *Structured Computer Organization.* Prentice–Hall, Englewood-Cliffs, N.J.

Teichrow, D., and Hershey, E. A. (1977) "PLS/PSA: A Computer Aided Technique for Structured Documentation and Analysis of Information Processing Systems." *IEEE Trans Soft Eng* SE-3(1), 41–48.

Tesler, L. G. and Enea, H. J. (1968) "A Language Design for Concurrent Processes." *Spring Joint Computer Conference, AFIPS Conference Proceedings,* Vol. 32, AFIPS Press, Montvale, N.J., 403–408.

Texas Instruments (1981) *The TTL Data Book.* Texas Instruments, Inc., Dallas.

Thornton, J. E. (1964) "Parallel Operation in the Control Data 6600." *Proceedings of the Fall Joint Computer Conference,* AFIPS, Vol. 24, Pt. 2, AFIPS Press, Montvale, N.J., 33–40. Reprinted in Siewiorek, Bell, and Newell (1982) 730–742.

Thurber, K. J. (1976) *Large Scale Computer Architectures.* Hayden, Rochelle Park, N.J.

Tokoro, M., Tamura, E., and Takizuka, T. (1981). "Optimization of Microprograms." *IEEE Trans Comput* C-30(7), 491–504.

Tomasulo, R. M. (1967) "An Efficient Algorithm for Exploiting Multiple Arithmetic Units." *IBM J Res Dev* (Jan.), 25–33.

Tomita, S., Shibayama, K., Kitamura, T., *et al.* (1983) "A User-Microprogrammable, Local Host Computer with Low Level Parallelism." *Proceedings of the 10th Annual International Symposium on Computer Architecture.* IEEE Computer Society Press, Los Angeles, Calif., 151–159.

Toong, H. D., and Gupta, A. (1981) "An Architectural Comparison of Contemporary 16-Bit Microprocessors." *IEEE Micro* (May), 26–37.

Touzeau, R. F. (1984) "A Fortran Compiler for the FPS-164 Scientific Computer." *Proceedings of the ACM SIGPLAN Symposium on Compiler Construction,* SIGPLAN Notices, 19(6), 48–57.

Tredennick, N. (1982) "The 'Cultures' of Microprogramming." *Proceedings of the 15th Annual Workshop on Microprogramming.* IEEE Computer Society Press, Los Angeles, Calif., 79–83.

Treleavan, P. C., Brownbridge, D. R., and Hopkins, R. P. (1982) "Data Driven and Demand Driven Computer Architecture." *ACM Comp Surv* 14(1), 93–144.

Trivedi, K. S. (1982) *Probability and Statistics with Reliability Queueing and Computer Science Applications.* Prentice–Hall, Englewood-Cliffs, N.J.

Troiani, M., Ching, S. S., Quaynor, N. N., *et al.* (1985) "The VAX 8600 I Box, A

Pipelined Implementation of the VAX Architecture." *Digital Tech J* Digital Equipment Corp., Hudson, Mass., 24–42.

Tseng, C. J., and Siewiorek, D. P. (1982) "The Modeling and Synthesis of Bus Systems." Technical Report DRC-18-42-82, Design Research Center, Carnegie-Mellon University, Pittsburgh, Pa.

Tucker, A. B., and Flynn, M. J. (1971) "Dynamic Microprogramming: Processor Organization and Programming." *Comm ACM* 14(4), 240–250.

Tucker, S. G. (1967) "Microprogram Control for System/360." *IBM Sys J* 6(4), 222–241.

Turing, A. M. (1949) "Checking a Large Routine." *Report on the Conference on High Speed Automatic Calculating Machines.* University Mathematical Laboratory, Cambridge, England, 67–68.

Uehara, T., Saito, T., Maruyama, F., *et al.* (1983) "DDL Verifier and Temporal Logic." In T. Uehara and M. R. Barbacci (Eds.) *Computer Hardware Description Languages and Their Applications* (Proceedings of the 6th International Symposium), North-Holland, Amsterdam, 91–102.

Ullman, J. D. (1984) *Computational Aspects of VLSI.* Computer Science Press, Rockville, Md.

Ungar, D., Blau, R., Foley, P., *et al.* (1984) "Architecture of SOAR: Smalltalk on a RISC." *Proceedings of the 11th Annual International Symposium on Computer Architecture.* IEEE Computer Society Press, Los Angeles, Calif., 188–197.

U.S. Department of Defense (1981) *ADA Language Reference Manual.* Springer-Verlag, Berlin.

van Cleemput, W. M., and Ofek, H. (1984) "Design Automation for Digital Systems." *Computer* 17(10), 114–125.

Varian (1975) *Varian Microprogramming Guide.* Varian Data Machines, Irvine, Calif.

Vegdahl, S. (1982a) "Local Code Generation and Compaction in Optimizing Microcode Compilers." Ph.D. Thesis, Department of Computer Science, Carnegie-Mellon University, Pittsburgh, Pa.

Vegdahl, S. (1982b). "Phase Coupling and Constant Generation in an Optimizing Microcode Compiler." *Proceedings of the 15th Annual Workshop on Microprogramming.* IEEE Computer Society Press, Los Angeles, Calif. 125–133.

Vernon, M. K., and Estrin, G. (1985) "The UCLA Graph Model of Behavior: Support for Performance-Oriented Design." In Giloi and Shriver (1985), 47–65.

von Neumann, J. (1945) "First Draft of a Report on EDVAC." Memorandum, reprinted in Randell (1975), 355–364.

Wagner, A. (1983) "Verification of S*(QM-1) Microprograms," M.S. Thesis, Department of Computer Science, University of Alberta, Edmonton, Alberta, Canada.

Wagner, A., and Dasgupta, S. (1983) "Axiomatic Proof Rules for a Machine Specific Microprogramming Language." *Proceedings of the 16th Annual*

Workshop on Microprogramming. IEEE Computer Society Press, Los Angeles, Calif. 151–158.

Wagnon, G., and Maine, D. J. (1983) "An E-Machine Workbench." *Proceedings of the 16th Annual Microprogramming Workshop.* IEEE Computer Society Press, Los Alamitos, Calif. 151–158.

Watson, I., and Gurd, J. (1982) "A Practical Data Flow Computer." *Computer* 15(2), 51–57.

Wegner, P. (1972a) "The Vienna Definition Language." *ACM Comp Surv* 4(1), 5–63.

Wegner, P. (1972b) "Programming Language Semantics." In R. Rustin (Ed.) *Formal Semantics of Programming Languages.* Prentice–Hall, Englewood-Cliffs, N.J., 149–248.

Wegner, P. (Ed.) (1979) *Research Directions in Software Technology.* MIT Press, Cambridge, Mass.

Weiss, S., and Smith, J. E. (1984) "Instruction Issue Logic for Pipelined Supercomputers." *Proceedings of the 11th International Symposium on Computer Architecture.* IEEE Computer Society Press, Los Alamitos, Calif., 110–118.

Weizenbaum, J. (1976) *Computer Power and Human Reason.* Freeman, San Francisco.

Wexelblat, R. L. (Ed.) (1981) *History of Programming Languages.* Academic Press, New York.

Whitby-Strevens, C. (1985) "The Transputer." *Proceedings of the 12th International Symposium on Computer Architecture.* IEEE Computer Society Press, Los Alamitos, Calif. 292–300.

Wilkes, M. V. (1951) "The Best Way to Design an Automatic Calculating Machine." *Report of the Manchester University Computer Inaugural Conference.* University of Manchester, Manchester, U.K. Reprinted in Swartzlander (1976) 266–270.

Wilkes, M. V. (1965) "Slave Memories and Dynamic Storage Allocation." *IEEE Trans El Comput* EC-14, 270.

Wilkes, M. V. (1968) "Computers Then and Now." 1967 Turing Lecture, *J ACM* 15(1), 1–7.

Wilkes, M. V. (1969) "The Growth of Interest in Microprogramming: A Literature Survey." *ACM Comp Surv* 1(3), 139–145.

Wilkes, M. V. (1975) *Time Sharing Computer Systems.* MacDonald/Elsevier, London.

Wilkes, M. V. (1977) "Babbage as a Computer Pioneer." *Historia Mathematica* 4, 415–440.

Wilkes, M. V. (1982) "The Processor Instruction Set." *Proceedings of the 15th Annual Workshop on Microprogramming* IEEE Computer Society Press, Los Angeles, Calif. 3–5.

Wilkes, M. V. (1983) "Size, Power, and Speed." *Proceedings of the 10th Annual International Symposium on Computer Architecture* IEEE Computer Society Press, Silver Spring, Md., 2–4.

Wilkes, M. V. (1985). *Memoirs of a Computer Pioneer*. MIT Press, Cambridge, Mass.

Wilkes, M. V. (1986) "The Genesis of Microprogramming." *Ann Hist Comp* 8(2), 116–126.

Wilkes, M. V., and Needham, R. M. (1979) *The Cambridge CAP Computer and Its Operating System*. North-Holland, New York.

Wilkes, M. V., Renwick, W., and Wheeler, D. J. (1958) "The Design of a Control Unit of an Electronic Digital Computer." *Proc. IEE* (U.K.), 105.

Wilkes, M. V., and Stringer, J. B. (1953) "Microprogramming and the Design of the Control Circuits in an Electronic Digital Computer." *Proceedings of the Cambridge Philosophical Society,* Pt. 2, 49 (April), 230–238. Reprinted in Bell and Newell (1971), 335–340.

Wilner, W. T. (1972a) "Design of the Burroughs B1700." *Proceedings of the Fall Joint Computer Conference,* AFIPS Press, Montvale, N.J., 489–497.

Wilner, W. T. (1972b) "Burroughs B1700 Memory Utilization" *Proc. FJCC* AFIPS Press, Montvale, N.J., 579–586.

Wilsey, P. A. (1985) "S*M: An Axiomatic Non-Procedural Hardware Description Language for Clocked Architectures," M.S. Thesis, Center for Advanced Computer Studies, University of Southwestern Louisiana, Lafayette.

Winner, R. I. and Carter, E. M. (1986) "Automatic Vertical Migration to Dynamic Microcode: An Overview and Example." *IEEE Software* 3(4), 6–17.

Wirth, N. (1971) "Program Development by Stepwise Refinement." *Comm ACM* 14(4), 221–227.

Wolfe, T. (1981) *From Bauhaus to Our House*. Farrar, Straus & Giroux, New York.

Wood, W. G. (1978) "On the Packing of Microoperations into Microinstruction Words." *Proceedings of the 11th Annual Workshop on Microprogramming*. ACM/IEEE, New York, 51–55.

Wood, W. G. (1979) "The Computer-Aided Design of Microprograms." Ph.D. Thesis (Technical Report CST-5-79), Department of Computer Science, University of Edinburgh, Edinburgh, Scotland.

Wulf, W. A. (1981) "Compilers and Computer Architecture." *IEEE Computer* 14(7), 41–47.

Wulf, W. A., and Bell, C. G. (1972) "C.mmp: A Multiminiprocessor." *Proceedings of the Fall Joint Computer Conference,* AFIPS, Vol. 41, Pt. 2, AFIPS Press, Montvale, N.J., 765–777.

Wulf, W. A., Levin, R., and Harbison, S. (1980) *Hydra/C.mmp: An Experimental Computer System*. McGraw–Hill, New York.

Yeh, P. C., Patel, J. H., and Davidson, E. S. (1983) "Shared Cache for Multiple Stream Computer Systems." *IEEE Trans Comput* C-32(1), 38–47.

Yourdon, E. N. (Ed.) (1979) *Classics in Software Engineering*. Yourdon Press, New York.

Yourdon, E. N. (Ed.) (1982) *Writings of the Revolution, Selected Readings on Software Engineering*. Yourdon Press, New York.

Zelkowitz, M. V., Shaw, A. C., and Gannon, J. D. (1979) *Principles of Software Engineering and Design.* Prentice-Hall, Englewood-Cliffs, N.J.

Zemanek, H. (1980) "Abstract Architecture." In D. Bjorner (Ed.) *Abstract Software Specification.* Springer-Verlag, New York, 1-42.

Zimmerman, G. (1980) "MDS—The Mimola Design Method." *J Digital Syst* 4(3), 337-369.

Zurcher, W., and Randell, B. (1968) "Iterative Multilevel Modeling: A Methodology for Computer System Design." *Information Processing 68* (Proceedings of the IFIP Congress), North-Holland, Amsterdam, D138-D142.

INDEX

Abstraction levels:
in computer architecture, 3, 5–7, 9–10
for endo-architecture, 163
as hallmark of complexity, 27
for management of complexity, 157
Adams, P. M., 224
Addressing modes:
absolute, 114
autodecrement, 140–141
autoincrement, 139–141
base-displacement, 111, 136–138, 142, 271
in Berkeley RISC, 271
capability-based, 138
classical, 140
as components of exo-architecture, 3, 132
direct, 133
display-offset-based, 246–247
effectiveness, 141–143
indexed, 135–137, 140–142
indirect, 134–135
for PDP-11, 138–141
register-based, 114, 133, 139, 142
relative, 111
stack-based, 138
stack marker-based, 247–248
for VAX-11, 141–143
in von Neumann model, 104
Advanced Micro Devices, 69
Agrawala, A. K., 224
Agüero, U., 93
Aho, A. V., 82, 114
Alagic, S., 95
Alexander, C., 75, 94
Alexander, W. G., 16, 118, 119, 147, 263
Amdahl, G. M., 25
Amdahl Corporation, 60, 315
Andrews, M. A., 224
Appel, K., 87
Arbib, M. A., 95

Architecture description languages:
ISPS, 276
purpose, 91
S*M, 122, 255
S*M descriptions, 235, 237, 249, 251
Ardoin, C. D., 219
Armstrong, R. A., 59, 62
ASCII code, 129, 329
Assignment statements:
frequency, 118–119
types, 118–119
AT&T Bell Laboratories, 59
Autoindexing, 136
Ayres, R. F., 71

Baba, T., 18
Babbage, C., 23
Backus, J., 110
Baer, J.-L., 25, 141, 255
Banerji, D. K., 208, 224
Barbacci, M. R., 276
Bartee, T. C., 217, 313
Barton, R. S., 21, 260
Batson, A. P., 304
Bauer, F. L., 232
Behavior:
definition, 13
at the endo-architectural level, 162
Belady, L., 85, 305, 306
Bell, C. G., 3, 26, 35, 71, 102, 108, 121, 151, 153, 154, 286
Bertsis, V., 320
Bilardi, G., 64
Binary tree, post order traversal of, 236
Birkhoff, G., 217, 313
Bit slice devices:
AMD 2900 family, 69–70
definition, 67
examples of, 67